From
International Law
To
World Peace

Problems & Turning-Points

VALENTIN TOMBERG

From International Law *To* World Peace

Jurisprudence, the Law of Nations, and the Right of Humankind Viewed in Philosophical-Historical Context

Problems & Turning-Points

Foreword by
Michael Frensch

First published in German as
*Von Völkerrecht zur Weltfriedensordnung:
Die Problemgeschichte der Völkerrechtswissenschaft*
© Novalis: Verlag des Valentin Tombergs-Archivs, 2022
First published by Angelico Press, 2024
English translation by Stephen Churchyard
and James Wetmore © James Wetmore, 2024

All rights reserved

No part of this book may be reproduced or transmitted,
in any form or by any means, without permission

For information, address:
Angelico Press
169 Monitor St.
Brooklyn, NY 11222
angelicopress.com

ISBN 978-1-62138-952-1 (pbk)
ISBN 978-1-62138-953-8 (cloth)

Cover Design: Michael Schrauzer

MOTTO:

OSSA ARIDA, AUDITE VERBUM DOMINI:
HAEC DICIT DOMINS DES OSSIBUS HIS:
ECCE EGO INTROMITTAM IN VOS
SPIRITUS, ET VIVETIS.
                    EZECHIEL XXXVII

O ye dry bones, hear the word of the LORD. Thus saith the LORD GOD unto these bones; Behold, I will cause breath to enter into you, and ye shall live: And I will lay sinews upon you, and will bring up flesh upon you, and cover you with skin, and put breath in you, and ye shall live.

                  Ezekiel 37:4–6

CONTENTS

Foreword i

Introduction v

PART I: How the Problem Stands
1 International Law and its Jurisprudence 1
2 The Fundamental Problem of the Jurisprudence of International Law 9
3 The Method of the Jurisprudence of International Law 17
4 The Historical Beginnings of the Jurisprudence of International Law 21

PART II: St Thomas Aquinas's Doctrine that Law has Three Stages, and the Significance of that Doctrine for the Fundamental Problem of International Law: *War* and *Peace*
1 The Augustinian Tradition 37
2 The Dispute over the Possibility of Knowing the Truth in Thinking up until the Time of Thomas Aquinas 42
3 Thomas Aquinas and the Doctrine of the Three Levels of Law 56
4 Thomas Aquinas and the Doctrine of World Peace 71
5 Thomas Aquinas and the Doctrine of War 75

PART III: Further Development of the Problem of International Law on the Basis of a Law with Three Levels
1 The Medieval Concept of Neutrality and Tolerance 87
2 Francisco de Vitoria 101
3 Early Modern Theologians and Jurists and their Doctrines of the State 132
4 Francisco Suárez 167

PART IV: The Transition from Three-Stage to Two-Stage Law
1 Albericus Gentilis 183
2 Hugo Grotius and His School 197

PART V: The "Conservative" and "Liberal" Ideas of International Law as a Rationalistic Law of Nature after the Twilight of Divine Law
1 Thomas Hobbes and John Locke 215
2 Samuel von Pufendorf and Christian Thomasius 245
3 The "Grotians": Leibniz, Wolff, Vattel 283

PART VI: The Twilight of the Rationalistic Natural Law and the Transition from a Law with Two Levels to a Law with One Level
1 The French Enlightenment's Ideas about International Law and the Revolutionary Politicizing of Law 345
2 Kant and Kantianism 358
3 Hegel and the Theory of the Sovereignty of the State 386

PART VII: International Law With One Level: Pure Positivism and Its Problems 406

PART VIII: The Dawn of One-Dimensional Law: Positivism as International Law 414

PART IX: The Present Movement Towards the Rebirth of International Law Through a Return to Natural Law and Divine Law 422

APPENDICES
Appendix A: Francisco de Vitoria 447
Appendix B: Francisco Suàrez 461
Appendix C: Thomas Hobbes 466
Appendix D: John Locke 473

Foreword

alentin Tomberg's final jurisprudential work, *From International Law to World Peace*, was written in England in 1952. At the time, the Cold War was becoming the determining political factor in Europe and throughout the world. It threatened to turn into a "hot" war at any time—for example, during the 1962 Cuban Missile Crisis. In our own time also, throughout the world, but perhaps especially in Europe, we teeter on the brink of war and peace—we need only call to mind the present conflicts in the Ukraine and Palestine. In short, the question of establishing world peace, and the role of international law in promoting it, is more relevant than ever. This is what prompted the Valentin Tomberg Archive to finally release this book, whose author, born in St. Petersburg in 1900, deals knowledgeably and with great clarity and depth of insight with the history of the jurisprudence of international law from its very beginnings in antiquity up to the middle of the twentieth century.

A further reason for the book's appearance at this time is that in the past few years Angelico Press has published English editions of several other works by Tomberg, including two shorter ones on questions of jurisprudence, for which the present book provides an exhaustive summary. It also offers insight into the period of Tomberg's personal reorientation during which these legal works were written.

From International Law to World Peace

Tomberg's first work in this field, initially presented as a doctoral dissertation, was written in Germany between 1944 and 1946 and published one year after World War II.[1] During the war also, often while sitting in an air-raid bunker, he wrote a work more specifically on international law, which was published in 1947.[2] Probably until 1948, he was also working on a habilitation thesis[3] for the Cologne Law School, apparently intended as a draft for a new legal order for postwar Germany. The fate of this draft has not been conclusively clarified, although there is much to suggest that Tomberg destroyed it after he realized that political and legal developments in Germany were taking a different direction, and that a divided Germany was on the horizon. Since he no longer saw a future for himself as a university lecturer in international law (as he had done until then at the Technical University in Aachen), he turned to England.

It was during the years following the move to England that Tomberg completed the present work, which had a notable genesis. Fritz von Hippel, the brother of Tomberg's closest friend Ernst von Hippel (and like his brother, a law professor also) had asked Tomberg if he would write a con-

---

[1] *Degeneration und Regeneration der Rechtswissenschaft*, published in 1946 by Verlag Götz Schwippert, Bonn. Reprinted in 1974 by Bouvier Verlag, Bonn. Published in English by Angelico Press in 2021 as *The Art of the Good: On the Regeneration of Fallen Justice*.

[2] *Die Grundlagen des Völkerrechts als Menschheitsrecht*, published in 1947 by Verlag Götz Schwippert, Bonn. Published in English by Angelico Press in 2023 as *Jus Humanitatis: The Right of Humankind as Foundation for International Law*.

[3] The *Habilitationschrift* is a post-doctoral qualification conferring the *venia legendi* ("right to read," i.e., to lecture) needed before an academic may take up a university professorship.

tribution on the history of international law and the jurisprudence of international law for the publishing house Herder. Tomberg took this request to mean that he should write an entire book on this subject, whereas, as matters turned out, Herder's intention was instead to publish a volume of contributions from a number of authors. So it seems we may owe the magnitude of this extraordinarily comprehensive text by Tomberg to a misunderstanding! Even after learning of this mistake, and of the uncertainty of publication, for his own reasons Tomberg saw the work through to completion, after which, remarkably, it was consigned (now more than 70 years ago!) to a desk drawer.

In his book, Tomberg provides an review of the overall development of international law, echoing the idea of his dissertation that the modern development of law consisted in its gradual degeneration. Based on Thomas Aquinas's conception of law, he sees at the top of the legal edifice and at the same time as its foundation the eternal law, the *lex aeterna*, which, as the essence of God, invisibly and immovably gives any law its legal character in the first place. This hidden eternal law reveals itself in the world as divine law, the *lex divina*. Divine law, in turn, underlies natural law, the *lex naturalis*, and gives it that efficacy which (among other things) evokes in man an unerring sense of right and justice as a basic orientation for the positive law established by man. The latter is the applicable law related to the earthly reality of life, the *lex positiva*.

Tomberg shows how, in modern international law scholarship, the originally comprehensive law was dismantled stage by stage—for Tomberg both an expression of and the cause of an ever-continuing decay—until it finally lay completely at the bottom.

From International Law to World Peace

The author does not limit himself to justifying his thesis that the stages of law are no longer to be found in today's rulings of law, but he also lists approaches as to how the process of degeneration that he diagnoses can be counteracted in the sense of regeneration. Ultimately, it is a matter of a Christianization of human consciousness. May the book in your hands contribute to this!

MICHAEL FRENSCH

Introduction

alentin Tomberg was born in St. Petersburg on February 26, 1900.[1] Baptized a Protestant, he entered the Orthodox church (which he never formally left) shortly before 1933, and, in 1945, became Roman Catholic. His father, Karl Arnold Tomberg, was the administrator of a high school in St. Petersburg, and worked from 1903 onwards as an official in the Russian Ministry of the Interior. After attending St. Peter's School, where he was given a classical education, with teaching conducted in both Russian and German, Valentin studied one semester at the Faculty of Law at the University of St. Petersburg; but the Russian Revolution of November 1917 prevented his further studies. During his life, Tomberg learned to speak fluent Russian, German, French, English, Dutch, and Estonian, and had a good command of Spanish, Polish, Ukrainian, Latin, Greek, and Church Slavonic. In 1918 he fled with his family to Estonia. There his mother, Juliana Umblia, was shot and killed by the Bolsheviks, an event that left deep scars on Tomberg, and shaped his view of communist Russia for the rest of his life. In 1920 he moved to Tallinn, where, between 1928 and 1938, he worked as an interpreter in the postal service administration.

---

[1] According to the Julian calendar then used in Russia the date was February 14th, that is, St. Valentine's day.

From International Law to World Peace

In 1925, Tomberg joined the Estonian Anthroposophical Society, becoming its vice-president in 1926 and its president in 1932. From the beginning of the 1930s he began to publish essays in anthroposophical journals. In 1933, he married Maria Belozvetova (1893–1973) in Tallinn, and in the same year his son Alexis (1933–1995) was born. Towards the end of that year there appeared the first of his twelve "Anthroposophical Meditations on the Old Testament"; twelve further such meditations on the New Testament followed between 1935 and 1937. Both sets of essays divided opinion in the Anthroposophical Society, since in them Tomberg developed his own spiritual inquiries, which in part went beyond the work of Anthroposophy's founder, Rudolf Steiner.[2]

In 1938 Tomberg emigrated to the Netherlands and began actively to lecture on Christological topics. Until the Russian occupation of the Baltic states in 1940, he earned his living as a secretary in the Estonian Vice-Consulate in Amsterdam; thereafter, he was dependent on the support of friends. In the middle of July 1940 he began to teach a weekly course on the Lord's Prayer to this circle of friends. This course, which was organized as a series of meditative exercises affording deep insights into Christian esotericism, was broken off in 1943 because of the threat posed by German occupying forces.

The longer the war went on, the more Tomberg sought to find an organization or a community with a Christian basis that had not been corrupted or destroyed by National Socialism—and he found it at last in the Catholic Church.

---

[2] See *Christ and Sophia, Anthroposophic Meditations on the Old Testament, New Testament & Apocalypse* (Great Barrington, MA 2006).

Introduction

Tomberg's trust in this institution rested, first, on its established hierarchy and its seven sacraments; and second, on the fact that a series of Catholic men and women had offered resistance to the Nazis and paid the price by perishing in concentration camps.

At the beginning of 1944, Tomberg moved to Cologne at the invitation of the legal scholar Ernst von Hippel (1895–1984), whose friend he had become. In the same year he was awarded the title of Doctor of Law for his dissertation on "The Degeneration and Regeneration of Jurisprudence." A second work on international law followed at the beginning of 1945. Tomberg then worked on his *Habilitationsschrift* in the Faculty of Law of the University of Cologne, probably until 1948, which was intended as an outline of a new legal order for post-war Germany.[3] The fate of this latter text remains unclear: there is some evidence that Tomberg may have destroyed it after realizing that German law and politics were developing in a different direction, and as the partition of Germany by the Allied forces began to look likely. Since he no longer envisaged working as a university lecturer in international law (as he had previously done at the Technical University of Aachen), he moved in 1948 to England, where he later completed his jurisprudential magnum opus, here published for the first time. As for the provenance of Tomberg's fourth and final jurisprudential text, completed in England in 1952 and published here for the first time, see the Foreword. A brief summary of the book is also given at the conclusion of this Introduction. Thus, Tomberg's four works in the field of jurisprudence were the fruit of a period of activity lasting from 1944 to 1952.

[3] Regarding these three works, see footnotes on page ii.

From International Law to World Peace

Stepping back in time for a moment, in July 1945 Tomberg, with his wife and son, had moved into a camp for "displaced persons" in Ossendorf, Cologne, where he worked for the British Army as a translator. In December 1945 the Tomberg family relocated to Mülheim, in the Ruhr region of Germany. In 1946 Tomberg began lecturing at the technical college in Aachen, specializing in ethics and law. There he led the rehabilitation of the adult education center. In 1948, as mentioned before, he moved with his family to London, then a year later to Reading, where he worked until 1960 as a translator for the BBC (monitoring propaganda broadcasts primarily from the USSR). In 1952 he became a British citizen. Between the years 1958 and 1967 Tomberg composed the text he is best known for, *Méditations sur les 22 arcanes majeurs du Tarot* (published anonymously),[4] now considered a spiritual classic. His final works were published posthumously.[5] He died on February 24, 1973, on the island of Majorca, and was buried in the cemetery in Palma de Majorca.

In the present book, Tomberg presents the *history* of international law in a broader overview, formulating his results in such a way that they are fruitful not only for the special

---

[4] In English, *Meditations on the Tarot: A Journey into Christian Hermeticism*, republished in an expanded edition by Angelico Press in 2020.

[5] Published in 1985 by Verlag Herder Basel as *Lazarus komm heraus! Drei Schriften von Valentin Tomberg*. A translation of this text was published in 2022 by Angelico Press in three separate volumes: *Lazarus: The Miracle of Resurrection in World History*; *Proclamation on Sinai: Covenant and Commandments*; and *Thy Kingdom Come: The New Evolution of the Good*.

Introduction

case of the existing constitutional arrangements of a particular nation, but can in principle serve the peaceful coexistence of *all* nations on earth when governed by *true* reason, *actual* justice, and *lived* humanity. Whereas in his earlier texts on jurisprudence Tomberg had demonstrated the collapse of the ideal of law and of the idea of law (the *lex divina* and the *lex naturalis*) into the positivism of the enforced law (the *lex positiva*) of the modern age, in this, his final jurisprudential work, he returns to subject of the step-by-step dismantling of the edifice of law. But he presents this now more particularly as the eclipse of the *lex divina* and of the *lex naturalis* by the so-called "law of nations"—a process that, according to his analysis, began as a purely methodological exercise, but in the end led to the *de facto* eclipse of the higher vocation of international law; indeed, so much so that this vocation came to be understood for all practical purposes (that is, positivistically) as nothing more than a legitimizing of *absolute power*, which then led further (as Tomberg was all too painfully aware)[6] to the final degradation of international law from its true foundation in the right or law of humankind to the absolutely sovereign (i.e., totalitarian) modern state.

As a final note, we point out that the deceptively simple-looking German title of Tomberg's second jurisprudential text (*Die Grundlagen des Völkerrechts als Menschheitsrecht*) calls for close scrutiny because this work may be seen as a

---

[6] Recalling in particular the murder of his mother by the Bolsheviks, his labors during the Nazi invasion of Holland, during the bombing raids in and around Cologne, and then again monitoring Soviet bloc propaganda broadcasts for the BBC.

stepping-stone to the present work. Whereas the term *Völkerrecht* ("international law") is standard usage in German jurisprudence, this is not the case with *Menschheitsrecht* ("right of humankind" or "law of humankind")—which tells us as well by implication that the related German legal term *Menschenrechte* ("human rights") was not adequate to the perspective Tomberg is at pains to develop in both works. This point is all the more important in view of the content of Tomberg's broader cultural and Christological writings, where he presents a perspective on jurisprudence of unexampled depth, garnered from the standpoint of the spiritual provenance and distribution of law and order as it cascades into our human world from the "celestial hierarchies" of Christian tradition.[7] More particularly, the hierarchy of law as described in these works may be brought into connection with the three lowest ranks of the ninefold celestial hierarchy: angels—guiding spirits of *individuals*; archangels—guiding spirits of *peoples* (folk), i.e., nations or states; and archai—guiding spirits of *humankind* for set cycles of time. Looked at in this light, we might consider Tomberg's unifying, overarching perspective on jurisprudence as associating the "right of humankind" (or "law of humankind") with the hierarchy of the *archai*, who exercise their guidance from one rank higher than that of the *archangels*, who guide individual peoples or nations, and two ranks above the *angels*, who guide individuals.

JAMES R WETMORE

---

[7] See *The Art of the Good: On the Regeneration of Fallen Justice*; *Proclamation on Sinai: Covenant and Commandments*; *Lazarus: The Miracle of Resurrection in World History*; and *Meditations on the Tarot: A Journey into Christian Hermeticism*.

PART I
How the Problem Stands

1

International Law and its Jurisprudence

he subject of the present work is the history of the jurisprudence of *international* law—that is, of the branch of jurisprudence concerned with legal relations extending beyond the borders of a single state. This concern is not, however, a merely phenomenological determination, description, and cataloguing of the domain of dealings among nations, but rather (as befits the nature of jurisprudence as such) a determination of those principles of law whose application transforms interaction among nations from being a collection of mere power relations into a rule of the power of *law*. That is, the principles in question order the concerns of the community of humankind in such a way that this community is able to elevate itself from the bestial struggle for existence to an order ruled by reason, justice, and humaneness—an order worthy of human beings. Such an order goes beyond the mere absence of cruelty and injustice; it imposes an obligation to active support. It is not enough for jurisprudence merely to know what human relationships are *like*; it must also know what they *ought to be like*. The jurisprudence of international law is not the mere knowledge of what current treaty commitments are in force and of infractions of them in the affairs of nations. It is, rather, the *critique* of these commitments from

From International Law to World Peace

the standpoint of principles that are not taken from dealings among nations, but have instead to *shape* those dealings so they will become what they *ought* to be. The *historical phenomenon* of international law is the degree of reason, justice, and humaneness at work in dealings among nations as the ordering element of those dealings. The *jurisprudence* of international law, by contrast, is both the knowledge of the principles of international law and also an examination of their correctness and fitness for their purpose, as well as their supplementation by new principles.

As an historical phenomenon, international law is ancient. It commences with the "archetypal phenomenon" (*Urphänomen*) of international law, i.e., with the fact of the existence of peaceful dealings among at least two groups of people organized in some way into communities. It is of no consequence, in this context, whether or not these communities regulated their dealings by means of explicit treaties (oral or written) that by "acts of confirmation" set up a network of "implicit contracts" which shaped their mutual dealings in a spirit of reason, justice, and humaneness. The fact of peaceful dealings between two communities suffices *in itself* to identify the presence of international law as such. International law prevails always and everywhere, whenever and wherever *peaceful* dealings exist between two independently organized communities of people. *Peace* as such is the prevalence of implicit or explicit international law. There is as much international law in the world as there is peace in it.

What we are saying is in no way contradicted by the fact that a so-called "law of warfare" also (and rightly) makes up part of international law. For, since there was never in recorded history a peace that was *absolute*, i.e., "free from the seeds of conflict," there was also never an *absolute* war that

International Law and its Jurisprudence

failed to harbor some elements of peaceful dealings, i.e., of reason, justice, and humaneness. Both states—war and peace—are mixed. In our experience, peace is the state in which law is "hot," and sheer power is "cold." Conversely, war is the state in which law becomes "cold" and power "hot." Any state of peace among men that must acknowledge Cain as its ancestor, and the Tower of Babel as its past, is a sort of "cold war." Yet we can also know that a "cold peace" is present in any state of war, since not only can we look back on a series of wise men and prophets, but we also date our very reckoning of time from the first Christmas. International law is peace. The presence of international law *even* in war as "the law of warfare" is nothing other than the continued operation of peace in time of war—nothing other than "peace *in* war." A war without a "cold peace" in it, i.e., an *absolute* war, would mean a relationship between two organized groups of people (tribes, nations, states) in which *every* member of one group was striving to destroy *every* member of the other group, not excepting women, children, and the elderly—and doing so *always* and *everywhere* and by *all* possible means. To the extent that this does *not* happen—e.g., to the extent that in the occupation of an enemy territory not *all* of its inhabitants are slaughtered—the peaceful effect of international law is present even amid war. International law is so strongly associated with peace that it strives to preserve as much as possible of the element of peace (i.e., of reason, justice, and humaneness) even in time of war, and does actually preserve it. This "fragment" of the world of peace, standing opposed to the assaults of war, is, precisely, the so-called "law of warfare" within international law.

The fact that in war today prisoners are taken, are fed, and after the end of the war are permitted to return home;

From International Law to World Peace

the fact that the enemy's wounded are given medical aid and cared for in the same way as one's own wounded; the fact that in the occupation of enemy territory its population is spared—all this and much else forms the domain that peace has wrested from war's grasp, the domain where *law* has successfully opposed sheer *power.*

Against this, the objection can be raised that what is here described as "international law" is nothing but human *culture*, the winning-out of reason and morality as these have been developed by religion, philosophy, art, and science. To this objection our response is to acknowledge that it is quite true. The peace-making, peace-preserving power of reason and of morality that restricts the evil of war even amid war (which is to say, the influence of *culture* in the domain of international relations) is, precisely, international law as an historical reality. It lives in treaties and in the conduct of governments and peoples, in peace and in war, to the extent that, in them, brute force has retreated in the face of the influence of culture. A history of international law would, then, be the history of the influence of human culture on the dealings of states and nations, and the "beginnings" of the history of international law would be identical to the beginning of culture as such. The beginning of the history of international law lies wherever the influence of reason and humanity on the relations among two groups of people organized into communities has shown itself. In other words, the first peaceful dealing between two communities of people is the beginning, the "archetypal phenomenon," of international law. Is this beginning to be found three thousand, four thousand, or eight thousand years ago? Who would dare assert that four thousand years ago there were no peaceful dealings among neighboring peoples? Or that such a state of affairs was impossible even eight thousand years ago? The beginning of international law lies in so distant a past that any question concerning it becomes trivial. It suffices for our present purpose to ascertain that, within the history known to us, there has always been international law—for there have always been peaceful dealings, or epochs of peaceful dealing, between peoples.

The case is different, however, when we shift from the historical phenomenon of international law to the *jurisprudence* of international law, which *does* have an ascertainable beginning within known history. Its germ was already contained (together with all other branches of science) in such knowledge as came into existence with the birth of logical thought out of mythological consciousness. It came alive as part of the indivisible complex of questions regarding the being and vocation of man himself. When in his work *Civitas Dei* St Augustine sketched the outline of a grandly-conceived philosophy of history, this latter, which was at the same time a theological soteriology, eschatology, and apologetics, was also a doctrine of the nature and meaning of human community and of the role of justice and injustice in its life. It was, that is, a philosophy of the state and a philosophy of law. St Augustine's thinking—the thinking of a legally-educated Roman who had risen to the episcopacy and was endowed as well with an historical consciousness—was a *total* thinking. He strove to answer essential questions essentially, rather than from the standpoint of a particular discipline. In our day, when thinking is not determined by the essential questions that originate in human nature, but by objects instead, matters are different. Objective or matter-of-fact thinking, adequate to its object, has of necessity become "specialized" thinking. One specialized kind of thinking, or "method of thinking," is theology, another is jurisprudence, another is philosophy, still another is natural science. For example, the question of the nature of man today receives very different answers, according to the kind of specialized thinking that undertakes to answer the question. For the natural scientist, man is a natural being: a higher animal or a "biological subject"; for the philosopher, man is a being organized in such a way that knowledge can come about in him: a "knowing subject"; for the jurist, man is a being endowed with rights and duties: a "legal subject"; for the theologian, man is a being standing between sin and grace: a "moral subject." To the layman, man is all of these at once. To the specialist, however, he is whichever one that specialist happens to specialize in.

The process of the division of the *one* legacy of culture into religion, knowledge, and art; of the division of knowledge into theology and philosophy; of the separation of philosophy from theology and its subsequent ramification into the various disciplines of the human and natural sciences; and finally of their fragmentation into special disciplinary fields—all of this commenced more than two-and-a-half millennia ago, with the birth of logical thinking out of mythological consciousness. Thus began the autonomy of knowledge as such. Over time, however, this autonomy splintered—affording us an intimation of the later development of politics into individual fields. For their part, these individual fields, as they became ever more self-sufficient, became equally matched and equally valued members of a "family of sciences" organized into a loose unity—rather as the Holy Roman Empire of the Middle Ages became the "family of nations" of the twentieth century. For several centuries, theology and philosophy jointly ruled over the life of knowledge, rather as did the emperor and pope over history. But then the "secular sword" of philosophy parted from the "spiritual sword" of theology. Once this goad to separation was given and the path of separation was embarked upon, the process of the dissolution of the life of knowledge into individual domains could no more be abated than could the process of the dissolution of "Christendom" into individual sovereign states—which led ultimately to the point that the "secular sphere" of the state declared and asserted itself to be unlimitedly sovereign. The struggle between "emperor" and "pope" ended in victory for the emperor. The dispute between a comprehensive, "synthetic" thinking and an investigative "analytic" thinking based in research ended in victory for the latter—a victory that is to be understood historically as holding good "until further notice." The victory of the emperor as that of the principle of the unlimitedness of secular sovereignty brought with it, however, encouragement for *all* secular sovereignty to become unlimited.

In this way, absolutely sovereign states came into being within "Christendom," while concomitantly the emperor became superfluous and disappeared. It was as if the emperor had been devoured by his own children (the unlimitedly sovereign states). Likewise, the victory of the unrestrictedly sovereign, investigating, and analyzing intellect led to the emancipation of secular thought ("free enquiry") from theological thought—but at the same time, led to the fragmentation of this secular thought into absolutely dependent areas. Thus, the unlimitedly sovereign secular philosophy that had claimed to encompass everything was also devoured by its own children and disappeared.

From International Law to World Peace

⊕

The development of modern jurisprudence in international law is one of the currents within the gradual emancipation of the individual areas of the life of knowledge and their growing autonomy. This development did not happen overnight. It made its appearance first as a particular coloration and emphasis discernible in all thoughts related to humankind as a whole—all thoughts, that is, concerned with striving for a human order in accord with reason, justice, and humaneness. The Stoics' idea of *civitas maxima*, St Augustine's idea of *civitas terrena*, Dante's idea of world monarchy, Thomas Aquinas's idea of just and unjust war, all make up part of the developing jurisprudence of international law.[1] That this jurisprudence *did* in fact emerge is a result of systematic and comprehensive work having been devoted both to the legal principles and to the practical phenomena of international affairs. This emergence of systematic consideration of the essential problems and phenomena of international law is precisely the point at which the jurisprudence of international law itself comes into view.

Naturally, to establish this point, we must first specify the essential problems and phenomena of international law, as also what is to be understood by a "system" that deals with them. To this we now turn.

---

[1] *Il Convivio* (Trattado IV. 4). Likewise belonging to the development of the jurisprudence of international law are the ideas and works of people like Pierre Dubois (*De Recuperatione Terra Sancte*, 1305), George of Podebrady, the King of Bohemia, and his chancellor Antonius Marini (who in 1461 set out a plan for a world federation of Christian states), as well as Sully, Henri IV's minister (who had a plan for a European federation made up of fifteen states)—all of whom were concerned with the problem of how to bring about world peace.

2

The Fundamental Problem of the Jurisprudence of International Law

griculture had been practiced for millennia before the science of agronomy came into being. People had been thinking for millennia before Aristotle wrote his *Organon*, Bacon his *Novum Organum*, and Hegel his *Logic*. Similarly, there was a *practice* of international law long before there was a *jurisprudence* of international law.

Now, international law is that limiting and mitigating governance by reason, justice, and humaneness that embraces the state of peace, and struggles against the state of war. The most essential *task* of international law thus consists in bringing about a peace that, on the one hand, bears within it as few seeds of war as possible—and on the other, sows as many seeds of peace as possible in time of war. In other words, the task of international law is both to make peace as reasonable, just, and humane as possible, and to preserve the greatest possible degree of reason, justice, and humaneness in time of war. This is the ever-present *goal* of the practice of international law. The *ideal* towards which this practice is oriented, however, is *world peace*—and that, not as a mere absence of military action, or as a truce extended over a long period of time, but as peace in the *real* sense of the word: a state embracing the whole of humankind and containing within itself none of the causes of war. Given historical experience, this ideal of international law may perhaps be *regarded* as a utopia, but it cannot be *treated* as one. For to treat the ideal of peace as a utopian dream is precisely the national etatism[1] of Hitler and the simultaneously national and international class etatism of Bolshevism.

The "utopia" of world peace is the very force that effectively drives international law! It is this force that over the course of centuries—indeed, of millennia—never tires of bringing reason, justice, and humaneness to rule over the relations between states and between their peoples. Prisoners of war who have returned home owe their life and their freedom to the belief in the "utopia" of world peace. Clever satirists and disappointed sentimentalists may describe the ideal of world peace as an illusion, but this "illusion" has lived on through the millennia, working and creating, making a mockery of mockery, surmounting all disappointments. If belief in world peace ("peace on earth among men of good will") disappears, the struggle for peace will have been given up as a hopeless affair, and the brute force of evil-doing will have free rein.

If international law is the practice of reason, the sense of justice, and humaneness oriented towards world peace, then the *jurisprudence* of international law is the systematic

---

[1] "Etatism" (German *Etatismus*, French *étatisme*) signifies in a broad sense "state socialism" or total control of the state over individual citizens, whereas "statism" is the general belief that the centralization of power in a state (sovereign polity) is the best way to organize humanity. ED

Fundamental Problem of Jurisprudence of International Law

treatment of the problems that international law encounters in its striving for world peace.

What, then, are these problems? There are two. They are the all-embracing problems denoted by the words "peace" and "war."

⊕

PEACE

Peace, as a problem, means the sum-total of the conditions that must obtain in the dealings of nations with each other in order that these dealings should become neither a battleground for mutually hostile forces nor the fiefdom of a single overmighty power. Thus, the three kinds of external state of peace that are to be observed historically ("balance," "hegemony," and "precedence") belong to the problem of peace. Let us briefly examine them in turn

Balance. Although in itself immemorially ancient, "peace as a balance of power" came to prevail in the Christian European world (both as a lasting situation and as a political doctrine) after the Treaty of Westphalia in 1648. The "balance of power in Europe," which so many wars have been fought to preserve, was for centuries regarded as *the* "realistic" basis for peace—at first within Europe, but then throughout the world. But the "balance of Great Powers" essentially means nothing other than a system of states that are in principle hostile to each other, that stand always in mutual fear and mistrust of each other, and that are ready to leap into action to attack and subdue in a timely manner any state among them that may have become stronger (and thus an enemy by virtue of its greater power) before it can become dominant. The series of "coalition wars" (for example, against Louis XIV, Frederick the Great, the French

Republic, and so on) that European nations have had to fight was a consequence of this same system of the balance of power and its political doctrine. For not only does this system signify the "necessity for a coalition" against those nations that grow more powerful, but it signifies as well the perpetual requirement for the latter to put the balance of power to the test and seek to replace it with hegemony.

Hegemony. Peace on the basis of the dominance of a *single* power is the other kind of state of peace taught by history. The attempt to repeat the *pax romana* lives on in the course of world history. After the collapse of the Roman Empire, and later of the Holy Roman Empire, somewhere in Europe there was always the intention, and not infrequently actual attempts, to bring about the unity of Europe on the basis of hegemony. This was the ultimate goal of the policy of Louis XIV. It was also the avowed program of Napoleon and of Hitler. In the post-WWII period, however, Moscow made no secret of the fact that the USSR was attempting to bring about world peace on the basis of a communist world order, to which there can hardly have been a greater obstacle than Tito's Yugoslavia, since the latter was both communist and at the same time claimed independence from Moscow. The peace that the Soviet Union wished to impose upon the world was that of dictatorship, and that in a twofold sense: as the dictatorship of a *single* class (the "proletariat") within all countries, but also as the dictatorship of one country over these other countries. Hitler's "new order" signified the hegemony of Germany. Stalin's "world peace with social justice" signified the hegemony of Russia. Thus, the succession of "hegemonarchs" in Europe has been as follows: what Napoleon wished to accomplish as "emperor" was sought in a new way by Hitler as "Führer," and was striven for by Stalin "as the leader of the working class and father of the nations" in yet a third way.

Precedence. Alongside "balance of power" and "dominance" (hegemony), there is a third conception of the order of world peace, that of "precedence"[2]—i.e., the presence of an authority *above individual states* that can stand equally independent of all other states. In other words, here the unlimited sovereignty of states ceases, and the states acknowledge a higher force standing above them—not the force of *one* state over the others, or that of a mere principle, but an authority possessing those powers and obligations that are directly or indirectly connected to world peace.

"Precedence" was the idea of the Middle Ages, in that the "secular" sword of the emperor and the "spiritual" sword of the pope took precedence over hundreds and thousands of other "swords." In essence, the same idea underpins the modern organizations of the League of Nations and the United Nations, which put themselves at the service of inalterable principles (i.e., the "pope") and represent an authority taking precedence over individual states (i.e., the "emperor"). True, the principles set out in the charter of the United Nations are entirely humanistic (i.e., they contain no revealed theological teaching); yet, when applied to the *practice* of international affairs, they are nevertheless *in accord with* the revealed teachings of the Christian religion. To this extent, their unconditional validity as a basis for the organization of the United Nations corresponds to the "spiritual sword" of the Middle Ages—just as the Security Council, as an institution, corresponds to the emperor's "secular sword."

[2] *Überordnung*, literally "superordination." ED

From International Law to World Peace

The three essential phenomena of the state of peace—peace as a balance of power, peace as the hegemonic dominance of one power, and peace as order—belong, then, to the *first* essential problem in the jurisprudence of international law: that of the true nature of the state of peace and of the paths leading to it. Connected to this problem are the questions of the *sovereignty* of states (that is, of the unrestrictedness or restrictedness of this sovereignty) and of the permissibility or impermissibility of intervening in the "internal affairs" of states; of the *jurisdiction* of states and their liability to punishment (that is, of how the trans-state judicature is to be organized and what powers it is to have); of how the trans-state executive is to be organized and what powers it is to have; and so on.

⊕
WAR

The other essential problem in the jurisprudence of international law is that of *war*. As a problem in international law, war cannot be regarded as the mere absence of peace, nor simply as the opposite of peace. No state, no nation in the world, however bellicose it might be, ever wishes to wage war as an end in itself—i.e., to wage war for war's sake. Ultimately, the objective in any war, however aggressive it may be, is to secure an advantage, or to obviate a disadvantage. It is a case, that is, of wishing for some alteration in a peaceful situation. War is a means to an end. As such, it must either be endured (if there is no other means available by which it could be replaced) or be declared an impermissible means and replaced by another means just as effective but more in accordance with the demands of reason, justice, and humaneness. In the life of those nations that are organized into states, war remains the *ultima ratio* ("the last resort") for so long as there is no alternative *ultima ratio*. The problem of war is thus essentially the question: how can the means of the use of force in war be replaced by an equally effective legal means?

In the *internal* affairs of the modern civilized state, the use of force in blood feuds and duels is no longer in use. In its place, we have the legal means of the court, sanctioned by the state. In *international* affairs, it is a case of the practical task of creating a legal means sanctioned, and thus enforceable, at a trans-state level, a means that would render superfluous the use of force in war as a way of securing those ends not in conflict with reason, justice, and humaneness.

The internal legal order of states, however, is sanctioned by the police force. Criminals and bandits are in the first instance held in check, not by the courts, but by armed police. The international legal order can likewise only be effectively sanctioned by an international force corresponding to the police force of an individual state. For neither can international criminality and banditry be fought with court judgments alone: the world must be in a position to bring international criminals to justice and to carry out sentences upon them.

In the practice of international affairs, the fact of a sanctioned international law will have the consequence (among other things) that war will no longer be a means to expand a nation's territory and to secure advantages of other kinds, but will instead be a means of protecting the legal order. The *sanctioned war* or *legal war* would then replace wars of conquest and defence.

This makes clear the essence of the problem posed by "war" to the jurisprudence of international law—the problem, that is, of the "just war" (*bellum justum*) and of its permissibility, purpose, nature, and limitations (issues already discussed in his day by St Thomas Aquinas). If pacifism simply condemns war as such, while militarism sees in war the ultimately decisive factor in regulating inter-state conflicts, then, for the tradition of treating the problem of war in an international law oriented towards world peace, the problem of war is how to put war *in the service of* peace, and (precisely because of its task of securing peace) how to gradually humanize and limit war, until, as a result of this gradual re-shaping, it becomes superfluous to a rational, just, and humane order of world peace.

Peace and war are thus the fundamental problems in the jurisprudence of international law. The systematic treatment of these problems is the task of that jurisprudence. The first result of such a systematic treatment—i.e., the first "system"—therefore marks the beginning of the history of jurisprudence of international law. But before that beginning of the *history* of the jurisprudence of international law can be established, we must first ask how the basic problems of international law are to be handled, such that they correspond to the condition of "scientificity." In other words, since the beginning, what has been the *method* peculiar to the jurisprudence of international law?

3

The Method of the Jurisprudence of International Law

xperience of the spiritual and intellectual life of humankind stretching over millennia teaches us that each particular *object* brings with it a particular *method* by means of which knowledge of that object can be acquired. It shows, indeed, that the application of a single method to all areas of existence is *unscientific*, i.e., cannot lead to knowledge that is true and adequate to the object concerned. Thus, the methods of chemistry cannot be applied in the realm of psychology. The life of the human soul *can* certainly be traced back to its "elements," and one *can* even search for the "indivisible simplest units of sensation" or "atoms" of psychic life, but the results of such an enquiry in fact turn into an artificial superstructure so complicated and so alien in nature to the life of the soul that it proves useless in trying to acquire actual knowledge of psychic life. The same holds true of the "projection" of economic modes of thought onto the realm of human spiritual and intellectual life, the realms of religion, art, and science. The "reduction" of religious ideals, of works of art, and of scientific ideas to "economic relationships" as practiced in Marxism is unscientific—i.e., is not

objective and not in accordance with the nature of the object of which knowledge is being sought. Indeed, "fantasy" is universally acknowledged to be unscientific precisely *because* it is an arbitrary treatment of an object that does not correspond to it. The fantasist projects ideas and concepts of an alien domain onto a particular area, and thus fails to do justice to the object. Presumably, hardly anyone would explain the puffing of a locomotive as a sign that it is "annoyed." In other words, since mechanical phenomena cannot be explained using psychological ideas (or at least not directly), to say that the locomotive is huffing and puffing because it is annoyed would be fantastical, and thus unscientific. Why, then, do we put up today with so much fantasizing in the opposite direction? Why do we tolerate "explanations" of soul phenomena drawn from mechanical phenomena, rather than rejecting them as unscientific? Why should "historical materialism" be any less fantastical or any more scientific than an "historical magic" claiming to explain the phenomena of economic life by appealing to supernatural powers, just as "historical materialism" tries to explain the phenomena of intellectual and spiritual life by appealing to "economic factors"?

In short, only those methods may be considered scientific that commence investigating the phenomena in any given field by means of ideas and concepts deriving from that field itself. Only after this has reached the point where connecting threads to other fields (especially those lying closest at hand) come to light, may the representations, concepts, and ideas prepared in this way be understood as having some essential relation to the representations, concepts, and ideas of other fields. Thus, for example, a "de-theologized," "de-economized," "de-socialized," and "de-psychologized"

Method of Jurisprudence of International Law

jurisprudence (in the spirit, say, of the "pure jurisprudence" of Hans Kelsen's Austrian school) may discern and acknowledge the substantive, historical, and functional kinship of its representations, concepts, and ideas to the fields of theology, philosophy, history, and the social and economic sciences. But it may not on this account try to turn these other fields into mere provinces of jurisprudence; nor, by means of borrowings and so on, may it try to become itself a mere province of another field. The great discovery of the harmony of all scientific fields (insofar as they rest on true scientificity) is thus reserved to sciences that are "individualized" in the sense set out above, and to their scientists.

In this sense, jurisprudence too is a particular method that corresponds to its particular object. Its object is the field of human "commerce"—that is, of the advantages and the disadvantages that can accrue through human relationships. Its method is to establish a connection between universal principles on the one hand and what is individual and concrete in human commerce on the other. If the empirical natural sciences progress by means of abstraction from the facts of experience to their universal laws, then normative jurisprudence moves from the universal principles to their applicability in concrete cases of lived experience. *Juridical thought is the assessment of the facts of human commerce in the light of principles.* For example, the purely juridical meaning of a table is the place tables occupy among the possibilities of human commerce (possession, property, use and enjoyment, sale, inheritance, donation, hire, pledge), which for their part lead to the conceptual principles of *freedom to dis-*

pose and *binding contract.* This brings us further to the principle of the freedom of the human person, which can be limited only by the freedom of other persons. But then again, for its part, the principle of the freedom of the person leads to the idea of law as such. The *gradual* ("continuous," in Leibniz's sense) connection between the idea of law and a given concrete idea is that of the juridical method of thinking. An organic interconnecting of the results of this method of thinking into a coherent and clearly laid-out whole is a—or rather *the*—system of jurisprudence.

This goes for the jurisprudence of international law too, since it is a branch of jurisprudence. There, too, it is a question of "cases" and "situations" that are to be considered, judged, and regulated in the light of principles. The history of the jurisprudence of international law thus begins at the point where a consistent enough use is made of this method (of treating in a principled manner the most important problems of international affairs in connection with war and peace) that a system results from this use.

4

The Historical Beginnings of the Jurisprudence of International Law

The historical beginning or "initial system" of the jurisprudence of international law can be determined in time and space in different ways, according to the requirements of those specifying the beginning. If, for example, only a positivistically-constructed jurisprudence of international law is deemed scientific (so that we quite naturally demand that the "initial system" in question be a comprehensive analytic treatment of the valid law of contract and custom), we will situate the "real" beginning at a later period and in a different area of culture than would a scholar who cannot omit from the "initial system" the principles of natural law, which transcend positive law. Anyone for whom a jurisprudence without law or right[1] seems just as impossible as a mathematics without the principles of logic, or a theology without God, will look for a *two-level* system of international law—i.e., a system that places the prevalent practice in a particular period in relation to certain principles of

---

[1] As appears, for example, in Leonard Nelson's *Die Rechtswissenschaft ohne Recht* [Jurisprudence without law or right] (Leipzig: 1917).

reason, justice, and humaneness—in which case he will most likely think of the works of Hugo de Groot (Grotius) as the beginning of the jurisprudence of international law.

But the claim made for jurisprudence can go higher still. Just as are there thinkers who cannot content themselves with a single-level jurisprudence limited to positive law, and who postulate the necessity of a two-level jurisprudence, so also there are thinkers who cannot rest content with these two levels (of positive law and of the natural law of emancipated human reason) and demand a *third* level of law as belonging without qualification to the totality of jurisprudence. For such thinkers as these, it is just as impossible to accept natural law without reference to divine law, as it is impossible for the champions of pure natural law to acknowledge the self-sufficiency of positive law. Just as these last cannot treat matters of principle as though they do not exist, so, for the supporters of three-level law, the ideals of divine law cannot be denied. For them, these ideals are the lodestars by which reason navigates—that same reason which for its part guides the technical element of positive law.

The juridical *concepts* of *positive* law would be empty, formal husks if they were not anchored in the *ideas* of *natural* law, which lend them substance. Moreover, the ideas of natural law would fall victim to a static self-satisfaction if they were not given movement and direction by the *ideals* of *divine* law. Just as a mental image lacking the concept thereof is a merely momentary experience; and just as a concept lacking the idea thereof is a merely formal summary; and just as an idea lacking the ideal thereof is a mere insight lacking any further reach—so, in the same way, positive law lacking natural law is a formalism bereft of ideas, and natu-

Historical Beginnings of Jurisprudence of International Law

ral law lacking divine law is an abstract system of thought closed in on itself and incapable of further development. Positive law, natural law, and divine law are related to each other and belong with each other, just as concepts relate to and rely on ideas, and ideas relate to and rely on ideals.

And so, since, in my view, these three conceptions of the nature and scope of jurisprudence *all* belong to the history of jurisprudence (and thus also to the history of the jurisprudence of international law), there is no reason to equate the beginning of that history with the beginning of a one-level or even of a two-level jurisprudence, especially as the three-level conception of jurisprudence comprehends the other two levels in itself. In the present work, it is a case not merely of the history of the positivistic school of the jurisprudence of international law, or even merely of the history of rationalistic natural law and the positivistic schools, but of the history of the jurisprudence of international law *as such*. A truly objective historical account, then, is obliged to take into account the three-level conception of jurisprudence also. And from this it follows that the beginning of the history of the jurisprudence of international law must be sought during a period when, for the first time, a *comprehensive system* of law appeared including the fundamental problems of international law. When might this have been?

⊕

Such a comprehensive system *did not* emerge on the basis of the Mosaic law within the history of Israel. The writings of the Old Testament do indeed include several indications and comments relevant to international law on relations in peace and war (for example, the prohibition of felling fruit-bearing trees in the course of military action, Deut. 20:19–

20), but these did not become the subject or the source of a system of ideas in the course of the history of ancient Israel. The laws of Hammurabi might have played the part of an Assyrio-Babylonian system of state and national law, but no such use of them appears to have been made over the course of the history of Assyria and Babylonia.

Greeks of the classical period were certainly aware of the three levels of law—i.e., the law of the native city-state, the law of the Hellenes (τὰ πάντων ἀνθρώπων νόμιμα τῶν Ἑλλήνων), and the "law of all people" (τὰ πάντων ἀνθρώπων νόμιμα) (Thucydides, I.3; I.118; Plutarch, "Pericles," 17)—which found expression in the dealings of Greek city-states among themselves and with the Asiatic barbarians, but was never systematically elaborated or formulated. The Greeks' "law of all people" was the natural law (φυσικὸν δικαίον) of the philosophers (Aristotle, *Rhetoric*, I.13), i.e., the human capacity to judge rationally and to decide justly. This capacity was held in the highest regard in Platonic and Aristotelian philosophy and in the philosophy of the Stoa.

The "laws of warfare" (οἱ τοῦ πολέμου νόμοι) and the "common laws of human beings" (οἱ κοννοὶ τῶν ἀνθρώπων νόμοι) to which Polybius of Megalopolis refers, are essentially identical to the Romans' *jus belli* ("the law of war") and *jus gentium* ("international law"). They represent the practical solution of the basic problem of international law as a law of humankind (as we have seen: war and peace) as they pertained to Greco-Roman Late Antiquity. Indeed, the "governing rules of the law of humankind" (τὰ παρ ἀνθρώποις ὡρισμένα δίκαια)—according to Polybius (II.8.58; IV.6) and also according to the principles of the Romans' *jus belli* and *jus gentium*—were the protected status of envoys and temples, fidelity to treaties, and the prohibition on plundering the territory of friends and allies.

After the emperor Caracalla (AD 211–217) had extended Roman civil law to all free inhabitants of the Roman world-empire, the *jus gentium* became universal law for the peoples of the Roman imperium. It was interpreted and formulated as such by the jurisconsults Ulpian, Gaius, and Hermogenianus; and at the emperor Justinian's behest, it was incorporated by Tribonianus and his collaborators into the digests and institutions of the *corpus juris civilis Justiniani*.

Now, civil law (*jus civile*) and international law (*jus gentium*) are distinguished from each other in the following ways:

> The laws of every people governed by statutes and customs are partly peculiar to itself and partly common to all humankind. Those rules that a state enacts for its own members are peculiar to itself, and are called civil law. Those rules that are prescribed by natural reason for all men and are observed by all peoples alike, are called the laws of nations. Thus the laws of the Roman people are partly peculiar to itself and partly common to all nations: a distinction of which we shall take note as occasion offers.[2]

This is how the definition of international law stood as it had resulted in the sixth century after Christ as the summary of a millennium of development and blending of Greek and Roman culture from Heraclitus to Boethius.

That the intuitions of the great Roman jurists of late antiquity represent a pointedly legal summary of the entire intellectual life of Greek and Roman antiquity is owed in particular to the fact that these jurists were for the most

[2] *Institutiones*, I. 2, 1.

part philosophers also. Through the mediation of Stoic philosophy, they knew of Aristotle's doctrine of justice, of Zeno's text *Of The Laws*, and, in particular, of the writings of Cicero, the preacher of Stoic philosophy. They also frequently quoted the philosophers. Caius quotes Aristotle and Xenophon; Ulpian and Celsus quote Cicero; Paulus appeals to "the Greeks" in general. The great Roman jurists started out from the view, common to Plato, Aristotle, and the Stoics (Zeno, Seneca, Epictetus, Cicero, Marcus Aurelius), that reason is not an exclusively human quality, but belongs to the world. According to this view, just as the materials that go to make up the body do not belong to human beings exclusively but are present in the natural world surrounding them, so reason is not something that catches light only in human beings and is absent outside them. Rather, both man and nature participate in the reason of the world, the *logos*. It is precisely because reason is no mere human "fabulation" within a realm of being that is deaf and dumb to reason, that it can increase and grow: man can always become wiser, because there is a wisdom towering above him that he can make his own. The universal law of nature holding sway through the universe, and ordering it, is one and the same with right reason (the *recta ratio* of the Stoics).

Obedience to this all-embracing world-law in life and in death was the principle of the Roman legal scholars. In the work of Caius, Paulus, and Marcianus, the *jus naturae* is the governance of reason that brings about harmony both in the universe and in the realm of men as a part of the universe. Within the universe, it is the ordering of the world, which it shapes and preserves as a cosmos in contrast to chaos. In the shared life of humanity, it is *natural law (jus naturae*), which shapes and preserves the ordered life of society, in contrast to chaotic savagery. Thus Ulpian, for example, defines the *jus naturae* as "that which nature has taught all living creatures" (*quod natura omnis animalia docuit*),[3] whereas he defines as international law (*jus gentium*) that part of the *jus naturae* which nature has taught the subgroup of all living creatures called "humankind." For his part, Caius does not make this distinction, since he does not discuss extra-human nature, and thus equates natural law (*jus naturae*) with international law.

The "international law" of the Roman jurists, however, is not the law of *inter-state* relations (as international law is today), but the law that underpins all particular forms of *civil* law. The tendency dominant in modern international law to treat only states as legal subjects is also foreign to the Roman jurists' conception of international law, for which only the human person endowed with reason (and consequently capable of being responsible) could count as a legal subject—that is, as capable of disposing of property, making contracts, and committing offences. The *jus gentium* of Greco-Roman late antiquity, which had coalesced into a single whole, was not international law in the sense of a mere law of treaties between sovereign states and their rules for diplomacy and waging war (rules resting on reciprocity). It consisted, rather, in the replies (*responsa*) of the jurisconsults, grounded in right reason (*recta ratio*) and justice (*justitia*), i.e., on the results of the practical application of *natural law* or of the *law of nature* (*lex naturae*). Here, natu-

---

[3] *Digest of Justinian*, 1.1.

ral law was the strict prescription of reason in *general* for fairness (*aequitas*), but also its application to *individual* relationships—that is, reasonableness, appropriateness, and consideration of mitigating and other circumstances. The *jus gentium* was the result of centuries of combined creative work on the part of reason and humaneness (i.e., of legal *knowledge* and legal *conscience*) to order the relationships of human life in a way as worthy of humanity as possible, i.e., justly and humanely.

For the Roman jurists, natural law was the source of positive law—its "meaning" and its criterion. The *responsa* of the jurisconsults, as well as the prior remarks of the praetor, had the force of law as soon as they were uttered and known. They received a positive legal significance in the *lex casus*, according to which the magistrates made their decisions and to which the emperors referred in their constitutions. Natural law was also the norm for the positive *lex ferenda*.[4] It was the norm as well for making decisions in all cases in respect of which there might be lacuna in positive law, or in its "meaning" or criterion. In cases of conflict, natural law prevailed, and what the natural law forbids, the *jus civile* could neither abrogate nor permit. In other words, natural law, which emerges from the natural kingdom—to which it owes its correctness, justice, and persuasiveness (inner authority)—was measure and inner ground of the validity of the positive law. "If everything that came about (merely) through decisions of nations, decrees of princes, and judges' summings-up were law," writes Cicero (*De re publica*, I.1643), "then theft, adultery, and falsely subscribed

---

[4] *Lex ferenda*, "the law as it should be" as contrasted with the *lex lata*, "the law as it is." ED

wills would be law as soon as they had been approved by the agreement and resolution of the crowd." Cicero thus shows by *reductio ad absurdum* that the natural law (or the *lex aeterna*, as he also calls it) is the basis and true source of positive law: "Law proceeds from nature; after that, many things pass over into the realm of custom; and at last, the things that have proceeded from nature and have been confirmed by custom (practice) are sanctioned by fear of the law and by religion."[5]

This is how Cicero conceived the coming-into-being of positive law from natural law by way of the intermediate stage of the law of custom (i.e., the principles of natural law *in practice*). This view that the law *in force* is the result of a "process of crystallization" remained the prevailing one even in the *Corpus Juris Civilis* of the Emperor Justinian (530–533) about six centuries after Cicero (who died in 43 BC). This view prevailed for so long, not just because it was the one taught throughout that period, but above all because it had remained *in practice* during the intervening centuries. Indeed, the *responsa* (replies) of the jurisconsults, the consequent application of these by the magistrates, and the coming-into-being as a result of this of the *lex casus* (law of precedent), was precisely the process Cicero had characterized: the crystallization of the principles of reason and justice into binding laws in the course of practice (*consuetudo*).

In terms of content, the Roman jurists described: the basic norms of family law (marriage, family, kinship) as belonging to natural law; the principle of fidelity and belief; the principle of appropriateness and reasonableness (*suum cuique*); the principle of the interpretation of professed

---

[5] *De Inventione Rhetorum*, II.53.

intentions from the actual will of the legal subject, as opposed to the literal form of professed intentions; the right of self-defense (*vim vi repellere*); and the principle (emphasized by Stoic philosophy in particular) of the original freedom and equality of human beings.

When applied, these principles produced the *jus gentium*, the law of all the nations of civilized humanity, precisely because these principles are rational, just, and humane. Present in this universal law, or *law of humankind*, are not merely the work of generations of jurists, but also the development of nearly a millennium of philosophy, epitomized by the Stoa. The high value the Stoics set on the dignity of the human being and on being a citizen of the world created the atmosphere in which this universal consciousness of law was able to develop. Indeed, that same atmosphere gave place for the fresh air and clarity in which the rising new sun of Christianity was able to shine out visibly to cultural consciousness. Christianity, which elevated trans-national values—and all else human—to a previously unimagined dignity, was the herald (like a heathen "making straight the way for the one who is coming") of the cosmopolitanism and individualism of the Stoa. The Stoic philosophers themselves made their start by "preaching in the wilderness" of an ethically-decadent world that had fallen into epistemological relativism. They also were clad, so to say, in the "camel-hair garments" of self-mastery, battling against softness and ethical laxity. They also "baptized" the spirits of their proselytes in the noble waters of a pure thinking elevated above the egotistical and personal, the local and the national. Thus, at a time when slavery existed right across the world, Epictetus taught that any laws declaring slavery to be just were "laws of the dead" and an abyss of crime. To the prevailing practice of slavery, Seneca opposed the formula of human dignity: *homo sacra res homini* ("a human being is a sacred thing to other human beings"). And Marcus Aurelius, emperor of the world empire, was of the persuasion that "we are like the limbs of a great body. Nature has inspired us with mutual love towards each other, since we are like each other and born of a like mould. Nature has grounded within us the idea of what is just and fair. . . . In that I am an Antonine, Rome is my native land; in that I am a human being, the world is my home."

The Stoa, as the noblest form of *humanism*, on one hand prepared the way for Christianity by resisting the spiritual values of scepticism, cynicism, and epicureanism, and on the other decisively contributed to the emergence of a universal consciousness that was crystallized in Justinian's *Corpus Juris Civilis*. The Stoa affirmed natural law against merely positive law; and it is to the Stoa in particular that we owe the two-level legal consciousness. It was reserved to the impact of Christianity, however, both to warm into life the pure natural reason of ancient humanism by revealing the mysteries of love for the supernatural, and to elevate legal consciousness to a *third* level—to the level of divine law.

The confluence of pre-Christian humanism and Christian revelation into their first comprehensive organic association took place about seven centuries after the time of Justinian (the epitomist of the legal life of antiquity) and Boethius (the epitomist of the philosophical life of antiquity) in the work of St Thomas Aquinas. Free from any kind of iconoclastic tendency (even of a piously Christian kind), free from any secret doubt and fear about the certainty of his faith, in Thomas Aquinas a sun rose above the horizon of world history—a sun in which ancient philosophy's clarity and audacious quest for knowledge were united with Christianity's warmth, great-heartedness, and absolute certainty in faith.

True, St Thomas Aquinas's work did not come out of nowhere: St Augustine (AD 354–430), who was a Roman jurist, Platonist, and Christian bishop of Hippo, created a Christian philosophy of history and a Christian political philosophy. St Isidore of Seville[6] formulated in his *Etymologiae* the foundations of a three-level Christian-humanist legal philosophy. St Anselm, Gratian,[7] and particularly St Albert the Great all prepared for the work of Aquinas by helping to honor humanistic study (Albert the Great), by collecting materials and building blocks (Gratian, Isidore), or, again, by championing the inner self-evidence and essential reality of the life of ideas as against mere faith in authority (Anselm). Thomas Aquinas's predecessors created the conditions that made his work possible and necessary. But

---

[6] Isidore of Seville was Bishop of Seville from AD 601. In the year 633 he chaired the Ecumenical Council of Toledo. His *Etymologiae*, a work of twenty volumes, was a complete encyclopaedia of the early Middle Ages. It appeared in printed form in 1585 as part of the collection *Auctores Latinae linguae in Unum Redacti Corpus*, edited by Guillelmus Leimarius.

[7] Gratian, a Benedictine, published at Rome in 1144 a compilation under the title of *Decretum*, which he had written in Bologna on the pattern of Justinian's *Corpus Juris Civilis*, and which became a pandect of Church law for the Western Christian world. It contained excerpts from the acts of Church Councils, papal bulls, and decretals from the Church Fathers, from Justinian's *Corpus Juris*, and from the later imperial constitutions.

Historical Beginnings of Jurisprudence of International Law

Aquinas's work itself was a spiritual and intellectual creation that embraced all the problems of the subsequent spiritual and intellectual life of the Christian West. In its way of posing the problems, in its method, in its conceptual language, Thomas's work unites the essential problems of theology, philosophy, morality, law, and social life in an organic whole. A doctrine of the nature and significance of the three-level idea of law, and of its necessary, possible, and actual task in peace and in war, is one limb of the organism of Thomistic doctrine also. This limb is itself, however, further membered into an articulated system that systematically and methodically treats the problems of jurisprudence, including those of the jurisprudence of international law.

In my opinion, then, it will be productive and entirely justified to commence an account of the history of the jurisprudence of international law with the concepts, ideas, and ideals of Thomas Aquinas. And all the more so, since these concepts, ideas, and ideals not only comprise the entire heritage of ideas from antiquity, but represent as well the ground and basis upon which every subsequent development of Western intellectual and spiritual life played out, *including the development of jurisprudence.* Whatever ideas may have been later extended, overthrown, justified, clarified, transformed, negated, or affirmed, they were always an extension of ideas present already in their essential outlines in St Thomas. This is because his intellectual work is the destined intellectual-historical foundation of the totality of the spiritual-cultural sciences of the West. His work is at once a summarizing "afterword" to antiquity and a prospective "foreword" setting the tone for modernity. The work of Thomas Aquinas is a "Noah's ark" of intellectual life. It rescues all the essential ideas of the past in "pairs" of thesis and antithesis, so they might be delivered safely to future shores. This, then, is how I justify beginning my account of the history of the problem of the jurisprudence of international law with an account of those of Aquinas's concepts, ideas, and ideals that are related to international law.

PART II

St Thomas Aquinas's Doctrine that Law has Three Stages, and the Significance of that Doctrine for the Fundamental Problem of International Law: *War* and *Peace*

1

The Augustinian Tradition

he spread of Christianity brought a new impetus to the problem of war and peace. Towards the end of the second century, the African radical *Tertullian*[1] penned an attack on military service, entitled *De Corona*. In the same vein, Origen testifies to the prevailing rejection of war in early Christianity when he says: "by overcoming the demons who provoke war and disturb the peace, we do better service to the rulers than those who bear the sword. More than anyone else, we fight for the emperor. *True, we do not go with him into battle, not even when he demands it,* but we fight for him by pitching a camp of our own, a camp of piety, whence we send our prayers to God."[2] Lactantius[3] forbids the Christian to commit any act of violence: "it is not permitted to the just man

---

[1] Quintus Septimius Tertullianus, probably born around AD 160 in Carthage, was originally a lawyer, but after his conversion became a priest and an ecclesiastical author. He joined the Montanist sect and left the Church c. AD 212. His most important writings include "To the Martyrs (197), "To the Nations," "Apologeticus," *Liber de praescriptione haereticorum, De Corona* (211).

[2] *Contra Celsum*, VIII. 73.

[3] Lucius Caecilius Firmianus Lactantius, fourth-century Christian apologist. He earned the title of "the Christian Cicero." His most important works are *De Opificio Dei* (AD 303 or 304), *Divinarum Institutionum Libri VII* (AD 304–311), *Epitome Divinarum Institutionum, De Ira Dei.*

to bear arms; his service is justice; he may not even accuse a felon, since it is irrelevant whether one kills someone with a sword or by means of words, for it is killing that is forbidden. There is not the least exception from this divine command."[4]

These views of the Christian minority in the powerful Roman world-empire had to undergo scrutiny when (from Emperor Constantine onwards) responsibility for the well-being, and even the existence, of this world-empire was entrusted to Christians themselves. Once the Roman empire became Christian, its protection and security became a matter for Christianity. True, the principle that *ecclesia abhorret a sanguine* ("the church abhors bloodshed") remained in force unchanged. Moreover, Augustine wrote that "whoever can think of war without feeling deep pain must have lost all sense of humanity,"[5] and that "peace ought to be dear to us all; there is no greater glory than to keep the peace. How contemptible, by contrast, is the glory of conquest won by means of abominations."[6] But war is no longer declared a crime, nor military service a sin. Augustine teaches the possibility of a just war[7]—that military service is service of the faith, and courage a gift of God, which are to be used in accordance with his will. For "peace is not sought in order to beget war, but war is waged in order to achieve peace. Be ready for peace, therefore, even when you are waging war, so that, by conquering, you may lead those whom you are fighting to the blessings of peace."

---

[4] *De div. instit.*, VI: 18, 20.
[5] *Civitas Dei*, LXIX. c.7.
[6] Ibid., L.III. c.14.
[7] *Contra Faustum Manichaeum*, Lib. 22, cc. 77–78.

The Augustinian Tradition

Just wars, according to St Augustine, are those that "avenge injustices whenever a state or a city is to be punished, either to punish the injustice committed by its citizens, or when it has failed to restore what it has unjustly taken away."[8] "For the just man, it is the injustice of the opposing party that allows him to proceed to a just war,"[9] and "whenever a just war is waged, the other side is fighting for sin."[10] Lastly, "Good people, when they are really good, do not fight against good people; a fight is either between wicked people and wicked people, or between good people and wicked people."[11] Thus, good people can never fight against good people, nor champions of justice against champions of justice. This basic idea of St Augustine's was adopted by Isidore of Seville (d. AD 636) in his *Etymologiae*:

> There are four kinds of war, namely the just, the unjust, civil war, and more-than-civil war (*bellum plusquam civile*). The just war, as follows from what has already been said, is waged so as to get things back or so as to defend oneself against one's enemies. The unjust war is a war that is not begun on grounds consistent with justice, but is begun out of passion. Of this war, Cicero said in his *Republica* that "those wars are unjust that are begun without just cause. For no just war can be waged except for reasons of punishment or to defend against an enemy. . . . Civil war results from tumult, discord, and passion among citizens, like the war between Sulla and Marius, who waged war against each other within a nation. A more-than-civil war is a war

---

[8] St Augustine, *Lib. Quaest.* VI, 10. This formulation of the just war is adopted by Gratian's *Decretum*: Causa XXIII, qu. 40.

[9] *De Civ. Dei*, XIX. 7.

[10] Ibid., I.c. XIX. 15.

[11] Ibid., XXV. 5

in which not only citizens, but also kin (*cognati*) take part, as for example the war between Caesar and Pompey, in which son-in-law and father-in-law fought against each other."[12]

This is how Isidore defines the four kinds of war, of which he recognizes only the just war as justified.

We find Isidore's definitions of the *jus gentium* unaltered[13] in the first *distinctio* of the first part of Gratian's *Decretum* (i.e., more than five centuries later). There, Gratian deals with eight questions, of which the first four are immediately related to the central problem of international law (i.e., war and peace), namely the questions: (1) Is the use of weapons (*militare*) a sin? (2) Which wars are just? (3) Are injustices towards allies (*socii*) to be prevented with armed force? (4) May punitive military actions (*vindicta*) be undertaken?

Gratian answers these questions in the spirit of St Augustine, whom he quotes on each point:

Regarding the use of weapons. The use of weapons is not in itself a sin, for otherwise (as Gratian concludes, with Augustine) Christ would have explicitly told the centurions and warriors who sought him out to give up their profession. Moreover, courage, which is a gift of God, can be used in accordance with God's will, especially if the war is being waged for peace (cf. Augustine's letter to Boniface). A

---

[12] *Etym. Lib.* XVIII, c.1.

[13] The only alteration of the text of the above definition from Isidore is to be found in the sentence: *justum bellum est, quod ex praedicto geritur de rebus repetitis*, etc., where, out of *ex praedicto* (or *proedicto*), Gratian makes *ex edicto*, so that the sentence has the meaning "the just war is waged *on command*, for the sake of things that are demanded back or for defence against one's enemies."

The Augustinian Tradition

war waged out of the "wish to do damage, the cruelty of revenge, a restless and irreconcilable spirit, the savagery of the rebellious spirit, or a lust for power or any other similar motives"[14] is to be rejected.

Regarding which wars are just. The question of the nature of the just war is answered by Gratian with the words of Isidore: "A war is just, when it is waged *on command*, for the sake of things that are demanded back or for defence against one's enemies."[15] Here it is irrelevant whether the war is waged and won by open force of arms or by means of a ruse.

Regarding preventing injustices to allies. It is the teaching of St Augustine, Ambrose, some of the popes, and the Council of Carthage that it is justified to protect allies using armed force. Anyone who is in a position to prevent the criminal action of an evil-doer by force, and who neglects to do so, fails in his duty. *Mali sunt prohibendi a malo et cogendi ad bonum* ("evil is to be forbidden the evil, and they are to be forced towards the good").[16]

Gratian's work confined itself to the important task of forming a link in the uninterrupted transmission of the Augustinian and Stoic intellectual legacy.[17] On the basis of this transmission there developed in the second half of the thirteenth century the comprehensive intellectual system of St Thomas Aquinas.

---

[14] Augustine, *Contra Faustum Manichaeum*, Lib. 22, c.74.
[15] Augustine, *Quaestionum*, 6.40.9.10.
[16] Augustine, *Ad Donatum*, epistle 204.
[17] The author provides no further comment here on point (4) above, regarding whether punitive military actions may be undertaken.

2

The Dispute over the Possibility of Knowing the Truth in Thinking up until the Time of Thomas Aquinas

longside the tradition of the intellectual legacy of late antiquity (which was preserved by jurists and canon lawyers in particular) lives another tradition that was, as it were, the mortal enemy of the first. For if the West owes all its remaining intellectual and spiritual foundations (such as, for example, law itself, or natural law, as well as those ideas, traditions, and institutions that cannot be argued away from Christianity) to the intellectual current of Socratic-Platonic-Aristotelian idealism (further fortified and crystallized by the Stoa, and animated, warmed, and elevated to new heights by Christianity), the counter-current is rooted in the views of the opponents of the Platonic-Aristotelian philosophy—the Sophists, whom the West has to thank, on the whole, for the disruptions and radical changes it has had to undergo in the wake of the influence of relativism, subjectivism, voluntarism, and the subjectivistic postulate of freedom. The devastating dialogue between Christ and Pilate resounds like a tragic drone-note throughout the history of the West, reprising itself in a thousand different timbres, voices, and settings: "for this cause came I into the world, that I should bear witness unto the truth. Every one that is of the truth

heareth my voice. Pilate saith unto him, 'What is truth?'" (John 18:37–38)

This drone-note resounds in the Medieval realists' championing of the objective validity of *universalia* against the nominalists, who saw in universal concepts "mere words" (*mere voces*); it resounds in the affirmation of love, which is stronger than death, and in its veneration of saints against the iconoclasts (who saw in the veneration of saints a worship of "mere images" and idols); it resounds in the unshakable conviction of the truth of the Christian revelation against the attacks of the "free spirits" who see in this revelation "a mere claim to authority" on the part of the Church and a "blind faith in authority" on the part of the faithful; it resounds in taking a stand on the ground of natural law and divine law against the would-be destructive critique of the "unscientific medieval postulates of natural law" by the legal positivists (who see in natural law a "mere postulate," or "wishful thinking"). Wheresoever this drone-note resounds, it is always *essentially* a matter of variations on the one original opposition—that between Christ and Pilate. People, and their languages, change. New problems are discussed by new people. But the encounter between Christ and Pilate is immutable. Their dialogue survives the centuries.

In contrast to such philosophers as Heraclitus, Socrates, Plato, and Aristotle, the Sophists emphasized the relativity of knowledge and morality. Their natural law was not a world-reason bidding unconditional obedience, but consisted instead of the claims of the individual person (grounded in the nature of the will) to a field of action in which he could run free. The natural law of the philosophers was a *law*; it was *binding* for all. The natural law of the Sophists was a *justification*; it gave everyone the right to specific *claims*. Thus, in ethics the philosophers emphasized *duty*, whereas the Sophists emphasized *law* or *right*. To the Sophists, laws were not sacred values conserved and transmitted through the life of the state; they were instead (as Thrasymachus taught),[1] artificial instruments that serve the interests of the ruling clique. Laws were merely declarations of will; moreover, they were declarations of the will of one group, which naturally made of law what they themselves wanted, what corresponded to their interests. When Callicles first proclaimed the proposition that "might makes right," he meant by this not only that the strongest will becomes the right, becomes the law, but also that the equal distribution of power to all those persons endowed with a will—i.e., all those who were entitled to power—was *just* in the sense of Sophistic natural law. By emphasizing the equal claim of all to power, the Sophists became the first pioneers of the "liberty, equality, and fraternity" of the "Enlightenment" and of the "great" French revolution of 1789.

> Three ideas are presented by the Sophists as belonging to natural law, although they are charged with social dynamite in the context of the Greek world. And these three ideas have served revolutionary thinkers ever since as forms and vessels into which they may pour their revolutionary feelings, reforming ideas, and political goals. First, the laws in force serve class interests; they are artificial instruments. Only the naturally-ethical and the naturally-just is ethical and just. Second, the idea of the natural-legal freedom and equality of all those who bear the countenance of human beings; and, following from this, the idea of human rights and the *civitas maxima*, the idea of humankind, which is

[1] In Plato's *Republic*.

higher than the *polis*. Third, the state, the polis, is contingent; it is the result of human decisions; that is, it originates in a free contract, and not in any kind of necessity. The political situation must therefore have been preceded by a state of nature [whether this is portrayed optimistically, as by Rousseau, or pessimistically, as by Hobbes—*Author*] in which natural law held sway.[2]

This characterization of the essence of Sophism by Heinrich Rommen is correct about Sophism in every respect. It exhibits, alongside its shallow intellectual life (a consequence of the skepticism that eats away at its root), its humanistic and humane impulse too. The Sophists as little wished to bring about evil as the pamphleteers of the "Age of Enlightenment" wished to bring about the abominations of the Jacobins' reign of terror. But even so, they formed their thinking in accordance with their *wishes*. To the Sophists, concepts, ideas, and ideals were not wandering stars, fixed stars, and constellations of stars in the sky of eternal being. They were mere instruments of the will, which could create these concepts, ideas, and ideals, and also use them—whether as utilitarian tools or as weapons—rather in the way the *words of language* can be used. To the Sophists, intellectual life (one could also say, the world of ideas) was the *language of the will*, whereas to the philosophers it was the shining characters, words, and sentences of the language of the world's Godhead, the *Logos*.

It is Sophism's *voluntarism* that makes of it in social life a revolutionary and subversive impulse: in the field of ethics, a utilitarian eudaimonism;[3] in the field of the life of knowl-

---

[2] Heinrich Rommen, *Die ewige Wiederkehr des Naturrechts* [The eternal return of natural law] (Leipzig, 1936), 118.

[3] The view that the highest ethical goal is personal well-being. ED

edge, a nominalism (a subjectivism and, finally, a scepticism). Indeed, voluntarism—as the primacy of the will over reason as expressed both in theory and in the practice of legal positivism and of politics—of necessity lends all knowledge the appearance of subjectivity and relativity, thereby removing from great thoughts their universal validity and supra-temporal authority.

The primacy of the will may indeed have first been proclaimed with an emphasis on the moral over the "merely cognitive," but the *direction* that was taken in the subsequent development (to which this proclamation gave the first stimulus) necessarily led ever further away from the binding, obligating, and orienting aspect of the principles, ideas, and ideals of the life of the mind. It led ever deeper into the field of the postulates, programs, and self-interested demands of the life of the will. In the end, it led even to the life of wishes and drives. There would at first certainly seem to be nothing in common between, on the one hand, the pious scholastic Duns Scotus, who emphasized and taught the principle of the primacy of the will over the intellect,[4] and on the other, Nietzsche's "will to power," Hitler's "Aryan-Germanic will to power," and Bolshevism's "proletarian and popular-democratic will to power." And yet, the modern glorifications of state tyranny, of the tyranny of a clique (one-party state), and of individual tyranny (the *Führerprinzip* or "leader-principle"), are all consequences of a voluntarism that is first theological, then

---

[4] The idea that something is good, not because it corresponds to the nature of God or to the nature of man formed in God's image, but because God *wills* it thus, so that natural law could have a quite different content if God's arbitrary will had so determined it.

philosophical, then legal and political, and finally social and political. Life's layers reflect each other: theological opinions become secularized legal theories, which in turn become political and social endeavors. Heinrich Rommen illustrates the connection between an earlier voluntarism and many later phenomena as follows:

> In pursuing the course of the development of doctrine, it is worth noting that the antithesis *lex ratio – lex voluntas*, which relates to the milieu of theological thinking, and, more generally, to the *lex naturalis*, which includes natural law, coincides structurally with the theories of God that are held by the respective thinkers. Even later on, however, when the theory of natural law detaches itself from its theological milieu—that is, when it becomes secularized—the same structures of thinking repeat themselves, now detached from the medieval form of the *summa*, and applied simply to law in the narrower sense. The result will be that natural law is a consequence of the theological and anthropological doctrines of the priority of the intellect over the will (law is reason), of the idea that we can know the nature of things and of their essential ordering, of their metaphysical being, and of a cosmos that is a hierarchy of values. Positivism is the consequence of the priority of the will (and *voluntas* means more than mere will; it means also passion and irrational aspirations, etc.) over the intellect, both in the theory of God and in the theory of man; it means renouncing knowing the nature of things (nominalism), as well as renouncing the metaphysics of being and the order of values. Positivism thus finds itself in the same intellectual structure even in the thinking of the nineteenth and twentieth centuries (and even if this is concealed by the difference of appellations). Relativism in ethics, legal positivism, a will-centered theory in state and international law, nominalism and agnosticism in episte-

mology and metaphysics: these have recently formed a single front with a mystical biological positivism presenting itself as a form of natural law. On the other side stands the conviction that there are inalterable principles of ethical life and of law, that the idea of law is the object of a philosophy of law, that there is natural law, that it is possible to know the nature of things, that there are objective values, and that there is in the end a unity of what is and what ought to be, as well as that a true theodicy is possible. And this antithesis, in an ever sharper form, continues into the theory of the different kinds of state. . . . [5]

The tendency, which began with the ancient Sophists, to deny the possibility of knowing objective truth by means of thought, and the assertion (connected with this) that what conforms to the will is decisive both for knowledge and for action, was revived in a different form in the eleventh century. This had been particularly so in the Neoplatonist Porphyry's earlier treatment of the relationship between what is thought, on the one hand, and reality as we are informed of it by our experience, on the other. Thinkers at that time were deeply preoccupied with this problem, formulated then as: "whether anything of general and specific concepts actually exists in reality, or whether they are found in the understanding alone." This question was at first answered in two ways: yes, or no. In the ninth century, Fredugisius, Rémigius of Auxerre, and Johannes Scotus Eriguena had already answered it in the affirmative, i.e., that universal concepts were not merely subjective but real (realism); so too did Gerbert and Odo of Tournai in the tenth century, and both St Anselm and Ivo of Chartres in the eleventh.

A contemporary of the latter two, however, Roscelin, a

[5] Ibid., 54–56.

monk from Compiègne, answered Porphyry's question in the negative. For Roscelin, universal concepts (*universalia*) did not exist outside the subject. In conformity with Boethius's terminology, universal concepts were at that time described either as *res* (objective realities, "things") or as *voces* (subjective creations, "voices"). In around 1087, Roscelin became the founder of the *sententia vocum*, the doctrine of the verbal value of universal concepts, i.e., of nominalism.[6]

Since then, nominalism has lived on in its two basic forms: that of "radical nominalism," or the complete denial of the possibility of knowing objective truth; and that of "conceptualism," or the assertion that we are permanently uncertain as to whether the knowledge we have acquired is truth or not, along with the consequences following therefrom—either scepticism such as the *ignoramus ignorabimus* of Du Bois-Reymond, the situation of "as if" (such as Voltaire's "if God did not exist, it would be necessary to invent him"), Kant's postulates of practical reason, William James's pragmatism, and Vaihinger's *Philosophy of As If.* Nominal-

---

[6] Otto of Freising says of Roscelin that "he was the first in our age to argue that the value of concepts was verbal." Roscelin was convicted of tritheism and was summoned to appear before the Council of Soissons (1093). He defended the view that the three divine persons were independent beings, like three angels, for otherwise God the Father and God the Holy Spirit would have been made flesh together with God the Son. According to St Anselm, Roscelin also taught that the color of a horse did not exist independently of the horse, and that the wisdom of a soul, similarly, did not exist outside the soul that is wise (*De fide trinit.* 1–2). The doctrine of the nominalists (*nam cum habeat eorum sententia nihil esse praeter individuum...*) was that the individual alone is reality: there is nothing apart from individual beings and things.

ism in its radical form was anathematized at the Council of Soissons in 1092–1093, but it was still cultivated thereafter, and was defended with particular success in its conceptualist form by William of Ockham in the fourteenth century. From there, thanks to the successive efforts of Francis Bacon (1561–1626), Thomas Hobbes (1588–1670), John Locke (1632–1704), David Hume (1711–1776), John Stuart Mill, Hippolyte Taine, Théodule-Armand Ribot, Herbert Spencer, Aldous Huxley, etc., nominalism became dominant in the area of natural science, and in the nineteenth century gradually began to get the upper hand in almost all scientific and scholarly thought in the West.

Nominalism remained the same in essence, however, throughout all these centuries. For its defenders, it was always a matter in the end of experiencing thinking as a shadowy *remnant* acquired from the realm of sense experience, and of the process of thinking as a busying oneself with this shadowy world of experience in accordance with the inclinations or "postulates" innate in the nature of the human will. Whereas the champion of "realism" experiences the content of thought as an essential and efficaciously convincing intellectual and spiritual light, and the process of thinking as the creation of that state of calmness of will and selflessness needful to allow the light of conceptual clarity to shine into the mind and for profundity of ideas and elevation of ideals, the defender of "nominalism" by contrast experiences only generalities of sense experience reduced to a shadow-existence subject to his will. The more shadowy the life of the mind appears, however, the more strongly the life of the will is foregrounded. Thus, nominalism leads inexorably to voluntarism, to the view that *voluntas nobilior facultas* (will is the nobler faculty).

Dispute over Knowing Truth in Thinking till Time of Aquinas

For its part, realism has also lived on since Plato and Aristotle in two basic forms: the Platonic theory of *ideas* and the Aristotelian theory of *forms*. In the Middle Ages, particularly in the period immediately before that of Aquinas, the two undercurrents of realism were alike in giving a positive answer to Porphyry's question, but with the difference that the "Platonists" attributed to the *universalia* an existence *independent* of their being embodied in individual appearances or of being thought in the consciousness of a thinker (*universalia ante res*, "universals prior to things"), whereas the "Aristotelians" denied that the *universalia* had being independent of individual appearances, and acknowledged them only as principles of form at work *in* individual things (*universalia in rebus*, "universals in things"). For their part, however, "conceptualistically" oriented nominalists (whose theory originated with Zeno the Stoic, just as the two currents of realism can be traced back to Plato and Aristotle) saw in *universalia* only "signs" (*signum* and *terminus*) for the common elements in things (*universalia post res*, "universals after things") acquired from sense experience.

Now, the so-called "universals controversy," or better, the dispute over the possibility of knowing truth by means of thought, was of the highest significance for the life of law. For the question at hand was whether "universal law" is a reality grounded in the being of the world, or merely a description contrived by human beings to cover a grouping of observed experiences. In other words, it was a question of whether there is such a thing as law-in-itself, or not.

Since the consequences of the outcome of this dispute (which continues to this day in various fields and under various nomenclatures) were also regarded as no less weighty in other areas of spiritual and intellectual life, the dispute was carried on in the most passionate and acute manner.

Albertus Magnus (Albert the Great, Doctor Universalis, c. 1280–1280), theologian, philosopher, and natural scientist of the Dominican order (as his contemporary Roger Bacon was of the Franciscan order), and teacher of Thomas Aquinas, established his intellectual output amid this very struggle over universals, an output that essentially not only reconciled Christian revelation with humanism, but also reconciled the three forms of humanism—Platonism, Aristotelianism, and Stoic conceptualism—among themselves. He taught in particular that three kinds of universal are to be distinguished from each other: ideal archetypes of divine reason, which precede things (*universalia ante res*); "type-determining" forms of things (*universalia in rebus*); and concepts gained by means of abstraction (*universalia post res*). These three kinds of universals correspond to divine law, natural law, and human law (*lex humana*)—the three levels of law. By projecting into human nature as the light of reason and the voice of conscience, the divine law becomes natural law. When laws are conceived by abstraction from natural law, however, human (positive) law comes into being. The latter consists of *concepts* that owe their truth and justice to their concord with the *ideas* of natural law that have created them, while the ideas of natural law in turn draw their orienting authority from the *ideals* of divine law. Concepts are thus the result of a perception of the analogical affinity among individual phenomena (universals "after" things), while that affinity *itself* is governed by the creating form-ideas (or "archetypal phenomena" in Goethe's sense) *in* the individual things (universals "in" things). This governance by form-ideas is directed in turn towards the realization of the final, essential ground and highest potentiality—towards the ideals or divine archetypes, which are not embodied (not "in" things) for so long as perfection is not yet present "in" phenomena, and which precede phenomena just as the ground plan of a building precedes the building itself (universals "prior to" things). "Know that man cannot become perfect in philosophy but by the knowledge of two philosophers, namely Plato and Aristotle," says the Doctor Universalis.[7]

In other words, progress in philosophy is not achieved by rejecting Plato's theory of ideas or by rejecting Aristotle's entelechies (his "forms"), but by bringing the two together. This means in turn, however, connecting the *universalia ante res* with the *universalia in rebus*—that is, connecting the archetypes of kinds with the creating forms within the individual appearances of those kinds. For their part, abstractions acquired by means of experience (*universalia post res*) are a way of becoming aware of what is shared in common among individual phenomena, i.e., of becoming aware of *universalia in rebus*. "The universal concept is formed by means of two factors: by means of the nature to which the universality belongs, and, in respect of the many individual phenomena, by means of that which fills them in their universal nature."[8]

Irrespective of the question of whether they might be considered valid in a Kantian or in an empirically scientific sense, these comprehensive insights of Albert the Great proved to be extremely productive. Not only did they

---

[7] *Metaphysics*, I.V. 15.
[8] Ibid., V. VI. 5, 6.

enable the man who held them to write nine treatises on theology, seven on logic, seven on physics, seven on biology, seven on psychology, two on morals and politics, and two on metaphysics (and perhaps more, since there is a series of writings ascribed to Albertus Magnus, but whose authenticity is doubted), but also decisively to contribute to forming the mind of a pupil who was to create a comprehensive basis for Western Christian intellectual culture: St Thomas Aquinas.

Thomas Aquinas (Doctor Angelicus, 1225–1279) stands on the foundation of his teacher's work. All of his thought is underpinned by the principle of analogy (the *analogia entis* or "analogy of being"), and it was Albertus Magnus who proclaimed with the greatest decidedness the basis of the analogy of being. He did so, moreover, not merely in the purely theological domain, in which it goes without saying, given that Moses's account of creation mentions it explicitly (man as the "image and likeness" of God), but also in the humanistic domain of philosophy, since, for about six centuries, the West owed its knowledge of the ancient source of the principle of analogy—*the Emerald Tablet of Hermes Trismegistus*—to no other than Albertus, who published the Latin text of it. (Only six centuries later were ancient manuscripts of it in Arabic discovered.) This source contains the ancient and venerable formulation of the principle of analogy: "what is above is like what is below, and what is below is like what is above: to accomplish the miracle of one thing." The principle of the *analogia entis* in the work of St Thomas Aquinas was what not only made it possible for him to keep theology and philosophy in harmony with each other, but also to answer Porphyry's question about the *universalia* in such a way that this answer has lost not one iota of its validity up to the present day: divine reason is reflected in the way nature is ruled, as well as in the minds of men; or, in other words, the *universalia ante res* become formative entelechies (*universalia in rebus*) that then become universal concepts of human knowledge (*universalia post res*).

3

Thomas Aquinas and the Doctrine of the Three Levels of Law

hen it is applied, the principle of the analogy of being means two things: on the one hand, things are graded (hierarchically articulated); on the other, what is thus graded is interconnected (is in harmony). "Human law is to be derived from divine law: a law that contradicts the prescriptions and the nature of divine law is not a law at all," as Albertus Magnus taught (*Summa de creaturis*). For his part, Aquinas says of natural law that "every law enacted by human beings has the character of law to the extent that it is deduced from natural law. If, however, it is not in agreement with natural law, it is no longer law but a perversion of law."[1]

These claims on the part of the Doctor Universalis and the Doctor Angelicus both contain the principle of the

---

[1] *Summa theol.* I–II. qu. 95, art. 2. (Tomberg's translations of Aquinas have been translated directly from his German here, since in certain cases the terms he employs in his translation—e.g., *Begriff* [concept], *Idee* [idea], and *Ideal* [ideal]—are also terms essential to his own argument. At the same time, Tomberg's sometimes highly abbreviated references to the text of Aquinas have been expanded (and sometimes corrected) so that readers can locate the text for themselves if they wish.) TR

Thomas Aquinas and the Doctrine of Three Levels of Law

analogy of being, together with its two fundamental consequences: that what is below is the "image" of what is above and may not contradict the latter. For

> holy science has come to be in us by means of another and higher thing that brings it about. It is a form of stamping, like a sealing of us with divine wisdom, so that the human spirit bears the seal of divine wisdom, and the stamp of the forms and concepts of the first cause which, in its wisdom, creates, restores, and transfigures what it has caused. Holy science thus comes into being without question by means of such an impression made upon us; and, indeed, by our rising up to God in it, as wax rises up to the seal, not the other way round. Thus it is obtained more by means of prayer and piety than by means of study.[2]

This is what Albertus Magnus says about how essential concepts, ideas, and ideals come into being in the human spirit (among them the concept, idea, and ideal of law), and about the relationship of what has come about this way to truth. The seal of truth corresponds to divine law. The imprint of the seal of truth on the human spirit corresponds to natural law. The practical application of the principle of natural law to particular relationships and particular groups of people corresponds to human or positive law.

This view underpins the whole of Aquinas's doctrine that law has three levels.

> Since the eternal law (*lex aeterna*) is the idea of government in the highest governor, all concepts of government among the lower governors must be deduced from the eternal law. Concepts held by the lower governors are, however, all laws outside the eternal law. Consequently all laws, insofar as they correspond to right reason (*ratio*

[2] No citation given.

recta), must be deduced from the eternal law. For this reason, Augustine also says in his book *On Free Will* (I.6) that everything that is just and lawful under temporal law is derived by human beings from the eternal law.[3]

What, then, *is* the eternal law or divine law? Law as such is "an ordering of reason to the common good, promulgated by the one who has care of the community (ibid., qu. 90, art. 3). . . . Presupposing, then, that (as we have seen in Part I (qu. 22) the world is governed by divine providence, it is evident that the whole community of the universe (*tota communitas universi*) is governed by divine reason, and that, since the reason in God that orders things is the prince of the universe, it is analogous to law. And since divine reason grasps nothing in time, but in eternity . . . this law must be called an eternal one" (ibid., qu. 91, art. 1).

What, however, is the relation of the eternal law to natural law, and what is the nature of the latter?

> Since the law is the norm and the measure, it can be present in a being in two ways: either as normative, or as measuring. . . . It follows that everything which is subject to divine providence, precisely because it is ruled and proportioned by the divine law . . . participates in some way in the divine law insofar as everything has an inclination to deeds and ends of its own through the imprint of the divine law. Among all other things, however, the creature endowed with reason is subject to divine providence in a much higher manner, insofar as this creature makes itself a participant in providence by being provident for itself and for others. It thus also participates in eternal reason itself, whereby it receives a natural inclination to the right deed and to the right end. This participation of the rational

---

[3] *Summa theol.* I–II, qu. 93, art. 3.

creature in the eternal law is called "natural law". . . . The psalmist says (Psalms 4:6) "Many say: who will show us any good?" to which question he gives the answer "the light of thy countenance is imprinted upon us, Lord." By "light" the psalmist seems to mean the light of natural reason, with the help of which we distinguish good from evil. This belongs, however, to the natural law, which is nothing other than the expression of divine light within us. From this it follows that natural law is nothing other than the rational creature's participation in the eternal law.[4]

If the eternal law is the governance of divine reason, and if natural law is the projection of the governing eternal law into the inner being of the rational creature, then "human law" is the projection of the natural law from the inner being of the rational creature into the external world.

Law is a dictate of practical reason. Now, practical reason and contemplative (pure) reason work in a similar way: they both draw particular inferences from specific principles . . . consequently it must be said that, just as in the domain of contemplative reason the inferences of the various sciences are drawn from principles that are naturally known and indemonstrable—principles whose knowledge is not naturally imprinted upon us but is found by means of the activity of reason—so the human intellect (practical reason) must draw conclusions from the dictates of the natural law, which are as it were universal and indemonstrable principles, so as to arrive at more particular (*magis partiulariter*) determinations. These particular determinations, however, which are acquired by means of the human intellect, are human laws if they are in accordance with the nature of the presuppositions that belong to law. . . .[5]

[4] Ibid., qu. 91, art. 2.
[5] Ibid., art. 3.

From International Law to World Peace

There are thus *four* basic properties of law. (1) Law must be an ordering of reason (*ratio ordinatio*). (2) Law must serve the common good (*bonum commune*). (3) Law must be promulgated (*promulgata*). (4) Law must be promulgated by the person or a corporation upon whom care for the well-being of the community in question devolves.

Alongside the eternal law (which is the governance of divine reason in the universe), the natural law (which is the imprint of the eternal law upon the inner being of man), and the human law (which consists of the inferences drawn from the principles of natural law and applied to particular cases), there is also a fourth kind of law, the so-called "positive divine law," or the divine law *as such*. This divine law (*lex divina*) has been given to humankind through revelation; its content is the eternal law, or that part of it which concerns humankind. Divine law cannot contradict eternal law or the natural law, since it is essentially identical with them. Nonetheless, it exists in the intellectual and spiritual culture of humankind as a self-sufficient phenomenon. The necessity for, and the meaning of, the "[positive] divine law" is explained by Aquinas as follows:

> A divine law (*lex divina*), as well as the natural and the human law, is necessary for the guidance of human life for four reasons.
>
> First, because the law directs people towards right actions in respect to the final end. If man were framed only for a goal not exceeding the measure of natural human capacity, then he would need no other guidance on reason's part than the natural law and the human law derived from it. But since man is framed for the end of eternal blessedness (*beatitudo aeterna*), which exceeds the

measure of natural human capacity (qu. 5), it is necessary that man should be guided towards his end not merely by the natural and by the human law, but also by the divinely-given (*divinitus data*) law.

Second, because human judgment is uncertain, especially in relation to particular and changeable things, so that different people arrive at different judgments about the same human actions, as a result of which different and mutually contradictory laws arise. So that one can know without any doubt what man is to do and from what he is to refrain, it is necessary that man should in his actions be guided by a divinely-given law, of which it is certain that it cannot err.

Third, because man can only create laws in respect of such phenomena as he is capable of judging; human judgment cannot extend to inward impulses, which remain unexpressed, but only to external actions, which appear. It is however required, for "perfection" in virtue, that man should be corrected in both kinds of action; moreover, the human law is incapable of compelling and ordering inward impulses, and for this reason it was necessary that a divine law should come to assist in this purpose.

Fourth, because, as Augustine says in his work *On Free Will* (bk 1, chap. 5), human law is not in a position to punish or to forbid everything that is wicked. If it were to wish to do away with everything wicked, it would thereby also at the same time have done away with much that is good, and would consequently have detracted from the common good necessary for human intercourse. So that nothing wicked should remain unforbidden and unpunished, there must be a divine law that forbids all sins.

These four reasons are mentioned by the psalmist (Psalms 18:18) when he says that "the law of the Lord is unsullied" (that is, it admits no spot of sin), "converting hearts" (since it does not concern only external, but also inward actions), "lending wisdom to the least" (insofar as it frames people for a supernatural divine end).[6]

Thus, divine law is twofold: on the one hand, it is the governance of divine reason in the world extending itself towards the inward man (*lex aeterna*, the eternal law); on the other, it is the revelation of this law in human language (*lex divina*, the positive divine law).

Is, then, the eternal law known to all?

> I answer that something can be known in two ways: either in itself (*in seipso*) or through its effect (*in suo effectu*), which shows a certain similarity, as for example someone does not see the sun in its essence (*substantia*) but nevertheless knows it from its shining. It must therefore be said that no one can know the eternal law as it is in itself apart from God alone and the saints who see God in his essence (*per essentiam*); but that every creature who is endowed with reason knows it by means of this or another measure of illumination, whether greater or smaller. *For all knowledge of the truth is a kind of illumination and is a participation in the eternal law*, which is immutable truth, as Augustine says in the book *Of True Religion* (chap. 31): "The truth, however, is known by everyone in one way or another, at least to the extent of the universal principles (*principia communia*) of the natural law. In other things some have more, others less, of a share in the knowledge of the truth—and thus they know the eternal law in a greater or lesser degree."[7]

Along with all of nature, all men are, however, subject to the eternal law. Indeed,

---

[6] Ibid., qu. 91, art. 4.
[7] Ibid., qu. 93, art. 2.

the good are *perfectly* subject to the natural law, since they always act in accordance with it; the evil, on the other hand, *imperfectly* in relation to their actions, insofar as they know the good imperfectly and have an imperfect inclination towards it. What they lack in their action is made up for in what they suffer (*quantum deficit ex parte actionis, suppletur ex parte passionis*), by suffering what the eternal law bids (*dictat*) them suffer, and this to the extent that they have neglected to do what is in accordance with the eternal law.[8]

The natural law, however, is nothing other than the degree of knowledge of the eternal law that is common to all people. What then is the content of the natural law?

As being is the first object of knowledge in general, so the good is the first object with which practical reason, which is directed towards action, is concerned. For every agent acts in accordance with a purpose that corresponds to the concept of the good. Hence the first principle of practical reason, grounded on the concept of the good, is as follows. If one desires something, one desires it because it is good. The first prescription of the (natural) law is thus: the good is to be done and to be striven for, while what is evil is to be avoided—and on this rest all the other prescriptions of the natural law, so that everything that is to be done and to be omitted belongs among the prescriptions of the natural law, because practical reason has known it by natural means as a human good [or as an evil—*Tomberg's note*].

Since, however, the good bears the concept of a purpose within itself, but the evil the concept of its opposite, reason considers everything to which man has a natural inclination as by its nature good, and consequently as worthy of being striven for, while it considers everything that con-

---

[8] Ibid., qu. 93, art. 6.

tradicts natural inclination as evil and as something to be avoided.

From this it follows that the order to be found in natural inclinations is also the order of the prescriptions of the natural law. In the first place, there is in human beings an inclination to the good that is in accordance with nature, that man possesses in common with all substances (*substantiae*). Every substance, that is, has a natural inclination to preserve its being in accordance with its nature. In accordance with this inclination, all prescriptions that serve the preservation of human life and prevent its opposite belong to the natural law.

In the second place, man has a natural inclination to more particular goods, which is peculiar to him (alone). Man has thereby a natural inclination to know the truth about God and to live in society (*societas*). In accordance with this inclination, all those prescriptions that relate to it belong to the natural law—such as, for example, that man avoid ignorance, that he do no injustice to other people with whom he has dealings, and other prescriptions that are connected with this.[9]

If, then, natural law is a natural disposition of human beings, how can we explain the fact that there are errors, i.e., opinions that contradict natural law, and even that there are several "systems of natural law" distinct from each other (the eighteenth century, for example, afforded a multitude of such systems)?

The answer Aquinas gives to this question essentially consists in the suggestion that there exists a level of inferences (*conclusiones*) between general principles and the treatment of particular cases in experience; a level that, to

---

[9] Ibid., qu. 94, art. 2.

the extent these inferences grow distant from the original principle and become more deeply involved in the domain of the particular, can fall victim to imperfection, one-sidedness, and error.

> It belongs to the nature of reason to move from the universal to the particular (Aristotle, *Physics*, chap. 1). This happens in different ways, however, in the case of contemplative reason and that of practical reason. Contemplative reason has what is inwardly necessary for its object, which cannot possibly be otherwise than it is; and the truth is found by contemplative reason without deviation, both in relation to inferences and in relation to universal principles. Practical reason, by contrast, has to do with what is mutable (*contingentia*), to which human action relates. From this it follows that, although there is a certain necessity in the universal principles of practical reason, it diminishes to the extent that one descends to the realm of the particular.... The natural law is therefore the same for all insofar as it is a matter of the first universal principles, and indeed in relation both to its correctness (*rectitudo*) and to its being known (*notita*). As far as individual inferences from the universal principles are concerned, however, it is in most cases the same situation as for the correct and the known. In a few rare instances it can, because of particular obstacles, be connected with defects either in relation to its correctness (as for example one can occasionally see in the arising and passing away of natural phenomena through deviations caused by obstacles) and in relation to its being known. This is because of the fact that there are people whose reason has become depraved by passion or bad habits or lack of aptitude (*male habitudo naturae*). Thus, for example, robbery was at one time not considered as unlawful among the Germans, although it

decidedly contradicts the natural law. This is reported by Julius Caesar in the sixth book of his *Gallic War*.[10]

Precisely because natural law is only universally known and recognized in its universal principles and at the first level of inferences (*primae conclusiones*), it requires to be supplemented by positive human law, which draws inferences about the way in which individual cases are to be treated in practice, and by the positive divine law, which comes to the assistance of "wounded human nature" (*natura vulnerata*) in these inferences insofar as it protects them from errors that might be dangerous to salvation.

If man were not fallen—i.e., had the Fall not taken place—then no positive human or divine law would be necessary: man would be able to draw all the inferences necessary to practice effortlessly and correctly from his own rational being, which participates in the eternal law. If, on the other hand, the consequences of the Fall had been of such a kind that human nature was *completely* ruined, i.e., *destroyed* in its nature, then natural law would have been impossible, since everything natural, everything in the disposition of human nature, would indeed have consisted only of wicked inclinations and errors. If one denies the Fall of human nature, i.e., if one believes in the infallibility of human reason and of naturally-disposed inclinations, then any positive law would have been superfluous—not only the Ten Commandments of Moses, but also all the statutes of private and public law. The Catholic theological doctrine that nature is wounded by the Fall, but not destroyed (*natura vulnerata, non deleta*) finds its consequences to be of powerful significance in the domain of law—not only in

---

[10] Ibid., qu. 94, art. 4.

Thomas Aquinas and the Doctrine of Three Levels of Law

Aquinas's theory of law, and that of Scholasticism as such, but in all theories of law and in all the legal practice of the past and present as well. For all law, all legislation, rests on the principle of the simultaneous trust and mistrust of those to whom legal norms are addressed. It must in the end rest on trust, since otherwise the chain of surveilling authorities or of burdens of proof would extend to infinity. *Quis custodiat custodes?* "Who will guard the guardians?" This is an old question, to which all law in the end gives only *one* answer: the person who is worthy of trust, i.e., the person of reason and conscience, the representative of natural law. On the other hand, all law-making rests on a conscious mistrust of human nature, precisely because it accompanies prescriptions with threats in the case of the law's being broken. Thus the formula *natura vulnerata, non deleta* underpins all valid laws, since this formula carries with it a simultaneous trust and mistrust towards human nature in general. This simultaneous trust and mistrust, however, is the basis for the whole world's legal practice.

Now, in Aquinas's theory, this same formula—*natura vulnerata, non deleta*—is also the answer to the question posed above. That is, if natural law is a natural disposition of man, how can the fact that there are errors and subjectivistic systems of natural law be explained? While the pure and authentic nature of man is not destroyed, he has only limited knowledge, and may err. The positive *human* law has, precisely, the task of remedying this. The positive *divine* law, however, has in addition the task of preventing this remedy itself from falling into serious errors.

> A natural striving towards virtue is innate in man, as has been said above (qu. 63, art. 1); but man achieves perfection in virtue only with the help of a particular discipline

(*per aliquam disciplinam*), just as we see that man, by diligence, provides himself with what is necessary to satisfy his needs, e.g., for nourishment and for clothing, although he possesses the necessary bases for this by his very nature, that is, reason, and hands. . . . A discipline that is enforced by means of fear of punishment is the discipline of the law.[11]

It belongs to the essential properties of human law that

law is framed by the governor of the community of the state. . . . Thus, human laws are distinguished according to the different forms of state, of which one is monarchy (following the Philosopher, bk III of the *Politics*), i.e., when the state is led by one person, and then we have the prince's ordinances (*constitutiones*). Another form of state is aristocracy, i.e., the rule of the best or highest in rank, and then we have the decisions (*responsa*) of the experts and the decrees of the senate (*senatus consulta*). A further form of government is oligarchy, i.e., the rule of a few rich and powerful people, and then we have praetorian, or "honorary" law (*jus honorarium*). Still another form of government is the rule of the people, which is called democracy, and then we have the decrees of the common people (*plebiscita*). Yet another form is a tyrannical government (*regimen tyrannicum*), which is corrupt through and through (*omnio corruptum*), and then we have no law at all.

There is also a form of state government that brings the forms mentioned above into a unity, and this is the best form of state, and then we have a law that is sanctioned both by the elders and by the people, as in Isidore (*Etymologiae*, bk 5, chap. 10).[12]

---

[11] Ibid., qu. 95, art. 1.
[12] Ibid., art. 4.

Positive law (human law) can thus be changed, not only because of the variety of forms of state, but also because of the progress and regress of nations, i.e., because of the varying degrees of human *reasonableness*.

Human law is dictated by reason, by which human deeds are regulated. There can consequently be two reasons for justified alterations of human law: one reason lies in the nature of reason, and the other in the people whose deeds are regulated by means of the law. From the side of reason, it corresponds to reason's nature to progress gradually from the imperfect to the perfect. For this reason, we see that in the domain of the theoretical sciences, the first philosophers handed down some imperfect things that were then brought into a more perfect form by later philosophers. The same is also true of practice: the first people who had the intention of inventing something useful to the human community, at first (since they were not in a position to think of everything on their own) created things that were in many respects imperfect, and were altered by subsequent generations in such a way that they only failed to correspond to the general good in a few respects.

In respect of people, however, whose deeds are regulated by law, changes in the law can be justified when the circumstances under which people live have changed, since different things are of use in different circumstances, as Augustine writes in his work *On Free Will* (bk 1, chap. 6), by using an example. He says that "if a people is sensible and serious and takes the general good into account as carefully as possible, a law is justified which confers on that people the power themselves to choose the magistrates (*magistratus*) upon whom the direction of the state devolves. If, however, the people later falls victim to ethical depravity, so that it sells its votes and entrusts the direction of the state to dishonest and bad people, then it is justified to take away from such a people the power to appoint public officials, and to hand this power over to a few good people instead."[13]

Practice (custom, *consuetudo*) is also a factor that plays an important part in alterations to the positive law: it "possesses the force of law, annuls laws, and is the interpreter of law."

The key to Aquinas's theory of law as having three levels is the consummately earnest thought (which is accorded its whole weight) that *there is law*—i.e., law-in-itself. Such law is not an expression of human personal interests, of class interests, of national interests, but is grounded in divine reason, and is efficacious in human reason. Moreover, upon all the laws that human reason makes, it confers their correctness, their justice, and their binding content.

---

[13] Ibid., qu. 97, art. 1.

4

Thomas Aquinas and the Doctrine of World Peace

he general theory that law has three levels also carries within it an answer to the fundamental problem of the jurisprudence of international law: the problem of true peace, and of how to make war superfluous as a means of justice.

According to St Thomas's fundamental idea, peace is not merely the state of warless commerce among states, but a state so ordered that it has no germ of war within itself. In other words, it is a matter in Aquinas's view not merely of equally justified sovereign states existing alongside each other, but of a hierarchically-graduated order of authority and connectedness, and thus of a hierarchical ranking—which is an image of the order of the cosmos itself. "Just as it is right and proper that the ordering of a city or of a kingdom should be patterned on the model of the ordering of the cosmos, so the governance of a state must also be in accordance with divine governance."[1] This is a principle of the *analogia entis*, which holds for the ordering of the state as well as for the ordering of humanity. Thus, the deeper

---

[1] *De Regno*, chap. 24, art. 1.

meaning and content of the concept of "peace" for Aquinas is an ordering of humanity grounded, not on the will of man (irrespective of whether this is the will of one person or that of many people), but on eternal law, natural law, and human law (the latter, insofar as it does not contradict natural and divine law). But this means there are three hierarchically-graduated sources of authority: the authority of the state, international authority, and divine authority—which correspond to human law, natural law, and divine law. The Middle Ages knew these three authorities in the form of the prince (or magistrate), the emperor, and the pope: "prince, emperor, and pope" signified the concrete embodiment of the legal order with three levels. This was the concrete expression of the *Medieval idea of peace*, whose champion and herald was Thomas Aquinas.

The *ordo* (order) patterned on that of the cosmos is peace; each disturbance of this order is war, whether "cold" or "hot," international or civil, class or economic, or whatever other form war might take.

In contrast to a truce and a latent state of war, true peace is the state of the world in which the *horizontal* level—in which persons, families, groups, and nations live alongside each other—is determined by the *vertical* level of the ranked hierarchy of human law, natural law, and divine law. St Thomas's idea of peace is the cross, which is formed along the lines of the relation of people to each other and the relation of people to God, or (which is the same thing) the realization of the all-embracing command: love God with all thy strength and love thy neighbor as thyself.

This, however, means that religion and humanism, as forms of expressing one's attitude to God and one's attitude to people (the "neighbor"), are the two forces from whose

Thomas Aquinas and the Doctrine of World Peace

concord results true peace in spiritual and cultural life, and in social and political life. A "godless" peace, a peace without God, is, accordingly, impossible, since there would then be nothing that could stand *above* the parties and could occasion their wills to any other conduct than that of mere requiring and desiring. Mere requiring and desiring, however, is war, since it is in principle insatiable. An "inhuman" peace, a peace without humaneness, is accordingly also impossible, since it means a coercion of the essential core of human nature: freedom. For the parties to such a peace are not conceivable as free partners, but only as commanding and obeying respectively. Where mere power commands, however, it need not stop in principle at any limit; indeed, in response to coercive power, even one who obeys it prostrate upon the ground will, in the end, not be obedient enough. Consider how modern Thomas Aquinas is (as though he knew all about the Fascist-Nazist and popular-democratic-communist practices of today) when he says that "tyrants seek to destroy every bond of friendship among their subordinates, and strive also to ensure that the latter do not enjoy the advantages of peace (calm), so that no one has trust in others, and thus nothing can be undertaken against the rule of the tyrant."[2]

In the domain of law, the concord of humanism and religion, as the essence of true peace, means the primacy of divine law and natural law over positive law—and, as well, the primacy of international law over internal positive state law. This is because international law (the *jus gentium*) rep-

---

[2] Ibid., bk 1, chap. 3.

resents the first stage of the transition from natural law to positive law: "the *jus gentium* is in a certain way natural to human beings, insofar as man is a being endowed with reason—natural, because it is derived from natural law by means of deductions (*conclusiones*) that do not stray far from the principles (*principia*). For this reason, it is easy for human beings to be united on this subject."[3] International law, i.e., the *jus gentium* understood in its ancient sense as the norms of law that hold among all civilized humanity, is the link connecting natural law with the *jus civile*, the particular law, of individual states. Thus, it immediately refers to the dealings, whether peaceable or martial, of states with each other.

If the individual civil legal systems form the legal foundations for the corresponding human communities organized into states, then international law is the valid legal foundation of the *community of humankind*—not merely the community of states, but the community of humankind too—i.e., the legal community that includes all human *persons*.

St Thomas's idea of peace, consequently, consists in a harmonic triad of positive, natural, and divine law. However, it still remains humankind's historical and practical task to find or to create the authoritative institutions corresponding to these three levels of law, and to provide the authority and sanctioning capacity due them. St Thomas simply establishes the principles, and emphasizes the immutable ordering of divine law, while granting to everything mutable the right to develop—indeed, the *necessity* of developing.

---

[3] *Summa theol.*, I–II, qu. 95, art. 4.

5

Thomas Aquinas and the Doctrine of War

homas Aquinas's teaching on war is expounded in four articles of his famous *Secunda Secundae* (the second section of the second part of the theological *Summa*, written in the years 1268–1270). His teachings on divine, natural, and human law as set out above are from the *Prima Secundae* (the first section of the second part of the *Summa*).

Drawing on St Augustine, Thomas sets out three conditions for the just war: a declaration of war by the highest state authority; a just cause (*justa causa*); and a right intention (*intentio recta*). In point of history, the first condition is directed against the law of brute force *practiced* in the Middle Ages, according to which every minor citizen or prince believed he had the right to wage war. But in point of *principle*, it is directed against all earlier, later, and modern forms of the law of brute force: e.g., against Roman wars of rivalry, Latin-American *pronunciamentos*, "black" and "red" partisan wars, etc.

Highest state authority. Following the above condition that only a just war is permitted, and that it has to be declared by the highest state authority, the presupposition for the justification of a war is the absence of a higher judicial authority standing above that of the state. Thomas says that "private persons" (by which he means all those who still have an earthly judge above them) may not resort to force when they can seek justice at the hands of a judge. If a state, then, is in a position in which it can appeal to a *judicium superioris* equipped with the necessary force, the justification for the state taking matters into its own hands disappears. When a trans-state, international judicial authority is *not* present, the one upon whom care for the state devolves must himself protect the state against attacks, and must take care that no injustice is done to the state entrusted to him. "And if, now, the forces of the state defend it with the sword in a permitted manner against *inner* revolts by punishing the evil-doers, conformably to the words of the apostle in the letter to the Romans (13:4)—'he beareth not the sword in vain: for he is the minister of God, a revenger to execute wrath upon him that doth evil'—then it is also his business to defend the state with the sword of war in the face of *external* enemies."[1]

In any case, the authority that can declare war in order to protect the state and in order to prevent an injustice must be a legal authority. The tyrant ("who oppresses by force, instead of governing by means of justice," *De Regno*), the oligarchic clique ("which is distinguished from tyrants only in that there are several of them," ibid.), and the rule of the mob ("in which the whole people is equal to a single tyrant," ibid.), produce no legal government (i.e., none corresponding with natural law and divine law) that could be in a position to declare or to wage a just war.

Justa causa. The second requirement for war to be permitted is the "just cause" (*justa causa*). According to Tho-

---

[1] *Summa theol.*, I–II, qu. 40, art. 1.

mas, there is only a single such cause (along with defence against an unjust attack, which he regards as self-evidently valid and therefore does not discuss): "that those against whom war is waged, deserve this because of their guilt." Thomas defines guilt, in the words of St Augustine, as when "a state or a city is to be punished, either in order to punish the injustice perpetrated by its citizens, or to punish their neglecting to restore what they have unjustly taken away." As for Augustine, so for Thomas, war is an act of pure retributive justice, excluding reasons of distributive, let alone of commutative, justice. In other words, according to Augustinian and Thomistic teaching, to the extent it is not an act of self-defence, a war waged for a just cause is an *act of international legal punishment*. This means, however, that there must be not merely a breach of the law, but also *guilt*, on the side of the state to be punished; and furthermore, that breaches of the law and guilt must be absent on the side of the punishing party or parties—as, for example, is the case with the police acting within a state when they overpower a band of criminals who are defending themselves. "If a just war is waged, then the other side is fighting for sin," says Augustine,[2] thereby giving the clearest conceivable formulation (even if it is not set out in legal terminology) of the punitive character of the just war. Later views to the effect that right does not always need full certainty to be on the side of the state waging war,[3] were relax-

---

[2] *City of God*, XIX. 15.

[3] E.g., that it suffices when there is *more* right or legal grounds on this side than on the other, or even that war can be waged on both sides without moral guilt, and thus justly, when it is occasioned by the "common good" and "public order."

ations of the strict requirements of Augustinian and Thomist teaching. When the doctrine of the "just cause" descended from the domain of retributive justice into that of distributive justice (where right is, as it were, unequally distributed), and then fell into that of commutative justice (where both sides are equally justified or unjustified), it was lost in the process of the relaxation of its strict requirement. Law lost thereby its moral content, and thus its moral curb, and became in the end an amoral question of political advantage, of baneful *raison d'état*. After centuries of experience, civilized humanity is now returning to the views of the Augustinian and Thomist school: the statutes of the League of Nations and of the United Nations are really nothing other than the recognition of the old doctrine of the punitive character of the only permissible legal grounds (*justa causa*) of war.

Right intention. Thomas gives "right intention" (*intentio recta*) as the third condition for a just war. By this he understands that

> one should have the intention of furthering what is good or of avoiding what is evil. For Augustine says in his book *De verbis Domini* that among God's true servants, even wars are peaceable, since they are not undertaken out of covetousness and cruelty, but for the sake of peace, so that the evil can be kept within limits and the good supported. Thus it can happen that although war has been declared by the legal authority and on the grounds of a just cause, it is nevertheless not permitted because of the perversion of the intention of the one who is undertaking it. For what Augustine justly reproaches, where war is concerned, is the wish to cause harm (*nocendi cupiditas*), the cruelty of wrath, an unpeaceable and irreconcilable intention, the

fury of resistance, the lust for domination (*libido dominandi*), and other things of this sort.[4]

The intention "of furthering what is good or of avoiding what is evil"—excluding the motives of expanding one's rule (imperialism), of self-enrichment (mercantilism), or the wish to annihilate races, peoples, classes, and religious communities (genocide)—must thus also be present in the case of a war waged for a just cause by the supreme political authority that owes its authority neither to the tyranny of a single man nor to that of a ruling clique or of a mob. If Thomas's conditions for war being permitted had been met, it would have made war so much more difficult among the civilized community of humanity (in which there is a consensus in principle about the good that is to be furthered and the evil that is to be avoided) that war would have become almost as infrequent as large-scale natural disasters.

All these conditions that a war has to meet in order to be just (i.e., to be permitted) relate to sovereign states, and *that* on the condition that there is no trans-state judicial force present. But *if* such a trans-state judicial force *were* present, how would the teaching of St Thomas then need to be understood?

If a judicially authoritative institution superordinate to states were present, war would either be a just war, i.e., a punitive action for protection and for punishment, or (if this trans-state institution broke down) it would be a *civil war* of international dimensions, and thus fall under the conditions of the permissibility or impermissibility of civil war (that is, of the resistance of subjects to their state power)—or, in the case of the breakdown of that state

---

[4] *Summa theol.*, I–II, qu. 40, art. 1.

power, of the struggle between two groups of citizens. Thomas's doctrine of the just (i.e., justified) civil war or of the "just revolution" is as clear as his doctrine of the "just war." If, where the just war is concerned, it is a case of the protection and restoration of the right of the states, then, where a conflict within a state is concerned, it is a case of the protection and restoration of the *fundamental rights of humankind*.

⊕

Although St Thomas drew up no list of the fundamental rights of humankind (such as, for example, the list of human rights contained in the thirty articles of the "Universal Declaration of Human Rights" made by the General Assembly of the United Nations on December 10, 1948), he nevertheless had very definite and clear views on the inalienable rights of humankind. Their content is defined and given by the nature of divine and natural law (*lex divina* and *lex naturalis*). It is distinguished, however, from the ideas about "human rights" current today by the fact that for Thomas, it is not a question of *claims* or demands ("rights") of individual people to a particular degree of arbitrary will, but of claims and demands that the divine law places upon human law and the state power.

The fundamental idea of the Thomist conception of human rights is that the *duties* of human beings towards God are at the same time their inalienable *rights* in the face of the state and fellow citizens. It is not a matter here of the claims of the human will (which can be inexhaustible), but of the divine and natural *order* that has allocated to human beings a vocation, and therefore also demands that the fulfillment of this vocation should be made possible and be protected. The just (i.e., justified) conflict within a state community comes about, consequently, only when the claims of arbitrary will on the one side, and the demands of divine and natural law on the other, are opposed to each other. In such circumstances, the state power can be opposed to the rebellious arbitrary will of the people, just as the people can rise up in opposition to the claims of arbitrary state power. The "voice of the people" is not *in itself* and without further ado the "voice of God." Nor is the "voice" of a given "authority" *in itself* and without further ado the "voice of God." It is so, only insofar and to the extent that the "voice of the people" or the "voice of authority" stands in accord with the voice of reason, which is in harmony with divine law. The teaching of the apostle Paul that "all authority is from God" means, in Thomas's view, that "authority" owes its authority to divine and natural law, but also that it relinquishes this authority, i.e., ceases to be an "authority," when it infringes divine and natural law.

> For this reason, the duty of obedience is for Christians a consequence of the derivation of authority (*praelatio*) from God, and it ceases when that ceases. As was already said earlier, however, authority can be lacking a derivation from God for two reasons: either because of the manner in which the authority was acquired, or because of the kind of use made of the authority. There are, in turn, two reasons that bring about the first case: either it is a defect in the person (if the person is unworthy) or it is a defect in the way the authority has been acquired (if it has been acquired by means of force or simony or in some other impermissible way). The first defect is not of a kind that can deprive the acquisition of authority of legitimacy. Since authority, by virtue of its form, is always derived from God (which is the cause of the duty to obey), those who are subject to it (*sub-*

diti) are obligated to show obedience even to unworthy superiors. The second defect, however, removes the right to authority (*jus prelationis*): whoever seizes power by means of force does not become a real superior or prince. It is therefore permissible, when it is possible, to resist such rule—except in the case when it has retrospectively become legitimate ("actual"), either by the consent of the subjects, or by means of the authority of a higher body.

As far as the misuse of authority is concerned, this can be of two kinds. First, when what is commanded by authority stands in opposition to the definition of authority as such—if, for example, a sinful deed is commanded, conflicting with virtue, for whose protection and care authority is afforded. In such a case, one is not only not bound to obey authority, but one is also obligated to refuse one's obedience to it, as the holy martyrs did, who preferred to undergo death than to obey the blasphemous commands of tyrants. Second, when the authority oversteps its own limits, "as, for example, when a lord demands that a bondsman should do something that the latter is not obliged to do, and in other similar cases. In such cases, the subordinate is free to obey or to refuse to obey."[5] It should be emphasized that Cicero speaks [here] of a case in which a person has seized rule by means of force, either against the will of his subjects, or by forcing them to consent, and in which there was no possibility of appealing to a higher authority that could have judged the usurper (*invasor*). In such a case, the one who frees his native land by killing a tyrant is to be praised and rewarded.[6]

---

[5] In *De officiis*, I.26, where he justifies the murder of Caesar—*Author*.
[6] *Commentum in IV libros sententiarum Magistri Petri Lombardi*, bk II, dist. xliv, qu. 2, art. 2.

Thomas Aquinas and the Doctrine of War

⊕

From the passages adduced above it can be seen that a "just revolution" (covering the whole scale from passive refusal of obedience through to the assassination of a tyrant) and a "just civil war" (in which two groups of citizens come into conflict, and where a higher judicial power is not present or is incapacitated) are only possible in a case where it is a question of defending the duties demanded, and the law established, by revelation, conscience, and reason (divine law and natural law). Material advantages, claims to power, and claims to "equality" resting on envy—claims that were and still are the driving forces behind most revolutions and civil wars—do not, according to St Thomas's doctrine, belong among the motives from which a "just war" (whether between nations or within one nation) can be undertaken and waged. The defence, on the other hand, of religion, of life, of family, and of property, against usurpation by force—by tyranny, by the mob, or by a neighboring state—is indeed justified, and indeed in many cases is commanded, when a higher judicial power is lacking.

PART III

Further Development of the
Problem of International Law on
the Basis of a Law with Three Levels

1

The Medieval Concept of Neutrality and Tolerance

ne of the most important and most essential characteristics of the Middle Ages was the seriousness with which the life of the mind—its concepts, ideas, and ideals—was lived. This seriousness grew out of the awareness that every thought is related to every other thought either by being in accord with it or by contradicting it, and that consequently every problem, whether directly or indirectly, concerns the absolute values upon which rest—in time and eternity—church, empire, rank, family, and the safety and salvation of the soul and the body of the individual. There was at that time no such thing as a "tolerance" grounded on relativism, scepticism, and indifference. Opinions were not a merely personal affair that belonged to the realm of a person's subjective freedom, but were deeds and events with social import that either furthered and helped to build the social, political, ethical, attitudinal, and religious temple of "Christendom," or else had an obstructive and destructive effect. At that time, ideas wielded an enormous weight: their expression signified a good deed or a crime, recognition and fame or infamy, prison, and death. The awareness of responsibility for the views one expressed corresponded to the grave consequences that expression brought with it. Imma-

ture, un-thought-out, or carelessly formulated ideas were hardly brought into circulation.

On the other hand, it was in no way characteristic of the Middle Ages to renounce creative intellectual work. On the contrary, there was an astonishing intellectual activity at work in that era, testifying to an eagerness and energy of a kind seldom seen in our age, overburdened as it is with factual data, and exhausted as it is by relativistic half-truths and even quarter-truths. Looked at from today's standpoint, factual data and a treatment of technical minutiae may have been sparse in the academies of Bologna, Toledo, Paris, Cologne, and Oxford, but as against this, the creative life of the mind, focused as it was then on the most essential questions of what it is to be human, was correspondingly richer than is the case in the same institutions today. Indeed, in the age of Thomas Aquinas, Albertus Magnus, Bonaventure, and Roger Bacon, less was known quantitatively than today, but there was a correspondingly deeper immersion in things. Ideas meant more than merely casting a light upon the causal connections between things: they were a ladder to a deeper immersion in the content of those things. For this reason, people held fast to ideas, and did not lightly, let alone easily, adopt "new" and "original" ideas. Thoughts had at that time a serious weight. They were acquired with difficulty, and sometimes carried grave consequences.

It is therefore not surprising that some concepts and doctrines that are current today and owe their existence to relativism and to the disappearance of absolute values into the blue yonder, were not present in the Middle Ages. Thus, the very concept of *neutrality* in war was lacking. Instead of today's concept of neutrality, there was a concept of *innocence*: only two parties could be in question in a just war—

The Medieval Concept of Neutrality and Tolerance

parties that, accordingly, stood on the side of right and the side of wrong respectively. There could be no "neutrality" in the sense of knowing the causes and the nature of a conflict while refusing at the same time to take sides. There could, however, be "innocent parties" (*innocentes*), i.e., persons who, because of their greater distance or because of their calling (monks), age (children), or gender (women), stood outside the conflict. There were "innocent parties" as well in the enemy country—indeed, they existed even in the enemy camp, as they did as well everywhere in the world. But there were not, nor could there be, any "neutrals," either in theory or in practice. For although in theory war was a dispute between right and wrong, in practice no member of the body of Christendom—of the Holy Roman Empire—could remain indifferent and unengaged in conflicts that endangered the life and prosperity of the empire of Christendom. If it was a matter of a war with the "other" empire—with the Caliphate of Islam—it was impossible to remain outside this conflict, because it was then unequivocally a case of the defence of everything life has to offer, in time and in eternity.

The fact of the opposition between the empire of Christendom and the world-empire of Islam[1] corresponded to the inner disposition of the medieval life of the spirit, and reinforced an "either/or" or "yes/no" attitude—thereby ruling out the "both/and" of compromise. For if medieval man took his religion and culture truly seriously, this was also

---

[1] Despite the schism in both empires: the separation of the Eastern Roman-Slavic realm from the Western Roman realm; and the separation of the Western Caliphate (or Emirate) of Cordoba from the greater world-empire of Islam.

From International Law to World Peace

because it was always seriously endangered. At the threshold of the Christian empire stood the empire of the Crescent, which had already wrested away more than a third of the Christian cultural area (Syria, Palestine, Egypt, North Africa, most of Spain—and, later, Asia Minor and the Balkan peninsula) from Christianity, and had for centuries alienated those lands from Christianity. This danger also contributed to the fact that the people of the Middle Ages, always alert to the meaning of its Christian spiritual values, were kept in a state of constant vigilance. Alongside the *memento mori* ("remembrance of death"), which did not allow them, in their temporal lives, to lose sight of the value of eternity, there also sounded throughout the centuries of medieval history and beyond, up until the end of the seventeenth century, when the Turks stood before the gates of Vienna, another warning cry: *memento Saracenis*.

This "remembrance of the Saracens," together with the "remembrance of death," left no room in their effects for "neutrality," as this notion until lately survived in the theory and practice of international law and politics. Today, the idea of neutrality has at least been severely shaken, if not recognized as untenable. For an "empire" of humankind and freedom has again emerged, threatened by another empire (no longer that of the crescent but that of the five-pointed star of communism) at whose summit stands a man who is the "caliph" of militant materialism, i.e., a man at once "pope" and "emperor" in the "state church" of a materialism bent on world domination.[2] Today we are in the position of better appreciating the seriousness of medieval

---

[2] Since this book was written, historical events have of course moved rapidly with respect to Soviet Russia and Islamic influence. ED

The Medieval Concept of Neutrality and Tolerance

intellectual and spiritual life, since our situation is becoming ever more like that of the Christendom of the Middle Ages. The more similar the situation of a hard-pressed and threatened "free humanity" (i.e., the "Christendom" of the twentieth century) becomes to the situation of a medieval Christendom strongly oppressed by an Islam bent on world domination (i.e., the "free humanity" of a thousand years ago), the more any neutrality becomes a betrayal of humanity in practice—and a conceptual husk in theory.

That medieval thinkers actually did regard neutrality as an insubstantial conceptual husk is shown by the fact that they did not take it seriously, and that the modern concept of neutrality was missing from medieval theories for as long as the absolute values of Western humanity—and the absolute danger to which these values were exposed—were alive in the consciousness of Christendom. Only after the wave of "secular" humanism had shattered the intellectual and spiritual discipline of Europe (and thereby allowed relativistic tendencies to insinuate themselves), and after the Reformation had subsequently destroyed the unity of the Western religious worldview, did the concept of *neutrality* in the modern sense emerge from the ever-widening atmosphere of uncertainty and insecurity about what, finally, is normative and absolute. Connected with this was the loss of standards and criteria, and the spreading confusion of moral judgment. Because a disintegrated Christianity's consciousness of mutual belonging had been lost, and especially given that there were now scarcely any longer any "brothers," a neutral person now found it all the easier to say "I am not my brother's keeper"—so that matters came to the point where one Christian state was able to contract with the Turks an alliance directed against another Christian state!

From International Law to World Peace

Medieval thinkers like Thomas Aquinas had "not yet arrived" at the development of the concept of neutrality, not because this concept demands a sharper and more energetic thinking than it was reasonable to expect of capacities "in those days," but because the thinkers in question were not afflicted with the degree of drowsy, deadening thinking necessary to be swayed by the concept of neutrality!

⊕

In relation to the history of the intellectual and spiritual life of humankind, it is an experience of the utmost importance to realize that the *absence* of certain concepts and ideas is not always attributable to weakness or imperfection, but sometimes also to strength, even to a higher degree of perfection. For example, the absence in the Middle Ages of the concept of "class struggle," which has become the cornerstone of the "ideological superstructure" of the modern Marxist intellectual current, is not to be explained by the notion that people of that time were not clever enough to grasp the idea that one could seize the property of knights and merchants by force and make what was seized common property, but by the fact that people placed no value upon such a way of acquiring goods because they lived for other, higher, values. That is, in the language of the preachers of class struggle, they were indeed "intoxicated by the opium of the people."

As far as the concept of neutrality is concerned, it was perhaps most saliently defined in the Declaration of Neutrality issued by George Washington on April 22, 1793 as "conduct friendly and impartial" towards the belligerent powers, and included a warning to all citizens to avoid any acts that might conflict with such conduct, and the stipula-

The Medieval Concept of Neutrality and Tolerance

tion that the United States would not only refuse protection to any citizens who might be engaged in such acts, but would provide for legal punishment, in their own land, of persons who had infringed upon this neutral status.

It was the statutes of the League of Nations that for the first time made the statutes of neutrality questionable in principle, since the idea underlying these statutes (that of a solidarity among states) is in principle irreconcilable with neutrality. The resolution of the Council of the League of Nations, made on Febuary 2, 1920 (on the occasion of Switzerland's joining the League), accordingly explained explicitly that the concept of the neutrality of members of the League was irreconcilable with the principle according to which all members of the League had to *act in concert* in order to fulfill their obligations under its statutes. At the conference of the International Law Association at Oxford in 1932, James Brierly declared that neutrality was henceforth completely "outlawed" (as he put it). In American jurisprudence of international law there is an especially strong trend against neutrality.

Now, what has just been described is already true for the time that preceded the establishment of the United Nations; but thereafter, neutrality became even more impossible for its members than had been the case for members of the League of Nations. This was because the intention and very raison d'être of the foundation of the United Nations in place of the League of Nations was a greater degree of solidarity and an increased obligation to act against states or groups of states guilty of aggression. It is true that the concept of neutrality has not yet been altogether extinguished—its feeble flame flickers on here and there—but its champions today lack any sort of legal or moral grounding, apart from the physical or moral incapacity to fulfill their obligations. For all practical purposes, then, it is now the case (since modern political and international legal practice has led to a recognition of the medieval theory of the "just war" grounded in reason and morality) that the concept of neutrality has been dropped. It is to be anticipated that the other modern concept of which the Middle Ages "lacked awareness"—that is, the concept of *class struggle*—will also be abandoned in due course by a free human community organized on the basis of the concept of solidarity.

The root of the concept of neutrality, refuted by practice today, and rejected by theory in the Middle Ages, lies in the domain of religious and moral worldviews. What was "missing" from medieval spiritual and intellectual life was the concept of *tolerance* in the sense given it by Frederick the Great, namely, that "each can be blessed in his own way." That is, the concept of tolerance was consciously rejected, not unknown! It was also known from the writings of antiquity, when it stood personified before the whole world in Pilate's question "What is truth?"

There is another concept of tolerance, however, one that does not rest on relativism, skepticism, and indifference, but is instead grounded upon the rock-hard conviction that truth possesses its own voice and persuasive power (a voice, that is, clearly demarcated from the voices of half-truths and lies), which selfless contemplation brings to light. This concept of tolerance means *uniting patience with respect* when faced with the intangible inner freedom of the other person. Patience, as the foundation of tolerance, is beautifully illustrated in a Jewish legend apparently of medieval origin. A stranger once came to Abraham and asked him for hospitality. As it was already time to perform evening prayer, the host suggested to the guest that they pray together. As it turned out, the stranger was a fire-worshipper, for he knelt down before the fire and prayed to it. Horrified and enraged by this idolatry, Abraham was about to turn the stranger out from his tent, when the Lord appeared to him with the words: "Is your understanding so small that you have not considered that I have tolerated this heathen throughout the many years of his life, whereas you are not even willing to summon enough patience to endure him for a single night?" Ashamed, Abraham renounced his intention, and let the stranger pass the night in his tent.

The import of respect for inner freedom is emphasized by Thomas Aquinas:

> There are, among the unbelievers, those who have never accepted the (Christian) faith, as, for example the Mohammedans (*gentiles*) and the Jews; these ought in no way (*nullo modo*) to be forced into faith, in order that they confess the faith; for faith is a matter of the will (*credere voluntatis est*). In certain cases, however, force is to be applied to infidels, if it is a matter of protecting the faith against blasphemies, evil rumors, or even open persecutions. For this reason, Christians (*fideles Christi*) have often waged war against the infidels, not in order to force them to believe (for even if they had defeated the infidels and brought them into captivity, the latter would still have retained the freedom to believe or not to believe), but in order to force them not to impair belief in Christ.[3]

The concept of tolerance that results from the Jewish legend and from the ideas of St Thomas in no way contains

---

[3] *Summa theol.* II–II, qu. 10, art. 8.

either an explicit or an implicit recognition that Abraham's belief in the invisible God and the worship of the element of fire are equally justified, nor that the Christian faith and that of Islam (in the case of St Thomas) are equally justified. Instead, it is an explicit recognition of the human being's claim *not to be coerced* in spiritual matters, i.e., the claim to freedom, and freedom's claim to be respected.

It is not relativism, but *humaneness* that underpins the medieval concept of tolerance.

It is hardly any more difficult to understand the fact that such frequent and severe infringements of this conception of tolerance took place in the Middle Ages than it is to understand the fact that, despite the concept of tolerance in force today, millions of people can be persecuted and annihilated solely on the grounds of their belonging to a particular nationality or class. Such a way of acting certainly lay far from medieval people, because in the Middle Ages it was a question of heresies that, as was then believed, people could freely choose,[4] whereas today it is a matter of relations of heritage and birth that the people concerned have themselves neither chosen nor could in any way alter. The systematic annihilation of the Jews and Gypsies, as well as of the Polish aristocracy and intelligentsia, on the part of the National Socialist empire, and the annihilation of the upper classes as well as the disappearance of the Crimean Tartars, the Ingush, the Chechens, and the Volga Germans from the population maps of Soviet Russia, are testimonies of mass murder and forced emigration that, although they do not in any way excuse medieval offences against humanity, at least seem to be of equal gravity.

---

[4] "Heresy" itself derives from a Greek root signifying "to choose." ED

The Medieval Concept of Neutrality and Tolerance

Nevertheless, the epoch of the Middle Ages was by no means only the age of the Inquisition, any more than the present epoch is only the age of the Gestapo and the Soviet NKVD.[5] Turning first to the present, we can see also how its achievements have made visible the previously invisible host of death-dealing microbes and bacilli; have made possible life-saving interventions into inner workings of the organism that were previously veiled in darkness; and have placed the previously hidden forces of the material world so powerfully in the service of humanity that all nations of the world are directly connected with each other. Consequently, the unity of the humanly inhabited world, with its cares, crises, and struggles, can be seen as an accomplished fact. All this and much more is owed to the light shed by this age of ours. But the Middle Ages, too, had its light, a light that will shine again throughout the whole future as it shone in the Middle Ages, and as the light of the present will shine again for our children and for our children's children.

The progress of humanity does not consist in radical changes, in revolutions, but in "fulfillments." An earlier age leaves its legacy to the following age in the form of an *achievement* and a *longing*. The longing, once satisfied, becomes a new achievement, while the former achievement becomes a vessel that receives the new achievement. The fulfillment of the law of Moses through Christ is, and remains, the archetype and pattern of all progress: "I am not come to destroy, but to fulfill."

In this sense, medieval catholicity was the fulfillment of

---

[5] The Soviet secret police during Stalin's regime; later the KGB. ED

the *pax humana*; and modern humanity is on the way to fulfilling the catholicity of the Middle Ages. The ascending scale of "fulfillments" stands in opposition to the "dialectical process" of the *other* current in history: that of thesis, antithesis, and synthesis (i.e., of a culture, a revolution in that culture, and the outcome of the confrontation between the two). The former path—that of fulfillments—is, however, the *true* path of humanity as it progresses towards the goal. When today, for example, we sing the psalms of David, or in our thinking make implicit use of the concepts of Aristotelian logic, we do not do this (in the case of the psalms) as a "synthesis" of the glorification of God by David as against the blaspheming of God by, say, the Soviet Russian poet Demyan Bedny, or as a "synthesis" (in the case of thinking) of Aristotelian logic as against a system of "anti-logic." Rather, we sing the psalms of David and we think in accord with Aristotelian logic because both possess a value that remains intact across the millennia.

True, a good deal has been *added* to the value of the psalms of David and also to Aristotle's logic in the course of the millennia, but David's psalms and the forms of Aristotle's thinking have lost nothing of their validity. This is because they belong to the line of progress: they belong to the true path of humankind. Consequently, the *actual* crisis of the present consists, not in the opposition between bourgeois culture and the proletarian revolution, but in the renewed assault upon the path of humankind's progress by the "barbarians" of the modern age—just as in the past the actual barbarian nomads and the Saracens attacked that path. The battle of the present-day is not between a thesis and an antithesis caught up in a dialectical process, but between, on the one hand, the "dialectical process" itself (as

The Medieval Concept of Neutrality and Tolerance

the modern form of fatalism) and, on the other, the "way, the truth, and the life" of the culture of humankind. Today, "revolution, planning, and affluence" are opposed—"like" an antithesis—to the way of progress, and to the life of its achievements through the strength of its truth. But this opposition is not an antithesis *on the same level*, but an assault on the level of human culture in an effort to force it down from its historical level to a lower, "subhistorical" or barbaric level, in order to make an end of the true history of humankind and to found a new history. The intention of this "new history" is to extinguish everything of antiquity and the Middle Ages that still survives into the present—that is, to extinguish Christian-humanist culture as such and to replace it with a "collectivist humanism of production."

The concept of tolerance in the relativistic sense, and the reflection of that concept in the field of political theory and of international law (that is, the concept of neutrality), were absent from intellectual life in the Middle Ages (up until Alberico Gentili and Hugo Grotius) because people of that time lived in an awareness of the existence of, and the possession of, absolute values—and thus they thought of history as the "way, the truth, and the life" of these values. They most surely did *not* think of the course of history and its values as a "dialectical process" in which the truth of one epoch becomes a lie for the next, so as to return as a half-truth in the epoch after that.

In this sense, the course of the history of the problem of international law as set within the *progressive* tendency (following Thomas Aquinas's view) was a positive continuation—in contrast to the *revolutionary* tendency. As Thomas himself took up the great ideas of Antiquity and of his predecessors with devout respect and understanding, so too

From International Law to World Peace

did his own achievements become the basis and the starting-point for a labor of thought that continues even today. This endeavor lives still—indeed, even in this text on which we are working here and now, in its relation to the jurisprudence of international law.

A series of treatises about war and peace were written in the fourteenth and fifteenth centuries, among which the oldest, *De Bello, de Represaliis et de Duello* [Of war, of reprisals, and of duels] seems to be the work of the Bolognese professor of civil and canon law Johannes de Ligano. It was written in 1360, but was apparently not published before 1477. These treatises do not, however, signify progress in the history of the problem of international law. Their only contribution (according to von Kaltenborn and T. A. Walker)[6] consists in the extension of the topic discussed by adding the argument that it was necessary to honor agreements in one's dealing with the enemy in war, as well as that the stipulations of truce agreements were binding.

To the Spanish controversialists of Reformation times (Francisco de Vitoria and Francisco Suarez) it was however granted to make a decisive contribution to the history of the problem of international law. Together with Fernando Vasquez and Balthazar Ayala, these two betokened a true renaissance of Scholasticism in an altered temporal setting. Like Thomas Aquinas, they devoted a considerable part of their work to the problems of international law.

---

[6] Karl von Kaltenborn and Thomas A. Walker, both of whom wrote studies on the present subject. Von Kaltenborn published in the mid-nineteenth century. Walker's *A History of the Law of Nations: From the Earliest Times to the Peace of Westphalia, 1648* was published in 1899. ED

2

Francisco de Vitoria

rancisco de Vitoria (known also as Fransiscus a Victoria) was born in 1480 in Navarre, Spain, before Ferdinand of Aragon incorporated the largest (southern) part of this small kingdom into the area he ruled. Vitoria received his education in Paris, whence he returned to Spain as a Dominican. There, in Salamanca, he won high renown as a professor of theology. He died in 1546 or 1549. Vitoria's thirteen *Relectiones Theologiae*, published for the first time in Lyon in 1557, include lectures on international law and on a world-organization as well. In other words, they discuss questions of the relation of the secular power of the princes and the emperor to the spiritual power of the bishops and the pope (*relectiones* 1 and 2), the nature and limits of state authority (*relectio* 3), the authority of the pope and of councils (*relectio* 4), the rights and duties of Christian states towards the primitive peoples of overseas territories (i.e., "colonial law," in *relectiones* 5 and 6), war and peace (*relectio* 6), and so on. In the sixth *relectio*, *De Jure Belli* [Of the law of warfare], Vitoria discusses the central problem of the jurisprudence of international law on a Thomistic basis, but now according to the tasks and requirements of an altered temporal situation.

The temporal situation had undergone an essential change (when compared with the century of Aquinas)

around the middle of the sixteenth century because the discovery of America and the schism within Christianity as a result of the Reformation had brought with them new tasks as well as new dangers for Christian and civilized humanity. The new continents presented a dangerous temptation to treat them as a mere space for the expansion of power and a source of enrichment, even though they were indeed inhabited by *people*, relations with whom—precisely because they were human beings—had to be in accordance with natural and divine law.

On the other hand, within Christendom itself, a new formation, almost a new spiritual "continent," detached itself from the continent of Christendom: the world of Protestant communities now existing outside the Catholic church. While new churches were being built in Vera Cruz, Mexico, and Lima, Peru, and new diocesan capitals of the Catholic church were being founded at the same time to the north of the original domain of Christendom, churches were being expropriated from the Catholic church and from their centuries-old diocesan capitals. On the one hand, the continents discovered overseas acted as a temptation to betray the spiritual foundations of the Christian West for the sake of power and wealth. On the other hand, the Protestant world acted as a standing temptation to relinquish the international unity of Christendom in the tradition and discipline of the Church for the sake of subjective inclinations and personal freedom. Furthermore, the Turks now stood (as the Saracens had once stood) at the very gates of Christendom. Two-thirds of Hungary belonged to the Ottoman Empire, and the crescent-banner of Islam had already flown for many decades over the Hagia Sophia in the former capital of the Eastern Roman Empire. In this situation, it was important not only to think of lasting values and of absolute and fundamental truths, but also to deduce from these values and truths those consequences which that altered age, with its attendant tasks and its dangers, demanded.

Out of awareness of this task, the "Spanish School" emerged. It was this school that set up the lasting values of a law consisting of three levels as a beacon for their age, and as well for subsequent centuries of the modern era. In his work *The Spanish Origin of International Law*, the commendable controversialist James Brown Scott says the following of the Spanish school's founder, Francisco de Vitoria:

> After wandering, as it were, in the wilderness—when it was not a desert—the publicists of today are disregarding the international law based upon force, unrelated to morality and rendered futile and inoperative in the international community by a conception of sovereignty descended from the divine right of kings and its successor, the divine state. They are leaving the paths marked out by false prophets of international law and turning to Vitoria's law of nations and the Vitorian principles that for four hundred years have pointed the path to an international law still of the future, in which law and morality shall be one and inseparable, in which states are created by and for human beings, and every principle of international law and of international conduct is to be tested by the good of the international community and not by the selfish standards of its more powerful and erring members. In Vitoria's doctrine, the duty of the more powerful is to observe the law as do the weak and, through his conception of the mandate, to lend a helping hand to less favored peoples.[1]

---

[1] James B. Scott, *The Spanish Origin of International Law: Francisco de Vitoria and His Law of Nations* (Oxford: Clarendon Press, 1934), 11*a*.

From International Law to World Peace

These thoughts, written in 1932, have lost nothing of their validity or defensibility today. On the contrary, the experience of the Second World War and of the communist war of aggression in Korea, as also, on the other hand, of the necessity for and the advantage of an organization of United Nations that is capable of acting, have lent even more weight to the idea that one should turn "to Vitoria's law of nations and. . . . Vitorian principles."

What, then, are these "Vitorian principles" that are recognized and defended by so many commentators today, and indeed even put forward as postulates for international political practice in the present day? In the final analysis, they answer in three ways *the question of the permissibility of war.*

(1) War is the *ultima ratio* of state policy and follows with absolute necessity from the unlimited sovereignty of states; it is beyond the "permissibility and impermissibility" of law and morality, since it is the state that determines what is right and wrong. Civil war is likewise an *ultima ratio*, in this case of the class struggle—since it follows with absolute necessity from the nature of unlimited class rule (class dictatorship). It is beyond the "permissibility and impermissibility" of law and of morality, since it is the ruling class that creates law and morality as a superstructure of its power, one that lovingly cares for that power. In a case of opposition between states that are at once unlimitedly sovereign and also proponents of opposed orders of class rule, war follows with absolute necessity from the fact of their unlimited sovereignty, as well as of their opposed social orders—a war that brings together both forms of war, i.e., that is at once a civil war and a war between states.

(2) War is not permitted in any case where it is a greater

evil and brings about a greater evil than that evil which is to be prevented or averted by means of it. Law does not suffice as a legal means, because war is an expression of brute force and thus not an appropriate way of refuting a claim or of demonstrating that a claim is true and justified (right and wrong cannot be proved or refuted with artillery). In other words, war contradicts the nature of humanity and of Christendom. War must therefore be replaced with a *court*. The path leading to world peace, however, is that of passive resistance to war, on the principle that the one who takes pleasure in attacking will at length become weary of intruding through open doors. *Legally*, however, and quite apart from its causes and motives, war is itself a crime, so that there can be no such a thing as a "just war" in the sense of the word "crime"—that is, as an act that has been committed. "The aggressor" will be treated as an outlaw, just as a pirate is. Yet the wrong of aggression and of the aggressor should not be thought to lie in a substantively affirmed guilt of war (in the sense of a cause of war), but rather in the *crime de l'attaque*, the crime of *aggression as such*... The problem of "just cause" lies outside the terms of this argument.[2]

(3) War, when no legally organized trans-state organization exists, is a last resort of protection and deterrence that remains at the disposal of individual states against attempts on the part of politically, socially, or ideologically aggressive

---

[2] Cf. "Francisco de Vitoria and the History of His Reputation" (since incorporated into Carl Schmitt, *Nomos!*) vol. 4 of the *Neuen Ordnung*, edited by the Albertus-Magnus-Akademie of the Dominicans (Walberberg, Cologne). (In the German text, inverted commas are closed at the end of this paragraph. However, it is unclear from the printed text where they are supposed to have been opened. TR)

states or organizations to coerce individual states politically, socially, or ideologically. War is also a last resort of protection and deterrence, as well as a means for enforcing legal decisions, at the disposal of a trans-state judicial power. War is, in the case of the presence of a trans-state organization, an international police action in defence of the international legal order, i.e., of peace. It is the means of defending and sanctioning international penal law.

These three points represent, in their essentials, the intellectual content of the problem of the permissibility of war as we are conscious of facing it today.[3] What, then, does Francisco de Vitoria say about this problem?

> I wish to consider four main questions here. First, whether Christians may wage war at all. Second, where the authority to declare or to wage war is situated. Third, what grounds can be given or ought to be given for a just war. Fourth, which measures, and of what scope, may be taken against the enemy in a just war?
> As far as the first question is concerned, it may appear that war is forbidden to Christians as such, since self-defence is forbidden in the passage from Romans 12: "Dearly beloved, avenge not yourselves, but rather give place unto wrath." And the Lord says in the gospel of Matthew (chapter five): "whosoever shall smite thee on thy right cheek, turn to him the other also"; and "I say unto you, that ye resist not evil"; and (Matthew 26): "all they that take the sword shall perish with the sword." Now, it does not suffice to say that all these sayings are not com-

---

[3] It appears that these three points essentially summarize text from the book cited in the previous footnote.

mands but advice, since, even were that so, it would be a sufficiently great impertinence if a war waged by Christians contradicted the Lord's *advice*. The view of all teachers (*doctores*) is, however, against this, and so also is the general usage of the Church.

In the further discussion of this [first] question, it must be emphasized that although all Catholics are at one on the essentials of this question, Luther, by contrast, who left nothing untainted, denies that there is any justification for Christians to make use of weapons, even against the Turks. He supports this argument not only with the passages from Holy Scripture adduced above, but also with the view that if the Turks were to attack Christendom, this would be God's will, which one may not be tempted to resist. In this point, however, Luther did not find so much success as with his other dogmas, given that he wanted to press this view upon the Germans, who were born soldiers. Tertullian seems also not to have been inclined to this opinion, since in his work *De Corona Militis* he considers the question "whether military service is at all permissible for a Christian," and arrives in the course of his discussion at the position that military service is forbidden to Christians, since, as he said, a Christian "may not even go to court."

Now I leave strange opinions to one side, and give an answer to the [first] question in the form of a single ruling on doctrine: Christians may undertake military service and may wage war.[4]

After Vitoria has discussed the reasons why St Augustine

---

[4] As in the case of quotations from Aquinas, and for the same reason, I have translated Tomberg's quotations from Vitoria directly from his German. For an English translation directly from Vitoria's Latin text, see Francisco de Vitoria, *Political Writings*, ed. Anthony Pagden and Jeremy Lawrance (Cambridge: Cambridge University Press, 1991), 295–97. TR

arrived at the same answer to this question,[5] he expands at considerable length on the principles of Augustinian and Thomistic doctrine concerning the preconditions required for the justice of a war,[6] which can be summarized from Vitoria as follows:

(1) Only a *just reason* justifies a war. Difference of religion is not, however, in itself any reason for war, as little as is the extension of the prince's dominions, personal fame, or other advantage to the prince—but only and solely an injustice suffered. But not every injustice, nor any arbitrary quantity of injustice, suffice for a war. (2) Accordingly, there must be a *grave injustice* on the side of one, and *only* one, of the parties in dispute. (3) There must also be a grave *formal moral guilt* on one of the two sides—a merely material injustice does not suffice. (4) Both the injustice and the guilt of one party must be indubitably *demonstrable*. (5) Military engagement must have been shown to be *unavoidable*, i.e., there must be a lack of a higher legal authority or court of appeal recognized by both parties; in short, all attempts to reach a peaceful understanding, undertaken in complete seriousness and with all the strength available, must have been shown to be fruitless. (6) There must be a moral *certainty* that victory will serve the just cause. (7) There must be a *right intention* present to further the good by means of the war and to avoid evil.

---

[5] In *Contra Faustum*, in *Liber 83 Quaestionum*, in *De Verbis Domini*, in *Contra Secundum Manichaeum*, in his sermon on the son of the Centurion, and in his letter to Bonifatius.

[6] To introduce the reader to Francisco de Vitoria's own exposition of the question of just war, a running quotation covering many pages was originally inserted here. This content has been placed for reference in Appendix A, so that the author's own line of thought can be more readily followed. ED

The good to the state that is to be expected from the war must exceed the evil to be expected from it. (8) The war must also be prevented from inflicting heavy damage on *other states* that are not immediately participating in the war, and in particular from damaging the *whole of Christendom*, still less placing it at risk of its survival. (9) The war, as a measure in the service of law and justice, must correspond to the principle of the just *proportion* between crime and punishment. (10) The *decision* both as to the justice of the reason for war and as to the necessity of war may not be left either to a *single* person, or to the mass of the people, but must be a matter for counsel taken as extensively as possible from wise and experienced people—which produces the basis and justification for the *declaration of war* on the part of the *authorized power* in the name of natural and divine law, which is necessary to a just war.

For Vitoria, if any of these ten preconditions is lacking, the war is unjust. It is also unjust if, despite conforming to the ten conditions set out above, it violates the *correct manner of waging war*, i.e., if it brings about or permits an *avoidable* killing of innocent parties, or even where it is conducted with cruelty towards guilty ones. Thus, for example, prisoners of war "under the international law that is in force among Christians" may not be made into slaves. Hostages may be taken only in a case in which the enemy cannot be trusted to keep faith, if those hostages belong to the "arms-bearing class." The killing of prisoners of war as an act of punishment may indeed not be unjust in itself, but contradicts the custom according to which, after a victory and after the cessation of danger, prisoners of war may not be killed—"and that which is the custom among good people is also to be followed as international law."

From International Law to World Peace

⊕

All the above, however, holds either for the realm of "Christians among themselves" or for their relation to the *hostes perpetui*—the Saracens and Turks. The discovery of America, however, presented a new problem: that is, the relation to the original population of the discovered area, which, since it was a population neither Christian nor hostile to Christians, necessitated a relationship to them that had to be clarified—that is, the nature of the *colonial problem*, with its moral and legal difficulties. This new problem is set out in its full extent by Francisco de Vitoria, who treats it in a spirit of incorruptible justice and moral awareness of responsibility that are among the most noble phenomena anywhere in world history.

Starting out from the proposition in Holy Scripture, "Go ye therefore, and teach all nations, baptizing them in the name of the Father, and of the Son, and of the Holy Ghost" (Matt. 29:19), Vitoria poses three basic questions: (1) With what right were the natives ("barbarians") subjected to Spanish rule? (2) What authority do the Spanish princes possess over the natives in secular and civic matters? (3) What authority do these princes, or does the Church, possess over the natives in spiritual matters? Once Vitoria has posed these three basic questions, he justifies his personal engagement with this field by saying that the rights of the "natives" constitute a problem that is not only a matter for jurists, but also for theologians, i.e., a problem of a three-level law, in which law, morality, and religion are all concerned. In view of this, he begins answering these fundamental questions by posing a fourth one: Were the natives really the owners (*veri domini*), as private and public law understand that term, before the arrival of the Spaniards?

Francisco de Vitoria

Vitoria makes a start in this regard by pointing out that it would only be possible that the natives were *not* the real owners, either because they were incapable of holding property rights or because they had lost them. Now, slaves are incapable of holding property, and the natives are (one might argue, with Aristotle) slaves by nature. Conversely, however, at the time of the Spaniards' arrival, the natives were in peaceful possession both of their private and of their public property. If they were not, however, actual owners, then they will have had to relinquish their right of ownership. This could have happened to them (a) as sinners, (b) as infidels, (c) as unable to hold property because deficient in reason, or (d) as insane persons.

Now, position (a), that the natives had lost their property as sinners, would be heretical, since the doctrine that property is founded on a state of grace is heretical. This is the error of the Waldensians and of Wyclif, and was condemned by the Council of Constance, which determined that "mortal sin in no way impairs civic and actual ownership." As far as reason (b) is concerned, according to Thomas Aquinas and Holy Scripture, "infidelity is not incompatible with actual ownership." Moreover, unbelief is less heinous than active sin. Heretics can indeed be despoiled of their property rights, but this can only be done according to human law (not according to the natural or divine law); and also, it does not take place before they are condemned. Moreover, even if one concedes that beings without reason or insane persons, (c) and (d), cannot bear property rights, the American natives are in fact not without reason.

> It follows from everything that has been said, then, that the natives were actual owners both of private and of public property, just as Christians are, and that they may there-

fore not be despoiled of their property on the grounds that they were no real owners. It would also be difficult to deny to those who have done no sort of wrong such rights as we grant to the Saracens and Jews, the continual enemies of the Christian faith, to whom we do not deny the right to own property, so long as they do not seize control of the lands of the Christians.[7]

Once the American natives have been recognized as the legal ("actual") owners of their country, and of all their moveable and immovable property, Vitoria subjects to a searching examination *fourteen* possible legal grounds for a claim on Spain's part (or on the part of any other country) to rule over the natives. Seven of these possible legal grounds are condemned by him as invalid, as "inapplicable or insufficient," while seven others are, conversely, recognized as valid.[8]

The *first* invalid legal basis for a claim on Spain's part to rule over the natives was the emperor's claim to be the ruler of the world. But, Vitoria says, the emperor is in fact not the ruler of the world. He is not such, even from the standpoint of law, since, according to *natural* law, all people are free; and according to *divine* law, the emperors were neither rulers of the world before Christ, nor was Christ himself, in the flesh, a ruler in secular matters. According to *human* law, however, the emperor has no claim to rule the world. Even if he did rule the world, he would not on this account have any right to occupy the provinces of the natives or to

---

[7] No reference given.

[8] What follows appears to be a close paraphrase of Vitoria's original text along with further context from the author.

install new rulers there and levy taxes upon them. Mere jurisdiction, such as that claimed for the emperor, does not justify such measures.

A *second* invalid legal basis for such a claim by Spain was the assertion that the pope ruled the world. Now, if it were, as Vitoria says, granted that the pope possessed the authority claimed for him by certain jurists—that he possesses complete jurisdiction in secular matters across the whole of the earth, and that secular authority is derived from him—the pope would indubitably have the power in his capacity as the highest secular ruler to appoint the king of Spain as prince over the natives. If the natives were then to oppose the secular rule of the Holy Father, war against them would be justified, and princes could be imposed upon them. However, the pope is not the political or secular ruler of the whole world in respect of ownership and political power. Christ himself, as has already been mentioned, did not have this power—and Christ's representative is not greater than the Lord himself. If it were granted that the pope possessed secular rule over the whole earth, then it would have been a question of a right belonging to the *papacy*, and no pope could have taken this right away from his successors. The pope does indeed have secular power *in ordine ad spiritualia* ("in the spiritual order"), and can for this reason, in order to ward off spiritual evils, arbitrate in cases of disputes between Christian princes, and may indeed even depose and enthrone such princes. But he has no secular power over the American natives or over other infidels, since he has no spiritual power over them, which is the necessary basis for his secular power. It thus follows that if the natives should refuse to acknowledge the authority of the pope, no war waged against them on these grounds, or any seizure of their property, would be justified. Consequently, the Spaniards, when they first arrived by ship in the lands of the natives, had no right to take possession of these lands.

A *third* invalid legal basis for Spain's claim to dominion over the American natives is that the claim of *discovery* could be made good. Regarding this, Vitoria makes the point that, in accordance with international law, only those things can be taken into possession that are not in anyone's possession. This land was, however, owned by the natives, who, as set out above, were its actual owners, and it was therefore not a "thing without an owner." Thus, the Spaniards as little gained a legal claim to the lands of the natives through the mere fact of the discovery of these lands, as for their part the natives would have had a legal claim to Spain if they had discovered Spain.

A *fourth* invalid legal basis for Spain's claim to dominion over the natives is their rejection of the Christian faith—once it had been proclaimed to them. According to Vitoria, those who have never heard the Word are in a state of invincible ignorance, and thus commit no sin (if they are heathens, or remain heathens), for sin always means some kind of negligence or neglect. Moreover, the natives are not obliged to accept the first simple preaching of the Word, without miracles or any other signs, as if they had committed a mortal sin by not conferring belief upon it. The natives' rejection of such preaching in no way justifies the Spaniards in waging war upon them, nor in asserting that they had the right to wage war on them. The natives are innocent in this particular point, and did not do the Spaniards any wrong in this matter. A just cause is, however, required for a just war. But if the faith were proclaimed to the natives "in a plausible way," using plausible and rational arguments, and were also accompanied by an unimpeachable mode of life and preached by natural, lawful effort (which are themselves a strong argument in confirmation of the truth)—and this not once only and superficially but rather with diligent exertion—then they would be obliged to accept the faith on pain of mortal sin. They would also be guilty of mortal sin if, after having been called and warned, they refused to listen to the Word in peace. It cannot, however, be satisfactorily demonstrated that the Christian faith had already been set out and proclaimed to the natives in such a way as to mean that they were sinning when they did not believe it. Here, Vitoria remarks that he himself has heard nothing of miracles or signs, or even of examples of Christian life, in the above connection. On the contrary, news had reached him "of many indecent and unworthy things, and also of much impiety." Even if the Word had been proclaimed to the natives in a convincing way and to a sufficient extent, it would nevertheless not have been justified to wage war upon them and to despoil them of their property. This is likewise the view of Thomas Aquinas and the universal opinion of the Doctors both of canon law and of civil law. In short, the acceptance of faith ought to be free. War is no way of proving the truth of the Christian faith. Coercion begets feigned assent rather than conviction.

Vitoria next mentions as a *fifth* invalid legal basis for Spain's dominion over the American natives in this connection, their sins (not, indeed, against the Christian faith, but against natural law) by pointing out that no Christian prince, even if authorized by the pope, has the right to restrain the natives from sins against nature, or the right to punish them for such sins. The pope has, as explained above, no jurisdiction over them.

From International Law to World Peace

The *sixth* invalid legal basis in this connection is free choice. The natives could doubtless accept the rule of the king of Spain of their own free will, but fear and ignorance are incompatible with freedom of choice. If the natives had chosen the king of Spain as their ruler, this would have been done without knowing what they were doing, and in the presence of the Spanish army.

As a *seventh* such invalid legal basis, reference could be made to a special authorization from God. It could, that is, be the case that God had condemned the natives to defeat on account of their cruelties. It does not however follow from this that those who are the means of this demise are therefore without guilt.

After the above seven *invalid* legal grounds for a claim on Spain's part to rule over the American natives, Vitoria follows with seven *valid* legal grounds, as well as an eighth, of still undetermined validity, for Spain's claim.

The *first* of these valid legal grounds lies in the natural-law principle of *natural society and commerce*.[9] According to this principle, the Spaniards are justified in traveling to the lands of the natives and in remaining there, on the condition that this happens without harm to the natives. The natives could not refuse this right to the Spaniards. That

---

[9] The following fourteen points (pp 116–122) collectively pertain to the *first* of the seven legal grounds just mentioned that might give Spain a valid claim to rule over the American natives. After presenting these fourteen points relating to the first of these seven grounds, the author more briefly describes the other six possible grounds for this claim.

this is so, as Vitoria explains, is, in the *first* place from the *jus gentium*, which is either itself natural law or is deduced from natural law: that which is held valid by the nations through natural reason is called international law. Now, all nations hold the poor reception of guests and strangers to be inhumane when it happens without any particular reason; it is, conversely, humane and dutiful to behave well towards guests, which however does not hold if strangers behave ill towards other nations. In the *second* place, it was originally permitted to everyone in the world (when everything was held in common) to betake themselves to any country and to settle there. This permission was not abrogated by the division of the world, for it was never the intention of the nations to destroy reciprocal commerce among people by means of this division.... In the *third* place, everything that is not forbidden is permitted, to the extent that it does not cause others injustice or harm. The coming of the Spaniards (in the sense of the above presupposition) is, however, not an injustice or harm to the natives; consequently, it is permitted. In the *fourth* place, it is not permitted to the French to forbid the Spaniards to betake themselves to France or to settle there, if no harm arises to the French as a result, and if no injustice is done them. The same goes for the natives. In the *fifth* place, banishment is a punishment, and, indeed, a severe one. Foreigners may therefore not be excluded without guilt. In the *sixth* place, it is part of a state of war to deny enemy foreigners access to one's city and country and to expel those who are already there. In the *seventh* place, since the natives were, however, not waging a just war against the Spaniards, it is not permitted to them—so long as the Spaniards are harmless—to deny the Spaniards access to their country.

From International Law to World Peace

Or, as the poet says:

> What men, what monsters, what inhuman race,
> What laws, what barb'rous customs of the place,
> Shut up a desart shore to drowning men,
> And drive us to the cruel seas again?[10]

In the *eighth* place, every living being loves what is like himself (Eccl. 13); consequently, friendship among people is also a command of natural law. Thus, it is against nature to avoid dealings with harmless people. In the *ninth* place, it is also said in Matthew 25, "I was a stranger, and ye took me not in." Since taking in strangers is part of natural law, this judgment of Christ goes for everyone. In the *tenth* place, according to natural law, both oceans and flowing waters, as well as rivers and harbors, are all held in common, so that, according to natural law, it is everywhere permitted to cast anchor. It is consequently not permitted to anyone to prohibit this—from which it follows that the natives would have done wrong to the Spaniards if they had refused them entry to their territories. In the *eleventh* place, the natives are themselves accustomed to grant entry everywhere to all other natives; consequently they would do the Spaniards a wrong if they refused the same to them. In the *twelfth* place, if, however, it were to be forbidden to the Spaniards to settle among them, then this must be done either on the grounds of natural law, or on those of divine law or human law. Now, it is certain that this settlement is permitted according to natural law and according to divine law; if, however, it is a question of a human law (*lex humana*) that forbids it without any grounds in natural or divine law, then this law itself would be inhumane and also irrational,

---

[10] Virgil, *Aeneid*, I, 539–540; translation by John Dryden.

and consequently non-binding. In the *thirteenth* place, either the Spaniards are subject to the natives or they are not. If they are not subject to them, the natives cannot deny them entry. If they are subject to them, then the natives must treat them well. In the *fourteenth* place, the Spaniards are the neighbors of the natives, in the sense of Luke 10 on the good Samaritan. But one ought to love one's neighbors as oneself (Matt. 22). Consequently, one cannot deny them entry to one's country without reason. For as Augustine says in *De Doctrina Christiana*: when "love thy neighbor" is said, every person is obviously meant as one's neighbor.

According to Vitoria, then, in the fourteen cases listed above, the Spaniards *are* justified in entering the lands of the American natives and in staying there. This, however, also means that the Spaniards are justified in peaceful dealings with the natives. Now, trade is a form of these dealings—consequently, the Spaniards may "import goods that the natives lack, or export gold and silver or other objects of which they have plenty. The princes of the natives may not prevent their subjects from engaging in trade with the Spaniards, nor may the Spanish princes forbid the Spaniards to engage in trade with the natives." For, in the first place, it is a principle of the *jus gentium* "that foreigners engage in trade so long as the that trade does not inflict harm upon the citizens of a country; in the second place, since it is also permitted according to divine law, as a law forbidding trade to foreigners would indubitably be irrational; in the third place, the prince is obliged under natural law to love the Spaniards, and so in consequence, he may not inflict harm upon them by withholding their goods without reason. Fourth, it would be against the saying 'do not do anything to another that you would not wish to be done to you.'"

In short, it is clear that the natives are no more justified in forbidding the Spaniards to trade with them than Christians would be justified in so forbidding Christians. It is obvious that if the Spaniards were to forbid the French from trading—not because of the good of Spain, but so that the French should draw no profit from it—this would be an evil law and one that conflicts with love; and it would be against natural law to create estrangement among people without reason. "For man is not a wolf to man," as Ovid says, "but a man." Everything that the natives regard as held in common for themselves and for guests must also be so held for the Spaniards, and it would be illegal to take discriminatory measures against the Spaniards so as to exclude them from commerce and from participation in it.

Thus, for example, if it is permitted to other foreigners to dig for gold in common land or to take it out of rivers or to fish for pearls in the ocean or in the river, then natives may not forbid the Spaniards to do this; rather, they must permit it to the same extent to which it is permitted to other foreigners and insofar as it does not molest their own citizens and the natural inhabitants of the country. This follows from the fact that if it is permitted the Spaniards to settle among the natives and to engage in trade, then the use of the same laws and freedoms applies to them as to all foreigners. Moreover, it follows from this that things (e.g., wild animals) that have no owner belong under international law to whoever first took them into ownership). Consequently, according to the *jus gentium*, both the gold in the fields and the pearls in the ocean and other things in the rivers, which are no one's property, belong to whoever takes possession of them. Since, then, a great deal is here deduced from the *jus gentium*, and since the *jus gentium* is also sufficiently clearly derived from natural law (*jus naturale*), it therefore obviously has the power to make law and to impose obligations. Moreover, even if it cannot always be deduced from the natural law, the consensus of the greater part of the world is validly sufficient—and, indeed, in the highest degree, to the common good of all. For if, after the earliest age of the creation of the world, or after its restoration following upon the great Flood, the greater part of humanity determined that envoys (wherever they might be) were inviolable, that the ocean was a possession held in common, that prisoners of war become slaves, and that it is right to not drive out foreigners, then these determinations were doubtless valid also with respect to those other people who resisted them.

Furthermore, children who have been born to Spaniards who have settled among the natives may not have the rights of local citizens withheld from them. "For it is held to be according to the *jus gentium* that one who is born in a state (*civitas*) is considered as a citizen of that state, and is justified in acting as a citizen of it."

If, then, the natives were to express a wish to prevent the Spaniards from claiming their rights under international law—i.e., entry to the country, settlement, trade, the use of the rights that are shared by natives and foreigners, and the enjoyment of rights of citizenship for the children born to the Spaniards in their country—then the Spaniards would be obliged in the first place to attempt to convince the natives by means of reason. If the natives should, however, have recourse to force, then the Spaniards would be justified in using similar means to defend themselves.

After the Spaniards had exhausted all other means, and once it had been shown that safety could not be secured without occupation of the natives' states and without subjecting those states to the Spaniards' rule, then they would be justified in acting in this way. If, despite all the Spaniards' efforts to convince them of their peaceful intentions, the natives remain of an evil disposition towards them, then the Spaniards have the right to wage war against them.

All this, then, is the *first* legal basis for a just occupation of the provinces and states of the natives by the Spaniards—i.e., *the legal basis for a war for a just cause in defence of natural rights.*

The *second* valid basis for Spain's rule over the American natives is connected with the question of the *dissemination of the Christian religion.* By appealing at every step to divine law, natural law, and international law—as well as to dogmas he has previously shown to be true—Vitoria established the following principles: (1) that Christians have the right to proclaim the Word and to preach in the lands of the natives; (2) that the pope—on the grounds of his secular authority *in ordine ad spiritualia*—can entrust the Spaniards with the work of proclaiming the gospel, and can prohibit all others from doing the same, and indeed even from having any commerce with the natives, should this further the interests of Christian mission; (3) that if the natives allow the Spaniards to proclaim the gospel freely and without obstruction, it is not permitted to wage war against them or to occupy their lands on the grounds of an appeal to the work of evangelization, irrespective of whether the natives accept the Word or not; (4) that if, however, the natives place obstacles in the way of the proclamation of the gospel, the Spaniards are nevertheless justified in doing everything necessary to convert the natives, and, if this can-

Francisco de Vitoria

not be done in any other way, they may occupy the lands and provinces of the unruly, may appoint new rulers, dismiss previous rulers, and make use of martial law. What St Paul says must, however, be very carefully considered: "All things are lawful unto me, but not all things are expedient." (1 Cor. 6:12)

Everything said above is to be taken in this sense. It could be the case, in particular, that the conversion of the natives would be more hindered by such wars, with killing and rapine, than it would be furthered and extended. For this reason one ought above all to take care not to place any obstacles in the path of the gospel. If one has, however, created an obstacle, then one must give up the argument from evangelization and seek other grounds.

Vitoria mentions only briefly the other [*third* through *eighth*] valid legal basis the for Spain's rule over the American natives, as summarized below.

The *third* valid basis for Spain's rule is the defence of the converted natives against any of their own (i.e., native) rulers who might attempt to compel them to return to idolatry. In such a case, the Spaniards may defend the newly converted with armed force. The pope also can have sufficient grounds, including at the request of those converted, to award this task to one Christian prince, this being the *fourth* basis. The Spaniards can intervene with armed force in order to protect all innocent people from the tyranny of their native rulers, this being the *fifth* valid basis. The natives can accept the king of Spain as their ruler in a real and free election, this being the *sixth* valid basis. The Spaniards can also acquire provinces of the natives' by means of war, by defending any of the natives with whom they have entered into an alliance against attacks from other natives, this being

From International Law to World Peace

the *seventh* valid basis. And finally, Vitoria proposes a comment on one other, *eighth*, possible valid basis for Spain's rule—i.e., the incapacity of the natives, even within purely human and civic limits, to found or to administer a legal state.

Vitoria's thoughts on war and peace—both for the Christian and for the non-Christian world—are in their essentials an elaboration and application of Thomas Aquinas's teaching. For Vitoria, too, international law is not merely the sum-total of valid agreements and of valid customary law in dealings between states, but is the natural law that is in force among all civilized nations. And this is authoritative for all nations as such, together with everything immediately following from that natural law.

The *jus gentium* is thus not one domain of law *alongside* other domains of law, but rather penetrates all areas of legal life as the very rationality and justice that they contain. The Spaniards and the French have different laws, but common principles underpin both. The common matter of principle in Spanish and French law is the common legal ground upon which Spain and France stand: it is the law of these two nations simultaneously; it is *international* law. The same also holds for all nations of the world, since all nations consist of people (i.e., of rational beings), and reason and justice are therefore binding for all normal people (i.e., reason and justice regulate dealings between nations). It is true that for the Christian part of humanity the divine law is also binding; but for *all* humankind (Christian as well as non-Christian), the postulates of that faculty with which it is naturally endowed—namely reason, or its expression in human interaction, the *jus gentium* (international law as a law of humankind)—are valid.

Both states and individuals are subjects of this law of humankind, because if, for example, the individual may only take things that lack any owner into his possession, so also states may only take into their possession uninhabited countries that they have discovered; and there is no such thing as "discovering" a country that is already inhabited, let alone "discovering" one that is organized into a polity, any more than an individual who believes himself subjectively to have "discovered" another man's garden has a right to take possession of it. In other words, the principles of reason are valid for persons and for states, and to the same degree. Both persons and states are "addressees" of the statutes of reason and justice. Both are obligated and justified by the *jus gentium* as a law of humankind.

States, according to Vitoria's doctrine, are indeed sovereign—"the state is a perfect commonwealth or community, which is a whole in itself, i.e., is not part of another commonwealth, but has its own laws, its own council, and its own magistrate (*magistratus*), such as the kingdoms of Aragon and Castile, Venice, and other similar states"—but they are not *unlimitedly* sovereign. The sovereignty of the state is limited to the realm of human (positive) law—and this, too, only in secular affairs concerning worldly goals (*in ordine ad finem temporalem*), while in purely spiritual affairs, which can serve or obstruct what is spiritual (*temporalia in ordine ad finem spiritualem*), the sovereignty of the state ceases and is to this extent subordinate to the authority of the Church. The sovereignty of the state is also limited by natural law. Any of the state's laws that contradict natural law are not valid.

From International Law to World Peace

It is not the state itself, however, that is to decide whether its legislation agrees or does not agree with natural law, but, in the first place, the Church, and then individuals, i.e., the people and other states, who are justified in intervening and in protecting people against unnatural laws—that is, tyranny. Thus, the sovereignty of the state is limited by the authority of the Church, by the conscience of the people, and by the rights and duties of other states. In Vitoria's view, the state is not the heavenly firmament above the heads of men, but the solid ground beneath their feet.

Since, then, the sovereignty of the state is not absolute, but *limited*, the state is also deprived of the preconditions for the (modern) claim that it is "a world unto itself"—the claim, that is, to absolute non-interference in its internal affairs, which finds physical expression in the Chinese wall of ancient times and in the "iron curtain" hung before the Soviet world in our own time. According to Vitoria, if it is a question of protecting "those who are oppressed and who are suffering injustice" (*De Indis*), intervention is, on the contrary, the natural law and a duty under the divine law. This is merely the practical consequence of the conception of humankind as a unity: "And the power of law possesses the whole globe, which, in a certain sense, is a single commonwealth, setting legal norms fitting for all, as they are expounded in international law (*jus gentium*) . . . and it is not up to the individual state to reject the connection through international law, since the latter owes its validity to the authority of the whole globe." Since intervention is permitted, and indeed in certain cases prescribed, then, together with the state's claim to absolute sovereignty and absolute non-interference in its internal affairs, the ideological basis for *neutrality* also disappears.

Just as the concept of neutrality had been lacking in the work of Thomas Aquinas two and a half centuries earlier, so is it also lacking in that of Francisco de Vitoria. For Vitoria, too, there are only "innocents," i.e., people who have no part in the injustice that had led to war. "It is not permitted to kill foreigners or guests who are staying with the enemy, since they are to be presumed innocent—and in reality they are not, indeed, enemies at all," says Vitoria, meaning by this that there can indeed be states that—because of distance, or for other reasons—are *incapable* of taking part in the just war, and that citizens of such states can be present even in the enemy camp. But these states and their citizens are not *neutral* in the sense that there could be a right to indifference concerning matters of legality and illegality in the life of nations. Just as in the private life of the individual there is no right to "neutrality" in the sense of standing aside without doing anything in the presence of the commission of a crime (even if in certain circumstances this is to be excused from weakness or fear), so there is in the realm of dealings between states no right to neutrality in the sense of a freedom in principle from the duty under natural and divine law to be "one's brother's keeper."

Non-participation in a just war can, however (apart from physical incapacity or ignorance), be excused by one further circumstance—that is, doubt as to the justice of the war. Not only states, but even their subjects, have the right to renounce participation in the war if they cannot acknowledge the justice of the war to the best of their knowledge and conscience, that is, "if a subject is convinced of the injustice of a war," as Vitoria says. This principle applies first of all to states,[11] but even here it is not a question of neutrality in the sense of a justification for indifference in the case of a war for a just cause, but of the right to form one's own judgment on the question of the justice or injustice of a war. It is a matter, here, of a different problem of legal life—the problem of "conscientious objection."

Consistent with the principles propounded by Vitoria (of the limited nature of state sovereignty, of the human commonwealth, of the *jus gentium* as the law of the human commonwealth, of the permissibility of the just war and only of the just war, of the permissibility of intervention, and of the rejection of neutrality as the "normal situation") is the principle, which he also champions, of the *obligation to accept arbitration by peaceful means*: "If one party wishes to end the conflict by means of arbitration, and has suggested a division or a compromise in respect of part of what is claimed, the other party is obligated to accept the suggestion, even if this party is stronger and would be in a position to seize all of what is disputed by force of arms; nor would it then have grounds for a just war," to which he adds, with as much clarity as definiteness, the principle that "law and treaty trump force and compulsion."

---

[11] The corresponding passage in Vitoria's *Relectiones* reads as follows: "Granted that there is a demonstrable ignorance either in relation to the facts of the matter or in relation to the legal situation, then it can come about that on the side *on which justice in reality resides, the war is just in itself,* whereas on the other side, *the war is just in the sense that it is to be excused as a sin* on account of good faith (*bona fides*), since invincible ignorance signifies a perfect excuse."

Francisco de Vitoria

Francisco de Vitoria's doctrine can be summarized as follows. International law is valid natural law, i.e., reason and humaneness. In a case of doubt, pure natural law decides. If further doubt should still remain thereafter, divine law decides. War is the last resort for the protection of law and for the overcoming of injustice: use of it may only be made once the justice of the cause has been irrefutably established, and only when all peaceful means have proved unsuccessful—but also, only if the good to be expected from the war is greater than the evil it brings about.

These principles are related to the international-legal ideas of the present [1952] in two ways. They stand in the starkest imaginable contrast to legal positivism, insofar as the latter survives from the time before the First World War and came to be propounded by the statism of the Fascist and Bolshevist camps. But on the other hand, these principles are in remarkable accord with the ideas to which the rest of humanity has been led by the experience of two world wars, and that underpin the former League of Nations, and now (to a still greater extent) the United Nations. Let us take a closer look at these two ways that Vitoria's principles are related to the international-legal ideas of the present.

To the *legal positivists*, Vitoria is a man who postulates "an absolute world order in which law is trans-historically rooted"; but for legal positivists, an "absolute world order does not exist." Nor, for them, is it a matter of "universal and neutral argument," since it is not the task of the theoretician of international law to "expound a trans-historical truth," but rather to "provide arguments in cases of inter-state conflicts between state governments." Moreover, since, for legal positivists, ethical life and law are two separate orders of thought without any essential relation to each other, progress since the Middle Ages has consisted "in moral, theological, and ecclesiastical argumentation finally being detached from juridical and political argumentation." For them, war is a historical necessity: "the thought of perpetual peace is a dream, and not even a pretty one." A discriminating concept of war (i.e., a concept that distinguishes between just and unjust war) only transforms a war between states into an international civil war. Modern international law, conversely, does not distinguish between just and unjust wars according to the reason for the war. The "unjust war" is not a state of affairs under *international* law. Every war is a relationship of *parity between sovereign states* that is permitted and acknowledged under international law, a relationship in which "*justi et aequales hostes* [just and equal enemies] oppose each other without any discrimination being made among them in international law." "Every war between states equally legitimately sovereign" is "a legal war." For legal positivists, the great progress in European inter-state international law consisted precisely in the fact that the doctrine of the *justa causa* was replaced "by the doctrine of the juridical equality of the *justi hostes* on both sides."

To summarize, for legal positivists, the progress made in international law since Vitoria consists precisely in the *overturning* of Vitoria's fundamental doctrines—i.e., of the doctrine of the primacy of natural law, of the doctrine of the just war, of the restriction of state sovereignty, and of the doctrine that both states and individuals are subjects of international law. This, then, is the relationship of legal positivism to Francisco de Vitoria.

Francisco de Vitoria

Against the legal positivists, however, voices are being raised, such as that cited above from James Brown Scott, or the text by Nikolaos Politis on neutrality and peace (Paris, 1935),[12] in which the author argues against modern neutrality as an expression of international anarchy, and appeals on the topic to Vitoria (and to Pierre Dubois's project).

The question of the role Vitoria's ideas play and could play in the present will be discussed at the end of this work. At this point, the nature of the controversy about Vitoria today can be brought to a close with Heydte's words:

> Vitoria knows only a single prescriptive order, which binds theologians as it does jurists; he knows only a single *jus naturale*, in which the *jus gentium* is indissolubly rooted; and he knows only a single God-given law, which stands over church and state, a law discovered, not invented, by both church and state in the same way—a law that is revealed, not constructed. The exposition of this law is, Vitoria emphasizes, a matter for theologians as well as for jurists, who are not, on their own, *satis peritus* ["sufficiently expert"].[13]

---

[12] *La Neutralité et las paix* [Neutrality and peace] (Hachette, 1935).
[13] Baron von der Heydte, "Francisco de Vitoria and the History of His Reputation (A Riposte)," *Die Friedens-Warte*, ed., Hans Wehberg (Zürich, 1949), 4–5.

3

Early Modern Theologians and Jurists and their Doctrines of the State

ernando Vasquez (1590–1566), a high-ranking Spanish official and an outstanding jurist, published in Venice in the year 1564 a remarkable treatise under the title *Illustrium controversarium aliorumque usu frequentium libri tres* [Three books of famous, and other, controversies occurring in practice].

In the first of the three books of his work, Vasquez, like Vitoria, rejects the idea of the world monarchy and the claims of the emperor to rule the world. It is therefore opportune to consider here more closely the medieval idea of empire and its gradual eclipse, which can already be discerned as early as the time of the Spanish jurists and theologians (Vitoria, Vasquez, and Ayala) and of the secular jurists (Jean Bodin, Albericus Gentilis, and Hugo Grotius).

As was pointed out earlier, the thinking that was authoritative in the Middle Ages was "realist"—i.e., it was permeated by the conviction that concepts, ideas, and ideals, together with the help of the intellect, are not creatures of the human will but belong instead to an extra-human reality, where they are as formatively efficacious as they are in the life of the human soul itself. As a result of the storms of the dispute with the iconoclastic heresy and with the influ-

Early Modern Theologians' & Jurists' Doctrines of the State

ence of Jewish and Islamic scholarship,[1] medieval Christianity had arrived at a consciously iconodule (image-revering) attitude to religious practice, and at an Aristotelian view of *universalia in rebus*. However different the honoring of images of the saints might seem from the doctrine that ideas are effectually present *in* individual appearances as their universal element, they nevertheless represent one and the same spiritual stance (that of recognizing the individual as the bearer of the universal) in two different forms of expression, relating to two different domains: the liturgical and the theoretical. This is a stance that in the final analysis rests on the becoming-human of the Logos. In other words, just as Jesus Christ is at the same time a true human being (that is, perfectly individual) and true God (that is, perfectly universal), so an image of a saint, or a relic, is worthy of reverence because it makes present a spiritual reality of universal scope in an individual form—or, in the language of the Aristotelian school, it is a *universale in re*, a universal-individual sacrament.

If the decision had instead gone the way of pure nominalism (that is, had it been taught that there are no *universalia*, but only individual appearances), then one would have had, instead of an iconodulic stance, an iconolatrous or idolatrous stance, that of honoring the *merely* individual—or *idol-worship*.[2] If a decision had been made in favor

---

[1] σαρακηνόφρων ("Saracen-minded") was the prevailing expression for the iconoclasts in the Byzantine East. In 723, Caliph Jezid II promulgated a decree forbidding the use of images in Christian churches.

[2] The distinction between the relation to natural appearances that, say, Goethe had, and the relation to them that a purely empirical natural scientist of the present day has, consists in particular in the fact that

of extreme idealism ("realism")—i.e., if it had been propounded that the *universalia* ("ideas") are not effectually present *in* things, but precede them (*universalia ante res*), and are merely *reflected* in individual appearances—then one would in time have arrived at a denial of the incarnation of Christ, and would instead have accepted gnostic docetism, which taught that Christ was only an illusory appearance. The iconoclastic attitude would then have triumphed too, for then one would not only have had no reason to honor the illusory appearances of the individual element, but would also have had reason to extirpate this reverence root and branch, since it diverts us *from* the truth of the ideal in the purely spiritual and *towards* the mere appearance of the concrete and earthly—and thus covers pure truth over with mere illusion. Between the dangers of idolatry and image-breaking in religious practice (or in cognitive life, the dangers of pure nominalism and extreme idealism), the *via media* or middle way of the Catholic

---

Goethe sought the universal *in* individual appearances (i.e., he was an iconodule of appearances in that he had the "primal phenomenon" in view), whereas the pure empiricist takes the facts themselves, reduced to their simplest and smallest component, as a sufficient answer and explanation. The pure empiricist is an iconodule of the idols "electron," "atom," and so on, if he considers them as the final basis and final cause. Conversely, the philosopher who thinks in the manner of Hegelian dialectic (who, for example, sees in world-history and in nature a "process" of the world-spirit's self-cognition), can only consider the individual element of appearances as froth, as a play of light and shadow upon surfaces. He is in principle an iconoclast, an image-breaker. Image-breaking, idolatry, and reverence for images, live on in the science of today, in that they give expression, respectively, to extreme idealism, pure nominalism, and "realism" as an immanent idealism.

Christian intellectual life of the Middle Ages, arrived at the "moderate realism" of Thomas Aquinas, i.e., at a recognition of the equal justification of the individual and the universal, of personhood and the *lex aeterna* of God—in other words, at the principles of *Christian humanism*.

The Christian humanism of the heyday of the Middle Ages was essentially expressed in a recognition of natural human reason and morality as values that are, indeed, completed and extended by grace and revelation, but are not made by them. Just as Jesus Christ was God *and* man, so the culture of Christianity was now to be the harmony of natural human capacities *and* divinely efficacious grace. But this also means that the individual and the universal belong together—that personhood and idea are not opposed to each other, but belong to each other. This is why the idea of the unity of Christianity in a worldly respect had to become not only a *postulate* of reason, but also a realized *fact*—indeed, a fact in which the idea was embodied in a human *person*, i.e., in the form of an *office*.

The office of the emperor of the Holy Roman Empire, which originated in Rome in the year 800, can neither be understood from the standpoint of a purely nominalist thinking, nor from that of purely idealistic thinking. For, as far as this office is concerned, it is neither a matter of idolatry (the emperor was never understood as *Führer,* "leader," in the sense of National Socialism or of Bolshevism), nor of an abstract symbol (the emperor did not merely signify an official function in state ceremonial, but had in fact to decide to act), but of the simultaneously ideal and concretely real apex of the pyramid of the Christian social order of the world. Thomas Aquinas says (in his *Summa contra Gentiles*) that the process of the derivation of creatures from their first principle can be imagined as a sort of pyramid, with unity as the apex and the utmost plurality as the base. This pyramid of the "derivation of creatures from their first principle" was at the same time also the system of *legality*, i.e., of the derivation of all secular authority from the embodied first principle of authority—the emperor. In other words, kings could be "kings" *because* there was an emperor. Accordingly, if the empire had collapsed, the fate of all monarchical authority would have been sealed, and its end would have been only a matter of time. But with the fall of the kings, the demise of dukes, princes, marquises, counts, and bearers of other such titles would also have been only a question of grinding to a halt according to the law of inertia, since the crowns of all these title-bearers owe their lustre to the *one* crown of the emperor. If this crown loses its allure, then, by and by, the lustre of all other crowns would necessarily be dimmed.

The hierarchical principle demands completeness, for an incomplete hierarchical order is in principle no real hierarchical order at all, and will collapse. Hierarchical order demands an apex. In the Middle Ages, a Christendom without an emperor would have been considered nonsense, rather like a king without a nation or a country. Accordingly, for the leading lights of medieval culture, the emperor was not held to be the ruler of the *world*, and still less its conqueror, for in the Middle Ages people were still aware of the fact of the Byzantine and Slavic Christian East, as well as of the seemingly limitless ocean of the nations of Islam and the half-fabulous India and Cathay. What it fell to the emperor to protect and conserve from inner disintegration, then, was not the *world*, but Christianity.

The emperor was, precisely, the head of Christendom in

the world and guardian of its three-level legal order: the guardian of the state as a positive legal order, of the state *and* the "church-*in*-the-state" together as a natural legal order, and of the "church-*above*-the state" as the order of divine law. The "secular sword" alone is state power, or *positive* law; the mutual operation and mutual relationship of the "secular sword" and "spiritual sword" is the rational basis of justice, or *natural* law; the key power, however, that stands above everything else, is *divine* law. Thus, the pope originally *crowned* the emperor. *In* the state, however, pope and emperor were equal, each representing his own domain. And in the arena of purely political (secular) affairs, the emperor was the sole authority, but only insofar as he did not infringe upon the natural and divine order. The primacy of divine law is expressed concisely by Eike von Repgow at the start of the *Saxon Mirror*:

> Zwei swert liz got in ertriche zu beschirmene de christenheit. Deme bâbste ist gesaczt daz geistliche, deme keisere daz weltliche. Deme bâbste ist ouch gesaczt zu rîtene zu bescheidener zeit ûf eime blanken pferde, und der keiser sal im den stegereif halden, durch daz der satel nicht entwinde; das ist die bezâchenunge: swaz deme bâbste widerstê; des her nicht mit geistlichem gerichte getwingen mag, daz ez der keiser mit wertlichem gerichte twinge, ab ez sîn bedarf.

> God left behind on earth two swords for the protection of Christianity: to the pope he gave the spiritual sword, and to the emperor, the temporal one. Now, the pope is also required to ride a white horse at a specified time, and on this occasion the emperor will hold his stirrup so that the saddle will not slip, which means any who resist the pope in a manner that he cannot control by ecclesiastical jurisdiction must be compelled by the emperor and his use of

secular law to obey the pope. And so, too, shall the spiritual jurisdiction assist the secular power when need be.³

When first the politics of particular *dynastic* interests (but then, also, those of particular *national* interests) arose to varying degrees, the idea of the emperor as the guarantor of the law of the nations of Christianity faded accordingly. National states arose, with their ever-growing claim to self-rule, and represented a centrifugal force (both politically and ideologically) within the organism of Christendom. This centrifugal force was at work of course, in political life, but it was also at work in the minds of commentators and scholars. In consequence, a sort of "early" Enlightenment came to be directed in particular against the emperor and the restrictions of national sovereignty associated with him. A "second" Enlightenment (the one directed not only against the authority of the emperor but also against the authority of the pope) subsequently led to the revolution usually described as the Reformation. The "third" Enlightenment (the one that led to the French revolution) was directed in turn against national monarchy itself, and against the aristocracy as such. The tidal wave of the "fourth" Enlightenment rose up with Marx and Engels and engulfed not only the monarchy and the aristocracy, but also—in particular—the property-holding class of the bourgeoisie. This then led to the Russian revolution and to the emergence of the communist state-of-states with its

---

³ *The Saxon Mirror: A Sachsenspiegel of the Fourteenth Century*, trans. Maria Dobozy (Philadelphia: University of Pennsylvania Press, 1999), 68. The passage is quoted by Tomberg in the Middle High German, without translation, for which reason the original text has also been reproduced here. TR

claim to world-rule. A coming wave of Enlightenment (as a continuation of the same centrifugal movement) may be directed against the state itself, and find expression in anarchist revolution.

The impulse behind this cascade of enlightenments and their attendant revolutions commenced with the principle of "enlightenment" itself (that is, destruction by criticism conducted on a lower level of thinking than the dignity of the object of the critique rightfully requires) having been brought to bear on the subject of the emperor in support of national princes and their claims. Thus, for example, Jean Bodin writes in *De la république* (1577) that "Bartol has written that all those who do not believe that the emperor is the ruler of the whole world are heretics. This view does not deserve a reply, given that the emperors of Rome were never rulers of even the thirtieth part of the earth, and that the German empire is not a tenth the size of the Roman empire."

Here we see the new brand of "enlightenment" argumentation being brought to bear on the so-called laughable thesis (which, according to Bodin, "does not deserve a reply") of the "ignorant" Bartol, who "did not even know that the emperors of Rome were never rulers of the thirtieth part of the earth," and that "the German empire is not a tenth the size of the Roman empire"! Everything essential and substantive about Bartol's treatment of the significance of the emperor as the temporal head of Christianity, and about his principled claim to the whole domain of the fulfilled apostolic task of the Church (that is, in the last analysis, to the whole world) is, according to Bodin's "enlightened" critique, not even worthy of being mentioned! Instead, the question is treated and "solved" quantitatively in a statistical and purely spatial manner. At *this* level, Bartol's thesis is indeed quite rightly one that "deserves no reply," since, if it is not a question of the visible head of Christendom, but of quantitative comparisons of territory and national claims (Bodin does not speak of the Holy Roman Empire, but of the "German Empire"), then these claims *are* groundless, and the emperor himself *is* actually not an emperor at all, but the national commander-in-chief of Germany, who is only using the title of emperor.

By allowing such "enlightened" thinking and argumentation to be conducted on a level essentially foreign to its *actual* object (Christendom), the emperor of Christendom is effectively dethroned as *emperor* and relegated to the role of *king* of Germany, alongside the kings of France, England, and Spain.

Later "waves of enlightenment" repeated this procedure with astonishing regularity, both in terms of method and in terms of consequences. On each occasion, the object upon which "enlightenment" was to shed light was dragged down to a plane foreign to its actual nature, and was there necessarily shown (according to this latest brand of "enlightenment") to be shabby and untenable, leading inevitably to a corresponding revolution. Crowns rolled from crowned heads, and altars were desecrated, until at last even heads bearing only the invisible "crown" of human dignity began to roll. The consequence of this most recent wave of enlightenment is precisely the latest stage in the series of "dethronings": once the emperor had been dethroned, once kings and princes had been dethroned, once property-holders had been dethroned, the time came for free human personhood to be dethroned. The revolutions that led to recent totalitarian regimes were concerned, precisely, with "disappearing" personhood in favor of the masses. These revolutions, however, bore recognizable seeds of a further stage of "enlightenment" and the revolution corresponding to it. Among such uprisings were the resistance of the sailors of the fleet at Kronstadt in Petersburg in 1921, which led Lenin to impose the "New Economic Policy" (i.e., the supplanting of the old economic order with a new one, essentially anarchistic in nature); the "Green" movement and the troops of Nestor Makhno during the Russian Civil War; and the leading role of the anarchists in Barcelona during the Spanish Civil War. All of these phenomena point to the fact that any regime owing its existence and power to the sword of "enlightenment" will also die by that sword, and that Bolshevist total collectivism would also soon enough face the prospect of itself becoming the object of an "enlightenment" at least as reckless and radical as that to which it owed its own power and rule.

The "wave of enlightenment" to be directed in due course against the collectivistic total state and its order will, however, not be a return to Christian humanism and the rule of law, but rather a *continuation* of Bolshevism itself. Till Eulenspiegel will come back to life in a thousand forms and wander the streets and villages of the all-powerful state, bearing in his bosom the cinders of his father who fell victim to a state concentration camp; and, using the fearful weapons of wit, scorn, irony, and other means of "popular enlightenment," will mercilessly reveal the hollowness of the omnipotent state, indeed of *any* state order as such, and will tear down the last idols: the state and its bosses, the party and its leaders. But he will not call for a return to the sacred and sanctified abandoned bonds of divine order and reason. No, his popular brand of enlightenment will encompass *all* the previous stages of enlightenment, and will thus be directed against *all* authority, in support of freedom from *all* authority. The revived Till Eulenspiegel will invoke the ideology of the wandering people, a "gypsy" freedom, and will call for a beggars' war against the state as such. His followers will gather in "werewolf packs," celebrating their freedom in deserted corners in the middle of the night—each bearing in his bosom the cinders of a loved one: freedom from family, freedom from marriage, freedom from society, freedom from Church, freedom from God. In their fires, both the works of Karl Marx and the Bible will be burned; and their victorious assaults on town and village will ensure that both priests and commissars hang from the same tree…

Such will be the end of the stepwise course of "enlightenment" that commenced with the emperors themselves, when they raised a claim to unlimited sovereignty (as Frederick II, for example, wanted) with respect to the authority of the Church. The same claim was then directed against them in turn by national kings and princes, and others "enlightened" about the emperors—a process in which, at the emperor's court, Mephistopheles offered up a rich trove of matter to be pressed into service. (Goethe, *Faust, Part II*) This stepwise course moved on to "enlightenment" against pope and emperor together, to the raising of a claim not only to self-rule in interpreting Holy Scripture, but to determining what is valid in Christian tradition and what is to be struck out of it. After this, came an "enlightenment" of reason not bound to "dogmas" or "common usages of thought," a reason that—in the name of equality, fraternity, and freedom—undertook to "cast down thrones and altars." Next came economic "enlightenment" with the claim of the propertyless class, not merely to equality, but to the role of ruler, of dictatorship. Finally comes the menacing, brewing storm of anarchistic "enlightenment"—which will break out in the name of freedom from any sort of social order whatsoever.

The process of the obscuring of the idea of Christian empire—that is, the idea of the "kingdom" of Christendom—and thus of the unity of Christianity as such, was indeed a slow one. But just for that reason it was one of a continual advance. There fell a waxing shadow across the once brightly illuminated "full moon" of the idea of the emperor. It was a shadow cast by the "earth" of the claims of nations—to be traced back to "blood and soil"[4]—until the idea of the emperor waned to a fingernail-thin crescent of light, before being eclipsed altogether.

What was eclipsed was not, however, the claim to *lead* the European nations, but only the idea of *Christian* empire. The claim to *leadership* in fact persisted and became the primary cause of a series of catastrophic shocks, first for Europe, then for the rest of the world. The medieval idea of the emperor is actually only "medieval" (in the sense of "obsolete" or "untimely") insofar as it is *Christian*. In other respects it is not at all obscure or untimely. On the contrary, it is supremely modern and full of contemporary relevance. When Napoleon Bonaparte, for example, assumed the title of emperor and became Europe's leader (after Franz I was

---

[4] "Blood and soil" [*Blut und Boden*]: a National Socialist slogan. TR

compelled on August 6, 1806 to abdicate from the office of emperor), it was not a matter of the restoration of the Holy Roman Empire through the French nation, but of the foundation of an empire of power that was made possible by—and resulted from—the preceding French Enlightenment. What Napoleon failed (or only for a short while succeeded) in doing was again attempted by Adolf Hitler. Hitler's "new order" in Europe was in fact nothing other than a taking possession of the "vacant" imperial throne in order to found, in the place of the former kingdom of Christendom, a kingdom of biological Aryanism under the watchful leadership of the German Aryans.

But this attempt also foundered, and a new one is underway,[5] this time not on a biological basis, but on one of economic class. Out of Moscow a "new order" is preached day and night in every language of the earth, a new order whose center is the Kremlin and whose capital is Moscow.[6] Stalin was daily described as the "leader of the world's nations" in countless resolutions, messages, eulogies, poems, and songs. If anyone still had a shadow of doubt about Moscow's claim to world leadership, this doubt must have disappeared after the treatment dealt out to Tito's Yugoslavia by Moscow and its vassal states. It is now absolutely certain that Moscow is attempting to rule the world by means of revolutions, conquests, and surprise attacks. This attempt, however, is in essence an expression of a claim not just to the empire, but also to the kingdom of the "Caliphate." Here it is not a matter of bringing Christendom together with the world of

---

[5] These words were written in 1952.

[6] While writing this book, the author was employed with the BBC, monitoring propaganda broadcasts from Eastern bloc countries. ED

Islam, but of the disappearance of the world of Christendom, the world of Islam, and of all remaining "worlds" within a new, finally "enlightened" world of collectivistic statism. This new world is the absolute state having become a church.

Of course, the idea of the world-state, that is, the idea of humanity organized into a state, does not begin with the Holy Roman Empire of Charlemagne.[7] The latter is actually the fifth step on the ladder of the metamorphoses of the world-empire. The *imperium Romanum* was inherited from the idea of the Assyrio-Babylonian world-monarchy, the Median-Persian world-monarchy, and the world-monarchy of Alexander the Great. The *pax romana* represents the *fourth* stage of the attempt to bring humanity together in a single state. This stage was distinguished from the previous ones particularly by the fact that it gave greatest centrality to the idea of a universal *legal order*. The *imperium Romanum* was principally an imperium of Roman law and of Roman justice. Alexander the Great's empire, conversely, was thought of more as a *cultural* unity. There it was above all a question of the universal validity of Hellenistic culture. Still further removed from the idea of a universal legal order was the ancient Persian world-monarchy. In that case it was primarily a matter of a universal relationship of obedience (tribute and obligatory allegiance) to the *will* of *one* man. In the Chaldean (Assyrio-Babylonian) world-empire it was also essentially a matter of universal subjection, but with the difference that the Persian ruler claimed to be "king of

---

[7] See the author's *Jus Humanitatis: The Right of Humankind as Foundation of International Law* (Brooklyn, NY: Angelico Press, 2023), chap. 3.

kings," whereas the Assyrio-Babylonian leaders tolerated kings neither alongside themselves nor beneath themselves.

The four world-empires thus represent the scale of transition from universal despotism (Babylon) through universal super-monarchy (Persia) and universal cultural-monarchy (Macedonia) to the universal legal state (Rome). Since these empires brought together several nations—that is, they were or wanted to be, both as a matter of fact and in principle, not national states, but universal states—they at the same time represented a scale of *conceptual* development through stepwise conceptions of human order to the realization of perpetual peace. *One* ruling will over *all* nations: that is the first conception of a world-organization embracing the whole of humankind, i.e., the first stage of the idea of a world-state. This conception later underwent a metamorphosis insofar as this single ruling will had to be, not merely a *will*, but more specifically also the bearer and champion of a universal *culture*. It had not only to rule, but also to serve a universal culture and cultural formation—this being the *Hellenistic* conception of the order of humankind. The *Roman* conception, however, rises to the rule of world-law as the universal order of justice, which the ruler (or the ruling nation) is just as much obliged to serve as are his or its subjects. Then, through the influence of Christianity, the Roman conception of the world-empire, the *Roman* Empire, as world-law metamorphosed into the idea of the *Holy Roman* Empire—which was henceforth to be, not merely the bearer of the world *legal* order, but also, in particular, the guardian of the world-order of *salvation*, i.e., of the Christian Church.

If the Roman Empire had to serve justice, the task of the "Holy" Roman Empire under Charlemagne was to place the legal order of justice in the service of the salvation of souls. This, however, meant that the state was not an end in itself, but had to serve a higher end. The emperor was then not merely a ruler, nor merely a judge, but was *specifically* a guardian and a protector. The Holy Roman emperor was the first *knight*. Like every knight, he served a lady and her child, in that he protected the Bride of Christ, the Church, and the tender beginnings of the growing Christian life of the heart, which were otherwise defenceless on this earth.

As tradition relates, St Francis of Assisi could actually make himself understood by the birds and fish, and could even soothe the wolf. But if he had been able to go on his way, would he have been able to bring the work of founding his order to completion? Indeed, would the world ever have known anything about him if he had lived in our age, in a state that, instead of serving, avidly insists on absolute subjugation? Men in leather jackets and trousers would have turned up in the night in a windowless armored vehicle, and he would have been "disappeared" without trace—perhaps to somewhere in the shafts of the salt mines in the Urals, perhaps into the forest work-camps in the Siberian taiga, perhaps into a gas chamber in one of Hitler's genocide camps. Birds and fish just want their seeds and worms, and even the wolf wishes only to appease his hunger; but the secret of those men in leather jackets and trousers consists in the fact that they are always looking for a *new* Francis of Assisi, and are there so there will never *be* any more Francises anywhere… The massacre of the innocents continues.

As long as Herod reigns—i.e., as long as a state aiming to be "unlimitedly sovereign" reigns, and as long as its "leaders" assert themselves against divine law—for just so long will they be searching for the *holy child*, in order to murder it, if not with the sword, then (what is even *more* cruel) with the means of "state education" of a "Marxist" or "national" kind, with the "enlightenment" of youth organizations, etc. Francis was able to sing his hymns and found his mendicant order because the Holy Roman Empire not only protected him from Saracens and Normans, but also took care over four centuries to ensure that what is higher, what is divine, what is miraculous, had a right not only to exist but also a right to be recognized—indeed, to be revered. Thus, St Francis was locked up neither in prison nor in a lunatic asylum, but was able, in his own way, to live entirely openly a life at once supremely holy and supremely poetic. The emperor of the Holy Roman Empire protected the child. He was not Herod, the child murderer; neither was he the indifferently "just" Caesar who "allowed tribute to be paid by all people."

The archetype of the Christian emperor is to be found neither in Pilate nor in Herod—that is, neither in neutral, formalistic justice, nor in the will to power—but instead in the carpenter Joseph, who guarded and protected his holy wife and his holy child on the flight to Egypt. In St Joseph we find the archetype of *knighthood*—and thus also the archetype of the Christian emperor as the head of the knightly order, to whom was entrusted the protection of those who are defenceless on earth—children, virgins, and saints. It was this task that made the Holy Roman Empire *holy*, that made it a *Holy* Roman Empire in contrast to Babylon and Persia, to Macedonia and Rome, in the past; and in contrast to the aggressively secularistic *république française* of the French Revolution and the Herodic kingdoms of National Socialism and Bolshevism in more recent

Early Modern Theologians' & Jurists' Doctrines of the State

times. Humanity may in our time fashion as many political theories as it likes, but they will in the last analysis (to speak as Goethe does) only switch around among the "archetypal phenomena" of Herod, of Pilate, and of St Joseph. In their search for a world-organization, they will be forced to opt for the "emperor of the Holy Roman Empire" (even if the "emperor" comes forward in the shape of a world-parliament), for the "emperor of the (merely) Roman Empire," or for world tyrants.

These three "archetypal phenomena" stand, in fact, as *orienting* tendencies, behind *all* theories of the state and of the world-organization, as these theories have been developed over the course of the post-Christian age up to and including the present. The three "world-organization" tendencies in the present day (the system of the balance of power, the world-state organized around one leading state, and the world federation of the United Nations) essentially signify nothing other but an attempt to solve the problem in Pilate's way (balance of power), in Herod's way (the state as sole ruler of the world), or in St Joseph's way, where the principle of knighthood (protection of those in need of it, and standing as one's "brother's keeper") is once more to come into force.

These tendencies, while prevalent in the present day, are (as has already been said) by no means new. They have had a formative effect through over two millennia of history after Christ, and are expressed in the minds of theoreticians as well as on the battlefields of combatant states. They were also at work in the age of the "Reformation" and "Counter-Reformation," around the time that the great Spanish Late

Scholastics taught law and theology. The latter, indeed, think through the whole problem of the Christian empire yet again, but no longer see it as an existing fact. Vitoria certainly believes that a great Christian *imperium* could once again be founded if Christendom decided to do so, but denies that it has any existence as a valid legal reality (*relectio* V, sect. II, subsections I and II, prop. 1). Vasquez takes up the same position when he teaches that the king of Spain has sovereignty within the borders of his kingdom (bk I, 20–23). And indeed he is right to do so, insofar as the gradually ascending new system of the "balance of power" had in his time already advanced so far among the plurality of sovereign states that one could no longer speak of a Christian *empire*.

The development towards the disintegration of the empire into a series of national states had by then reached the point where it could no longer be a question of the *empire* of Christendom, but only of Christendom as a *family* of nations. When regarded *historically*, the "Western Christian family of nations" is the fragmented Holy Roman Empire, whose parts, despite their separation from each other, have nevertheless conserved so much in common from the time of their prior unity that they still do form a *family* of nations, a "community of international law." From a *legal* perspective, the "community of international law" is the legal successor to the Holy Roman Empire, even as the latter was the legal successor to the Roman Empire.

The bond that tied the original community of international law together as a community was the echo of the common past: the echo of the *one* legal order and the *one* faith. This community of international law remained unaltered until the fifties of the nineteenth century. The independence of the American colonies from England, Spain, and Portugal was only the continuation of a "centrifugal" development within Christendom. In due course, the "family of nations" simply became more numerous. It even extended beyond the boundaries of *Christian* culture when *Turkey* was received into the "European concert" (Acts of the Congress of Paris, art. 7) and when Japan opened for trade in 1854 and established its legal position within the community of international law through a series of treaties. With the *League of Nations*, however, the community extended itself almost to the whole of humanity, in which process it was always a question of adding or receiving nations into the "family of nations" or the "community of international law" as successor of the Holy Roman Empire—i.e., rather than adding members of an erstwhile Christendom to a new framework essentially foreign to Christendom.

The conception of Christendom as a plurality of *sovereign states* came gradually to dominate in the epoch in which the fragmenting forces came to a head, the forces of the self-assertion of the individual, of nationalism, and of particular religious phenomena in the Renaissance and Reformation. What is new in this conception, in any case, is *not* the recognition of a plurality of equally justified states as the basis for the community of international law (since the Middle Ages already had to deal with a plurality of states), but the fact that this equal justification was no longer thought of as an equal *connection to* the temporal and sacred head of Christendom, but as an equal *freedom from* this connection. Even in the Middle Ages, the idea of the family of nations, and indeed of a family standing beneath the paternal and maternal strength of emperor and Church, was a living idea. What was new in the age of the

Renaissance and Reformation was the idea that the "family" now consisted only of siblings—that is, it was now a family without parents. The empire and the emperor, who had for centuries been thought of as the *champions* of the fate of the Christian community (as it were, the eldest member of the family), was now no longer regarded as the head of Christendom, but only as *primus inter pares*, first among equals. Thus, for example, the Swedish king Gustavus Adolphus, in a text written to Emperor Ferdinand II, addresses him with the following words: *Serenissime et trés puissant empereur, cousin* ("Most serene and most powerful emperor, cousin"). The emperor has become now a "cousin" within the family of European nations.

Hand in hand with the progressive removal of imperial authority, and the eclipse of the idea it embodied, went the process in which the individual national sovereigns took over its essential functions. If international law as such rests on the joint operation of two facts—the *unity* of humankind on the one hand and the *plurality* of politically organized communities on the other—what happened during the centuries of the Renaissance and the Reformation was a decided and decisive shift in the basic significance of the two foundational facts of international law. For whereas in the Middle Ages it was the *unity* of humankind that stood above the plurality of politically organized communities, in the centuries of the waning of the Middle Ages and early Modernity it was the *plurality* of particular self-asserting national structures that came to dominate. Each individual state gradually became an "empire" unto itself, and each ruling head an "emperor." In the domain of theoretical reflection, this shift or transition from the medieval *ordinatio ad unum* ("aspiration towards unity") to a modern *ordinatio ad plures* ("aspiration towards plurality") was specifically expressed in the fact of the rise of the doctrine of "unlimited sovereignty" of the (individual) state, and of the linked doctrine of the "balance of power in Europe."

The doctrine of the plurality (i.e., of the *possibility* of the plurality) of unlimitedly sovereign states emerges gradually from the fourteenth century onwards; and then, in the age of the Reformation (or, more precisely, in the age of the so-called "Counter-Reformation"), it crystallizes into two fundamental views: the doctrine of the omnipotent state, the *civitas superiorem non recognoscens* ("the community not having a superior is its own prince") and the doctrine of the state as the *summa potestas in suo ordine* ("the highest power in its order"). The doctrine of the omnipotence of the state (that is, of its absolute self-rule) was specifically prepared for by the political doctrine of the civil lawyers, the glossators, and their successors, and was later particularly championed by secular jurists and politicians. The doctrine of the state as the highest power within a given order is, however, the work in particular of theologians of the Scholastic School.

Bartolus (d. 1375) already puts forward the concept of the *civitas superiorem non recognoscens* as the basis of a doctrine of the self-sufficient state. He develops this doctrine, indeed, to the effect that the individual states have the same power over their territory as the emperor does over the whole globe—i.e., that the states are absolutely sovereign so far as their internal affairs are concerned, but that in universal matters the emperor must decide.

Marsilius of Padua (author of *Defensor Pacis* [Defender of peace] c. 1324) defines the state as the community that suffices to ensure and preserve the necessities of life (*sufficientia vitae*) for human beings. Although he does not make the doctrine of absolute sovereignty a part of his concept of the state, he does declare that the priesthood is an office of state (*Defensor Pacis*, pt I, chap. 6)—thereby putting forward a proposition that is a significant contribution to the development of the doctrine of the state's omnipotence.

It was left to Jean Bodin (1530–1596), the French commentator, to announce the doctrine of the unlimited self-rule of the state power. Bodin taught that state power is itself completely free from the laws, since it is itself the source of law. Law is no more than the command of the prince, who is in any case subject to the natural and divine law insofar as he himself, as the living image of the all-powerful God, embodies, or must embody, the natural and divine law. Nevertheless, the prince's being bound by natural and divine law has a thoroughly "subjective" character here. From outside, the prince is "sovereign" in the sense of his complete independence both from those above and those below him; and his commands are laws because he is both the one who is authorized to issue them and the guarantor of their being in agreement with natural and divine law. Georg Jellinek comments that it was through Bodin that "the comparative adjective 'sovereign' became a superlative, that *superioritas* became *suprema potestas*."[8] Bodin's *jus majestatis* ["right of majesty"] as the "supreme power over citizens and subjects, a power that is free from the laws,"[9] was of course not meant by Bodin himself as *carte*

---

[8] Georg Jellinek, *Allgemeine Staatslehre und Politik* [General theory of the state and politics] (Berlin: Julius Springer Verlag, 1922), 453.

[9] *De republ.*, bk I, chap. 8.

Early Modern Theologians' & Jurists' Doctrines of the State

blanche for a tyrannical arbitrariness of state or princely power. The presumption was of course that the prince would be a faithful Christian, and that in fashioning human laws it was the task of the prince to create them out of the law of reason and of revelation. This, however, is a presupposition of a *subjective* kind—i.e., it is a private matter for the prince. And so, from an *objective* point of view, Bodin's concept of sovereignty can become a *carte blanche* for arbitrary state power. For this reason, *Althusius* (1556–1638) objected to Bodin's concept of sovereignty, pointing out that the law of the state (*jus regni*) was "neither the supreme law nor the established law, nor a power free from law." It is "not the supreme law, since every human power recognizes divine and natural law as standing above itself."[10] Bodin indeed in no way denies the *presence* of binding divine and natural law; he merely denies that the *authorities* standing outside the individual state (the emperor and the pope) are justified in examining the actions of the state power to determine their agreement or non-agreement with natural law and divine law. The state power is sovereign precisely in the sense that it does not need to account for itself to anyone on earth, and is not obligated to obey anyone on earth.

In other words, the new concept of sovereignty (which found expression in the French crown's struggle with the emperor, Charles V, and in the English king Henry VIII's resistance to the pope) contains the claim of state power to decide on its own account what is in accordance with natural law and what is not, and thus, in the final analysis, to be itself emperor and pope within its own territory. This claim was first made, and made good, by Henry VIII. It was

---

[10] *Politia*, chap. 9.

acknowledged in the international arena, however, only after a century of struggle, in 1648, when the Peace of Westphalia acknowledged the principle of *cujus regio, ejus religio* ("who governs the territory decides its religion") as the basis for the settlement of religious disputes among the populations of Central and Western Europe. State power, accordingly, was awarded authority not only to preside over the ordering and well-being of its own subjects, but also to decide what was necessary to the salvation of their souls. This settlement was, however, a purely political *compromise*—seen as being necessitated by the whole situation that had emerged, rather than as a *solution* according to the principles of law and religion. It was also never acknowledged by the popes, and was later decisively rejected by the assertion of reasoning focused on the rights of man, and, in the end, by public opinion across the whole civilized world.

It emerged again, however, in our own day, in the form of an attempt to draw and maintain "lines of demarcation" between territories under forced communist rule and those free from that rule. The borders between the Soviet and the Western occupied zones in Germany, and the "thirty-eighth parallel" in Korea, are examples of such lines of demarcation, which, as facts established by treaty, implicitly revive the principle of the Peace of Westphalia: *cujus regio, ejus religio*. That is, as regards the actual extent of the communists' rule of force—the rule of a group of leaders over the communist party by means of "party discipline," of the party over the "proletariat," and of the "proletariat" over the peasants and the remnants (scorned for whatever reason) of the erstwhile middle and upper classes—to this extent they may, in the lands subjected to them, do their worst unimpeded. And the Moscow conception of Marxist materialism may there be imposed upon the population by any means necessary.

The settlement of the Peace of Westphalia was, however, in *one* respect more humane: it allowed Protestants in countries ruled by Catholics, and Catholics in lands ruled by Protestants, to migrate—an option that has *not* been allowed for under the present settlement. To this extent, the state's claim to power over human persons has grown in the three centuries since the Westphalian compromise; for at that time, the right of the individual to migrate was recognized, whereas now it is denied, as attested in the existence of an "iron curtain." Indeed, the claim of the most modern state power (the communist one) with respect to individual people goes beyond forbidding them to emigrate from the land where an individual might be unhappy. It even claims the right to command individual people, and indeed whole national groups, to leave their homeland and to settle wherever the state power wishes them to. Thus, the German population east of the Oder-Neisse line was driven from their dwelling-places; the Crimean Tatars were driven out of Crimea; the Ingush out of the Caucasus; and the Volga Germans were resettled away from the Volga region. The new state forbids and prescribes to the individual his home and his homeland: it is, indeed, unlimitedly sovereign.

If one were not aware that God's presence had already come about on earth at an earlier date, and that it was expressed in the fact that the actual God who appeared on earth washed the feet of human beings, one might be tempted to say that here the state has actually become "the presence of God upon earth." Thus, the *theoretical* concept of "unlimited sovereignty" forged in the course of around four centuries gradually became the *fact* of unlimited state sovereignty. Hitler's state of yesterday, and the state of those in the Kremlin today, is henceforth the complete realization of the absolutely sovereign and omnipotent state.

⊕

The concept of state sovereignty developed by the theologically trained representatives of the Scholastic School in the sixteenth century—especially by Francisco Suárez—is quite different. Here it was a case, not of unlimited state sovereignty as such, but of the state as the highest power *in suo ordine*—"in its own sphere"—and *only* there.[11] This sphere is limited, on one side, by natural law and divine law, and on the other by the fact of the political and moral unity of the community of states: "although the human race is apportioned into different nations and states, it is also always, nevertheless, in a certain sense a unity, and that not only as a concept and as a species, but also as a political and moral unity,"[12] writes Suárez.

This idea—of the "political and moral unity" of the plurality of states—is precisely *the* basis of what we know today as "international law" in theory and in practice. And it is thanks to the proponents of *this* idea that humankind has retained an international law right down to our own age, i.e., that humankind has not finally disintegrated into a plurality of "little worlds" or "absolutely self-ruling states" that are in principle opposed to one another.

Morally speaking, international law as a law of humankind, whose task is to achieve peace in the world, rests on the principle of the moral unity of the plurality of free state

---

[11] *Defensio fidei*, bk III, chap. 6, sect. 2.
[12] *De Legibus*, bk II, chap. 19, sect. 9.

communities with equal rights; *juridically* speaking, it rests on the principle of the superiority of the freely-acknowledged law of humankind to the particular law of the state communities; *politically* speaking, it rests on the principle of "universal federation," that is, the realization in the first place of a world league of states that can then develop into a world federal state, which, as a political realization of world legal order (or even of a world-order of peace) would be the end of international law as the law of dealings between states—"end" in the sense that it would have *realized* its task. It would then actually have become the law of humankind as such—it would have become the basis, and the essential content, of the political constitution of the "state" of humankind.

The fundamental thought of the Late Scholastic commentators on the relation of states "sovereign in their own sphere" to the community of humankind carries within itself not only the possibility, but the fundamental stimulus as well, to a development from the empire of Christendom to the community of states under international law; and from the community of states under international law to the legal state of humankind. It is the line of development from the *jus gentium* of antiquity to the Christian natural law of the Middle Ages; from natural law to the international law of the modern era; and from international law to the law of humankind of the future. This line of development is (to use Goethe's language) that of the "metamorphosis" of law through the stages of root-formation in the ancient *jus gentium*, to stem-formation striving towards the heights of medieval natural law, to the plurality of the foliage-formation of an expressed inter-state international law, to, finally, the crowning blossom of the law of humankind.

From International Law to World Peace

Just as little as the stem signifies the death of the root, or the leaves the death of the stem, or the blossom the death of the leaves, so little does medieval natural law signify the death of the *jus gentium* of antiquity, so little does the modern inter-state international law signify the death of the high ideas and principles of medieval natural law, and so little, likewise, will the future law of humankind signify the death of the international law of the present day. It is only ever a question of *cumulative* stages of development. Moreover, perfection is neither an *end* nor *death*.

A contrasting line of development is, however, also possible, and is indeed already present and observable. This is the line of development towards a "rootless" stem to "stemless" leaves to "cut" flowers. This contrasting line of development is that of "progress" in the sense of negation and annihilation of what has gone before. It is the line of *revolution* as opposed to that of *evolution*, whose moral content goes back to the command "honor thy father and thy mother." This revolutionary line does lead to an *end*—that is, to the *death* of international law, indeed of all law as such, by replacing *jus gentium* ("international law") with *jus gentis* ("law of nations"), natural law with the law of nature ("the struggle for existence"), and international *law* with international *power*. When "liberated" from its medieval Christian elements of loyalty to the emperor and to the pope (and followed through to its ultimate consequences), the doctrine of the unlimited self-rule of the state, or of state power—first formulated by Jean Bodin, then by Thomas Hobbes (1588–1679)—inescapably bears within it both a *negation* of the human legal order that binds the individual state, and the *assertion* of the "will of state power" as the sole and supreme source of law: i.e., the assertion of *pure positivism* together with its cornerstones of power and profit.

Pure positivism, however, also means the abolition of divine and natural law as legal norms of human validity, because the positive law of the individual state cannot operate in contradiction to them. Such a denial of divine and natural law necessarily brings with it a striving for "emancipation from the haunting ghosts of the past" and for their replacement by "realities adjusted and brought up to date." In the final analysis, however, these "up-to-date" realities can be summarized as the biological law of the struggle for existence expressed as the struggle among races, among nations, and among classes in the domains of politics and the economy, together with the decisive factor in this struggle: *power*, for which pure positivism is *the* meaning of civilization as such.

From the perspective of the struggle for existence, science signifies nothing more than a means to acquire power over nature, a power to be brought to bear as well in the struggle among races, nations, classes, and other such groupings. Pure positivism, then, replaces international law as a law of humankind (the *jus gentium* of the ancients) with the "current system of power-relationships among states in the world"; replaces "natural law" (as reason, justice, and humaneness valid for human beings) with the "law of nature" of the struggle of existence; and replaces divine law with naked power, or at least with the "will to power." Thus could it come about, in the course of "evolution" towards the pure positivism of the unlimitedly sovereign state, that for the National Socialist dictatorship the "will of the Führer" and "the law" signified one and the same thing, and

From International Law to World Peace

that for the communist dictatorship of Stalin everything furthering communism and world revolution was "law" and everything impeding communism's victory in the world was a "against the law."

We see, then, that the two paths for the theory and practice of international law (which had appeared already quite clearly in the age of the Reformation and Counter-Reformation) ultimately lead, respectively, to the *perfection* of international law in the form of the human order of the world-federal-state as a "metamorphosis" of an organically-developing international law, or else to the *end-point* of international law in the guise of a state power-politics that rules the world; lead, that is, to *anarchy* (if there is more than one such state) or to *tyranny* (if a single state succeeds in subjugating the entire world).

This dichotomy, then, comes into focus above all in connection with the idea of the sovereign state. One group, the Spanish Late Scholastics (to whom Gentilis and Hugo Grotius subsequently adhered) thought of this sovereignty as limited to a determinately circumscribed territory, i.e., to the state's "own sphere"; the others, secularist commentators such as Jean Bodin, and later Hobbes, declared this sovereignty to be unlimited and absolute. What exactly, then, is the teaching of Late Scholasticism, the teaching that makes possible international law and its progress towards a law of humankind?

The doctrine of the state in Late Scholasticism is established upon St Thomas Aquinas's basic idea that the foundation of the state is the nature of human beings. The human beings who make up the state are constituted in such a way as to be reliant on one another. Thus, an existence worthy of human beings (that is, an existence corresponding to the nature of human beings upon earth) can only be achieved in community, which is to say by means of mutual aid and by neighbors' furnishing each other with what they need. Man needs the help of his neighbors even for the most ordinary necessities of life, such as food and clothing. He is not as self-sufficient as the animals (*non de facile invenitur homo sibi sufficiens*). This quality of human beings is at the root of society. Organized society, however, is the *state*. Moreover, the state is not absolute, since its "worldly power is subject to spiritual power, as the body is subject to the soul."[13] The state power has the task of striving on the basis of *natural* law for the common good in *worldly* things, and of striving on the basis of *divine* law for the common good in *spiritual* things. In other words, the state has a particular sphere in which it is sovereign, but this sphere is limited by the fact that another and superior sphere is present also. This idea forms the basis of the doctrine that Suárez put forward at a later time, the doctrine of the *suprema potestas in suo ordine*, "the supreme power of the state in the sphere proper to it."

The teaching of Scholasticism in its entirety agrees with Thomas Aquinas that the state is grounded in human nature. Since, however, human nature is not limited to one particular nation, but belongs to all humankind, each state is, as Francisco de Vitoria taught, a part of the whole, and consequently is not absolutely sovereign, but is subordinate to the whole—subordinate, that is, to international law as a law of humankind. The fact of the primacy of the law of

---

[13] Aquinas, *Summa theol.*, II–II, qu. 60.

the human community is what makes "just war" possible, since, if there were no single legal order binding for all states, measures to protect and restore this legal order—"just war"—would not be conceivable.

In his work *De Justitia et Jure* [Of justice and law], published in 1566, Domingo Soto, a pupil of Vitoria, put forward the idea that the state as such owes its origin to the essential nature of human beings. Since man's essential nature is derived from God as His image and likeness, state power also ultimately comes from God. Nevertheless, state power is not absolute, insofar as the bearers of state power only possess that power with the consent of the members of the community. The bearer of state power is thus not the personal owner of everything found in the state (since this would be against the will of the members of the state community), but may only make use of those things insofar as it is necessary to do so for the protection and administration of the state. Otherwise, his sovereign jurisdiction is limited to the rights and duties of the highest guardian of the legal order—that is, to the authority and obligations of exercising jurisdiction. Moreover, he is also subject to the laws insofar as he does not stand *outside* the body of the state but, as the head, is also one of its *members*. He stands, however, not under the "compelling" force of the laws (*vis coactiva*), but under their "guiding" force (*vis directiva*), since his function in the state, as its head, is not to obey the state, but to guide it. The binding force of the laws derives, not from the *person* of the head of state, or from the *institution* of supreme state power, but from "human law, which binds the conscience because it is derived from eternal nature."[14]

---

[14] *De Justitia et Jure*, bk IV, qu. 6.

Early Modern Theologians' & Jurists' Doctrines of the State

For Robert Bellarmine (1542–1621), the state is so closely bound up with and rooted in the essential nature of human beings that he can say that political supremacy is a principle of such necessity to the human race that it "cannot be done away with without destroying nature itself."[15] Such authority is, among other things, necessary for the reason that justice can only be exercised within the state community. This community is the proprietor of state power, which—since it is grounded in human nature, created by God—is ultimately grounded in divine law. Divine law, however, has not bestowed power on any individual holder of it. Power rests, consequently, with the whole community, which then *entrusts* it to one or more of its members.

The doctrine of the power-holding community and of the entrusting of power to the individual or to the collective head of state, is the seed from which later (in the work of Grotius, Hobbes, Locke, and Rousseau) the doctrine of the original "social contract" (*le contrat social*) grew into a mighty tree. This doctrine had two basic themes: the *pactum unionis* (the grounding of the community in a contractual basis) and the *pactum subiectionis* (the entrusting of power to the head of state). It played a central role in the Glorious Revolution of 1688 in England, in the French Revolution of 1789, and in the American Declaration of Independence in 1776.

In essence, these views of the state were also shared by other representatives of Late Scholasticism, such as Covarruvias, Vasquez, Molina, and, as already mentioned, Suárez. For all of them, the state was an institution that had originated in *human* nature. It was an institution in the service

---

[15] *De controversiis Christianae fidei*, etc.

of *human* beings. Its anchoring in the divine law was, then, not *immediate*, but had come into being by way of *human beings*. The task of the state is *sufficentia vitae*, the securing of the necessities of life for its citizens. Thus, the state is a servant tasked with ordering, safeguarding, and protecting human life and human commerce. The state is neither obligated nor authorized to do anything beyond this. This idea not only makes possible the theory and practice of international law, but makes possible as well its gradual development towards an actually valid law of humankind—that is, towards a world legal order.

On the other hand, the conception that postulates the state's unlimited self-rule, and omnipotence *in principle*, leaves no room for the theory and practice of international law, but rather permits international law to disappear into "politics," into the playing-out of factors of power in the world, which lead in the end either to a war of all against all or to a world tyranny.

4

Francisco Suárez

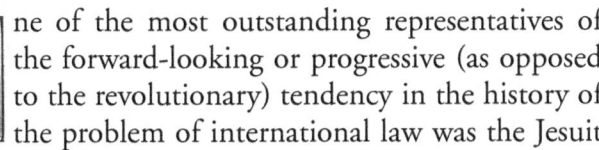ne of the most outstanding representatives of the forward-looking or progressive (as opposed to the revolutionary) tendency in the history of the problem of international law was the Jesuit scholar Francisco Suárez (1548–1617), a professor at the University of Coimbra. The ethical seriousness of his life, which was wholly devoted to work and to research, can be better expressed by means of a short phrase he uttered on his deathbed than by any collation of outward biographical data. As he was dying, Suárez said *nunca hubiera creido que fuera tan dulce morir*: "I would never have thought that it would be so pleasant to die." This statement illustrates his relationship to life and to death. Another statement reveals his relationship to his work. When he learned that his work *Defensio fidei catholicae* (a reply to King James I of England) had been ordered to be burned by that king, Suárez said, "May it please God that the fate of my book grant me the opportunity to support with my blood and my life the teaching that my pen has until this day defended."

Statements of this sort from such a clear-thinking and reflective scholar have the effect of inclining the reader of his works to take seriously what has been so seriously intended. Thus, for example, Hugo Grotius (de Groot) wrote that "Suárez is a philosopher and theologian of such great acumen that there is hardly anybody his equal." And

From International Law to World Peace

Menendez y Pelayo says "and Suárez, who is an outstanding psychologist in *De anima*, is, with his treatise *De legibus*, one of the founders of the philosophy of law—a science of specifically Spanish origin, for which Europe has him, Vitoria, Dominga de Soto, Molina, and Balthasar de Ayal to thank, rather than Grotius and Pufendorff."[1] More recently, in their foundational text on questions of international law, L. Oppenheim and H. Lauterpacht say of Suárez's *Tractatus de Legibus ac Deo Legislatore* that in it "for the first time the attempt is made to found a law between the states on the fact that they form a community of states."[2]

As for Vitoria, so for Suárez: When it comes to anything connected with war and peace (i.e., anything in the domain of international law), only a law oriented towards morality and religion is valid. Politics, on the other hand, stands outside law, religion, and morality. War and peace are questions of law, and indeed are so specifically in the sense of penal law, i.e., of a law grounded on enforcing justice, or just punishment (*justitia vindicativa*). Vitoria regards "pure" politics (in the sense of the playing-out of factors of power and weakness, advantage and disadvantage, surprise attacks, and so on) merely as a domain that is to be regulated—i.e., as a domain of lawlessness that is to disappear into the domain of law. Indeed, such a disappearance of political lawlessness was precisely the goal Suárez had in view when in his works he dealt with questions of war and peace.

Over three hundred years later, Lauterpacht[3] showed the

---

[1] *Heterodoxes espanoles*, II, 711.
[2] *International Law: A Treatise* (presumably vol. 2, on "Disputes, War and Neutrality"), 85. ED
[3] *The Function of Law in the International Community* (1933).

logical absurdity of the distinction between "legal" and "political" disputes—a distinction that amounts to giving *carte blanche* to every state arbitrarily to declare that individual disputes are either "political" (i.e., important) or "legal" (i.e., less important), and to so treat them. Either there are only political disputes (this being the position of the adherents of unlimited state sovereignty and the official doctrine of the totalitarian states) or there are, in principle, cases of legal dispute (this being the position of the proponents of the international legal order and of a limited sovereignty for the state). Now, this same standpoint was also adopted three hundred years ago by the great representatives of the Spanish school, Vitoria and Suárez, and will also (so far as anyone can judge) be championed in the future, for so long as there shall in the history of humankind continue be a plurality of states. Moreover, Suárez's doctrinal standpoint on the right to declare war is completely in accordance with this view:

> The right to declare war is a right belonging to the administrator of justice, the exercise of which belongs to the enforcement of justice, which is especially necessary to the state in order to be able to curb evildoers. Just as the sovereign prince, therefore, may punish his subjects if they have broken the law in any way, so may he also be avenged upon any other prince or state that has become subject to him because of a breach of law committed with respect to him. Since, conversely, he is unable to seek reparations from any other judge, because the prince of whom we are speaking has no one above him in worldly matters, he may, if the guilty party is not prepared to offer reparations, enforce them by means of war. [...] I used above the words "or state" so as to include any form of state, since the same argument holds for all forms of state. In relation to monar-

chical forms of state, it must be observed, however, that once the state community has entrusted its power to a particular person, such a state cannot declare war without the agreement of this person, since it no longer possesses supreme power, unless the prince so far neglects his duty to avenge or defend the state that public and very serious harm is done to the state as a result. In such a case, the whole community (*tota respublica*) has the right to enforce the law, and it may take over the supreme authority in question from the prince. For the state community is always regarded as authorized to do this if the prince does not fulfill his obligations.[4]

This position contains the fundamental views Suárez held on the main questions of international law. War is, for him, in principle, not a political act but an act of *vindicative justice*. That is, it belongs to the domain of international *penal law*. This, however, means that there is a pan-human *legal* order—that is, natural law and valid treaties, a breach of either of which on the part of an independent state against another independent state justifies the latter (in a case where the injuring state refuses to make voluntary reparations to the injured state) in resorting to force. In other words, such a case in principle makes the injured state *ruler over the injuring state*. Thus, a new relationship comes into being between the two previously equally independent states. The state guilty of breaking the law becomes dependent on the state victimized by this breach of the law. This relationship is in all essentials that between a judge and the accused. But this relationship is only possible and necessary in a case where there are no judges superordinate to the parties; that

---

[4] Suárez, *De triplici virtute theologica: fide, spe, charitate* (1621), "Disputatio XIII, De Bello," section II, 1.

is, if they are not parts of an empire, and neither has any *ad hoc* court of arbitration been put in place above them, nor (if the case concerns a Christian state) has the pope claimed the right to settle the dispute. For, were the parties members of an empire, the use of force would be "contrary to natural law, since, where there is a court and a power superordinate to both parties, it is contrary to natural law to resort to force to defend one's right and to act on one's own initiative." This point, since it is grounded in natural law, holds both for Christians and for non-Christians.

Where Christian kings are involved, however, one further circumstance must be attended to: the spiritual head (*summus pontifex*), although exercising no power in worldly matters outside his own territory, nevertheless possesses such a power indirectly, as is indicated in certain passages of the *Decretals* (bk i, pt vi, chap. 34; bk ii, pt i, chap. 13). This is why he has the right to require that the reason for war be set before him, and is authorized to give a judgment on the matter—a judgment binding for the parties unless his decision is obviously unjust (*nisi manifestam faciat iniustitiam*). For such an authority (as that held by the pope) is certainly necessary for the spiritual welfare of the Church and to avoid what could be almost innumerable evils. Accordingly, Soto (*On the Epistle to the Romans*, chap. 12) says that a war between Christian princes is only rarely justified, since they have another effective means at their disposal for settlement of their disputes. On occasion, however, he continues, the pope *omits to exercise his authority*—perhaps so that greater evil shall not result. In such a case, the princes are of course not obliged to obtain the agreement of the pope, and may proceed along the path of enforcing their right, so long as it is not expressly forbidden them to do so. Nevertheless, they must take care to ensure that it is not their own fault that the pope does not dare to interfere in the matter, for in such a case they would deprive themselves of the grounds on which they can be exculpated. If the pope in his supremacy and power imposes a justified prohibition of the war in question on the grounds that the war imperils the spiritual welfare of the Church (and thus the princes lose the right to wage war), then the prince who has nevertheless gone to war sins against justice, and is obliged to make restitution.

War is thus permitted, according to Suárez, only when there is no other way of protecting the *law* and of combating *unlawfullness*, i.e., when there is no superordinate judicial power. So far as the purely *political* idea of war as one of the most important means of obtaining advantages for the state is concerned, Suárez says:

> an error once prevailed among the heathen, who were of the opinion that the rights of nations were grounded on their military strength, and that it was permitted to wage war merely for the purpose of increasing a nation's prestige and wealth, which is in the highest degree absurd even from the point of view of natural reason [today we would say "common sense"—*Author*]. For this reason, I assert, first, that there can be no just war without a compelling underlying legal reason.... It is a just and sufficient grounds for war to have suffered a severe injustice that cannot be made good or avenged in any other way. For, with the exception of the protection of the state from harm, war conflicts with the welfare of the human race.[5]

Moreover, since in the case of an attack the legitimacy of self-defense is beyond question, and "this is especially a war of aggression, which is often waged against non-subjects, it

---

[5] Ibid. (presumably, as no separate citation is given here).

is necessary that the non-subjects must have committed a breach of the law, for which reason they become subjects. Otherwise, for what reason would they deserve punishment or should they be subjected to foreign jurisdiction?"

And so far as extra-legal, purely *political* grounds for war (of a *raison d'état* nature), "such as ambition, covetousness, and even vanity or cruelty" are concerned, "if they were recognized as legal and sufficient grounds, then each state could strive to satisfy them, and consequently war would be just on both sides ... which is perfectly absurd, since two opposite legal claims cannot simultaneously be just."[6]

Suárez goes into considerable detail[7] on the just-mentioned question of extra-legal, purely *political* grounds for war based upon natural reason, then takes up the question whether a Christian prince can have such grounds for war. After having given four such grounds from several other authors (Aristotle, Major, Sepúlveda, Alfonso de Castro, Alvaro Paez, Gabriel, Hostienses), and having rejected them as grounds for war—that is: (1) infidelity, or refusal to recognize the true religion; (2) punishment of insults offered to God by means of unnatural sin and idol-worship;[8] (3) the emperor's or the pope's claim to universal secular supremacy; (4) the incapacity of the native peoples ("barbarians") themselves to create or to preserve a civilized social order[9]—Suárez concludes:

---

[6] Ibid., (this and the preceding two short quotations).

[7] See Appendix B.

[8] Alfonso de Castro, *De Iusta Haereticorum Punitione*, II.14.

[9] Aristotle, *Politics*, bk 1, chaps. 1 and 3, supported by Major "On the Sentences," bk 2, chap. 44, quest. 3, and Sepúlveda, *De Regno et Regis Officio*, bk 7, chap. 2.

From International Law to World Peace

It must therefore be affirmed that there are no grounds for war that would be exclusively reserved to Christian princes, rather than being grounded in natural law, or at least standing in a particular relation to natural law, and that would thus not also apply at the same time to non-Christian princes. In order to elucidate this assertion, *first*, it follows from it that a Christian prince must *only* declare war in a case either of having suffered a legal injury or in order to protect innocent parties . . . for the law of grace does not destroy the law of nature, but perfects it. *Second*, it must be said that the protection of the innocent can be carried out by Christian princes in a special way—which is also, in a certain sense, true of the punishment for legal injuries they have suffered. Thus, for example, Christian princes, in the case of a country in which the population wishes to accept the law of Christ, but where they are prevented from doing so by an unbelieving prince, have the right to defend those innocent persons. But if, for example, the same country wishes to accept another, non-Christian law—Islam, for example—and has been prevented from doing so by its princes, then in such a case a non-Christian Turkish prince would have no analogous right to wage war against those other princes. The reason for this distinction lies in the fact that preventing the acceptance of the law of Christ would be a heavy injustice damaging to those who were so prevented, whereas to forbid the acceptance of another law[10] would cause no harm whatsoever. . . .

---

[10] By "law" and "another law," Suárez always means belief in a God and the natural principles of justice and morality. It is a question here, therefore, of Jewry and Islam, rather than of the worship given to their gods by the Aztecs, which is connected with human sacrifice, or the fetishism of certain African tribes. If it is a matter of the conflict between monotheism (even non-Christian monotheism) and the heathen (as

Moreover, the same holds also in the case of non-Christian princes who persecute preachers of the gospel of believing Christians, since

> this is a legal injury to the Church, which has a law of its own for expulsions and punishments. *Third*, I assert that all the above considerations rest on natural reason in such a way that they can also to a certain extent and in the right context be valid for non-Christians. Thus, for example, if a country wishes to serve the One God, and to follow the law of nature or to listen to preachers who proclaim these things, and if the prince of this country prevents this by force, then this situation produces a just cause for war on the part of another prince, even if he is not a Christian, who merely allows himself to be guided by natural reason. For such a war would be a just defense of the innocent.
>
> In a similar way, a nation that honors the One God and holds the laws of nature in reverence would have the right to send missionaries to teach another nation that has abandoned the worship of God and is living in a way opposed to natural reason, and to free that nation from errors. If it is attempted forcibly to prevent this (i.e., the sending of missionaries), then this can lead to a just war, because this right is completely in accordance with nature and because it is a matter of defending the innocent. For in general, there will always be someone who wishes to be taught about the natural truths that are necessary for an honorable and virtuous life and who is unjustly prevented from being so taught. . . .

---

defined by their worship), then the analogy of the conflict between the law of Christ and "another law" comes into force, i.e., the corresponding monotheistic prince then has the right to declare war to protect the innocent.—*Author*

From International Law to World Peace

So far as the question of *certainty* in relation to the justice of the grounds for war requisite to a just war is concerned, the following holds:

> Three kinds of person must be distinguished here: sovereign kings and princes; leading personages and generals; and ordinary soldiers. It is to be presumed that each of these kinds of person must possess factual certainty, which finds expression in the following declaration: "It is permitted to me to wage war." It is therefore a matter of theoretical certainty whenever there is a question of doubt, that is, of the certainty that can be expressed in declarations such as the following: "This justification for war is just in itself" or even "This thing that I want to obtain by means of war belongs to me."
>
> First, I assert that the *sovereign head of state* must initiate an exhaustive investigation of the grounds for war in respect of their justice, and that that power should act, after the examination has been completed, according to the knowledge that has been acquired by means of it. Where the result of the investigation is that the claim is legally tenable on both sides, the king must act like a just judge. Accordingly, if he finds that the opinion favorable to his own side has more justification, then he may enforce his right . . . if, however the opinion of the opposing party should be better justified, then the prince may not under any circumstances resort to war.
>
> But if the justification on both sides is equal, or if at least both standpoints are equally uncertain, then priority is held by that party which is in actual possession. If, however, it is a question of a dispute about a thing that is not in the actual possession of either of the parties, and in which probability and doubt balance each other out, then either a partition must take place or, if such a partition is not possible, both parties must come to an understanding about

how they may both be contented. The matter can also be entrusted to the decision of "good men," which is "obviously the best way," and use should therefore be made of it.

Second, I am of the view that *commanders* and other important personages of the kingdom are obligated to make a searching investigation of the matter when they are called to give counsel and asked for their opinion as to whether a war should be started or not. If, however, they are not called upon to give counsel, then they are under no greater obligation than common soldiers. . . .

Third, I am of the view that common soldiers, the prince's subjects, are not in any way obliged to conduct a searching examination of the matter, but may go to war when they are told to do so, provided they are not convinced that the war is unjust. . . . This also follows from the fact that the bailiffs of the court who are subordinate to the judge may execute the judge's judgment without first investigating it, provided that the judgment is not obviously unjust. [ibid.]

If, after an investigation has been carried out, the decision of the head of state for war is correct, then reason, justice, and humaneness (i.e., natural law) impose further conditions that, if they are not followed, may transform his just war into an unjust one. Suárez (and Bellarmine) add, in particular, to the three conditions named by St Thomas (the declaration of war by the highest state authority; the presence of a just cause; and the right intention) a fourth—i.e., the right way (*debitus modus*) of waging war. What, then, is the right way of waging war? "In every war, three periods must be distinguished from each other: the beginning of the war, the waging of the war until victory, and the period after victory." The first period demands the fulfillment of the following prescriptions:

From International Law to World Peace

The prince who is making the attack is obliged to make the other state aware that there is a just cause for war, and to suggest corresponding reparations that that state might make. If the other state now declares itself ready to provide such reparations, the prince is obliged to accept them and to refrain from making war, for otherwise the war would be unjust.... Full reparations must meet the following conditions. *First*, the whole of the property that has been unjustly seized must be returned. *Second*, reparation for all the expenses that the breach of the law has brought with it must be paid, so that if it has come to war, reparations may be claimed for all the costs of that war. *Third*, in addition to this, a service may be demanded as a punishment for the injustice that has been committed, because in the case of war it is a matter not only of compensatory justice but also of vindicative justice. Moreover, everything that is needed to keep and secure the peace in future can also be demanded, since the main aim of war is indeed to secure such a future state of peace. Once the war has been begun, and until it comes to a victorious conclusion, it is permitted to cover all one's losses at the enemy's cost, whether as reparations or in order to secure victory, unless this means inflicting substantial damage upon innocent persons, which would be an evil in itself. [Moreover], I am of the opinion that after the victorious end of the war, the prince has the right to inflict upon the conquered state such losses as will suffice to a just punishment, satisfaction, and reparation for all the losses incurred.... I believe that a war will not be unjust if all the foregoing rules are observed, along with all the other universal rules of justice—and yet such a war can also contain evil characteristics that are in conflict with love or one of the other virtues. [ibid.]

In other words, even the most just war is not immune from evil, since war as such is only an emergency measure taken by states to protect themselves against injustice when there is no better means to do so. This "better means," however, is self-evidently visible to the modern reader of Suárez's argument. It is a trans-state court of justice with an international jurisdiction over states, and a court whose decisions are sanctioned by the whole international-legal community.

PART IV

The Transition from Three-Stage to Two-Stage Law

1
Albericus Gentilis

ith Albericus Gentilis (1552–1608), there begins the epoch of transition from three-stage law (and thus also from three-stage *international* law) to two-stage law, i.e., to a law that consists of "rationalistic" natural law and the positive law of states.

Albericus Gentilis was born in 1552 in San Genesio in the province of Ancona. In 1572, he was made a doctor of civil law, and practiced as an attorney for a long time in Castello di San Genesio. Since his father, Matthew Gentilis, considered it advisable to leave Italy on account of his Protestantism, Albericus moved with him to Austria, until in 1580 he traveled to Oxford, where in 1581 he began to write and teach. The three parts of his magnum opus, *De Jure Belli*, [On the law of war] were published in London in 1588 and 1589. In this work, Gentilis first briefly discusses the nature of international law, the *jus gentium*. In his view, the sources of the *jus gentium* are to be sought in what has become customary practice, and in natural law. He hardly mentions divine law as a source of the *jus gentium*.

"War is a just contest waged through public armed forces," runs Gentilis's general definition of the concept of war. According to this definition, war is, then, a *contest*, and as such must meet three conditions. First, it must be waged by force of arms; second, it must be public; third, it must be just. But how exactly are we to understand the third condition?

"*Just* means not only what is lawful, but what is completely unobjectionable." The use of armed force must be public on both sides and the parties to the dispute must be sovereign. A prince has no judge over him. If another has power over him, then he is not a prince, not a sovereign. Thus, cases of dispute between princes can be adjudicated only by negotiations or by force. True, princes do sometimes very appropriately make use of a *court of arbitration*, but they are also justified in the last instance in having recourse to war. The justification of war is thus the *necessity* of war. "When there is no necessity for it, war cannot be just. For it is necessity from which war is the conclusion to be drawn. A voluntary settlement, then, is to be striven for by means of negotiations, using natural reason: 'that judge,' as Seneca says, 'of justice and injustice.'" Since princes such as the dukes of Parma, Mantua, and Ferrara, as well as those of various German princedoms, are subject to feudal overlords, it is a question of fact as to whether they are justified in waging war, one that is to be decided with reference to the conditions of their investiture. The machinations of pirates, robbers, and deserters have no claim to be described as "wars." "Robbers do not wage war." Those who break all law, have no rights. An opponent in war is one who has a commonwealth, a council of state, a state treasury, and the agreement and concord of its citizens, as well as (if it comes to this) the capacity to conclude peace treaties and to contract alliances. Wars of aggression and retaliation can, despite this, be just. A war can also be just on both sides, if there is sufficient reason for doubt about the legal situation. Vitoria and others teach the same.

Albericus Gentilis

The reasons for a war can be various. A war that is waged at God's direct command is necessarily just. It is not just, however, if it is waged for the sake of religion, for religion is an affair between God and individual human beings. No person incurs injustice through the beliefs of another. A prince has therefore no right to compel his subjects to accept his own faith by means of force, unless the state would otherwise be damaged. Uniformity of faith is indeed highly desirable, but this unity cannot be the result of compulsion. For their part, subjects may not wage any war against their princes because of those princes' wish to change faith or to retain the old faith. God, who is above everyone, may alone exercise compulsion. A prince, who is neither a subject nor a private person, may uphold his right to his faith along with his other rights.

Are there causes of war grounded in nature (*utrum sint causae naturales belli faciendi*)? No, by nature all human beings are each other's kin. There is no discord between one human being and another that is grounded in nature.[1]

Although war is not the natural state of human beings, there are nevertheless circumstances in which war has nature's agreement. Thus (1) *self-defense* is a natural reason for war; and likewise, the refusal of what nature provides. War is just, when it is necessary. It is therefore not one of the basic conditions of a just defense that one must first wait to be attacked. A just defense also obtains when it works to avert a danger that has been planned and prepared for—or even when it has not been planned, but is merely probable and possible. The fear that has given occasion for

---

[1] The antithesis of this principle is the application of the Darwinist doctrine of the struggle for existence to the realm of the life of the human community, as in the Marxist doctrine of class struggle.

the preventative action must be defensible by reason, however; mere suspicion is not enough. "The Turks and the Spaniards, whose object is world conquest, can justifiably be resisted, and a common danger must be prevented in common." Self-defense, however, is not the only reason for a just war. All people are members of one body, and the world is one great commonwealth (*res publica*). Individual people are obliged to render each other service—this duty, however, applies to princes also. If one member of the body intends to damage another member, then it is fitting for all to render help to the limb that has been damaged. (2) It is *just* to help someone who is threatened by injustice.

May the subjects of a foreign prince, however, be assisted against their commander? Now, no lack of clarity ought to be tolerated in distinguishing either the territory or the responsibility of one head of state from that of another. It would thus be appropriate, in controversies between private persons, to apply to someone other than the natural head of state; and in cases of dispute between a subject and the head of state, the *courts* should as a rule decide the matter. When, however, it is not a case of individuals, but of the state itself, then there are no state judges, nor can there be any. If a large number of subjects oppose their ruler, so that it is actually a matter of a war, this is a public matter. In such a case, it can be justified for foreign heads of state to intervene for the sake of justice.

What if, however, the cause of the subjects is unjust? May foreign assistance be provided to them in such a case? Now, kingdoms are not there for kings; kings, rather, are there for kingdoms. One may provide assistance even to subjects who have devoted themselves to an unjust cause, in order to set limits to the cruelty of their ruler or in order to alleviate an excessive punishment. The head of state ought to be protected against himself. For example, there were good reasons for the English to become involved in the cause of the Dutch: close ties created by mutual need; an ancient tradition of friendship with the dukes of Burgundy; trade ties and the original blood ties of the two nations. Thus, if the Dutch had been conquered, the situation of the English would have been completely altered, and this is an important point. It ought not to be forbidden to anybody to work in the cause of freedom. On the other hand, the presence of a good neighbor is of great importance. Finally, it is not just to treat subjects in such a way that harm or danger results to those who are not subjects.

According to Gentilis, war can be waged for reasons of *necessity*, *utility*, or *honor*.

Necessity. A war is waged for reasons of necessity if (1) one cannot exist without war, as was the case for the early Romans when the right of *connubium* (marriage) with their neighbors (the Sabines) was denied them; if (2) it is a matter of exiles who are in search of the ability to settle somewhere after having been driven out of their native land by force. The occupation of an uninhabited territory is regarded as justified under natural law. Undeveloped estates can indeed be allocated to immigrants, but they remain under the supreme rule of the native prince. Exiles are not always to be admitted. Admission can be refused them if (a) they might endanger the state or (b) they might bring war with them by causing a dispute with those who have conquered them.

Utility. A war is waged on the grounds of utility if it is a question of revenging an injustice that has been suffered.

From International Law to World Peace

This is useful because one who refrains from revenging an injustice thereby calls down a further injustice upon himself. It is also useful to get back what has been lost. Kings and kingdoms maintain themselves through their name and reputation. Their good name must be protected. When are our rights being injured? Our rights are injured when people refuse us what nature freely provides. The refusal of a right of way, of a harbor, of a market, of trade, and of commerce are cases of such an injury. Anyone who refuses a harbor, a market, or commerce, offends against human society. The Spaniards thus had just grounds for a war against the natives of the New World, who refused to trade with them. But in this connection one should note that the Spaniards were not fighting for trade but for rule. A prohibition must be of a general kind in order to count as a just reason for war. It is by no means impermissible to forbid the introduction of particular kinds of goods held to be damaging for the country's population. Foreigners are not justified in changing local laws and customs. If a nation forbids foreigners to conduct trade within its borders but does permit trade at its borders, it cannot be maintained that commerce is being refused. This was the custom of the Britons in the past, and the Chinese act in this way even at the present day. The export of particular objects, such as, for example, gold and silver, may also be prohibited. The Spaniards and the English both enacted such prohibitions in the past.

A further reason for a just war is the obstruction of free use of the ocean for ocean voyages. For the ocean is open to the common use of the whole human race, like the air we breathe. The same goes for the shores of the sea, the banks of rivers, and the rivers themselves. The claim of the Venetians to the Adriatic sea as their sole possession, and to the

Albericus Gentilis

right to close it to foreign maritime traffic, is nothing other than usurpation. The Venetians can exercise jurisdiction or protection in the Adriatic sea, as other nations do in other seas, but the ocean itself remains open to maritime traffic for all nations. There is no right of property over the oceans. A prince who forbids free ocean voyages thereby affords a good reason for war. In addition to those grounds for war that are provided by an injury to natural rights (to right of way, accomodation in a harbor, to markets, to commerce, and to free ocean voyages), such grounds also result from injuries to positive human rights. In cases of injury to a positive right, however, recourse may not be had to war if it is a matter of things of little importance.

All the above considerations have to do with injuries to rights that were committed by princes or heads of states. We turn now to infractions of rights by private persons. According to Gentilis, the state is not responsible for the offences of its citizens, unless the state knowingly allows these offences to be committed when it is obliged to and able to prevent its citizens from committing offences. The state is also justly held responsible for offences committed and often repeated by its citizens. The perpetrators of repeated breaches of the law were guilty when—placing the kingdom of England and its allies in great danger, and exposing them to great harm—they provided food, munitions, and weapons to the Spanish. They broke the instruction to give up their trade, appealing to the *jus gentium* and the freedom to conduct trade. This is a question of the greatest significance. Equity was on the side of the English, but the letter of the law was on the side of the traders. The latter wanted to avoid loss of the profit that the trade with the Spanish brought them; the English, however, protested against this, because their safety was being endangered. The rights of traders are to be respected, but the security of the state still more so. "The former belong to the *jus gentium*, but the latter to nature. The former are the rights of private persons, the latter those of the kingdom. Trade thus gives way to the kingdom, the private person to nature, money to life." These arguments in favor of the English are also turned, however, against the English, and against others who, while Gentilis was writing his work, provided munitions to the Turks, who were at war with the emperor: "Do not do to others what you do not wish done to you." For how long do just reasons for a war apply? Ancient grounds may not be revived. Public legal causes can go out of date just like private ones. A war is justified, however, if it is waged against the heirs of those who committed the offence. Individuals die, but states are immortal.

Of the three categories of reasons for a war (necessity, utility, honor), two have now been discussed. It remains to consider war as a matter of honor.

Honor. "A war is a matter of honor when it is waged not in one's own interest, but as a common cause and for the benefit of others." This applies to wars against cannibals and against nations that practice human sacrifice. It cannot be said, however, that the Spaniards' war against the natives of America can count as a matter of honor, if the reason behind it was the refusal of the natives to listen to the proclamation of the gospel. Christian love cannot be a just ground for war against unbelievers. War against pirates, however, is justified, since they offend against common international law. Subjects who wage an unjust war—irrespective of whether it is a war of aggression or of defense—are to be excused, but the heads of states are not.

Albericus Gentilis

⊕

The right way of waging war. War ought not only to be *undertaken* for a just reason [that is, on account of necessity, utility, or honor, as just discussed], but ought also to be *waged* in a just way. This includes, in the first place, fulfilling the just requirement that the decision to wage war should be made known to the party against whom war is being waged. A declaration of war may, however, be omitted in the following cases. (1) If it is a question of self-defense against an attack; (2) if it is a war against rebels. Stratagems that are not otherwise permissible in single combat proper are permitted in war. In earlier times, war was much simpler. The place and time of the battle were often specified in advance by mutual agreement. Although we have now abandoned this custom, it is nevertheless not the case that any kind of ruse whatever is permitted in modern war. Stratagems are indeed permissible, *but stratagems and malicious perfidy are different things*. For example, the use of poison in war is absolutely to be condemned, and the same goes for poisonous animals and the use of magical arts. Assassination is also to be condemned. The enemy may of course be killed, but not at any time or in any way whatsoever; nor may any enemy whatsoever be killed. The mode of action of "a Scaevola" or "a Judith"[2] are in no case to be approved; but reconnoitering the enemy, as

---

[2] According to legend, Gaius Murcius Scaevola, a young man at the inception of the Roman Republic, volunteered to infiltrate the camp of Lars Porsena, king of Clusium, who besieged Rome (c. 508 BC) with the intent to kill the king, at which he failed. The Book of Judith included in the Septuagint tells the story of Judith, a daring and beautiful widow who, upset with her Jewish countrymen for their lack of trust in God, goes with her loyal maid to the camp of the enemy general Holofernes,

well as the use of secret agents, are permitted. Spies may be harshly treated when captured and detected, because of the danger they import. It is also permissible to make use of the work of traitors against traitors. The commander-in-chief alone is empowered to negotiate with the enemy. His power over things directly connected to the waging of war is, however, limited. The commander-in-chief does not have the authority to conclude a lasting peace, but he does have the authority to arrange a truce of limited duration. A truce is an agreement in good faith. During the truce, the combat forces of either party may neither retreat nor advance. Prisoners of war are usually released on condition that they may no longer fight, or may not fight again for a particular period of time. They are also released when an agreement for their release is concluded.

Although a captured enemy is only treated as a prisoner of war once he has been brought into the camp or to some other seat of his opponent's, he may not be killed unless he resorts to force or attempts to escape. In all other cases, those who give up resistance may not be killed. "Anyone who prefers to kill people whom he could take captive is unjust. Prisoners of war may not be killed—this is what divine and natural law taught, irrespective of what the customs of individual nations might have been." Even if one admits that the killing of prisoners of war might be permitted, it is still the case that "not everything that is permitted is honorable." Henry II of France had prisoners of war

---

with whom she slowly ingratiates herself. Having gained his trust, she is allowed access to his tent one night as he lies in a drunken stupor. She cuts off his head, which she takes back to her fearful countrymen. The Assyrians, having lost their leader, disperse, and Israel is saved. ED

hung, after a city was stormed, for having defended themselves too obdurately. It is disgraceful and cruel to treat people in this way for having followed the orders of their prince. The killing of the Spanish prisoners of war in Ireland was also an offence against the law of war. One who surrenders while waging war also makes thereby an implicit claim to keep his life. Humanity and the law of war both demand that the life of an enemy who surrenders should be spared. And surrender is surrender, even if it follows a lost battle or happens as a result of fear. An offer to surrender must always be accepted, where there are no special grounds to reject it. A surrender that takes place after a consultation also protects those who opposed it. In interpreting the stipulations of a capitulation treaty, the rule is that they must be in accordance with valid law and with the will of a good human being. Thus, expressions such as "by mercy," "as far as can be judged," and so on, if they appear in the capitulation agreement, are to be understood in the sense that a just and good human being would attribute to them. There are six cases, however, in which prisoners of war and enemies who have surrendered may be treated harshly. These are the following: (1) if they have abused the victors; (2) as a reparations measure; (3) when enemies are guilty of perfidy; (4) when enemies have offended against the law of war; (5) when enemies are turncoats and traitors; (6) when prisoners of war have been released and captured a second time.

The philosophers, legislators, poets, and historians of the Romans, Greeks, and barbarians are all in agreement that supplicants ought to be spared. Religion may protect those who are fleeing in its sanctuary—since there it is a question of bonds that war cannot untie—but the community of nature is everywhere open for those who beg for protection.

From International Law to World Peace

As for the enemy himself, he may be killed anywhere; and enemy property may anywhere be treated as booty, except in the case where the territory of a third country is at stake. Foreign territory grants protection, and it is therefore the case that enemy property looted on foreign territory does not pass over to the looter, but must be restored at his request to the head of state of the country where the booty was seized. It makes no difference in this respect if the flight began in an area in which the seizure of booty was lawful; a change of area means a change of powers. Accordingly, the Spaniards who fled from their French enemies into English territory were not handed over to their pursuers; conversely, the Spaniards who fled to France in 1588 from the English fleet found protection in that country.

The life and property of non-combatants are never to be infringed upon, as a matter of principle. Foreigners must, however, take care not knowingly to do anything that might support the enemy, so as not to become an enemy themselves—for anyone who gives aid to the enemy makes himself an enemy too. Those who supplied military equipment to the Saracens that could be used against Christians, or who lent them ships, were excommunicated by the Lateran Council; their property was confiscated and they themselves, if captured, became the slaves of their captors. Anyone who supplies the enemy army with military equipment is to be considered as belonging to the enemy army himself (following Queen Amalasuntha's letter to Justinian).[3] When the Hanseatic cities complained to Queen

---

[3] Queen Amalasuntha (*c.* 495–535), daughter of King Theodoric the Great and ruler of the Ostrogothic Kingdom from 526 to 535, was influential in politics and a correspondent of Emperor Justinian. ED

Albericus Gentilis

Elizabeth that the English fleet had plundered their ships—in contravention of the treaty according to which those cities were friends of England's enemies and were permitted to conduct trade with them with impunity—she replied that damaging the interests of one side and assisting the other was not only incompatible with friendship with both sides, but meant supporting the enemy and making common cause with them against the other side. It is, however, the will of the persons in question (i.e., whether that will is completely or largely on the side of the enemy) that decides if they are to be regarded as belonging to the enemy state.

How are enemy citizens who live abroad to be treated? A Spaniard who lives outside Spain remains a Spaniard for so long as he has not "in any explicit way" ceased to be a Spaniard. "One's heritage is not altered, nor is one easily separated from one's native land. Settling in and becoming a citizen of another country do indeed add another citizenship to one's citizenship, but they do not erase the first citizenship. By means of naturalization (*allectione*) one can become a citizen of different places." The natural citizenship of heritage and birth is never relinquished, except as a punishment in one particular case—that is, desertion in a time of threatening danger.

After the end of the war, the limits of penal action must be strictly observed. These limits are set by the main goal of the war, by the peace, and by the reason for the war. They include damages, safeguarding against the guilty parties and others who might be inclined to follow their example, and the recovery of their unjust gains.

Political reasons may indeed move the victor to grant the defeated state its freedom, yet he may also change the constitution of the defeated state so that it is more in accord with the political arrangements in his own state. The reasons most commonly put forward in favor of a compulsory alteration of the religion of the defeated party are usually only illusory. The victor may, however, prohibit in the defeated state such things as are against nature. It is against natural law (*jus naturae*) to destroy the harbors of the defeated country. The defeated parties may, however, be disarmed. In all cases in which the victor imposes his own law, fairness is to be preferred to the letter of the law, and honor to bare utility.

Gentilis concludes his work on the law of war with words whose magic can perhaps be best preserved in their original Latin form:

> *Deus optimus maximus faciat principes imponere bellis omnem finem et jura pacis ac foederum colere sancte. "Pax plenum virtutis opus, pax summa laborum, pax belli exacti pretium est, pretiumque pericli: sidera pace vigent, consistunt terrea pace: nil placitum sine pace Deo." Etiam Deus, etiam impone tu bellis finem: tu nobis pacem effice: placatus iniquitatibus nostris: propitius nobis in Filio tuo, servatore nostro, Jesu Christo.*[4]

---

[4] May God most Great cause the princes to put an end to all wars, and to honor the laws of peace and covenants in a holy way. "Peace is the full work of virtue, peace is the sum of labors, peace is the price of exacting war, and the price of danger: the stars prosper in peace, the earthly rest in peace: nothing is pleasing without peace to God." Yes, God, dost thou also put an end to wars: you make peace for us: appeased by our iniquities: more propitious to us in your Son, our Savior, Jesus Christ.

2

Hugo Grotius and His School

or more than two hundred years, Hugo Grotius (de Groot) (1583–1645) was almost universally described and considered as the "father of international law." Thus the *Encyclopedia Britannica*, in its article on "International Law," asserts that in his work *De Jure Belli ac Pacis* [On the law of war and peace] (Paris, 1625), Grotius provided an exhaustive theoretical grounding of international law "for all times." In the present day, on the other hand, more and more voices have made themselves heard that find the real "father of international law" not to be Grotius, but Suárez, or Vitoria (as does James Scott), or even Gentilis. Thus, one of the basic textbooks of international law (L. Oppenheim, ed. H. Lauterpracht, Cambridge, 1946), takes the position that the honor of having founded the jurisprudence of international law belongs, not to Grotius, but to Albericus Gentilis: "Gentilis's book *De Jure Belli* supplies, as Professor Holland shows, the model and the framework of the first and third book of Grotius's *De Jure Belli ac Pacis*. 'The first step' (Holland rightly says) 'towards making International Law what it is was taken, not by Grotius, but by Gentilis.'"

If however one consults the "first step" of the Dutch jurist himself—that is, his first writing, *The Free Sea* (*Mare liberum*), published in November 1608—one finds that *the*

whole work is largely based on the teaching and the arguments of the famous Spanish jurist Ferdinand Menchaca Vasquez (1509–1566), whose work *Controversiae illustres* [Illustrious controversies] is extensively quoted. It is also based on Francisco de Vitoria (*De Indis*), Alfonso de Castro (?–1559), a professor of theology in Salamanca and father confessor to the emperor Charles V, and on Diego Covarruvias (1512–1577), the "Bartolus of Spain." Grotius also draws important principles of doctrine from the works of Cajetan, St Thomas Aquinas, St Augustine, and from Roman legal writings and the writings of classical antiquity. Grotius provides precise references to his sources.

The just-mentioned work *Mare liberum* contains no "modern" teaching, no new principles for a "new international law," but is, on the contrary, a concise summary of the international-legal views of Late Scholasticism generally (especially as it flourished in Spain), together with their Christian and ancient background, insofar as these views bear on the problem of the freedom of the seas. As a text, *Mare liberum* does not owe its origin to any intention of replacing, or need to replace, old doctrines with new. It is, instead, both expressly and implicitly in all its parts an energetic *defense*, informed by deep conviction, of the old views against their distortion by new ones that had in the meanwhile arisen as a result of political interests. Grotius sets the authority of immutable natural law, which is rooted in divine law, against the mutable and groundless play of political interests covering themselves with the mantle of "law." This new element was, precisely, a rising pure positivism, in which states wished to bestow upon the interests of their own power the validity of legal norms. The old element, conversely, was that "law-in-itself" which lived in

Scholasticism, in the works of the Church Fathers, and in Roman jurisprudence. Grotius placed himself on the side of the old. He opposed politics to law, and asserted the primacy of law. Thus, in the preface to *Mare liberum*, Grotius says the following:

> It is a delusion as old as it is damaging by which many people, and especially those who because of their wealth and power have the greatest influence, convince themselves that justice and injustice are not distinct in their natures, but only by virtue of human opinions and habits. Such people therefore think that both laws and also the appearance of fairness were invented only to serve the purpose of suppressing disagreements and revolts among those people born into a lower station. At the same time, they assert that they themselves, since they are placed high, determine justice according to what they think good; but can, however, direct what they think good according to their own advantage.
>
> There have, on the other hand, in all times been independent, wise, and pious men who have worked to blot this false conviction out of the souls of the simple, and to bring to light the shamelessness of the champions of this doctrine. For they showed that God is the founder and guide of the world, and that He, as the Father of the whole human race, did not divide that race into various kinds and categories, as He did in the case of other living beings, but willed that it should be known as one race under one and the same name. Moreover, he gave human beings a common heritage, a common organization, and the capacity to look each other in the face, the capacity for language and other means of commerce, so that they should recognize their natural community and kinship. These people also showed that God is the Lord and Father of this family, and that he issued, for the household or state that he founded, laws that are not chiseled in brass or stone tablets, but which are written in

the understanding and the heart of every individual human being, where even the unwilling and the unruly must read them, and that these laws bind great and small alike; that kings have no more power to go beyond the provisions of the magistrates than the magistrates do beyond the decrees of the governors, or the governors beyond the orders of their kings—indeed, that the laws of individual nations and cities stem from that divine source, and owe to it alone their sacredness and majesty.

This passage from the preface to *Mare liberum* is in reality nothing other than Grotius's "profession of faith" in the philosophy of law, and is indeed a declaration also of his adherence to the *realism* (the view that ideas are objective realities) of the "wise and pious men" whom "there have in all times been," and together with whom he works to "blot" the "delusion as old as it is damaging . . . out of the souls of the simple"—the delusion, that is, of *nominalism* (the view that ideas are only descriptions and words of a subjective kind). Grotius thus puts himself on the side of the Spanish Late Scholastics, on the side of St Thomas Aquinas and St Albertus Magnus, of St Augustine, and of Plato and Aristotle, and declares himself the foe of the sophism of antiquity and its cynics, sceptics, and epicureans, of the nominalists of the Middle Ages, of Machiavellianism, and of all the legal positivism of modernity—as well as of a rising nationalism against whose claims he undertakes to defend the rights of the one and undivided human race, that is, *international law as a law of humankind*.

The Portuguese and Spanish, like the Venetians and the Genoese before them, and the English after them, claimed the sea as their exclusive possession. Grotius stands up against this in the name of humankind and its law, writing his *Mare liberum* for the purpose of refuting the claims of national states insofar as those claims signify an attack on the law of humankind or on international law. For humankind does not consist of "different kinds," like the other living beings of nature (each with its own laws), but is "known as one race under one and the same name" and has "a common heritage, a common organization [of body and soul], and the capacity to look each other in the face, the capacity for language and other means of commerce, so that they should recognize their natural community and kinship."

This in turn is one of the cornerstones of the Catholic (i.e., "universal") thinking of High and Late Scholasticism, and Grotius is at pains to conserve that thinking in the age of the increasingly separatist tendencies of nationalism, individualism, and subjectivism—as well as to carry the henceforth non-Catholic current of the culture of Christian humanity safely through all the successive stages of the Reformation and Enlightenment.

In this, Grotius comes forward not so much as the "father of international law," as he does the "Noah" of international law: its savior in the face of the flood of rising individualism, subjectivism, particularism, nationalism, and the subjective "revaluation of all values." This "ark" he built by reclothing in legal argument the essential element he was attempting to keep safe. It was his primary task and achievement. He "built" the ark from the materials furnished him by his precursors in the Middle Ages and in Antiquity. But the *content*, the *essential element* that was to be rescued with the help of this "ark," is an item of ancient Catholic heritage that, through Grotius, was posited also as the foundation of the Protestant world's thinking about international law. Addressing the Christian princes of all denominations, Grotius puts it thus:

From International Law to World Peace

There are none among you who has not publicly declared that every human being is justified in freely disposing of his own property; there are none among you who do not insist that all citizens have the same right to use watercourses and public spaces; there are none among you, even, who do not defend the freedom of travel and trade with all your might. If, then, we are of the opinion that that small community (*parva illa societas*) which we call the "state" cannot exist if these principles are not put into practice, why should these same principles not be equally necessary to preserve the community of the whole of humankind and its harmony? [If] a king commits a crime against a king, or a nation against a nation, does that then signify a breach of the peace in that universal state (*magnae illius civitas*) and an offence against the supreme governor? Nevertheless, there is a distinction here, namely that, . . . although the King of the universe has reserved to himself final punishment of your own offences (a punishment that is indeed slow and invisible, yet unavoidable), he has nonetheless appointed two judges who are authorized to judge human affairs, and whom not even the most successful of sinners can escape, namely *conscience*, as condemnation of oneself, and *public opinion*, as condemnation by others. These two tribunals are open to all who lack access to any other; to these tribunals the powerless appeal; in them, those who wish to conquer through power alone are themselves conquered. . . .

Grotius repeats here with full emphasis the principles that, for example, Vitoria too, and indeed Thomas Aquinas, had endorsed. But at the same time he takes a step in a direction of which his great predecessors would not have approved. *He exiles divine law to heaven, and allows it to be valid on earth only as natural law*, that is, on the subjective stage of conscience and public opinion. Of the three levels of law—divine, natural, and positive—Grotius separates off the highest level, divine law, making it transcendent. He exiles it to a sphere of being that lies beyond the practical realm of validity of legal life. For Grotius's great predecessors too (as for his contemporaries in Late Scholasticism), divine law was equally sublime; but for them it was not only transcendent, it was also historically immanent in humanity. Divine law was present *within* the culture of humanity, and it was *in force*. To these great precursors, the Church was the immanent—objectively present—divine law, which by means of revelation was alive within it as an orienting component of the three-part organism of the *valid* law of humankind. Just as the transcendent God became immanent in human nature in Jesus Christ, so for the likes of Vitoria and St Thomas, the transcendent divine law became immanent in the Church. It became a component of the spiritual life of humanity *on earth*, and, indeed, the supreme norm ruling it.

For Grotius, however, divine law *forfeits* its quality of being objectively present on earth within the course of the history of humankind. It is with God. True, it is revealed in Holy Scripture; but understanding, enforcing, and validating that revelation depends upon the understanding and the conscience of the individual. It is thus referred to the *subjective* tribunal of the individual person. For Grotius, then, it is not valid in the older sense that there is one definitive and binding interpretation and explication of divine law: i.e., that the Church is called to be the interpreter, protectress, and representative of the divine law on earth, and to be in charge of teaching it.

Grotius does, indeed, strive to *conserve* the principles of his Catholic predecessors for the future, and, where necessary and possible, to provide them with a new foundation.

But he is nevertheless obliged to *adapt* to the universal fate of Protestantism. Within the historical and earthly realm of human existence, the Church falls away as protectress and bearer of the revealed divine law; and what also falls away for Grotius is universally and objectively valid divine law itself, which becomes a personal affair for the individual, with a merely subjective validity. It is certainly the case for Grotius that "the laws of individual nations and cities derive from that divine source, and owe to it alone their holiness and majesty." But even so, for him the source itself is henceforth in the beyond, while on the stage of human affairs "only two judges are appointed": the conscience of the individual and the community's public opinion. The *third* judge, the Church as a court of objectively valid universal divine law standing above both the individual and the state community, is for him no longer present. His great precursors acknowledged *three* "judges": the conscience of the individual, the community's public opinion, and the vocation of the Church. Grotius can henceforth acknowledge only the first two judges as "authorized to judge human affairs." The third is exiled to the beyond.

Whatever one thinks of the Protestant doctrine of faith (or rather, of the Protestant doctrines of faith), it necessarily entails at least *one* profound effect on the whole life of the civilized Christian human community: the disappearance of the sanctioned, objectively valid divine law from the realm of the political, social, and cultural life of humankind. In its place, the *subjective* element of conscience and of public opinion becomes the highest criterion. Since, however, there is no *objective* supreme authority or institution of conscience, in practice conscience and public opinion become the criteria that play a determinative role in the life of the *state*, in the life of monarchs, government representatives, and parliamentarians. In other words, the *state* becomes the highest authority—as it were, the institution of the "organized conscience"—on whose stage it is left to the now transcendent divine law to unfold its supernatural effects of grace. That is, the state takes over the function of the Church which, on whatever grounds, is denied it, but which humankind cannot do without for the preservation of an orderly social life.

Hugo Grotius is, then, not *the* "father of the jurisprudence of international law"; he is, rather, *one* of the most prominent early champions of the school of the jurisprudence of international law that attempts to adapt a tradition rooted in the Catholic intellectual world into a form acceptable to the Protestant intellectual world. Only because Grotius proved outstandingly successful in this adaptation, did he become "the father of the modern jurisprudence of international law." It would be more correct, as was said earlier, to see him as the "Noah of the jurisprudence of international law." In this sense, he can perhaps be accounted a father—the father, that is, of that jurisprudence of international law that was *rescued* from the storms and floods of the so-called "Age of Reformation."

As regards Grotius, Thomas A. Walker is of the view that there was "little or nothing new in his general treatment of the subject. His system is fundamentally identical with the ideas outlined by Suarez."[1] The structure of the *first two* books of Grotius's chief work, *De Jure Belli ac Pacis*, does

---

[1] T.A. Walker, *The Law of Nations*, I, 330.

indeed correspond exactly to the structure of Gentilis's work *De Jure Belli*. Grotius also drew freely on the works of his immediate precursors, such as Vitoria, Covarruvias, Vazquez, Ayala, Gentilis, and Bodin, as well as on the works of Classical Antiquity, Christian Patristics, the Scholastics, and the canon and civil lawyers of the Middle Ages. He did this precisely because this was the best way to accomplish what he intended: to make nothing new; only to save what was old. The "ark" of his system contains everything living that was threatened by the revolutionary flood of modernity.

In the foreword to his book *De Jure Belli ac Pacis*, which appeared in Paris in 1625, Grotius expressly says that he was "impelled to write his work by the ignorance and unhappy state of public opinion in his time with respect to international law, as well as by the resulting savage lawlessness and barbarity in the waging of war." It was Grotius's task once again to point to the law, in war and peace, and to show that humanity is not freed from the rule of law in its dealings merely by having been fragmented into various state communities, and that justice does not remain silent even amid the clanging of weapons. His work *De Jure Belli ac Pacis* is an appeal to all humankind, in a time of lawlessness, to be mindful of the timeless principles of law, reason, and justice.

The fundamental intuitions on which *De Jure Belli ac Pacis* rests can be traced back to two basic concepts, namely those of natural law (*jus naturale*) and of positive law (*jus voluntarium*). Natural law is the governance of world-reason as it reveals itself in human reason. The *jus voluntarium*, by contrast, is the governance of the will. It consists, that is, of the commandments and prohibitions of a will (whether divine or human) with respect to another will, whereas natural law consists of the dictates of right reason, which reveals either the essentially reprehensible or the morally necessary character of a particular action by virtue of its agreement or non-agreement with the nature of reason itself—and then either forbids or commands this action in the name of God, the author of nature. The actions in which these dictates come to expression are *in themselves* either obligatory or impermissible, so that they are understood as necessarily commanded or prohibited by God Himself. Thus, this law differs not only from human law, but also from divine positive (*voluntarium*) law, which does not command and forbid things that are in themselves and by their nature (*natura*) obligatory or impermissible—but makes them impermissible by *forbidding* them, or necessary by *commanding* them.

"Natural law is so immutable that God Himself cannot change it."[2] The positive law (*jus voluntarium*) can originate in the *divine* will (*jus voluntarium divinum*) or in the *human* will (*jus voluntarium humanum*). The *jus voluntarium divinum* [divine positive law], then, is the express *will of God* that is made known by means of revelation, either to the whole of humankind or to a particular nation. Three times has God made His will known to humankind in the form of direct law-giving: immediately after the creation, at the restoration of humankind after the Flood, and at the redemption of humankind through Christ. Each of these three laws is universally valid for human beings.[3]

Such a divine positive law was also given to Moses, in which case, however, it was valid only for the nation of Israel. Nevertheless, the Mosaic law, since it is divine, cannot contradict natural law. This is why the prescriptions of

---

[2] *De Jure Belli ac Pacis*, I.I.
[3] Ibid.

the Mosaic law concerning virtues that Christ demanded also of his disciples are at least as binding for Christians as they are for Jews—if not more so.

Human positive law (*jus voluntarium humanum*), for its part, embraces three kinds: first, the *jus civile*, or the particular law of a state; second, a kind of law *narrower* than the *jus civile*; and another, third, kind of law, *broader* than the *jus civile*. The *jus civile* is the law of a particular state, and originates in state power, understanding by state "a perfect coming together of free human beings, who have united for the purpose of the flourishing of the law and of the common good." International law is thus, according to Grotius, an intermediate level between natural law and the internal law of states. It is *universal* to the extent that it participates in the nature of natural law (i.e., insofar as it brings natural law into force by means of treaties and practice), but is *individual* and *regional* to the extent that it is shaped by the particular wills of individual states. Thus the *postliminium*,[4] for example, is a postulate of natural law, because of the necessity in principle of the restoration of peaceful relationships in respect of persons and property after the end of a war. The *degree* of the restoration, however, depends upon the treaties, customs, and usages of the states in question. Natural law is indeed included within international law (II. 18, "De legationem jure"), but it often goes beyond the boundaries of international law. Thus, to give one example, the killing of prisoners in the storming of a city is not forbidden according to the letter of international law, whereas honor and "natural justice" (*justitia interna*) forbid it.

---

[4] The right of a banished person or a captive to resume civic rights on return from exile, recovery, or restoration. TR

Hugo Grotius and His School

⊕

These are the basic intuitions as to the nature and division of law that lie at the basis of Grotius's system of international law. Starting out from these intuitions about matters of principle, Grotius now poses the "first question" that is most important for Christians and for all civilized human beings: Is war as a means of regulating international affairs permitted under natural law, under the *jus gentium voluntarium* (international law), and under the *jus voluntarium divinum* (positive divine law)? In answering this question, Grotius follows the ideas of the tradition of St Augustine, the Scholastics, and his immediate precursors, the Spanish Late Scholastics Vitoria, Vasquez, Molina, Suárez, and so on. And his answer to the question accords with this tradition and these ideas—i.e., that under certain circumstances war is not irreconcilable with natural law, that it is practiced by civilized nations, and that it is not entirely forbidden by the law of Christ.

In treating of the concept of the just war too—a war that can be occasioned only by the infliction of an injury—as well as the just grounds for preventive, reparative, and punitive wars (military preventive measures against legal injury, military measures for the restoration of an injured right, and military punitive measures for the restoration of the certainty of law), Grotius remains true to his task of being the "Noah" of international law.[5] His arguments essentially rep-

---

[5] "The division of law into natural law, divine law, and international law, and the precise division of international law, was achieved long before Grotius by *Suárez*, and we must stop celebrating the Dutchman as the founder of international law. That founder is Suárez." (Hans Mayer, *Geschichte der abendländischen Weltanschauung* [History of the western worldview], Würzburg, 1950, iv, 70.)

resent a newly formulated way of justifying views which the part of humanity that took ideas seriously had worked out over the best part of two thousand years.

On one point, however, Grotius takes the opposite stance to Vitoria, Vasquez, Molina, and to those who share their views. Whereas they hold the view that the head of state, the prince, is only justified in waging war if either *he himself* or *his state* has suffered an injustice, or if the law-breaker stands under *his own* jurisdiction, Grotius takes the position that princes are justified in proceeding, and are called to proceed, against anyone who has substantially offended against natural law and international law—irrespective of whether this offence concerns himself and his subjects, or the prince of another state and that prince's subjects. Grotius is of the view that kings, and persons whose position of power is the same as a king's, have the right to protect the human legal order and human society *as such*. "It is truly more honorable to revenge injustices that have been done to others." Thus, just wars can be waged against *all* those who do not honor their parents, who kill foreign travelers, or who practice cannibalism or piracy. In other words, the right to punish is *not* granted by the law of a *particular state*, as Vitoria, Vasquez, and others seem to accept, but by *natural law*.

Here Grotius foregrounds an essential principle that only appears to be new when he is compared with his immediate precursors; for in reality, it is not a case of a new principle set in opposition to an "obsolete" mode of thinking, but of Grotius's effort to *restore* an older principle to its place of honor—a principle that was at risk of becoming forgotten owing to the modern inclination to make room for ever further powers for the national state. This is not an "individualistic" and "liberal" Grotius, contesting the "Catholic" mode of thinking of Vitoria, Vasquez, and Molina. Rather, Grotius here takes up a position that is *more authentically* Catholic than the standpoint of some of his influential Catholic contemporaries! Grotius, that is, courageously and uncompromisingly professes the principle that from the beginning lay at the basis of all Christian and Catholic thinking, to the answer that humanity always, in the name of the fratricide Cain, owes to heaven: that is, "I *am* my brother's keeper."

In reality, Grotius neither will nor *can* come to terms with the disintegration of the empire of "Christendom" into a series of absolutely sovereign states, into several "empires" or little "Christendoms." Since it has now come about that the emperor is no longer the actual head of Christendom, and that there no longer exists any "empire," any political organization that embraces the whole of Christendom, its place is taken by natural law and international law. And every prince of a sovereign state is henceforth bound to obey the "invisible emperor" (natural law), and the "invisible empire" (international law), just as in the past he was obliged to obey the visible emperor within the political organization of the empire. *This* is the idea that Grotius, as the "Noah" of international law, wishes to rescue for the future. It is also the idea that governed the entire Middle Ages, and that, in the last analysis, is and will forever be the root, the meaning, and the goal of all legal life, of any international legal order and of any world organization. It is the idea that humankind must realize, so that in place of giving Cain's answer, "Am I my brother's keeper?" it can give the answer truly worthy of humanity: "I *ought to be* my brother's keeper."

From International Law to World Peace

In this sense, in Grotius's sense, all states, all heads of state, and all governments are, as a matter of principle, guardians of law in the world, and thus also guardians of each individual state—and, indeed, finally, of every individual human being. If, anywhere in the world "cannibalism" is being practiced—i.e., wherever human bodies, human life forces, or human capacities are being forcibly "devoured" (as is happening to a monstrous degree today)—then, for Grotius, it is the duty and the right of all states to intervene by any means necessary, including war. If, anywhere in the world, the ideas and ideals of the fathers are forcibly and impiously suppressed (as is happening to a monstrously excessive extent today), it is, according to Grotius, the duty and the right of all states to intervene by any means necessary, including war. If, anywhere in the world, foreigners are not tolerated, and piracy—whether state piracy or piracy of some other kind—is practiced (as is also happening to a monstrous degree today), it is, according to the principle "I am my brother's keeper," the duty and the right of the whole community of states to intervene by any means necessary, including war. This duty and this right *are* international law as Grotius understood it, and as it has always been understood by all those who have humankind and its fate at heart.

PART V

The "Conservative" and "Liberal" Ideas of International Law as a Rationalistic Law of Nature after the Twilight of Divine Law

1

Thomas Hobbes and John Locke

ince the time of Plato and Aristotle, Western thought has been governed by the idea that all social life (including, therefore, the state and the community of states) rests on the "social nature" of human beings, who are endowed with reason. That man is by nature a "social being" was taught by Aristotle, Thomas Aquinas, and Hugo Grotius. It is therefore a doctrine whose power of conviction has been confirmed over two millennia. Indeed, it has retained this power through all the disturbances brought by the transition from pagan Hellenic antiquity to early Christianity, from early Christianity to the Middle Ages, from the Middle Ages to the Renaissance, as well as through the tempests of the Reformation. *Naturale autem est homini ut sit animal sociale et politicum* ("man is by nature a social and political animal") says Thomas Aquinas.[1] It is indeed "natural" for human beings to be organized in communities, because their varied capacities and incapacities make them dependent on such an organization; and also because the faculty of reason—which elevates human beings above the natural kingdom—demands it.

The idea that man is by nature a "social being" held the field as one of the most certain and universally valid truths,

---

[1] *De regimine principum*, I. 1.

a truth that was not to be shaken so long as the view was maintained that reason was higher than the will (*intellectus nobilior potestas*) both in general, and more specifically in the realm of theological thought. So long as the wisdom of God was understood as the governing and ordering principle of the world, man, who was made in the image of God, was seen as a being who—by virtue of his reason—bestowed upon the will a purpose, a direction, and a way of acting. And so long as reason was seen as the guiding power both in the wider world and in the little world of the human interior, it was certain too that the light which, as reason, shines within the inner life of the human being—ordering it and setting its goals—was essentially the same as the light ordering and guiding the wider world. The view was thereby professed that reason bridges the split between the outer world and the inner world: that it is neither "subjective" nor "objective," but is a third element above both the purely-subjective element of the soul and the purely-objective element of the factual. Natural law, accordingly, was what human reason both prescribed and proscribed, as well as being the governance of the *lex aeterna*—the divine reason in the world. And man, as by nature a social being, is such because he participates in the universal, both through his reason and through his body. He is not in principle a solitary being condemned to the loneliness of the subjectivity of the life of his will. Reason lifts him above the isolating nature of his wishes to an insight into, and a recognition of, the universal.

The case is quite otherwise, however, if the primacy of the *will* is asserted. Then it is not God's *wisdom* that orders and guides the world, but His *will*. And His creatures then no longer participate in the great work of world history in the sense of being moved to do so by the insights of reason, but in the sense that their will is obedient to the will of God, which is ranked above human will. If *voluntarism* is consistently followed through to its conclusion, the command "Thou shalt not kill" is valid, not because killing *contradicts* the ideas of the true, beautiful, and good, but because God's will has *commanded* that it be so. Had God felt like giving the Ten Commandments the opposite content, we would have been obliged to follow opposite commandments just as absolutely, since their "correctness" lies not in their ethical and rational content, but in the authority of the superordinate (because more powerful) will of God.

In the "little world" of the human being it is then, correspondingly, also the will that makes use of reason as its instrument. Thus, with its concepts, ideas, and ideals, reason then no longer bridges the opposition between the subjective inner world of the human being and the objective world of facts outside the human being by means of ideas (or *universalia*, as they were customarily called in the Middle Ages)—both lighting up as insights in the minds of human beings and shaping with their governance the world of facts outside them—for at this lower, second level of law, concepts, ideas, and ideals become forms through which the activity of the will is expressed: mere external orderings of the realm of experience according to the groupings and postulations of urgings exerted from our own interior. Universal *concepts*, acquired now in this voluntaristic setting by means of abstraction, are henceforth mere external descriptions of collections of data, mere *names* (nominalism); and as for values and ideas, they are nothing but postulates of the will. "God," "immortality," and "freedom" are not truths, but are postulates of the will; "man," "beast," and "plant" are not realities of the world of facts, but are descriptions of a sum-total of similar experiences that a person has had and that serve the purpose of allowing these experiences to be more conveniently sorted through by memory. *Voluntarism* and *nominalism* are twin brothers. Each requires the other; neither can subsist without the other.

This was the exact setting in which the great revolution in theological thought of the Reformation broke out: the exhaustion of the powerful intellectual edifice of the medieval world alongside its "dictatorship of metaphysics" (as many experienced it), and a move towards emphasizing the *will* over against the governance of the "absolute truths," "absolute institutions," and "absolute values" of the Church, the Schools, and the Empire of the Middle Ages. Both Luther and Calvin elevated the will to a leading role. By giving a central place to a "return to Scripture," Luther inked out, as it were, the entire metaphysical edifice of ideas that had grown up over the course of more than a millennium. For him, in Scripture (and in it alone) lies the *word* of God; not the ideas and truths of "realism," but, precisely, God's word (i.e., what God commanded, forbade, and promised), while everything subsequent to that is only "the work of man." "The work of man," however, does not mean the product of reason illuminated by God's truth, but rather a product of the *will*, which *of itself* cannot bring about anything good, because, since the Fall, it has become "incapable" of the good and the true. The only thing of which the will *is* capable is to receive the efficacious *grace* of God's *will*—that is, *belief*—and indeed belief in God's *word*, as it is contained in Scripture. Everything else is brought about by the will of God. In short, man is justified by faith.

Luther sees human beings as creatures in whom will is

the decisive capacity. But this capacity is incapable of producing what is good and true, either in outer works of action, or in the inner work of metaphysical knowledge. Everything true and good is owed to the workings of God's will. Through faith, man *surrenders* to God's will. In Luther, then, we have a voluntarism (hence also a nominalism in the life of cognition) that is *negative* in human beings, and *positive* in God.

Calvin takes theological voluntarism still further than Luther. For Calvin, it is divine will, not human will, that accomplishes election to eternal salvation and to eternal perdition. Since it is pure will that determines who will be saved and who will be damned—and thus (seen from a human point of view) an arbitrary choice made by God—this pure will of God is an absolute *mystery* for human consciousness. No person can ever know whether he is saved or damned, precisely because it is not a matter of "truth," but of an act of God's will.

Theological voluntarism was first taken to its ultimate conclusion by Islam. In Islam, the will of God is the only power that determines everyone's individual fate in all details, in both time and eternity. "Islam" means "submission" of the will to fate, which is the governance of God's will.

In its essentials, the Reformation, as a spiritually revolutionary movement, inverted the formula "reason is the nobler capacity" (*intellectus nobilior potestas*) to produce the formula "will is the normative capacity." In other words, just as in His creation, revelation, work of grace, and miracles, God does not reveal Himself by means of a series of thought-processes or "dialectical processes of development" but by means of *deeds* expressing His will, so man does not express himself through his views and speculations, but through his *deeds*. Since the Fall, however, the latter are valueless, for they can only be an expression of the corrupted nature of the human will. If one *has* faith, grace brings about everything good that comes about in human life. If one *does not have* faith, however, every action remains a merely human work; that is, it remains in the realm of error and of what is evil. Fallen man—man as what he has now become—is bad by nature.

Thomas Hobbes. But if the nature of man is bad in itself, then man is by no means a "social being" in Aristotle's sense! On the contrary, he is a being of will who is in principle hostile to all other beings. It is just this view that was championed by Thomas Hobbes (1588–1679), who followed its consequences very far indeed (even if not to their ultimate conclusion), and realized them with great precision and consistency. According to Hobbes, man is *not* "an animal born fit for society" since "all society . . . exists for the sake either of advantage or of glory; i.e., it is a product of love of self, not love of friends," because "the origin of large and lasting societies lay, not in mutual human benevolence, but in men's mutual fear."[2] This fear is explained by the fact that "in the state of nature there is in all men a will to do harm," so that "men's natural state, before they came together into society, was war; and not simply war, but a war of every man against every man."[3]

---

[2] Thomas Hobbes, *Of The Citizen*, ed. and trans. Richard Tuck and Michael Silverthorne (Cambridge: CUP, 1998), 22, 24.

[3] Ibid., 26, 29.

Thomas Hobbes and John Locke

How does Hobbes arrive at such views, and what are his ideas of the nature of society—both of the state and of the community of states, or of community of international law? Hobbes devoted his chief work, *Leviathan: or the Matter, Forme, and Power of a Commonwealth Ecclesiastical and Civil* (1651), to just this problem of human social life. [*Editor's note*: Here the author inserts an extended series of excerpts (with brief commentaries) from the work just cited. In the interest of keeping focus on the primary points under discussion here, these excerpts now make up Appendix C. They serve to illustrate exhaustively the line of thought and mode of argumentation of Hobbes, who, as early as the seventeenth century, already set out clearly and systematically—in broad daylight—ideas that even today form the basis (explicitly or implicitly) for great, world-shaking political and ideological currents. A central result to be drawn from these excerpts is that, for Hobbes, religion "must depend on the laws of the state," not on "arbitrary" human beings: that religion "is not philosophy, but law, and hence it is not to be discussed, but obeyed."]

Now, at the center of the doctrine of the state (a point that especially sharply distinguishes Hobbes from Grotius and the Traditional School) stands his theory of the final and complete transfer of all the natural rights of the individual to the state power, or rather to the ruler, with the explicit or implicit promise of unconditional obedience. Such a transfer of the person's natural rights to the head of state, in compensation for which only the capacity to rule and keep order is expected, is in Hobbes's view, the "social contract" that underpins all political life. Hobbes, in contrast to Grotius, admits no unlimited diversity of social contracts in which individuals might to a greater or lesser degree renounce their natural rights to the benefit of the state power. He acknowledges only *one* kind of social contract—unconditional and complete subjection, including in matters of conscience and religion. His social contract is an unconditional *pactum subiectionis*, in which all natural rights are renounced in favor of the ruler, and in which unlimited power is thereby lent to the latter. Any resistance on the part of citizens to the ruler or to the state power is, accordingly, frowned upon. Should such resistance prove successful, however, then the social contract ceases to be valid, and the citizens revert to the original, pre-contractual state of affairs, and it is then open to them to subject themselves to another ruler or to another state power. "The Obligation of Subjects to the Sovereign, is understood to last as long, and no longer, than the power lasteth, by which he is able to protect them."[4] The mortal sin of state power is to be weak. For all law, including natural law, is grounded on its enforceability (sanctions). "And Covenants, without the Sword, are but Words, and of no strength to secure a man at all."[5] There is no "legitimacy" without power. A government that has relinquished actual power thereby ceases to be "legitimate." Conversely, *any* government is legal, if and for so long as it is in possession of actual power.

Moreover, there is, according to Hobbes's doctrine of the social contract, no other form of society alongside and outside that of the state. Everything that is not a state—i.e.,

[4] Ibid., 121.
[5] Ibid., 93.

everything that is not subject to a government—is only a formless and anarchic mob. No self-governing corporations *sui juris*, such as guilds, estates, and so on, may exist in a healthy state, since they would be "like wormes in the entrayles of a naturall man."[6] The Church, too, is completely and unconditionally subordinate to the state; and so the head of state is the head of the Church as of all other corporations. The head of state has no natural law and no divine law above him, to which one could appeal against the head of state. The "errour" that "setteth the Lawes above the Soveraign, setteth also a Judge above him, and a Power to punish him; which is to make a new Soveraign; and again for the same reason a third, to punish the second; and so continually without end, to the Confusion, and Dissolution of the Commonwealth."[7]

Hobbes's doctrine of the social contract is thus (to characterize it in modern language) the theoretical equivalent of the totalitarian state or of state totalitarianism outright, which even today corresponds admirably to the totalitarian regimes of the present. It rests on the founding intuition that man—in contrast to Aristotle, to the Scholastic School, and to Grotius—is not a "social animal" by his nature, but an animal who lives in a struggle for existence. In other words, man is *a being who is naturally involved* in a war of all against all (an anticipation of Darwinism), who—on rational grounds, i.e., the grounds of utility and advantage—allies with others in order to rule together over another group or to struggle against them (an anticipation

[6] Ibid., 169.
[7] Ibid., 164.

of Marxism). The same "rational grounds" then necessarily lead them to unconditional subjection to a power, i.e., to state formation (an anticipation of the totalitarian state of fascism, National Socialism, and communism).

Hobbes's doctrine of the social contract is distinguished from the traditional social contract by the fact that it excludes values of morality and reason such as justice, freedom, and human love. The difference soon becomes clear if one compares Hobbes's doctrine with that of Plato, which contains the basic ideas of the traditional doctrine of the social contract. In book II of the *Republic*, Plato says of the origin of the state that "those who have done and suffered injustice and tasted both, but who lack the power to do it and avoid suffering it, decide that it is profitable to come to an agreement with each other neither to do injustice nor to suffer it. As a result, they begin to make laws and covenants, and what the law commands they call lawful and just."[8] The principles of the doctrine of the social contract are comprised here, but these views on matters of principle are distinguished from those of Hobbes by the fact that the formation of the state presupposes, as it were, a revolt of the higher nature of humanity, of morality and reason, against injustice; and not only on the part of those who have suffered injustice but also on the side of those who have practiced injustice.

The *pactum subiectionis*, the contract of subjection to a power, is preceded by the *pactum unionis*, the contract of joining together for the sake of justice. Subjection (*pactum subiectionis*) is, however, according to Plato, not an uncon-

---

[8] The view here attributed to "Plato" is, in the dialogue, spoken by the character Glaucon. TR

Thomas Hobbes and John Locke

ditional subjection to an external power, but to "laws and agreements" to which both the subjects and the bearers of power are subject. The social contract is, according to Plato, first of all an act of the universal acknowledgement of particular principles and rules (*pactum unionis*) and subsequently an act of the sanctioning of its validity (*pactum subiectionis*) through the setting-up of a power that can embody, enforce, and protect these principles and rules—in other words, a *legislature*, an *executive*, and a *judiciary*.

The state of nature in human society that precedes the social contract has, in the course of history, been represented in different ways by different thinkers. For some it is a paradise-like state of innocence, freedom, and equality (Locke, Rousseau); for others, it is a kind of hell of the war of all against all (Hobbes). A third view is that it is a kind of purgatory of mingled human nature and society in which, by way of error and suffering, man's lower nature comes to acknowledge the demands of his higher nature (Plato, Grotius). Still others regard the state by no means as the result of social contract but only as the expression of human nature, and thus as being as old as human nature itself, so that even in the state of innocence there existed a social compact and subjection (Aristotle, Thomas Aquinas): "and this subjection would have existed even before sin";[9] "in a state of innocence, man would have been able to dominate man."[10]

The social contract itself has also been imagined variously. Some, like Grotius, conceived of it as an external historical

[9] *Summa Theol.*, I, qu. 92.
[10] Ibid., I, qu. 96.

event. Others, conversely, think of it as a theoretical construction or even as a postulate of reason (Rousseau, Kant). For the representatives of Scholasticism and Late Scholasticism, however, it was neither a real historical event that had once occurred, nor a purely subjective construction, but the perpetual and eternal relationship between reason and the natural drives in humankind—so that it can be thought of on one hand as a recurring event of state formations and reformations, but on the other as the constant relationship of natural law to positive law, and of positive law to the forces of lawlessness on the scene of human conscience. It is a matter, for these thinkers, merely of the dialogue between reason and the conscience, on one hand, and the forces of self-assertion and will on the other: between law and wilfulness, or between the legal order and sheer force.

Up until the rise of voluntarism, the whole Western tradition, whether Platonically oriented (built on the idea of justice) or Aristotelian (founded on the justice that indwells human nature) had as its shared essential feature the primacy of reason and natural law over the will and positive law. The obligations of natural law stood above both the ruler and his subjects. The state (and thus also the community of states) was agreed, that is, to be a *legal order*, an order that was not permitted to contradict the principles of reason and justice, irrespective of whether the state in question was a monarchy or a republic. *This view was now rejected by Hobbes*. His "natural law" is not justice, with its ideal and ethical content, but the claim of the human will to possess and enjoy all things. His "natural laws," of which he counts nineteen, are not norms derived from the ideal, the idea, and the concept of justice, but are instead laws of human action, acquired by means of observing and evaluating human nature. Hobbes rejects the *ought* of the norms of the traditional school of natural law. He replaces the *ought* with the *must* of the laws enforceable by means of state power. For this reason, the state is for him not a legal order served by the state power, but an order of force served by the law in force (positive law). His doctrine of the social contract is in the last analysis nothing but a justification and grounding of *absolutism*: the subjection of the nation to the state power, a subjection that is irrevocable once it has taken place. After this, the state power is *the* person of all the persons subordinate to it.

In Hobbes, the outcome of a development that spans centuries becomes clear. The revolt against the authority of the Church that began in the Renaissance and had been prepared for by the struggle of the emperor with the pope—a revolt in support of the freedom of opinion and inquiry—now led to the granting to the state of powers more extensive than any ever before imagined, even by the most fanatical adherent of the supremacy of the papacy in the Middle Ages. The head of state ought, according to Hobbes, simultaneously to possess a secular power greater than that possessed by any emperor of the Holy Roman Empire, *and*, as the supreme head of the Church in his country, a spiritual power that at least equaled that of the pope. The revolt against the spiritual authority of the Church produced as early as the seventeenth century, in the shape of Hobbes, the demand for an authority that would signify the greatest possible amount both of secular and of spiritual authority. As an idea, Hobbes's *Leviathan* is the new, or rather, the *other* Church. If the Church is (as believers imagine it to be) the mystical body of Christ, whose limbs and component parts are individual Christians, then the Leviathan (the absolute or totalitarian state), is a "great . . . artificiall Man," whose limbs and component parts are individual citizens. Hobbes laid at the feet of the absolute secular state authority the freedom from commitments that had been won for the Church through the Reformation. And what Hobbes had done as an individual in the seventeenth century was done by millions in the twentieth.

Of what significance for the history of the jurisprudence of international law are Hobbes's doctrine of the state and the doctrines of the "social contract" we have compared with it? For Hobbes, the state, the "artificiall Man," is the highest form of social organization on earth. Since, however, there are simultaneously several such artificial men or states, there pertains to them, according to Hobbes's line of thought, exactly what pertained to human beings in the pre-political state of nature—that is, in principle, a war of all against all.

Hobbes is so consistent in his doctrine of the state that it is not difficult—particularly since his doctrine concerning problems of international law proceeds from the principle that natural law consists of two parts (one of which concerns individuals, and the other the state)—to think further along the lines of thought he has so sharply delineated and to extend them beyond the borders of the individual state to the community of human states. In this connection, one cannot see in the so-called "community of states" anything other than a number of "artificiall men" or Leviathans, each in principle staking a claim to everything—i.e., to political, economic, and cultural world rule. And each these states, since they are prevented from achieving this by the other states staking the same claim, is in principle the enemy of all other states. From this, however, it follows that the weaker states—which, precisely because of their weakness, are not in a position to overpower the other states—are continually worried about protecting their existence against those states strong enough to overpower them. Thus there emerge alliances of states that always have the goal of defence against a threatened danger. The powerful states, by contrast, are either in a state of open war with each other, or they conclude briefer or more lasting truces ("peace treaties" between independent and lastingly independent states are always truces). They put off the decisive and final dispute in order to extend and strengthen the "spheres of influence" won at the cost of these truces, so that they may once again undertake uninterrupted war against their rivals, because they now consider themselves as having a viable prospect of ending the struggle in a way favorable to themselves. The whole process must—according to Hobbes's line of thought—lead in the end to a dispute between two great powers (that have already absorbed all the smaller states), a dispute that will last until one of them triumphs. At that point, the end of the war among states will have been reached, for the world becomes a single state—the great, the greatest, and all-embracing Leviathan.

The conquest of the world by a single state would be the final result of a war lasting for centuries. The other possibility of ending the war between states might consist in a situation in which states and governments, instructed by bitter experience, came to the view that loss of independence (or "absolute sovereignty") might be a lesser evil than an almost endless war that in the last analysis could only lead to the same result. So it might come about that a *pactum subiectionis* took place in the international arena, as it had already done in the formation of individual states. Since, then, the meaning and nature of force is *power*, such a "social contract between states" would (still according to Hobbes's line of thought) have to consist in all the sovereign states' subjecting themselves to a single most powerful state—without waiting for this state to conquer them. These conclusions follow with the greatest naturalness from Hobbes's presuppositions. Indeed, these conclusions were in fact drawn exactly as they are set out here—and that in short order. For the thesis that Moscow today [1952] champions and justifies in the world is precisely the thesis that world peace can and must be realized only through the world-rule of one state (or the dissemination through the world of a social "order" led by one state). The omnipotent state that has unlimited power over worldviews, science, art, education, health, life, all material goods and their production and distribution, is in the meantime the most perfectly realized Leviathan, which tries to destroy everything that stirs and lives outside it. Hitler's "new order" essentially meant the realization of the same idea by other means. Here it was a case of a "world-state of races," whereas Moscow wished to found a "world-state of classes"—the world-state of the proletariat, or of "Leviathan Man" *par excellence.*

Why, then, we may well ask, has Hobbes not officially and publicly been elevated to the ranks of the classics or of the most honored predecessors of the modern Marxist-Communist or National Socialist doctrines of the state and of the world order? Indeed, it is even conspicuous how little his work is mentioned. The great leaders, Hitler and Stalin, never referred to him in their speeches and writings. Perhaps another fact can help us answer this question. It is well known that Benito Mussolini highly prized Machiavelli's

The Prince, and always had it by him as a kind of vademecum. Nevertheless, he did not usually base his political and social views on quotations from Machiavelli's work. He preferred to cite anything else, rather than that book. He did, however, read Machiavelli—and acted accordingly.[11] Just as Machiavelli is not to be cited if one draws on him for stimulus and advice, so, today, Hobbes is not to be cited if one is a "believer in Leviathan." Even Hitler never referred to Nietzsche's *Antichrist*. But were not all his deeds and conduct replete with hatred and scorn towards those who were weak, vulnerable, humble, and willing to make sacrifices, and a glorification of everything strong, proud, and villainously heroic? Just this very hatred, this very scorn and glorification, are the spirit and the letter, the sense and the literal text, of Friedrich Nietzsche's *Antichrist*. Political leaders, and especially those of totalitarian states, have a sort of "esoteric doctrine," which is indeed not spoken of, but according to which they act. A corner of the bookcase also belongs to this "esoteric doctrine," a corner where stand books that are certainly read, but never mentioned.

In his already cited work *Die ewige Wiederkehr des Naturrechts* (101–4), Heinrich Rommen, gives a summary of Hobbes's doctrine, together with all its consequences for the state and for the community of states, that runs as follows:

> Hobbes's whole theory essentially comes down to a denial of natural law. He resembles a dark fellow-traveler of Epicurus, of joyful antiquity; he teaches that the state of nature is a wild and lawless situation of the war of all

---

[11] Mussolini did, however, state in his *Preludio al Macchiavelli* (1934) that Macchiavelli's teaching was more relevant then than it had been four centuries previously.

against all—that it is chaos. Here again is displayed the correspondence with epistemology and moral philosophy. For Hobbes the Ockhamist nominalist, reason is incapable of cognizing *universalia*, the Ideas. . . . The "war of all against all" is the reverse side of the *ius omnium in omnia* ["the right of all in all things"] that was taught with so much pathos . . . so that the natural law, despite everything, is exhausted in Hobbes's work in the phrase *pacta sunt servanda* ["agreements must be kept"] that is cited here and there. . . . In Hobbes's work, natural law thus, in a paradoxical fashion, becomes a *ius inutile* ["useless right"] squeezed into the sole legal form of the social contract, the contract of subjection. Natural law contains only the basic norm *pacta sunt servanda*, if one disregards the even more paradoxical natural law of the state of nature, with its norm of egotism. All else is pure will, the secularized theodicy of Ockham, the furthest extreme of the maxim "law is will."

John Locke. Now, if the application of Hobbes's doctrine to the field of the community of states—and thus to the field of international law—would have meant the coming into existence of a *treaty of subjection* between the weaker states and a supremely powerful great power, so that the latter would have become a world-state, then the doctrine of Hobbes's younger contemporary John Locke (1632–1704), if applied to the affairs of humankind, would have had the result of the coming into existence of a *treaty of union* (*pactum unionis*) of all states—that is, of a federal world state. For if Hobbes conceives of the social contract as an exclusive *pactum subiectionis*, Locke conceives of it precisely as a *pactum unionis*. According to Locke, the state originates, not in the subjection of wicked men—living in a war of all against all—to a single powerful (i.e., a particularly clever and strong) man or group of such men, but in an agreement between decent and rational men of good will, who join together in a community in order to preserve and to save, so far as is possible, a natural state of freedom and equality that is placed under threat by bad men. To illustrate this point, we include in Appendix D a series of citations from Locke's *The Second Treatise of Government*, chap. 2.

The significance Locke ascribes to *property*—whose inviolability, in certain cases, he sets even higher than that of life itself—is by no means an expression of materialism (understood as the prizing of material goods above everything else), or an expression of the "ideology of the rising middle class," as people who look at the world through the prism of the Marxist system, for example, would like to see it. Locke is an individualist; that is, he considers human personhood as an intrinsic value, which has nature and its creator to thank for its existence—but not the state, society, its kinship group, or even its function in the economic process of production. Man is by nature a free being, and he gives up a part of his freedom only for the reason, and to the extent, that this concession is necessary to protect and to secure his freedom. This protection and this security are provided precisely by the state, to which the individual transfers only so much of his freedom as is absolutely necessary in order to secure for himself, against encroachments, the greatest possible freedom. Property is both the most concrete form of this freedom and its bulwark. For just as the body is a piece of the world that provides the stage on which the free development of the life of the soul can take place, so, for Locke, property is another piece of the world that signifies the stage for the free development of the *whole* human being, of the life of the soul *and* of the body—that is, of *action*. Property is the realm of the human being's freedom in the external world. At the same time, it is, as it were, the projection, the extension of his or her body outwards. Property, however, as the secure and inviolable possession of material goods, is for Locke by no means identical in its significance with freedom, such that he could imagine freedom as the mere possibility of disposing, and the capacity to dispose, over material goods. Rather, property is merely the *most concrete* expression in the world of external facts of the same freedom that man possesses in his inner life.

In his text on toleration (*A Letter Concerning Toleration*), Locke set out his views on the inviolable right of human beings to freedom of conscience and understanding, and pointed out the duty, which follows from this right, to renounce all external means of coercion in the fields of knowledge, conscience, and faith—that is, the duty of tolerance. Human convictions are for Locke, as it were, an "inviolable property" of the spirit, while their external property "belongs" to human beings just as much as do the ideas, thoughts, and impulses of the life of the soul. Property—as the sphere of freedom—stretches from the most intimate impulses of the life of the soul right through to the external things of material fortune. Such external things are, however, a bulwark for the freedom of the person *per se*, because they represent, as it were, a protective wall around the body of the person. For its part, the body of the person (insofar as it is inviolable) protects the freedom of the life of the soul.

If the state, however, were to fail to acknowledge private

property, then a step would have been taken towards the destruction of freedom, a step along a path that, once taken, can in principle lead to further stages of the restriction of freedom. For if private property is no longer respected, why should the body of the human being be treated any differently? If the state can "expropriate" my house from me without compensation, why should it not also forcibly deploy my labor in the mines?

Locke's state, grounded on the *contract of union*, is in principle a *minimal state*, a state whose claim upon human freedom—that is, upon the freedom of property, body, and consciousness—is as small as possible, or *minimal*. Hobbes's state, conversely, the state grounded on the *contract of subjection*, is in principle a *maximal state*, a state whose claim upon the freedom of the individual human being (its claim, therefore, upon his property, his body, and his consciousness) is *maximal* in the highest degree. Thus, for Hobbes, religion is an affair to be regulated and governed by the state, because subjects have *wholly* surrendered their freedom, including the freedom of conscience. Hobbes's "Leviathan," the maximal state, makes individual human beings into its members—its organs—and leaves them only so much freedom as it does not need for its own ends. Locke's "commonwealth" of the minimal state is the common organ or organization of individual human beings, which places only so much of their freedom at its own disposal as is absolutely necessary to it in order to protect this same freedom.

⊕

How, then, can Locke's minimal state be capable of acting in a case where its citizens have differing and mutually opposed wishes and views? How can it be capable of acting, that is, if it wishes to remain faithful to its most essential principle, which is to respect the freedom of *all* its citizens? The answer Locke gives to this question is that the state can do so by means of the *will of the majority*, by the decision of the majority. The majority thus has the same power over the minority in Locke's minimal state as the ruler or the government has over everyone in Hobbes's maximal state. Not even natural law can actually provide an immediate and unconditional protection for the minority against the possible arbitrary will and rule of force on the part of the majority; this is because, according to Locke, natural law merely *instructs* human beings what to do and what not to do, whereas in Grotius, natural law "points out" what to do. Consequently, it is always possible that the majority may turn a deaf ear to the teachings of natural law, and may instead permit itself to be guided by personal, national, class-based, or other passions. In the domain of international law and the affairs of humankind (or "world politics"—a phrase that can hardly be freed any longer from the pejorative associations attaching to it), the principles of Locke's doctrine of the state would have led to the concrete consequences detailed below.

The states—in contrast to the members of each individual state community, the citizens—are still in a state of nature, i.e., in the state of freedom and equality (or, are "unlimitedly sovereign" and equally independent of each other), where there is no judge and no court above them and where each of them, depending on the case, can take on the role of judge or the role of criminal. Since there are now states that threaten such freedom with force and make its survival ever more questionable, the necessity arises (in order to preserve for these states as much as possible of the freedom of the state of nature) for the "decent" and peaceful states to unite by means of a treaty of union (*pactum unionis*) into a community of states, with the associated renunciation of (as small as possible) a part of their freedom, i.e., of their sovereignty and independence, to this community of states.

This community or federation of states would have the duty towards its members of conserving and protecting that degree of freedom and independence which remains to them after the transfer of that part of their freedom and independence which is necessary for the foundation of the federation of states. The community or federation of states would also have the rights connected with this duty. The decisions and actions of this federation of states would come about by majority decision. Thus, the voice of a small state, such as Luxembourg is today, would have the same weight on the scales of decision as the voice of a large state, such as the United States of America is today. The member states of the federation of states would have to bind themselves to obey the will of the majority, just as every citizen explicitly or implicitly binds himself to the will of his state community. This obligation would, however, sooner or later lead to a situation in which the minority would wonder whether they might not enjoy a greater degree of freedom if they were to separate from the federation of states and found a new federation of states, consisting of members of the outvoted oppositional minority (as happened, say, with the Confederacy of the southern states of the United States in the sixties of the nineteenth century). This second, new, federation of states would, however, with time (if it held fast to the principle of majority decision) get into the same situation: a discontented minority, tired of being

From International Law to World Peace

compelled by the majority, would again be formed, leave this new federation of states, and found yet a third federation of states, and so on, until, in the end, there were once again only individual states left—states that would thereby have returned to the "international state of nature" of unlimited self-rule.

In order to preserve the community or federation of states from an otherwise unavoidable disintegration, obedience to the will of the majority must, then, be enforceable. Any exit on the part of member states or of a group of them must be declared and recognized in advance to be impermissible; that is, in the very way in which the federation of states is constituted. This enforceability of the majority decision, together with the absence of any exit clause, would mean the same thing as the foundation of a *federal state* and not, any longer, a *federation of states*, which was indeed the actual result of the American war of secession between the Confederacy of southern states and the Union of the northern states—i.e., the absorption in principle of the formerly independent states into the creation of a new state within which the former states would become self-administering areas.

From the above considerations, we see that the *formal* final result both of Hobbes's theory of power and of Locke's majoritarian principles is the same. The real difference consists in practice only in the fact that, according to Hobbes's principles, the strongest state destroys all other states, whereas according to Locke's principles, a *new*, all-embracing state emerges from the combination of all the states, both weaker and stronger. Neither Locke's principle of the majority, nor Hobbes's principle of power, however, really has anything to do with the *principle of law*. For the *will* of the majority, like the *will* of the ruler or of the ruling group, has in principle nothing in common with *law* as such. The concept, the idea, and the ideal of law—corresponding with the tradition of realism, and in opposition to nominalism—can indeed be striven for and brought about by the will, but they can never be given their being nor their content by the will. The very fact of the choice of the word "law" [*Recht*] rather than, say, "what is desirable" or "the purpose," speaks to the fact that any purpose and any object desired can be "right" [*recht*] or "wrong" [*unrecht*]. Law stands above the will as its judge, but it is not created by the will.

Accordingly, the realists of Antiquity and the Middle Ages, of Late Scholasticism, of the Grotian School, as well as Leibniz and Wolff, thought of the state as a *legal* state, and of the community of states as a *legal* community, not because they are ruled by the *will* of the ruler (or the ruling group) or by the *will* of the majority, but because they are ruled over by *legality*. It is not a question either of a dictatorship of the *minority* or of a dictatorship of the *majority*, but (so to say) of a "dictatorship" of certain *immutable principles of law* that neither can nor may be shaken either by a majority or by a minority. In other words, it is a question of the legal order of the community of states, or of the community of states of legally organized humanity.

Here, however, it is a matter of the duties and rights of the community with respect to the individual, and of the individual with respect to the community, according to acknowledged, inviolable, and immutable principles of law. These principles express the governance of reason, justice, and humaneness, which applies to everyone, and is bind-

From International Law to World Peace

ing. They are also guaranteed, protected, and enforceable (i.e., "sanctioned") with all the means at either the community's or the individual's disposal. This in turn means nothing less than the replacement of the authority of the quantitative majority, or of the more powerfully qualified minority, with the authority of natural law—an authority independent of majority, minority, and individual alike. Natural law does not *derive* from the will, but rather *limits* and *directs* it.

What is meant here is a legal state, or an international legal order, whose basis is not the will of the legislator or of those to whom the laws are addressed, but natural law, which instructs this will and prescribes and proscribes to it. Or, as the *Decretum Gratiani* (c. 1140) says, it is a legal order in which "natural law in its dignity has absolute priority over custom and statute. Anything whatever that may be accepted custom or that is laid down in writing must be considered as null and void if it contradicts natural law."[12] And as the commentator on the *Decretum* then still more emphatically stresses, "It must be considered null and void because the Lord has said *I am the Truth*, not *I am Custom or Constitution*."[13]

Gottfried Leibniz. It was the primacy of natural law in international legal practice, in the form of, for example, a suprastate court of justice, that led Leibniz, a Protestant, to suggest an international court of appeal, to be presided over by

---

[12] *Decretum*, I.8.2.

[13] Quoted from A.P. D'Entrèves, *Natural Law: An Introduction to Legal Philosophy* (New Brunswick, NJ: Transaction Press, 1994), 38.

both pope and emperor.[14] Of this suggestion, a jurist of the Middle Temple, John Hosack, remarked as follows:

> By a sentence of excommunication, or by the still more dreaded process of interdict, the proudest thrones of Christendom might be shaken to their base. But powers of so extensive a kind, it is obvious, could only be exercised at a time when the head of the Church was an object of superstitious veneration. But such a state of things was wholly incompatible with the progress of knowledge and the dignity of independent states. It is therefore with surprise that we find the learned Leibniz proposing, even in the eighteenth century, the establishment of a tribunal of international appeal over which the pope and the emperor of Germany should jointly preside.[15]

The author of this history of international law "from the earliest times to the Treaty of Utrecht" would have been spared his surprise had he taken more trouble to think not only about "general usage" and the treaties of the period he was discussing, but also about the intellectual world of this century. For the "progress of knowledge" with which he believes Leibniz's efforts "even in the eighteenth century" to have been irreconcilable, has in the meantime led to theoretical and practical results according to which an international court of justice and even a kind of international executive power have been recognized not only as reconcilable with the "dignity of independent states," but even as essential to saving their independence. Those of us who live in the middle of the twentieth century are not at all sur-

---

[14] *Opera* IV, 330–31.

[15] John Hosack, *On The Rise and Growth of the Law of Nations, as established by General Usage and by Treaties, from the Earliest Time to the Treaty of Utrecht* (London: John Murray, 1882), 62.

prised by Leibniz's concern in the eighteenth for a court of justice superordinate to individual states, presided over by the representatives of the highest spiritual and secular authorities. We are, much rather, surprised by the ease with which scholars of the nineteenth century dismiss the past results of such clear thought, deep thoroughness, and high consciousness of responsibility, as if they were of lesser value. In reality, in the case of Leibniz (who was a contemporary of Hobbes and Locke) it was not a matter of a "superstitious veneration" of the "head of the Church" (a Church to which he did not in any case belong). Nor was it case of a *parti pris* in favor of the emperor, whom he never served, as against the princes, whom he actually did serve. Instead, it was a matter of the setting-up of a supra-state judicial power whose being and task would be to constitute a legal institution superordinate to the wills of the majority and minority, a guardian and protector of the *law as such*— i.e., of natural and divine law. Leibniz saw in such a supranational court of justice a practical solution to the problem (still just as relevant today) of the regulation of the relationship between politics and law in the international dealings of states. This was to be a solution of the problem that Locke expresses in the following way:

> Men living together according to reason, without a common superior on earth with authority to judge between them, is properly the state of nature. But force, or a declared design of force, upon the person of another, where there is no common superior on earth to appeal to for relief, is the state of war: and it is the want of such an appeal that gives a man the right of war even against an aggressor, though he be in society, and a fellow subject. Thus a thief, whom I cannot harm, but by appeal to the law, for having stolen all I am worth, I may kill, when he

sets on me to rob me but of my horse and coat; because the law, which was made for my preservation, where it cannot interpose to secure my life from present force, which, if lost, is capable of no reparation, permits me my own defence, and the right of war, a liberty to kill the aggressor, because the aggressor allows not time to appeal to our common judge.... §21. [109] To avoid this state of war (wherein there is no appeal but to Heaven, and wherein every the least difference is apt to end, where there is no authority to decide between the contenders) is one great reason of men's putting themselves into society, and quitting the state of nature: for where there is an authority, a power on earth, from which relief can be had by appeal, there the continuance of the state of war is excluded, and the controversy is decided by that power.[16]

Locke sees the possibility of world peace through the states' being subject to legal judgment—that is, by setting up a court authority superordinate to the states, whose composition and whose sanction he bases, however, on the *will of the majority*. With this, he fulfills the task of international law and solves the problem of the jurisprudence of international law, *if*, in the text quoted above, one replaces the words "man" and "I" with "state" and "my state." Hobbes, by contrast, sees the possibility of world peace in subjection to a single power that is equipped with a monopoly over judicial, executive, and legislative power. A third line of thought—as expressed, for example, by Leibniz's suggestion of an international court of justice presided over by the pope and the emperor—sees the solution of the problem in a supra-state judicial authority of natural law entrusted to persons who by virtue of their outlook on the world and

---

[16] Locke, *The Second Treatise*, 108–9.

their rank acknowledge natural law, and who are absolutely obligated to acknowledge it. The task of this authority would then consist, not in the preservation of *peace at any price*, for peace's sake, but in the preservation of a *just peace*, i.e., in the protection of the eternal principles of justice, beyond the realm of power relations, *including* expressions of the will of the majority or minority.

These three lines of thought surface towards the end of the seventeenth century with growing definiteness. It is these three lines of thought that have ever more powerfully influenced and marked out the political and legal intellectual life of humanity since that period. They are:

the tendency in which law is ever more identified with the will of the majority;

the tendency in which law is identified with the will of the current state power;

the tendency in which law is indeed a *norm* superordinate to the will, but in which it gradually threatens to fall victim to the subjectivism of personal opinion, since it wishes to be free from its connection to the superordinate divine will, and to become only an expression of "autonomous human reason."

Pufendorf's rationalist system of natural law, to which we next turn, is a stage on the path of the transformation of law with three levels (divine law, natural law, and positive law) into a law with two levels, in which autonomous human reason attains sole rule, and in which this reason smooths the way for the coming sole rule of positivism, a law that will henceforth have only one level, by allowing natural law as such to seem ever more merely "relative."

2

Samuel von Pufendorf and Christian Thomasius

Hugo Grotius, as the "Noah" of the jurisprudence of international law, had (to continue the biblical metaphor) three "sons." His work combined the traditional Scholastic approach, the rationalist natural law approach, and the positivist approach. But in the work of his successors, these approaches tended ever more to become independent currents.

Leibniz (1646–1716), the herald of the principle of continuity in science, and its champion in philosophy as a contributor to the preservation and progress of the *philosophia perennis*, brought together theologico-political, philosophico-juridical, and juridico-political thinking in Grotius's sense, and even to a greater degree than Grotius himself. Against Hobbes and Pufendorf, he asserted the reality of the society of states as a field for the operation of a law with three levels. At the same time, however, he also wrote one of the foundational works in the codification of international positive law, his *Codex Juris Gentium Diplomaticus* (1693–1700). Meanwhile, Pufendorf (1632–1697) championed the rationalist, natural-law side of Grotius's work, while Bynkershoek (1673–1743) dedicated his juridically-trained intellect exclusively to the practice of international law, from whose factual material he drew conclusions about matters of principle, instead of concerning himself with shaping practice in international law according to general principles. Three schools of the jurisprudence of international law thus followed Grotius: (1) The school of "naturalists" or of rationalist natural law, represented by Pufendorf, Thomasius, Rutherford, and Barbeyrac; (2) the school of "positivists" or of positive law, which ascribes primacy to the law actually in force, and to practice; and (3) the school of the "Grotians" or "eclectics," which championed a natural law that demanded the development of scholarly research on positive law. Leibniz's pupil Christian Wolff (1679–1754), and Wolff's pupil Emer de Vattel (1714–1767) were the most significant representatives of this latter school.

These three schools, however, had one thing in common. They all depended upon Grotius's work. This fact meant, in the first instance, that they owed both their origin and their continued existence to the pure and direct formulation of the problem in the jurisprudence of international law; whereas the international-legal influences on following generations of international lawyers, such as Locke and Hobbes, came via the indirect route of projections made from the basis of political philosophy and legal-political thought. Montesquieu and Rousseau, as "sons" of Locke, certainly had an influence on thinkers who were wrestling with the problems of international law, but this influence came via the translation of their views on political philosophy and state law into the realm of the theory and practice of international law, by way of analogy. The three "sons" of Grotius—the "Noah" of the theory of international law—however, remained *his* sons. The *immediate* problems of international law (i.e., the *questions concerning the law of humankind*), were and remained at the center of their thinking. Their having taken separate directions can be understood through that proposition which Grotius himself understood as laying the basis for scholarly work in international law:

> If many people in different times and in different places have held the same thing to be certain, this must be traced back to a universal cause. In respect of the question being discussed here, this cause can only be either a correct conclusion drawn from the principles of nature itself, or a universal consensus. The first cause shows us what natural law is, while the second shows us what international law is.[1]

Grotius makes use of two methods simultaneously: the Scholastic method of deduction from the founding propositions of revelation and reason, on one hand, and, on the other, the "empirical" method of drawing general propositions from experience, i.e., from the historically transmitted or currently present factual material of international law. He thus deduces international law from two sources, that of natural law as the essential revelation of human reason, and that of universal custom in the dealings between the states of civilized humanity. For this reason, he emboldens his successors (who incline more to one-sidedness) to give themselves over exclusively either to the speculations of pure reason or to the systematic reworking of the factual material of dealings in international law. Champions both of the rationalist natural law school and of legal positivism in the jurisprudence of international law see Grotius, in some respects rightly, as the founder of the jurisprudence of international law itself with respect to international law's particular methods and direction.

---

[1] *De Jure Belli ac Pacis*, prologue, xli.

From International Law to World Peace

Unfortunately, it often happens that what is at first a conscious and purposive self-limitation to *one* particular method becomes later on a narrowness—an habituation to an exclusive method; subsequently, it becomes a denial, and even a contestation of all other methods and views. The "legal positivists" of the end of the seventeenth and eighteenth centuries, such as G. F. von Martens (towards the end of the eighteenth century), did not deny that natural law was the source of "just law," but simply did not concern themselves with it, Instead, they devoted their forces and their time to discovering and getting to know the factual field of international legal practice, as well as to critically reworking, systematizing, and codifying it. Nor, for their part, did the champions of the natural law school deny the usefulness of experience in the law actually in force, and of systematically reworking it.

Only later did it gradually come about that the "natural lawyer" began to look on the "positivist" as if he were a mere artisan and technician, and the "positivist" began to look upon the "natural lawyer" as a sort of dogmatist and daydreamer. Still later, however, in the second half of the nineteenth century, the *positivist* method, oriented towards facts, became scientific method as such, and the *speculative* method, oriented towards natural law, became in the generally prevailing view a non-method. Indeed, natural law itself, as well as individual views about it, were scorned and banished from intellectual discussion. The positivist method of working turned gradually into the dogmas of positivism, and jurisprudence became "jurisprudence without justice," as Leonard Nelson described it. This development is summarized in the words of warning that conclude Nelson's work:

Samuel von Pufendorf and Christian Thomasius

Only through a sincere return to the concept of law, and thus to an honest metaphysics of law—which means to a theory of law grounded in a renewed critique of practical reason—can it be hoped to banish from science those unclean spirits that have taken control of the jurisprudence of our time, and thus to guide the theory of law back to scientifically sound paths, as well as to those paths that are fruitful for the highest practical purposes of life.[2]

In this process, a conscious *ignoring* that is grounded in method becomes actual *ignorance*. As a consequence of neglect and disuse, what was originally consciously ignored disappears gradually into the distance, becoming ever more "foreign," and at last vanishing from consciousness's field of vision altogether—to be "forgotten" by both head and heart. In the area of the jurisprudence of international law, the process began with an effort to "de-theologize" legal scholarship, that is, to free it from elements of the Catholic tradition of Scholasticism. Such de-theologization was followed by "de-metaphysicalization," that is, by attempts to "cleanse" jurisprudence of elements of metaphysical philosophy. The effort that followed this consisted of a "de-legalization" of jurisprudence, of an attempt, that is, to expel the concept of a law just-in-itself (in the sense of the Latin saying *jus quia justum*), and indeed the very idea of "correct law," from the realm of scholarship—and to replace it with "purpose," "utility," an "index of the social situation," or

---

[2] Leonard Nelson, *Die Rechtswissenschaft ohne Recht: kritische Betrachtungen über die Grundlagen des Staats- und Völkerrechts, insbesondere über die Lehre von der Souveranität* [Jurisprudence without law: critical reflections on the foundations of state and international law, especially on the doctrine of sovereignty] (second ed., Göttingen and Hamburg, 1947), 207.

even simply "imperative of power" (in the sense of the Latin saying *jus quia jussum*). At each of these stages of scientistic "cleansing" of jurisprudence, it was believed that it had thereby been rendered "more realistic" and "more objective," and that its "progress" had thus been furthered. Yet, for jurisprudence as a normative science (an "ought-science"), the "progress" from a law with three levels (the concord of divine law, natural law, and positive law), and from a law with two levels, to a "law" with only one level (i.e., to the fact of the validity of mere particular prescriptions and proscriptions), is in reality a process of atrophy and dying away. It is a process in which ideals disappear, ideas become ever more paltry, and even the concepts shrivel to mere verbal descriptors for relations between facts. The final result of this process is a technical apparatus of interpretation and construction that can be turned to face in any direction, and is fitted only to serve political and other power interests (which it accomplishes by providing them with the interpretations and constructions they desire).

Samuel von Pufendorf was a jurist who sought to free jurisprudence from its theological foundations and also from its historical foundations in humanism, and who wished it to rest exclusively on the laws of human reason and on the nature of things. As the first professor of natural law and international law (*juris naturalis et gentium*) in Heidelberg, he wrote, in the preface to his work *De Jure Naturae et Gentium* (1672), as follows:

> Indeed, it has been believed not unjustly that first place has thus far been held by Hugo Grotius, who was apparently the first to call his generation to the consideration of that study, and was also so grounded in it, that in a large

part of the field he has left all others nothing further than the task of gleaning after him. But, however much we cherish the fame of that man, so much so that we have been accorded the special designation of his "son," it must after all be acknowledged that he has entirely omitted a few matters, has accorded some but a passing touch, and has introduced certain other matters which prove that after all he was only a man. . . . Certain learned men have, indeed, essayed to remedy these defects by editing the books of his *De Jure Belli ac Pacis* with notes, and one or two of these commentators have rendered a service not to be scorned. Yet others have felt that it would be far more useful to lay all that material a second time on the anvil and reshape it into a different form.[3]

It was precisely this "reshaping" that Pufendorf undertook. In what, then, does it consist? First of all, in altering Grotius's method by no longer using humanist historical testimony (for example from antiquity) as primary sources, but offering them henceforth merely as supporting statements for the theses of reason. Second, in ignoring all the results of the work by jurists from the Catholic tradition of his own time—jurists of whose work Grotius had made extensive use, and thus breaking the tradition that was used to handle the problem.

> That I have not detracted from the honor due to antiquity is clear from the way in which on every occasion I prefer to cite ancient authors to witness to my theses. To add to them by calling in a cloud of more recent writers seemed superfluous. The reason why, especially, I have excluded

---

[3] Samuel Pufendorf, *De Jure Naturae et Gentium Libri Octo*, ed. and trans. C.H. Oldfather and W.A. Oldfather (2 vols, Oxford: Clarendon Press, 1934), 2:v–vi.

from my work those writers who, among the followers of the Roman sect, have undertaken to direct to their liking the customs and consciences of men, and whom even Grotius and others like to call to their side in such great numbers, will be patent, I fancy, to all men of judgment. It is this: Those men as a general thing lay down no fixed foundation or hypothesis for their traditions, but, in addition to what they habitually borrow from the Juris-consults, just as they are content for the most part to establish idle connections with equally idle and trivial logic-chopping, and in general hold it a great accomplishment to have adduced whole legions of writers of their sect (to know one of whom is to know them all), so they all devote futile labor to utter trifles, with the result, however, that there is scarcely any question on which they do not break up into factions. The hidden reason for this condition is that, inasmuch as it is one of the pillars of their sacred Commonwealth for the consciences of men to be directed, not by reason, but by the authority of priests, these should always have ready at hand a cloud of authorities capable of supporting any view whatsoever, according as it is to their interest for any man to be persuaded. And therefore we feel that they deserve very ill of the commonweal, who, in the full brilliance of the solid sciences, still strive to guide the youth to such persistent follies, which are the offspring as well as the mainstay of the kingdom of darkness. Nay, they make poor use of their time, yoke foxes to the plough and milk he-goats, who put themselves out to list their views on one side or the other and to reconcile them with sound reason.[4]

Pufendorf thus declares almost all the intellectual work that had been done between the time of the "jurisconsults" (the Roman teachers of law) and Hugo Grotius to have been

---

[4] Pufendorf, *De Jure Naturae et Gentium*, 2: viii–ix.

useless. He also "reshapes" Grotius's work, on the one hand, by "cleansing" it of the Catholic and theological elements of the "Roman sect," and on the other, by "correcting" its numerous divergences from the "accepted teachings of the orthodox Church," that is, deviations from the teachings of Lutheranism.[5] This is a standpoint he also takes up with regard to Hobbes, of whom he says:

> even where he goes astray, he still causes a man to think about matters, which, in all probability, would otherwise never have occurred to him. And yet, by virtue of the abominable theories that he has elaborated in the field of religion, and that are peculiar to himself, he has turned many against him, and this not without reason, although you may see it happen often enough that he is censured with the greatest scorn by those who have read and understood him the least.[6]

In short, Pufendorf reproaches Grotius with having made a pact with the "Roman sect," and Hobbes with having founded a sect of his own.

How, then, is Pufendorf's claim to apply the method of pure reason—because, as he says, "I have found no other principle that all men could be brought to admit without violation of their natural condition and with due respect to whatever view they might hold on matters of religion"[7]—to be made consistent with the importation of Lutheran theological views into the realm of jurisprudence; with the ignoring, denial, and contestation of Catholic theological views; and with other views that differ from Lutheran ones?

---

[5] Ibid., 2:vi.
[6] Ibid.
[7] Ibid., 2: ix, 1.

From International Law to World Peace

⊕

Each of the three fundamental modes of observation that are open to thought and knowledge as such, as they have been revealed over the millennia in the intellectual history of the West (but also of the East, as in, for example, India)—the "theocentric," "anthropocentric," and "naturalistic" or "physiocentric" approach to the search for knowledge—find full expression in the domain of jurisprudence.

The framing of the questions, research methods, and knowledge resulting from Scholasticism and Iberian Post-Scholasticism (or Spanish Late Scholasticism), were thoroughly "theocentric." Their proponents started out from God and from the cosmic *ordo rerum* ("order of things") that revealed Him—that is, from the divine world-order. In the light of what they knew, or thought they knew, from supernatural revelation as it is set out in Holy Scripture, from natural revelation as it is proclaimed in the order and lawfulness of the world, and from the light of reason that shines within mankind, they then discussed particular questions. They considered these questions solved when they had succeeded in integrating their topics with what was universal, so that no conflict remained with the truths of salvation and of Holy Scripture, nor with reason or with the rational order of the world. They held to the basic proposition that "the enigmatic character of a thing resides in its not having been related to God." For this reason, law was for them a problem only insofar as it stood in need of being *related to God*. This relatedness was seen precisely in the fact that law was regarded as a graduated connection between God and man. *In* God, law prevailed as divine law; *in* human beings, law was present as natural law; and *from* human beings, law was projected out into the social order as positive law. In this "theocentric" approach—a way of proceeding related to God—theology naturally played the leading role, since theology's topic was at the same time the realm in which the final answer to all questions, and the solution to all enigmas, was to be found.

Anthropocentric approach. The attempt to "de-theologize" philosophy and jurisprudence is the distinguishing feature of the transition from a theocentric to an anthropocentric viewpoint. The latter consists in no longer finding the solution to the riddles and the answer to the questions in *God*— and thus no longer either in Holy Scripture or in the world as a work of creation, i.e., as God's "Scripture"—but in *human beings*. Henceforth, the basic principle is that the enigmatic character of a thing resides in its not having been *related to human beings*. "Things in themselves" are enigmatic; even their existence is questionable. But once they are "humanized"—that is, once they can be brought into relationship with the forms of thinking and intuition innate to the human power of understanding—they become components of "necessary and universal" cognitions. The necessity of these cognitions is owed, not to the essential character of the things themselves, or to their order of being, but to the essential character of the *human being*, of his forms of thought and intuition. The universality of these cognitions is owed, then, not to the universality of the world order, but to the shared nature of the categorical structure of the human power of understanding. The *knowing* human being (the human being endowed with pure reason) and the *ethical* human being (the human being endowed with practical reason) become the measure of all things.

Theological approach. For a scholar taking the anthropocentric approach, law is the form and the categorical framework of *human reason*. A scholar with a theocentric approach acknowledges that there is in man an "image and likeness of God" that was not wholly destroyed by the Fall. He could thus rest entirely satisfied with the "anthropocentric" approach to law *if* he could be certain that "practical reason," for example, really does express only the *likeness* of God in man, and that "pure reason" really does reveal only the *image* of God in man: for egoism, which is the very meaning of the Fall, has become almost a "category"; as has also "the arrogant attempt to become like gods by means of knowledge." Until he is certain of these things, however, he will be of the view that the divine law contained in revelation must *complement* the law of reason by providing a criterion for how much of the postulates of practical reason is to be derived from the categorial structure of the "image and likeness of God," and how much is to be derived from the structure of the human being fallen into sin—a structure that has become just as "categorial" (as in, for example, the "will to power"). Until the ideal of the New Jerusalem is realized ("there shall be no night there; and they need no candle, neither light of the sun; for the Lord God giveth them light" Rev. 22:5), and until the ideal of the complete ethical and cognitive autonomy of human beings is realized, the proponents of the theocentric law with its three levels will maintain that the revelation of divine law remains necessary as touchstone and lodestar.

Naturalistic approach. The third, naturalistic, point of view is reached when scholars object both to the "subjectivism" of the anthropocentric standpoint, and to speculations drawn on the basis of the defective factual assertions (defective as concerns worldly knowledge) of theocentrism, and thenceforth seek the solution of the riddles and the answer to the questions in the extra-human and "objective" facts of the outer world. Here the basic proposition is that the enigmatic character of a thing resides in its not having been *related to other things*. The particularity of a phenomenon is the problem. Finding causal and other connections between this phenomenon and other phenomena is the solution to that problem.

In the domain of law, this point of view means renouncing *any* metaphysic, and thus the *idea* of law itself (whether in a theocentric or in an anthropocentric sense), and restricting oneself to the *phenomena* of the law in force in an attempt to demonstrate the existence of an order of causal, historical, social, political, and other connections that *results from these phenomena themselves*.

Theocentrism is to be regarded, in connection with the cognitive tendencies revealed in the medieval quarrel over the *universalia*, as resolutely realist, whether as extreme realist (*universalia ante res*) or moderate realist (*universalia in rebus*). Anthropocentrism is to be regarded as nominalist, either in the form of a moderate nominalism or conceptualism (William of Ockham: *universale signum et terminus*) or in the form of an extreme nominalism (*universale mere flatus vocis*). Naturalism, for its part, is to be regarded as an expression of resolute nominalism in thinking.

The transition from the theological approach to the anthropocentric approach is thus at the same time a transition from realism to nominalism; and the distinctive attempt on the part of the anthropocentric approach to "detheologize" philosophy and law is at bottom nothing other than an expression of the turn away from realism. Whether this turn away from realism concerns "Scholasticism" or "dogmatic metaphysics" is of only secondary importance. The transition from realism to nominalism also entails a renunciation of the attempt to cognitively penetrate particular domains of being and normativity. For the human power of understanding, then, the "intelligible world" of the "absolute truths and values" of the past is henceforth an empty, dark, and silent realm. For the *anthropocentric approach*, that realm is stuffed full of and plastered over with the dogmatic assertions of the "uncritical" spirits of the past. For this approach, what is given to human beings is solely man himself, as a sort of "piece" of being, and so one should stick to knowing from the human standpoint—and surely not seek for answers that *cannot be given* by human reason! Moreover, one should take whatever is unavoidably at work in the world, but inaccessible to the human will to knowledge (which makes use of human reason), simply as the decree of a higher power, and obey it! This, roughly, is how one can imagine the inner process of the transition from realism, where *is* and *ought* are one, to a moderate nominalism, where *is* and *ought* separate into two different domains: the domain of human reason and that of the will.

What happens in this process is the shrinking of the domain of the knowable, while what lies outside the knowable (i.e., the "unknowable") is consigned to the will. Here we have the first attempt to distinguish the faculties of pure and practical will in Kant's sense. Now, the domain consigned to the will is of the greatest practical importance, for it embraces everything that lies outside human reason. And so, this part of being must be taken into account. A conscious, rational approach must be taken towards it. One way to solve this problem would be to elevate those contin-

Samuel von Pufendorf and Christian Thomasius

uous and universal requirements of the human will that do not conflict with reason to the status of "postulates" of practical reason. Another way to solve it would be to hand over the work of formulating the propositions of the "sphere of faith" to other people, or to a vocational body (e.g., the Church), rather than doing it oneself.

The first way of solving this problem was taken by Kant, the second by Pufendorf. The role that "practical reason" plays in Kant's work (by "postulating" God, the soul, and immortality) was played in Pufendorf's work by the Lutheran church. For the Lutheran church, which also championed belief in God, the soul, and immortality, did so *without claiming* any ability rationally to ground that belief (thus without, for example, the *quinque viae*, the five proofs of God given by St Thomas Aquinas). The Lutheran church made it possible to draw a sharp line between "knowledge" and "faith," between reason and will, and thus to free reason from theological connections that were becoming ever more burdensome, and give back to the will "the original, unspoiled purity of childlike faith." The Lutheran church of the end of the seventeenth century was the home for people "whose understanding was free from faith and whose heart wished to believe," of whom Pufendorf was one. It represented a line of development that came to full flower in Kant.

Pufendorf thus "de-theologizes" the realm of reason, yet at the same time banishes the elements of reason from the realm of religion, which realm he leaves wholly to human and divine will. Justice and injustice, good and evil, are not such because they are thus in themselves and are revealed to reason's insight, but because they correspond to, or contradict, the decree of a superordinate will. The good is good because God *willed* it so. The true is true because it corresponds to the essential nature of man. And this nature, for its part, is as it is because God has willed it so. Pufendorf further develops his line of thought as follows.

> Now, in order that this knowledge of natural law with which we are now concerned, and which includes all moral and civil knowledge that is genuine and solid, may meet the full requirements of a science, we feel that we need not declare, with certain writers, that some things are noble or base of themselves without any imposition, and that these form the object of natural and perpetual law, while those, the good repute or baseness of which depends upon the will of a legislator, fall under the head of positive laws. For since good repute or moral necessity, and turpitude, are affections of human actions arising from their conformity or non-conformity to some norm or law, and since law is the bidding of a superior, it does not appear that good repute or turpitude can be conceived to exist before law and without the imposition of a superior. According to Selden: "The distinction in acts between good and bad, or base and reputable, is produced by law. Thence arises among persons obligation and indebtedness toward the performance of a duty."[8] And indeed, they who set up an eternal rule for the morality of human actions, beyond the imposition of God, seem to me to do nothing other than to join to God some co-eternal extrinsic principle that He Himself had to follow in the assignment of forms of things [at the moment of creation]. Furthermore, everyone must admit that God created all things, man included, of his free will. It must follow, then, that it lay within His own pleasure to assign whatever nature He wished to this creature whom He was about to create. How, then, can an

---

[8] *De Jure Naturali et Gentium,* bk. I, chap. iv.

Samuel von Pufendorf and Christian Thomasius

action of man be accorded any quality if it takes its rise from an extrinsic and absolute necessity, without the imposition and pleasure of God? [...] it does not follow . . . that any morality can exist of itself, without any law, in its own motion and [28] the application of physical power. [...] [30] The reason why many men cannot understand such an indifference in actions, is because from childhood on we have been imbued with a hatred of such vices; and this hatred, impressed on a mind still simple, appears to have grown to the strength of a moral judgment, the result being that few have thought of distinguishing between the material and formal in such actions. Hence it is patent that Grotius, *On the Law of War and Peace*, bk. I, chap. i, §10, had not considered this matter thoroughly when he refers the wickedness of some human actions to the class of things to which the power of God Himself does not extend because they involve a contradiction. Twice two, indeed, can only be four because twice two and four are one and the same thing, differing only in the name and in the point of view. It is, however, a contradiction for something simultaneously to be and not to be the same thing. But surely, such a contradiction does not appear in the case of actions that are opposed to natural law. For the same reason, Grotius shortly thereafter undertakes to derive this wickedness from a comparison with *nature when following sound reason*. And yet, in the words *sound reason*, as attributed to man, there is involved a reference to the law of society as given to man by the Creator. Again, in §12, he says that the absolute existence of any natural law is tested by its necessary agreement or nonagreement with *rational and social nature*. And yet man received this social nature not from any necessity, but from the pleasure of God.[9]

---

[9] Pufendorf, *De Jure Naturae et Gentium*, 1:27–30.

From International Law to World Peace

⊕

According to Pufendorf, then, the foundation of ethical life and law is not to be sought in the roots of human reason, but rather in God's *will*. The thesis of St Thomas Aquinas, which governs the thinking of the teachers of his School—the thesis of the *analogia entis*, the analogy of being—is henceforth rejected. This rejection, however, means at the same time the denial both of the knowability of a being superordinate to man, and also of the primacy of reason over the will, a primacy that follows from the analogy of man's having been created in the "image and likeness" of God. For Pufendorf, there is no *lex aeterna* (no eternal law) as the principle of the metaphysical and substantial necessity of God's wisdom, which reveals itself with the human being as "natural law."[10] The place of the "eternal law," of reason and necessity, is now taken by what God "prefers" or "deems good." With this, the essential content of the grounding of ethical life and law falls away. The actions of the human being are *in themselves* neither good nor evil, neither just nor unjust, because there no longer is *in itself* any good or evil, any justice or injustice; there is only God's command, which makes these actions into good or evil ones, just or unjust ones, insofar as they correspond to this command or contradict it. "Good" is that which God bids

---

[10] That is, in the sense of 8:22–35 of Wisdom's speech in the Book of Proverbs: "The Lord possessed me in the beginning of his way, before his works of old. I was set up from everlasting, from the beginning, or ever the earth was. . . . When he prepared the heavens, I was there: when he set a compass upon the face of the depth . . . then I was by him, as one brought up with him." (In the translation quoted by Tomberg, Wisdom says *da war ich bei Ihm und ordnete alles*—"then I was with him, and gave order to everything." TR) See also Baruch 3:9–38.

us do; "evil" is what he forbids. It is impossible for human beings to make "moral judgments" of their own: they merely *appear* to be their own as a consequence of hatred of things held to be "reprehensible," a hatred accumulated in the consciousness from the past through education and through external influences—or, as would be said today, in the unconscious.

There is however for Pufendorf a natural law, not indeed as the intervention of an eternal law or of the wisdom of God within the inner lives of human beings, but as the *predisposition* of human nature that corresponds to the will of God. Human nature is formed "as clay is formed by the potter," so that things *willed* by the Creator appear to human beings to be nothing but "rational," i.e., inwardly necessary. In Pufendorf's sense, then, natural law is a "human nature predisposed to community" (*socialitas hominis*), which is at the same time *reason* (i.e., appears to be rationality). It is not reason governing the world, however, but (so to say) subjective human reason, with its categories and postulates.

According to this view, the source of natural law—which is common to all human beings and thus also the source of international law as a law of humankind[11]—is man. The

---

[11] Pufendorf is also regarded as founder of the "natural law school" in that he denies the existence of international law, of a *jus gentium voluntarium*, as a special area alongside natural law. For him, natural law and international law are one and the same. In this he starts out from Hobbes's proposition that natural law consists of a natural law of persons and a natural law of states (Hobbes, *De Cive*, XIV, 4), and that the *latter* is international law (Pufendorf, *De Jure Naturae et Gentium*, II. 3., §22). Pufendorf's standpoint is that there can be no positive international law that has the obligating force of actual law (*quod quidem legis proprie dictae vim habeat, qua gentes tamquam a superiore profecta stringat*).

"theocentric" conception of natural law is abandoned by Pufendorf and left to the "Roman sects," whose proponents are best ignored. In its place comes the "anthropocentric" conception of natural law as *the* natural law.

"I have felt it fitting also to point out that I have made the basis of all natural law *the social life of man*, because I have found no other principle that all men could be brought to admit without violation of their natural condition, and with due respect to whatever belief they might hold on matters of religion," explains Pufendorf in the introduction to *De Jure Naturae et Gentium*.[12] Thus, for Pufendorf, the laws of human social life are in accordance with God's commandments, insofar as they correspond (by way of a detour through the social nature of human beings) to a human nature that has been formed for sociality at God's command. These laws are valid for all human beings, irrespective of their religious or other commitments, and thus represent a *jus gentium*, an international law as a law of humankind. Since natural law, which is at the same time international law (*jus nature et gentium*), consists of God's commands (which are revealed and take effect by way of a detour through human social nature), it cannot owe its origins to any sort of social contract—that is, either to a *pactum unionis* or to a *pactum subjectionis*. The natural law also came into force, independently of any contract, at the same time as human nature itself. Human social life is thus also not the result of a contract,[13] but results instead from the

---

[12] I, ix.

[13] Even if Pufendorf, in his political text "On the constitution of the German empire" (written under the pseudonym of "Severinus von Monzambano" and edited by H. Bresslau in the *Klassikern der Politik*

Samuel von Pufendorf and Christian Thomasius

the social nature of human beings, which nature, for its part, is as it were the imprint of the seal of God's command.

The state, as a form of human social life, is the result and expression of the relationship between commandment and obedience—not as an arbitrary commandment, but as the expression of a rational human nature oriented towards social life. The theory of "enlightened absolutism,"[14] as it is found in the second half of the seventeenth century, in the eighteenth century, and in the nineteenth century (until the dissolution of the Holy Alliance), is a consequence of Pufendorf's basic views, and was also put forward by Pufendorf himself. A "Holy Alliance" encompassing the whole world was the form in which an order of world-law or world-peace was to be realized, an order corresponding to the natural-legal and political-legal views of Pufendorf. This

---

[Classics of Political Thought], vol. 3, 1922), does speak of a contract for rule that consists of two contracts (the social contract and a contract that determines the form of government) and of a decree, these contracts represent, as it were, a "juridical construction" that sets out the relationship between command and obedience in the sense of mutual obligations (that is, in the sense of *socialitas* as such). This relationship rests on the *socialitas* of human nature, with the fourfold root of self-love, dependency, the inclination to give aid and to protect from harm, and the balance of these inclinations. What matters, in this interpretation, is that the citizens swear obedience and the king is obliged to take care of the state.

[14] According to Pufendorf, sovereignty is the highest power of the state, but not an absolute power: it can be restricted by the constitution. What we have here is, precisely, an *enlightened* absolutism, in which "being enlightened" can limit the arbitrary will *even* in the form of a constitutional arrangement. However, this constitutional limitation is not intended as a rule; it is merely acknowledged as being permissible. (*De Jure Naturae et Gentium*, VII. 6, §§ 13 ff)

was not a matter of a world-ruler with unlimited powers, of a majority-ruled world-parliament, or of a world-court equipped with the means to enforce its judgments, but of an "aristocratic" council of heads of state, of which each thus represented the God-willed "social nature" of humankind and expressed this nature in such a way as to enjoy the trust of his nation and thus to be able to judge and act in its name. An aristocratic world-constitution was the form of the practical realization of Pufendorf's principles in the domain of international law, i.e., in the human sphere.

In actual fact, Pufendorf's method of treating the problems of international law and the main problem of the jurisprudence of international law (the problem of war and peace) differs very little from that of his predecessors, especially from that of Hugo Grotius. Thus in chapter 6, "On the Law of War" we read:

> Since individuals who live in natural liberty have no less power accorded them than states to defend themselves against an unjust threat of violence, and to have recourse to force in maintaining their rights . . . I feel that it would be fitting to examine first, what the wars of individuals and states have in common, and secondly, what belongs in a special way to the later by their nature, or by the customs of nations.
>
> Now it is one of the first principles of natural law that no one unjustly cause hurt or do another damage, as well as that men should perform for each other the duties of humanity, and show especial zeal to fulfill the matters upon which they have entered into particular agreements. When men observe these duties in their relations one with another, it is called peace, which is a state most highly agreeable to human nature and fitted to preserve it, the creation and preservation of which constitutes one of the

chief reasons for the law of nature being placed in the hearts of men. (See also Polybius, bk. XII, chap. xiv) Nay, peace is a state especially reserved to human nature as such, since it springs from a principle that belongs to man as distinct from animals, while war arises from a principle common to them both. Of course [1293], even animals depend upon a natural instinct to defend and preserve themselves by force, but man alone understands the genius of peace. For it is characteristic of him voluntarily to do something for another, and to refrain from injury, by reason of a certain obligation residing in one, and of a certain right residing in another person, all of which is unintelligible without the use of reason. Of course, domestic animals perform services for their masters, but that is due to a fear of blows, or an expectation of food, and not to any obligation, which, indeed, is beyond their powers to comprehend. Animals also refrain from doing harm to men and to other animals, but that is due to weakness, or to the fact that they find nothing in them to whet their appetite. Finally, there are some that show affection for one another or render mutual assistance, but that does not mean they understand they are obligated to act in that way. . . .

[1294] The causes of just wars may be reduced to the following heads: To preserve and protect ourselves and our possessions against others who attempt to injure us, or take from us or destroy what we have; to assert our claim to whatever others may owe us by a perfect right, when they refuse to perform it for us of their own accord; and, finally, to obtain reparation for losses that we have suffered by injuries, and to extort from him who did the injury guarantees that he will not so offend in the future. As a result of these causes we have the division of just wars into offensive and defensive, of which we consider the latter to be those in which we defend and strive to retain what is ours, the former those by which we extort debts which are denied us, or undertake to recover what has been unjustly taken from us, and to seek guarantees for the future. Although sometimes the credit for defence stands with him who is the first to take up arms against another, if, for instance, a man has been troubled time and again with sudden border raids, the enemy always retiring on his approach, or if by a swift movement he overcomes an enemy who is already bent upon attacking him. . . .

But in general, the causes of wars, and of offensive wars in particular, should be clear and leave no chance for doubt. [...] [1295] Therefore, in the matter before us, neither should we rashly advance any vague claim, nor, on the other hand, fly at once to arms; but we should by all means try one of three courses in order to prevent the affair from breaking out into open war—to wit, either a conference between the parties concerned or their representatives; or an appeal to arbitrators; or, finally, the use of the lot. [...]

The unjust causes for wars are reviewed by Grotius, bk. II, [...] [1297] On the other pretexts [for war] adduced by Grotius in the passage cited above, we must reach the same conclusion. Thus we cannot agree with Bacon of Verulam in *The Advancement of Learning*, when he holds that sufficient cause for waging war upon the Americans can be found in the fact that they can be held condemned by the very law of nature, because it is their custom to sacrifice men and eat human flesh. On this matter we should carefully consider whether a Christian prince can attack the natives, as men condemned by nature, merely because they eat human flesh like any other food, or because they eat that of strangers. And in connection with their treatment of strangers, we must again inquire whether those foreigners come to their shores as enemies and robbers, or come as innocent guests, or driven by storms. For only in the last

Samuel von Pufendorf and Christian Thomasius

case does a right of war lie with those whose citizens are treated with such cruelty, not in the others.[15]

Pufendorf, like Grotius, comes to essentially the same conclusions at which Vitoria had arrived in his *De Jure Belli* over a century before them. However, he departs from Vitoria (whom he never mentions) on one essential point—on the question of *tempera = mentia*, i.e., the question of restraining war, of the limits within which a just war may be waged. On this, Pufendorf says the following:

> [S]ince according to the law of nature there should be a mutual performance of the duties of peace, whoever takes the first step in violating them against me, has, so far as he is able, freed me from my performance of the duties of peace; and therefore, in confessing that he is my enemy, he allows me a licence to use force against him to any degree, or so far as I may think desirable. . . . For this reason even open wars partake somewhat of the nature of a contract, like this: "Try whatever you can, I will likewise use every means at my disposal." And this holds good not merely if an enemy has undertaken to use every extremity against me, but also if he simply wishes to injure me within certain limits, for he has no greater right to do me a slight injury than a severe one. . . . Nor is it in fact always unjust to return a greater evil for a less, for the objection made by some that retribution should be rendered in proportion to the injury, is true only of civil tribunals, where punishments are meted out by superiors. But the evils inflicted by right of war have properly no relation to punishments, since they neither proceed from a superior as such, nor have as their direct object the reform of the guilty party or others, but the defence and assertion of my safety, my property, and my rights. To secure such ends it is permissi-

[15] Pufendorf, *De Jure Naturae et Gentium*, 2:1291–97.

ble to use whatever means I think will best prevail against such a person, who, by the injury done me, has made it impossible for me to do an injury, however I may treat him, until we have come to a new agreement to refrain from injuries for the future.[16]

But now the law of humankind would not only have one consider how much an enemy can suffer without injury, but also what should be the deeds of a humane and, above all, a generous victor. Therefore, we should take care that, so far as it is possible, and our defence and future security allow, we suit the evils inflicted upon an enemy to the process usually observed by a civil court in meting out justice in offences and other quarrels. This proportion and measure is treated in [1299] detail by Grotius, bk. III, chaps. xi–xvi, just as the understanding of the licence of war is greatly aided by the three rules laid down by the same author in bk. III, chap. i, §§ 2–4.[17]

Here Pufendorf puts forward a principle of law *acquired from reason, uninfluenced by theology or morality*, that the victim of an attack is justified in any sort and any degree of waging war. Then, however, this proposition is moderated by an appeal to *humaneness*, insofar as the victor is exhorted to show clemency, and to make use of his unlimited power,

---

[16] This is a doctrine that contradicts the principles of modern penal and civil law. In English law today, for example, if someone has been attacked, the burden of proof lies on the victim of the attack, *if* he has physically injured the attacker; he must also limit his use of force in *self-defence*; this defence must be *necessary* (if, for example, it was impossible to run away) and the injury must be in *proportion* to the severity of the threat. The same three limitations apply in the USA, while in Germany the first two limitations are specified in the *Strafgesetzbuch* [penal law code] and the third in the *Bundesgesetzblatt* [federal law sheet]. In France, only the first two limitations apply (*Code Pénal*, articles 328 and 329).

[17] Pufendorf, *De Jure Naturae et Gentium*, 2:1298–99.

where possible, within the framework of civil justice. "Where possible": that is, to the extent that the primary interests of his self-protection and his security, which alone are to be consulted, permit. War itself however is not an act in the service of justice, where, in the absence of a superordinate judiciary, the party unjustly attacked becomes a judge and is thus obligated to show the moderation and the self-limitation of a judge; rather, it merely signifies a measure taken to protect oneself for the present and to secure oneself for the future. In this respect, it is chiefly a matter of whether the measures to be applied are suitable for their purpose, not of their justice or of their permissibility.

The concept of war as an act of justice, with the purpose of restoring an injured legal order (as it was understood in the tradition of the Schools), is now reduced to the merely practical task of rendering the opponent harmless for the present, and where possible in future too. In this respect, even a small, or indeed the smallest suffered or threatened injustice suffices to begin a war. Against this, Vitoria says that "not every kind, nor every degree, of injustice suffices to justify a war. . . . It is not permitted to repay the authors of a small injustice with war, since the gravity of the punishment ought to be in accordance with the gravity of the injustice suffered (Deuteronomy 25)." He also says "the victor ought to consider himself as the judge between two states, one that has suffered injustice, and another that has inflicted it, and he ought, indeed, to come forward *as a judge and not as a prosecutor* . . . so that even the guilty state should suffer a degree of unhappiness that is as small as possible."[18]

---

[18] No reference is given here by the author. TR

From International Law to World Peace

Here we have an example of the "de-theologized" legal thought that determined Pufendorf's legal propositions, as well as an example, in Vitoria's case, of a thinking "mixed with theology" (resting on an appeal to Deuteronomy 25). Pufendorf's purely "anthropocentric" intellectual approach put forward the principle that war is a breach of law, and that consequently, until there is a new treaty (a peace treaty), no limit can be set to the kind and degree of war that is waged. Vitoria's "theocentric" intellectual approach, by contrast, produces the principle that there belong to the concept of a "just war" a "just kind" and a "just degree" of waging war. Centuries have gone by since then, which have brought with them lessons from experience.

What *is* now the "last word," as it were, of the text of the experience humanity has undergone in the catastrophes of the twentieth century? The last word is that there is a "just" and an "unjust" way of waging war (the Hague Convention): that the party attacked must exercise a judicial function over the aggressor (the Nuremberg trials and the foundation of the United Nations, with the International Court of Justice); and indeed, that the task of the victor consists not merely in passing judgment on the conquered aggressor, but also in making of him a friend—that is, an *ally* (the peace treaty with Japan)!

The experience of these catastrophes has vindicated Vitoria, with his citations of Deuteronomy from the Bible, and has refuted Pufendorf's principle—Pufendorf, to whom we owe a "detheologized" thinking that is "more enlightened," and grounded in human reason alone. Pufendorf further says regarding the problem of war:

> Let us now consider the questions that concern in a peculiar way wars waged by states and their heads. . . .

Samuel von Pufendorf and Christian Thomasius

[1300] A common distinction is drawn between a war that is *formal* and one that is *less formal.* The former requires that it be conducted on each side by the authority of the supreme sovereignty of a state, and that proper notice be given of its opening, while the latter designation of "less formal" is given to such a war as is not proclaimed, or that is waged against private citizens. . . . In this connection we should observe, in the case of formal wars, that the peoples who wage them along with their commanders are usually called lawful enemies, as opposed to robbers and highwaymen. . . . [1301] Although a state should not be considered as no better than a band of robbers merely because it has officially, in a way, been guilty of unjust practices, neither should a band of robbers receive the dignity of a state, even though they treat their members with some show of justice. (See also Grotius, Bk. III., chap. iii, §2).[19]

A double standard is applied, on the other hand, when Pufendorf continues:

Grotius . . . is wrong when he says: "And surely, if the matter be viewed without reference to the laws of particular states, it would seem that every public official has the right to wage war for the protection of the people entrusted to his charge, and also in order to maintain his jurisdiction if assailed by force." For, the protection of the people is the proper province of the supreme sovereignty; whereas a magistrate, whose province is the administration of justice, protects the people only to the extent that he defends the right of the weak against the more powerful, which end can be achieved without the right to wage war.[20]

Pufendorf sets out the relationship between the responsibility of the state and that of the individual as follows:

[19] Pufendorf, *De Jure Naturae et Gentium*, 2:1299–1301.
[20] Ibid., 1301.

> But just as those who live as individuals in natural liberty cannot be punished by law, except for injuries which they themselves have committed, so it is a point for further inquiry as to how, in states, the guilt of an injury and the reason why war may be begun, passes from those who are immediately guilty over to the entire state. Now, it is clear that a community, whether civil or of any other kind, is not responsible for the actions of individual members, except by some culpable act of commission or omission on its own part, for no matter how much a state may threaten, there is always left to the will of citizens the natural liberty to do otherwise, so that in no wise can a state stand good for the actions of its individual subjects.[21]

Intervention to protect a third state is subject to the following condition:

> An injury done another can only give us cause for war when the injured party calls upon us for aid, so that whatever we do in such a case is done not in our name but in that of the person wronged. But can a man also take up arms to protect another's subjects, that is, from the injuries of their own sovereign? . . . In our opinion the safest principle to go on is that we cannot lawfully undertake the defence of another's subjects for any other reason than they themselves can rightfully advance for taking up arms to protect themselves against the barbarous savagery of their superiors.[22]

The passages quoted from Pufendorf's work give a general impression of the method of *Enlightenment rational law* in its initial stage. Georg *Stadtmüller* summarizes this rational

---

[21] Ibid., 1304.
[22] Ibid., 1307.

law, which claimed to have acquired the objectively universally valid norms of law "from reason alone" (*ex sola ratione*):

> Enlightenment rational law fell into *one* dangerous error above all. It limitlessly overvalued the capacities of human reason, and completely overlooked its capacity for error. The reflective self-criticism with which the classical Medieval doctrine of natural law and Iberian Post-Scholasticism claimed inalterable universal validity only for the most general principles, and with which all individual conclusions were referred to the circumstances of each particular case, *was lost*. Now began a project of boundless deduction that aimed to settle all legal questions (even the most technical), from the most universal self-evident principles; and indeed, to settle them by means of "exact calculation" (*ratiocinatio*), whose model was geometry. This deduction-crazed rational law of the Enlightenment period gave rise to a plethora of systems, which in large part contradicted and mutually excluded each other. In the name of reason and of "natural law," all parties, trends, and tendencies of the age championed their own demands and ideals, and sought to make them universally binding. Locke championed the constitutional democratic legal state in this way; Hobbes championed absolute monarchy; and later, Pufendorf championed enlightened despotism—all by appealing to so-called "natural law," which was in this way degraded to the depths of the political power struggle, and distorted from a metaphysical idea to a political ideology.[23]

The inevitable consequence of "anthropocentrism" is this fragmentation of rationalistic legal naturalism (an approach recognizing only two levels of law) into many, and ever

---

[23] Georg Stadtmüller, *Das Naturrecht im Lichte der geschichtlichen Erfahrung* [Natural law in the light of historical experience] (Recklinghausen, 1948), 20–21.

more, mutually exclusive systems of natural law, is If one starts out from *human beings* as at once criterion, object, and creator of jurisprudence, one necessarily falls into a plurality of systems, since human beings differ from each other. "Nominalism must, if consistently followed through, lead to extreme individualism."[24] The primacy of the will necessarily enforces itself. Ockham (1300–1350), Hobbes (1588–1679), and Pufendorf (1632–1694) all contributed to turning "truth" into truths, that is, to truth's falling victim to relativism. Pufendorf's pupil Christian *Thomasius* (1655–1728) took a further step in this direction.[25] Whereas Pufendorf tried to separate reason and ethical life from theology, it was Thomasius who postulated a separation of ethical life and law, and thus became a precursor of Kant.

Christian Thomasius is usually credited with the distinction drawn between the "external" character of law and the "inner" nature of ethical life, a distinction that is universally considered an important one. In his work *Fundamenta Juris Naturae et Gentium* [Foundations of the law of nature and nations] (1705), and in some of his other writings, Thomasius put forward the view that law, as an order enforceable by the state, was (precisely because of its enforceability)

---

[24] Heinrich Kipp, "Nominalistisches oder realistisches Rechtsdenken," [Nominalist or realist legal thought] in *Forum der Rechtsphilosophie*, ed. Ernst Sauer (Cologne, 1950), 106.

[25] Christian Thomasius, a pupil of Pufendorf, was a jurist, philosopher, and one of the first champions of the Enlightenment. Through his intervention in favor of a humane and enlightened penal system, he made an essential contribution to the abolition of witch trials and of torture (*Grundlehren des Natur- und Völkerrechts* [Halle, 1705]).

entirely alien to the realm of ethical life. Since the essence of the ethical is freedom, that which is enforced, or even just enforceable, has nothing to do with the ethical. It belongs in another sphere—the sphere of law. The just (*iustum*) consists in setting down and keeping the conditions under which dealings among human beings are at all possible. The *foundational* prescription of the just is *do not* do to others what you do not want them to do to you. The *ethical* prescription, however (*decorum* and *honestum*), goes further in its demands. It demands of us that we *do* for others what we wish them to do for us. This, however, is a duty of conscience. It is an affair of the inner life of the human being, and lies entirely outside the realm of the state and its laws. Legal prescriptions can thus only relate to external conduct—to *doing* and *not doing*—and have nothing to do with the inner life of thought, with ethical life, or with religion.

This separating off of law from ethical or moral life of which Thomasius speaks became, in time, the foundation of the modern, secular, tolerant state. "Every man is to be saved after his own fashion": this maxim of Frederick the Great simply testifies to another way of asserting the difference between the moral and the legal, since Frederick's maxim contains an unspoken condition that completes it: "Every man is to be saved after his own fashion, providing that he fulfills his duties towards the state." The first part of this proposition expresses the *indifference* of the state towards the moral and religious; the second, however, expresses the state's interest in the legal and political.

The *distinction* between the legal and the moral, between the *forum externum* and the *forum internum* is, however, not Thomasius's own discovery. It can be traced back through many centuries. What is new in Thomasius is not his having formulated this distinction between law and morality, but to have drawn the line of *separation* between them. For so far as the distinction between law and morality is concerned, Thomas Aquinas had already emphasized it with sufficient clarity in the thirteenth century: "Man, as the creator of human law, can alone judge of external actions, 'since man sees things as they appear' (as the book of Kings tells us), whereas God, the divine legislator, can alone judge of the inner motives of our will, for He is 'the searcher of hearts and reins,' as the psalmist says."[26]

The Anglican Protestant Richard Hooker expresses the same thought over a century before Thomasius when, in complete agreement with Aquinas's doctrine, he says that "the difference between human laws and divine laws [is that] the first of the two are content with *opus operatum* [external action], the second require *opus operantis* [the *whole* action, including the motive]; the first do but claim the deed, the second especially the mind."[27] [author's brackets]

However, as early as the fourth century AD, St Ambrose, bishop of Milan, made a clear distinction between the two domains: "The law of God has taught us what we are to believe, what human laws cannot teach us. They can indeed compel particular outward conduct on the part of those who fear them, but they cannot effect faith."[28]

It is not, therefore, the case, in the great tradition of a law with three levels before Thomasius, that law and moral life

---

[26] *Summa Theologiae*, I–II, qu. 100, 9.
[27] Richard Hooker, *Of The Laws Of Ecclesiastical Polity*, ed. Arthur Stephen McGrade (2 vols, Oxford: Oxford University Press, 2013), 2:189.
[28] *Epistles*, 21.10.

were confused with each other, but rather that a *separating out* of the two domains (such as Thomasius proposed to be necessary) was not intended in that great tradition. Instead, the two domains were considered as, and treated as, parts of an organic whole. Just as ice, water, and steam are clearly distinct as phenomena, and yet are also only three states of the same one substance, so law, moral life, and religion are no less clearly separated from each other, yet in the view of the teachers of the tradition are also only states of the same one substance. Those teachers do indeed distinguish the spheres of faith in revelation, of conscience, and of enforceable laws, but they also saw how these spheres were interconnected. Just as steam, when it cools, becomes a fluid, and just as through further cooling this fluid becomes ice, so does the religious worldview "condense" as it were into the moral worldview, and the moral worldview into the moral-legal worldview—because through the process of "cooling," a progressive externalization gives more and more shape (through external rules and laws) to the intimate nature of the inner life.

Law, as the result of the crystallization of morality, and morality as the condensation of religion into a fluid, are indeed *distinct* things, yet not *separated* things. The tradition saw their unity; a later age emphasized their distinctness. The modern age, however, separated them out into completely isolated, even opposing, domains.

On the problem of the separating-out of the domains of the moral and the legal, a modern author says the following: "The differential characters between law and morals were the transformation into a political programme of an ideal which was inherent from the outset in Western civilization. We ought not to forget the blood and the toil which it cost to secure what could henceforward appear as a 'neat philosophical theorem.'"[29] Nevertheless, the reader's attention is also drawn to a different sort of critique, a more thoroughgoing one, of the doctrine of the "essential difference" between law and morals. That critique is mentioned briefly here because it furnishes further arguments to justify the work of the theoreticians of natural law and their long-forgotten efforts. What is emphasized here is that these stipulations of the essential difference between law and ethics—stipulations that are to be derived from a particular historical experience—can only be approximate and changeable. Indeed, on closer inspection they do not prove to be absolutely valid criteria for the distinction of *legal* prescriptions from *ethical* ones.

If we take the *social* character of law as opposed to the *individual* character of ethical life, it is self-evidently true that modern man has arrived at a position in which law is almost exclusively connected with the state, and ethical life is almost exclusively connected with the individual person. Are there not, however, moral values that also presuppose and require society just as much as, or even more than, the legal order can do? Are there not laws beyond the realm of the state, laws that we are accustomed to obey and that are often experienced by individual people as being even more binding than those of the state? An exclusively individual morality is unthinkable; and law, if we consider it in its broadest sense as a "measure of conduct," is experienced by us every day in our practical life (even Robinson Crusoe,

---

[29] A.P. d'Entrèves of Oxford, previously Professor of International Law at the University of Turin, in *Natural Law: An Introduction to Legal Philosophy* (London, 1951), 89.

who made it a rule to read the Bible a little every morning and every evening, resolved to make his life as regular as possible, so as in this way to save himself from despair and to retain an existence worthy of the dignity of humankind.)[30]

The same author (d'Entrèves) also points out that not all valid laws and legal norms are enforceable—such as, for example, the norms of international law and the fundamental laws of a state's constitution—and that it is often hardly possible to draw a line between the "inner" (i.e., moral) and "external" (i.e., legal) character of an action, as when, for example, the state today not only imposes on its citizens a duty to serve in the military, but also expects that they will be "good soldiers." "How can we prove," he continues,

> that law is never concerned with the internal side of action? What do we make of such legal concepts as *bona fides* (good faith) or *dolus* (malicious intent), which involve a subtle valuation of motives? And what of that "mental element" which plays so decisive and elusive a part in criminal liability? Clearly, criticism such as this can lead only to the conclusion that the distinction between law and morals should not be based merely on a generalization from our present experience, but on a deeper analysis of the inmost nature of legal and moral obligation. It also leads to the recognition that there must be closer links between the two spheres than is realized *prima facie*. . . . The theorists of natural law . . . may have unduly stressed the moral aspect of law or the legal aspect of morals. But, as has already been shown, they were well aware of the differences between them and showed a surprisingly clear insight into their real nature.[31]

---

[30] *Robinson Crusoe*, section 10.
[31] D'Entrèves, *Natural Law*, 90–91.

From International Law to World Peace

The separation of law from the world of moral life finds expression in the formula given by Thomasius: *In omni societate jus est, extra societatem jus non est* ("in every community there is law; outside the community there is no law"). *Thus does moral life become an internal affair of the state.*

3

The "Grotians":
Leibniz, Wolff, Vattel

n the second chapter of this fifth Part, the contribution of one of the three "sons" of the "Noah" of international law has already been examined—the school of natural law as a pure law of reason, which was inaugurated by the "son" Pufendorf. The basic features of what we might call the "Japhetic" tendency of "anthropocentric" rationalist natural law were thus characterized. Now we must set out the distinguishing feature of another current, that of "Shem," as it were: the school that synthesizes deductive speculation with inductive research work. As for the "Hamitic" current of pure positivism—in its various stages as a method of research, as historicism, as relativism, and in the end as a doctrine of pure positivism—it will be discussed in chapter 7.

Gottfried Wilhelm Leibniz (1646–1716), Christian Friedrich Wolff (1679–1754), and Emer de Vattel (1714–1767) are the three individuals who not only represent three generations of creative continuation and further development (in an age during which "throwing the baby out with the bath water" became an eagerly pursued practice) of the Grotian value of saving the *jurisprudentia perennis*, but also brought that value to *pre-eminence* for around a century and a half, thereby providing a philosophical and scholarly grounding to the work of Grotius. For despite his astonishing learning and many-sidedness, Grotius was no philosopher, and was a stranger as well to the rising mathematical and physical "exact sciences." Whereas Grotius, therefore, based his work on the intellectual achievements of his precursors (that is, on the great Christian and humanist tradition), Leibniz, Wolff, and Vattel provided a new intellectual achievement that provided Grotius's work with a fresh foundation, so that it could not only endure as a monument of the past, but could also stand up in the light of the present—and even, indeed, from the perspective of the future. To the grounding acquired from the past, they added a "modern" one, without however thereby making a break with the value and truth-content of the tradition. It was the philosopher, mathematician, physicist, historian, theologian, political scientist, and jurist *Leibniz* who gave Grotius's approach a new grounding in a philosophical worldview, which persuaded a number of clear heads and closed hearts; it was the philosopher and mathematician *Wolff* who conquered the world of universities and scholarship for this approach; and it was the jurist *Vattel* who won over the courts, embassies, and salons.[1] The basic principles and stimuli given by Leibniz were developed and elaborated by Wolff, and popularized (not without alterations) by Vattel.

---

[1] "Thanks to Vattel, Wolff's ideas, cleverly presented, shake off the dust of the schools and find their way into courts, embassies, and the 'polite world.'" A. De Lapradelle, "Introduction" to Emer de Vattel, *Le Droit des Gens ou Principes de la Loi Naturelle* (3 vols, Washington: Carnegie Institution, 1916), 1: viii.

The "Grotians": Leibniz, Wolff, Vattel

The goal that governed almost all of Leibniz's outwardly directed activity was to create (or, more correctly, to restore) a European culture on a Christian basis. A new unity of "Christendom" was the goal towards which his lifelong efforts were directed. He wished to contribute to this unity by working for the reunification of the Protestant and Catholic churches. And he himself contemplated, together with Peter the Great, a world council with the object of uniting Christendom. Leibniz also sought to further unity by founding scholarly academies in all civilized countries. The *Societät der Wissenschaften zu Berlin* [Berlin scientific society] was actually founded by Leibniz, who presided over it until 1710, while he was also the "spiritual father" of the academies in Dresden, Vienna, and St Petersburg. He also wished to save the unity of the Empire, which had fallen victim to disputes among the princes, and wrote in 1670 a memorandum in support of this endeavor.[2] Lastly, by developing the plan for an expedition to Egypt and having it presented to Louis (he undertook a journey to Paris for this purpose)—so that the French king could in this way be transformed from a fragmenter of Christianity into Christendom's "general," with the unity of Christendom behind him—he sought to render the aggressive policy of expansion adopted by Louis XIV harmless to the unity of Christendom. He recommended the conquest of Egypt to Louis as the conquest of "the bond between Asia and Africa, the dam between the ocean and the Mediterra-

---

[2] *Bedenken welchergestalt Securitas Publica interna et externa und Status praesens im Reich iezigen Umbständen noch auf festen Fuß zu stellen* [On what form of *securitas publica interna et externa* and *status praesens* to adopt as a firm footing in the empire's current circumstances].

nean, the granary of the East, the principal port between India and Europe."

Leibniz's activities of unifying, collecting, reconciling, and "peace-building" were not limited, however, to the spheres of politics and culture, but also furnished the basis for his worldview and the essence of a scientific research method. The "unity that explains everything" (*unitas omnia explicans*) of Nicholas of Cusa, and his own "multiplicity reduced to unity" (*varietas reducta in unitatem*), are the two poles of Leibniz's worldview and method—poles he successfully connected in theory and in practice. Many-sidedness (jurisprudence, history, mathematics, physics, linguistics, theology, and philosophy) was not only a personal preference for Leibniz; it was, rather, his *method*. "Great things are seldom achieved without marrying different disciplines to each other, and creating from these nuptials a new and distinct discipline that the researcher would never otherwise have thought of."[3]

The application of the "combinatory method," which, however, Leibniz never distorts into any sort of eclecticism or relativism, not only led to a charitable tolerance—that is, to the art of learning from everything—but also to views that were all-embracing, bridge-building, and "peace-building."

> Consideration of this system also shows that when one gets to the bottom of things, one discovers more reason in most philosophical doctrines than one had previously believed

---

[3] From a treatise dating to the last decade of the seventeenth century, *Spongia Exprobationum seu quod nullum doctrinae verae genus sit contemnendum* [Sponge of reproaches, or that no kind of true doctrine is to be despised]. (The quotation has here been translated from Tomberg's German. TR)

them to have. The limited substantial reality of sensuous things which the skeptics taught; the derivation of all things from harmony or from numbers, from ideas and proportions, that the Platonists taught; the identical, all-embracing One of Parmenides and Plotinus that nevertheless remains far removed from all Spinozism; the Stoical necessity that is nevertheless identical with self-reliance; the philosophy of life of the Kabbalists and the Hermetics according to which there are discoveries to be made everywhere; the forms and entelechies of Aristotle and the Scholastics that nevertheless do not exclude explanations of a mechanical kind: all these are found here as if unified from a perspectival center, from which the object that looks confused when seen from any other vantage-point allows its regularity and the agreement of its parts to be perceived.[4]

This "objective perspectivism," as Dietrich Wahnke characterizes Leibniz's method, made possible a reconciliation (not only at "first glance" but also at a "second glance") between apparently irreconcilable opposites:

> Everyone also knows that, through the continual connection between reason and sensibility—the concept of *petites perceptions*—Leibniz overcomes the opposition between *Plato*'s aprioristic ideas and *Aristotle*'s inductively acquired universal concepts, and, in connection to this, the opposition between the innateness of ideas according to *Descartes*, and their originating in sensation and reflection according to *Locke*.[5]

---

[4] Quoted from Hans Meyer, *Geschichte der abendländischen Weltanschauung* [History of the worldview of the west] (Würzburg, 1950), 4:178.

[5] Dietrich Mahnke, *Leibnizens Synthese von Universalmathematik und Individualmetaphysik* [Leibniz's synthesis of universal mathematics with individual metaphysics] (Halle, 1925), 317; compare Leibniz, *Nouveaux essais sur l'entendement humain* [New essays on human understanding].

From International Law to World Peace

Harmony as the unity of analogy and continuity: this is the key formula of Leibniz's method and worldview. This means, among other things, that Leibniz certainly *distinguished* individual disciplines—e.g., theology, ethics, and law—from each other, but that at the same time he *connected* them by means of analogy and continuity. In his later years, Leibniz says about his work of distinguishing and connecting:

> I already got to know Aristotle when I was a child, and even the Scholastics did not frighten me. And in no way do I lament this. But Plato as well as Plotinus also gave me a certain satisfaction, not to mention others of the ancients whom I consulted. When I had grown out of elementary school, however, I threw myself upon the moderns, and I still remember a walk in the Rosenthal, a grove in Leipzig, when, at the age of fifteen, I wondered whether I ought to retain the substantial forms. But mechanism won the upper hand, and made me decide to study mathematics, into whose depths I first went in my dealings with Huygens in Paris. But when I sought for the final grounds of mechanism and the laws of motion, I was amazed to see that it was impossible to find them in mathematics, and that I had to return to metaphysics. This led me back to the entelechies, back from matter to form.[6]

In other words, the young Leibniz for the first time has an insight into the connection between "substantial forms" and their expression: the world of movement. This world of movement, henceforth taken for itself, displays a lawlikeness that can be specified by number, weight, and measure. This specifiability of the mechanical leads to an insight into the connection between the intellectual activity of mathe-

---

[6] Quoted from Meyer, *Geschichte*, 4:174.

matics and the world of external motion. An *ideal* is expressed in *real* processes, and is decisively at work in those processes, so that the future can be determined in advance. The spiritual *moves* (and thus, among other things, also *forms*) the material. It is the "substantial forms" that, as a result of the efficacity of the entelechies or monads (as unities of consciousness), form the basis of the visible world. With this the circle is closed: once each has rendered its service, Scholasticism, mechanism, and mathematics remain within it, each in its place, so as to render further services for all future time. As steam becomes water and water ice, the mechanical originates in the living and the living from the spiritual. The three states are clearly *distinct* from each other, forming, as it were, three "distinct domains." But the *continuity* of the transitions from one state to another also brings their unity to light. Thus, theology, philosophy, ethics, and law are also "distinct domains" as clearly distinct from each other as are gases, fluids, and solid bodies. Yet a bond of continuity also exists between them—a bond of gradual, gapless transition. Who can draw a sharp line, for example, between theology and philosophy? At what point do the theological concepts "God," "soul," and "immortality" cease to be "theological," and at what point do they become "philosophical"? Where is the exact border between philosophy and ethics? What is the point at which moral life and law are distinguished from each other? Where are justice and law foreign to each other?

> I am not sure that, even after so many distinguished writers have discussed them, the notions of *right* and *justice* may be considered sufficiently clear. *Right* [*jus*] is a certain moral power, and *obligation* a moral necessity. Now, by *moral* I mean that which is equivalent to "natural" in a

good man [*viri boni naturaliter*].... [283]. Further, a good man is one who loves all men, so far as reason allows, for it is reason which guides that inclination so that it becomes *justice*.[7] *Justice* ... is ... the *charity of the wise man* [*caritas sapientis*].... [284] *Charity* is universal benevolence, and *benevolence* is the habit of loving or esteeming. But to *love* [285] or *esteem* is to take pleasure in the happiness of another.... [286] *Divine love* excels other loves, for God can be loved with the happiest result, since nothing is happier than God and nothing more beautiful or more worthy of happiness can be conceived.... [287] *Wisdom* is nothing but the very science of happiness. So we are brought back again to the notion of *happiness*.... Now, from this source flows *natural right* [*jus naturae*], of which there are *three degrees: right in the narrow sense* [*jus strictum*] in commutative justice, *equity* [*aequitas*] (or charity in the narrower sense in distributive justice), and lastly, *piety* (probity or uprightness) in universal justice. [288] Hence come the precepts: that we should do injury to no one, that we should give to each his own, that we should live virtuously (or rather, piously) the universal and commonly accepted principles of right.[8] [...] The precept of bare right or *right in the narrow sense* is that *no one is injured*: lest if it be within the state [*civitas*], the person should have ground for an action at law; or if it be without the state, he should have the right to make war. For from this there comes the justice that the philosophers call *commutative*, and the

---

[7] The final clause here, from "for it is reason" to the end of the sentence, does not appear in Latta's version and is translated directly from Tomberg's German. TR

[8] The three *generalissima et pervulgata juris praecepta* of which Leibniz speaks—*honeste vivere, alterum non laedere,* and *suum cuique tribuere,* represent a summary of the legal prescriptions of Justinian's *Institutions.* Cf. *Institutions,* I.1.3.

right which Grotius calls *right proper.* [289] The higher degree I call *equity,* or if you prefer it, charity (that is the narrower sense), which I extend beyond the rigor of bare right to those obligations also on account of which those to whom we are obliged have no ground of action to compel us to perform them, such as gratitude, pity [*eleemosyne*] and the things that are said by Grotius to have *imperfect right* [or *fitness, aptitudo*]—not right proper [*facultas*]. And as the precept of the lowest degree was to do injury to no one, so that of the middle degree is to do good to everybody; but that so far as befits each person or so far as each deserves, since we cannot equally befriend all men. Therefore, to this place belong *distributive* justice and that precept of right [*jus*] that bids us *give to each his own.* And to this, political laws in the state are related, laws that have to do with the happiness of subjects and usually bring it about that those who had only a moral claim [*aptitudo*] require a jural claim [*facultas*]: that is to say, that they are [290] enabled to demand what it is fair that others should give. But while in the lowest degree of right no regard was paid to the differences among men (except to those that arise from the particular matter in hand), and all men were regarded as equal, now in this higher degree merits are weighed, and hence privileges, rewards, and punishments appear.... For equity [291] itself leads us in business to act upon right in the narrow sense [*jus strictum*], that is, the equality of men, unless when a weighty reason of greater good requires us to depart from it.

I have called the highest degree of right by the name of uprightness [*probitas*] or rather *piety.* For what has been said so far may be understood in such a way as to be limited to the relations of a mortal life. And indeed bare right or right in the narrow sense has its source in the need of keeping the peace; equity or charity [292] strives after something more, to wit that while each to the other does as much good as possible, each may increase his happiness through that of others; and, to put it in a word, right in the narrow sense avoids misery, while right in the higher sense tends to happiness, but of such a kind as falls to our mortal lot. But that we ought to subordinate life itself and whatever makes life desirable to the greater good of others so that it behooves us to bear patiently the greatest pains for the sake of others, this is beautifully inculcated by philosophers rather than thoroughly proved by them. . . . But in order that it may be concluded by a universal demonstration that everything honorable is beneficial and that everything base is hurtful, we must assume the immortality [293] of the soul and the ruler of the universe, *God*. Thus it is that we think of all men as living in the most perfect city under a monarch who on account of His wisdom cannot be deceived and on account of His power cannot be avoided; and a monarch who is also so loveable that it is happiness to serve such a master. Therefore, he who spends his soul for Him gains it, as Christ teaches. By His power and providence it comes to pass that every *right* passes into fact, that no one is injured except by himself [294], that nothing done rightly is without a reward and no sin without a punishment. For, as Christ divinely taught, all our hairs are numbered, and not even a draught of water is given in vain to one who thirsts, and thus nothing is disregarded in the commonwealth of the universe. It is on this account that *justice* is called *universal* and comprehends all other virtues, for things that otherwise do not seem to concern anyone else—as, for instance, whether we abuse our own body or our own property, and such matters that are beyond the range of human laws—are nevertheless forbidden by the law of nature, i.e., by the eternal laws of the Divine Monarchy, since we owe ourselves and all that is ours to God. For as it is of importance to a commonwealth [*respublica*], so much more is it to the universe, that no one should make a bad use of that which is his own. Accordingly, from this is derived [295] the force [*vim accepit*] of that highest precept of right, which bids us live *virtuously* (that is, piously).... Thus I think I have very fitly explained the three precepts of right or three degrees of justice, and have pointed out the sources of natural law.[9]

In this short portion of Leibniz's treatise *On the Notions of Right and Justice*, we have a work that has constructed a sort of "rainbow" arching from antiquity (as it is contained in Justinian's *Codex juris*) over the whole Christian tradition of the eleven intervening centuries to the time of the Reformation, Counter-Reformation, and Enlightenment. The individual domains are indeed clearly distinguished from each other, but are at the same time understood as levels of an overall framework. The concepts are demarcated, but are at the same time seen as milestones on the *path* of their metamorphosis into higher concepts—and in such a way that the previous stages of the metamorphosis retain their validity, and, indeed, are required and strengthened by the subsequent stages. Just as, in a plant, the stem that rises up from the root does not render the root superfluous, and just as the leaves that grow from the stem do not render the stem dispensable, and just as the emergence of the blossoms and the fruit is not only *not* hostile to the root, the stem, and leaves, but on the contrary lends them all at once a

---

[9] G.W. Leibniz, "On the Notions of Right and Justice," in *The Monadology and Other Philosophical Writings*, trans. Robert Latta (NY: Garland, 1985), 281–96, 282–95. (Tomberg's long quotation brings together a number of passages, and includes the majority of this discourse. His elisions are indicated here. The Latin glosses enclosed in square brackets are provided by Tomberg; page numbers from Latta's translation are once again provided for convenience. TR)

higher value and a higher meaning, so Leibniz's "stages of law" are *not* stages of the "overcoming of the erroneous, obsolete, and imperfect" and so on, but are *stages of the developmental building of a whole*. As such—as a whole—this process is of lasting value and lasting significance. Moreover, it needs and includes all the prior stages, as if they were its various members. Just as Goethe's *Faust* is not a sequence of botched attempts at representing the final scene, but a work of which the opening monologue in Faust's study and the Prologue in Heaven belong for all time (i.e., just as much as the concluding scene of the Second Part), so the three levels of law, in Leibniz's sense, belong for all time together—since a stepladder is *not* there in order for the lower or higher steps to be broken off, but so that one can use it to climb up (and so is usable *only* if all the steps are present.

However, pictorial comparisons with plants or with a ladder do not by themselves suffice to illustrate Leibniz's method. For that, we also need the simile of the rainbow offered above. For not only does the rainbow illustrate the simultaneity of the colors as stages between light and dark (in the sense of Goethe's theory of color), not only does it display each color with radiant clarity as a sort of "special domain," but it also expresses their "dynamic" connection, i.e., the *continuity* of the transition between them. Just as red passes over into orange, orange into yellow, yellow into green, so, for Leibniz, *law* as the expression of equalizing justice becomes *fairness* as an expression of distributive justice, which in turn becomes moral *integrity* of the disposition as an expression of universal or general justice. At the first level it is a question of combating unhappiness (or of harming no one); at the second, of furthering temporal

The "Grotians": Leibniz, Wolff, Vattel

happiness (of securing for each his own); and at the third, of participating in timeless blessedness (a God-fearing life). The three stages are those of the potentiation of one and the same element. Law, justice, and moral life are, as it were, metamorphoses of the same "water" that appears as solid ice and also as a fluid and as steam.

⊕

Leibniz applies his method of "objective perspectivism" (or as we have put it, of "an overall view of the rainbow") not only to the concepts of law and ethical life, but also to the history of those concepts. Just as he explicitly adheres to the *philosophia perennis* in philosophy (the expression was coined by Augustinus Steuchus)—that is, to the great rainbow spanning the "flood" of limitations, one-sidednesses, and passions as a covenant between the eternal truth of God and the world of temporality (Genesis 9:12–15) set there as a sign that "the waters shall no more become a flood to destroy all flesh"—so Leibniz also pledges allegiance in the "concluding actions" of his general conduct to a *jurisprudentia perennis*. This pledge is the real meaning of the closing sentences of the treatise quoted above, the treatise *De Notionibus Juris et Justitiae* [Concepts of law and justice]. This is the meaning of the way in which the learned have referred to natural law and international law, and to the sublime and divine teaching of the wise, handed down according to Christian teaching, i.e., according to documentary records of Christ. This "teaching" of the wise is the rainbow of *jurisprudentia perennis* that arches over the tide of world history, that binds God and humankind in justice, and that Leibniz solemnly acknowledges.

Even the positive legal efforts and achievements of Leibniz must be understood and evaluated in this light. His pioneering work on the codification of valid natural law, as seen in his *Codex Juris Gentium Diplomaticus* [Diplomatic code of international law] (1693, the same year as the treatise on the "notions of right and justice" quoted above) and in his *Mantissa iuris Gentium Diplomatici* [Addendum on international diplomatic law] (1700), is also to be seen as an attempt to achieve an "overall view of the rainbow"—not only of its concepts, ideas, and ideals, but also of the *factual* material of the phenomena. *Phenomenology*, as an application of the method of "objective perspectivism," can be as fruitful for the *ars combinatoria*, for the logic of discovery, as an organic system of principles can be (i.e., a *harmony* of analogy and continuity). Even the factual material, clearly set out, has a corrective significance for speculation, just as speculation also has the truths of revelation on its other flank. As one schooled in the disciplines of mathematics and physics, Leibniz understood the danger of generalizing from faulty data; and as a believing Christian familiar with the course of theology over the centuries, he understood also the devastating consequences that even an apparently small deviation from such truths (for example, in respect of the relationship between grace and works, or of transubstantiation in the sacrament of Holy Communion) could have for the general spiritual life of humankind. Speculation, when it is able to develop freely, is assisted from two sides: on the one hand, empirical experience provokes speculation to find new problems and discoveries, and warns it against haste and one-sidedness; on the other, revelation sets speculation eternal problems and shows it which direction is of lasting validity.

The "Grotians": Leibniz, Wolff, Vattel

⊕

This same year, 1693, saw the completion both of Leibniz's work of codifying the treaties and documents under international law, and his treatise on the nature of law and justice, which views the foundation of law and of justice as residing in God's governance. Here, too, it is a question of finding the "rainbow of peace" between the domains of empirical fact, pure speculation, and religious revelation. Between the facts taken from the realm of experience and the domain of faith lying *above* all experience, stretches the "rainbow" of knowledge—at one of whose ends is found the gathered work of codifying the documents of international law; and at the other, the gathered spirit bowing in reverence before God.

Leibniz's method also connects the extremes of the opposition between independence and originality on one hand, and collaborative work and tradition on the other. This distinguishes Leibniz from Kant and from Grotius. For Kant wished to both set and to solve all problems under his own steam alone, or, in Dietrich Wahnke's words:

> through a "Copernican turn," Kant acquired an entirely new and superior standpoint, and henceforth needed no external influence, but rather, in proud solitariness, like a completely isolated Leibnizian monad (as these monads are usually, but wrongly, conceived of), was able to think through his entirely original thoughts—thoughts that had never been thought before—in ever deeper detail and in ever greater comprehensiveness. He was, so to speak, able to "spin" everything out of himself to its conclusion. The great synthesizers, Leibniz and Hegel, are quite different. They experience themselves, in comparison to their prede-

cessors, not as discoverers of wholly unknown worlds, not as revolutionaries or as radical new initiators, but as conservative guardians and augmenters of inherited possessions, as mature ripeners of a long and ancient process of cultural development. Always and everywhere, they follow their predecessors, think those predecessors' thoughts through to a conclusion, and reconcile their oppositions in higher syntheses.[10]

Grotius, by contrast, the "Noah" of tradition, stood wholly within the tradition, which he wished to preserve for the Protestant world too, whereas Leibniz, although wholly oriented towards discovery and invention, knows himself at the same time to be a member of the great working community of the spiritual culture of humankind, a community that embraces all civilized ages and all civilized nations. For as a *monad*, which is a "mirror of the universe," the individual can know the totality of universal truths. As a *member of humankind*, however, he can accomplish the empirical tasks of securing knowledge and bringing about progress in the social and cultural life only in company with the whole of humankind. Here Leibniz and Goethe share the same standpoint. For Goethe too believed both in the collective work of humankind toward the goal of comprehensive knowledge and ability, and that the entelechy of the individual (which, in conversation with Eckermann, he declared to be the same as Leibniz's monad) can creatively express the full lawlikeness of creation.

---

[10] Dietrich Mahnke, *Leibnizens Synthese von Universalmathematik und Individualmetaphysik* [Leibniz's synthesis of universal mathematics and individual metaphysics], 307.

The "Grotians": Leibniz, Wolff, Vattel

⊕

These fundamental methodological insights also influenced Leibniz's relationship to the complex of questions informing international law—questions concerning a just order in the world that would bring an end to war. He saw the foundation of such an order as lying in a unified culture, in a universal human culture that could progressively permeate the consciousness of all humankind. Now, an organized world-order presupposes a spiritual *civitas maxima*, and "Christendom" is the foundation of just such an order—which, if it is to exist, must necessarily be an analogue or reflection of the world-order, i.e., a monarchy. Since the unity of Christendom had been almost fatally weakened by the Reformation, its reconstruction had to begin again from the beginning. To put forward a program for a unified Christendom, in which Louis XIV, the Hapsburgs, Sweden, Holland, Spain, and England would somehow come together, was however nothing if not utopian, and Leibniz was too much of a realist for that. Reunification, the work of bringing together a Christendom fallen to pieces, had to begin with religious peace—peace as the reunification of the confessions, not merely a "making peace" with "lines of demarcation" of the Peace of Westphalia. Then, after such a religious peace had been established, the unity of the empire could be restored, so that in the end the empire and its emperor could bring together the remaining states of Christendom with a guarantee of their self-rule and their "princely" independence. The memorandum of 1670 mentioned above was aimed at instituting a stronger central power (*Directorium Imperii*) together with a standing imperial army (*perpetuus miles*) and an imperial treasury (*perpet-*

uum aerarium). In the memorandum we find, among other things, the following:

> But here we find the greatest difficulty, and one which, given the current state of the empire, is hardly to be overcome; that is, how such an everlasting *Directorium Imperii* is to be organized, and whence it should derive the means to cater for either itself or the nations. For the empire ought to be a *persona civilis*. Just as in a *persona naturali*, or human body, there are found a spirit, blood, and limbs, so a *persona civilis* needs a *perpetuum consilium*, which represents the understanding and the spirit, a *perpetuum aerarium*, which represents the blood and the veins, and a *perpetuus miles*, which represents the limbs; and just as the limbs are fed by the blood, and the blood cannot move without the *spirituum*, so the *perpetuus miles* cannot be catered for without an everlasting *aerarium*, nor the *aerarium* nor *miles* be kept nor governed in ordered motion without a *consilium perpetuum*.
>
> A *consilium perpetuum* would, admittedly, be desirable for the empire, but there is no hope of this in the empire's current situation. It is well-known how the military council has fallen apart, partly from want of support, which has certainly decreased not a little in our nation, and partly because of the different maxims of the emperor and the princes.

Here Leibniz points to the first step that would need to be taken in order to restore "Christendom," namely that the empire should actually become a state, a *persona civilis*, by receiving a settled government, a standing army, and an imperial treasury. However, these decisive demands, so necessary to the preservation of the empire, seemed to Leibniz himself to be something of which there was "no hope . . . in the empire's current situation." A draft written in Latin in Leibniz's own hand from the period between 1668 and 1672

The "Grotians": Leibniz, Wolff, Vattel

provides more information about this matter. The draft contains Leibniz's thoughts on the question of whether the emperor possesses a claim to world rule (*aliqua praetensio Imperatoris Romani in orbem terrarum*). The argument is as follows, paraphrasing:

> The Roman Catholic church has a claim in principle to world jurisdiction (*jurisdictionem in orbem terrarum*) insofar as it does not infringe upon sound conscience (*salva conscientia*). Now, it can however also be shown from the declarations of the Protestants that they have not refused to obey their spiritual leaders as a matter of principle, but only in cases where they considered that there was a valid objection. An individual jurisdiction, however, makes no broader claim to power. Now, the emperor is the legal advocate for the Roman church (*advocatus ecclesiae Romanae*). Consequently, the emperor has a claim to the world insofar as he is the legal advocate of the Church in respect of what concerns the Church. All Christians are obliged to obey those to whom has been lent that power which is the legacy of sin, insofar as such obedience does not conflict with sound conscience. The power to remit sins, however, was first given to Peter alone, and then to all the apostles together. Consequently, the same power was lent to Peter as to all the apostles together. The power given to the apostles was not given to them as single individuals, but as members of a body, a corporation. Their jurisdiction is therefore not one that only some of them have to exercise, nor is it only for particular people, but is instead the same for all the apostles, and relates to all people—since otherwise the apostles might contradict each other, which would be absurd. The power of the apostles is also, as is universally agreed, conferred upon their successors. Consequently, every Christian is obliged to obey Peter's successor, as well as all the apostles' other successors. It is the

From International Law to World Peace

Roman church, however, that is Peter's successor. Consequently, every Christian is obliged to obey the Roman church. Anyone who is obliged to obey the Roman church and who nevertheless does not obey it, can be forced to do so by the legal advocate of the Roman church, the emperor. Consequently, the emperor has a claim to jurisdiction over the world, where any matter of defending and disseminating the Christian religion is concerned.[11]

Obviously, this draft must not be taken to contain "Leibniz's own legal and world-political standpoint." It is simply a question of a draft. And given that he himself considered it hopeless to wish for a standing central power for the empire "in the current situation," Leibniz was too much of a realist to believe in the possibility of the emperor's attaining universal supremacy at that date. The value of the draft is just that it illustrates his *method* in dealing with important questions. The topic is to be thought through at the level of the truths of *pure reason*, resting on the principle of non-contradiction and the principle of sufficient reason, *and* at the same time on the level of *factual knowledge*, which rests on experience and on the principle of sufficient reason. By bringing together knowledge derived from pure reason (i.e., as things *ought* to be) and factual knowledge (i.e., as things *actually are*), a program for praxis in all domains can be produced, a program that rests on truth and reasonableness.

Thus, for example, at the same period during which Leibniz wrote the draft concerning the emperor's world primacy, he also presented to the French court his plan for an

---

[11] G.W. Leibniz, *Politische Schriften* [Political writings], ed. Prussian Academy of Sciences, vol. 1, 1667–1676 (Darmstadt, 1931).

The "Grotians": Leibniz, Wolff, Vattel

expedition to Egypt (he visited Paris for this purpose in 1672, and the draft dates from between 1668 and 1672); and again, at around the same period (1670), he wrote his memorandum on the need for a reorganization of the empire. The draft thus contains a "truth of reason" that was, however, unreasonable, given how things then stood and given the views of the people who then reigned and formed opinion. Knowledge of the facts, however, enabled Leibniz to advocate only for so much of this "truth of reason" as is contained in his efforts towards strengthening the unity of the empire and towards diverting Louis XIV's drive for expansion, and as is directed towards that end and determined by it. When, therefore, Dietrich Mahnke (like Bertrand Russell in England in our own day) speaks of an "esoteric doctrine" of Leibniz, or of his "esoteric views and writings," these "esoteric views" are nothing other than insights and postulates that Leibniz either could not ask his contemporaries to agree with, or did not think he could ask them to agree with, if he was not to worsen the already existing plague of confusion. Just as Moses, when he came down from Mount Sinai, where he received the statutes of divine law, had to cover his face because the people could not bear the radiance of the reflection of direct, strict, and absolute truth, so too Leibniz—who from personal experience knew the most authoritative scholars of his time and was familiar also with the courts of Hanover, Berlin, Paris, and Vienna—considered it unreasonable to expect people to grasp absolute truths of pure reason in their totality. For him, these truths were therefore to play the role of guiding stars, showing the way by shimmering and sparkling from the distance in the night sky.

In Leibniz's spiritual cosmos, such guiding truths showing the way included a human community that would be legally and politically organized on the basis of a shared human culture, the *civitas maxima*, as a reflection of the "great republic of spirits" in the world, with God as its monarch. This human community, this world-state, ought to be nothing other than the final stage of the gathering of the small states into larger and more capacious state-formations. Spiritually, this future community of humankind is already prefigured in the form of the "republic of science and arts" and the *one* supreme and true religion (which, in principle, can only be cultivated and be lived in *one*—reunified—Church).

According to Leibniz, the *state* is a result of human beings' striving for happiness. Indeed, it corresponds, in its stages of perfection, to individual happiness, shared happiness, and supreme happiness in God. The conception of the state community and its purpose in Leibniz is, once again, that of a "rainbow." This rainbow connects the utilitarianism of the later scholar Jeremy Bentham (1748–1832), which aims at "the greatest happiness of the greatest number" as the purpose both of the state and of any given legal order, and the Augustinian ideal of the "state of God" (*civitas Dei*). In other words, the ideal of happiness need not be a purely earthly ideal. It can be conceived of as part of setting a larger and more all-embracing goal. Leibniz combined utilitarianism (as a *stage*) with a theological and teleological conception of humankind, of history, and of the world.

Setting as a goal the *perfection* of the individual and of the community, Leibniz distinguishes *three stages* of the disposition of souls towards this goal: (1) *utilitas*; (2) *humanitas*; (3) *religio*. Later stages in this sequence are always higher than their predecessors. *Utilitas*, as the first stage, corresponds to the ideal of happiness in utilitarianism; but it is ennobled and internalized by virtue of its relation, as a preparatory stage, to the two subsequent stages. The stage of *humanitas* has as its goal the community of *free human individual persons*. To it corresponds the third prescription of Justinian's *Institutes*: *honeste vivere, alterum non laedere, suum cuique tribuere*. The *suum cuique tribuere*, "give to each his own," is the basic legal rule that corresponds to the stage of humaneness, while the rule *alterum non laedere* (Leibniz uses the formula *neminen laedere*), "not to harm others," is valid for the stage of utility. The *third* stage of justice, however, which is based on the command *honeste vivere*, "live honorably," strives towards the goal of the religious man who, as *vir bonus* ("good man"), lives in concord with God.

These three stages of justice correspond to three stages of the natural *community*: (1) the family community; (2) the civic community; (3) the religious community. Each of these levels of community in turn corresponds to a level of *law*: (1) *jus strictum* corresponds to the family community; (2) *aequitas* corresponds to the civic community; (3) *pietas* corresponds to the religious community.[12]

On the first level, human beings live and work towards the realization of true happiness through *individual* perfection; on the second level, human beings strive for *collective* perfection as a community; on the third level, human beings live as a community in community with God.[13]

Accordingly, the "family of nations" is a stage on the way

---

[12] J. Jacoby, *De Leibnitzi studiis Aristoteles*, 33–38.

[13] Cf. the author's *Degeneration und Regeneration der Rechtswissenschaft* (Bonn, 1946), 53 ff. English translation: *The Art of the Good: On the Regeneration of Fallen Justice* (New York: Angelico Press, 2021).

through the world-state community to the world-church. The church is thus the highest level of the development of the community. In Leibniz's work, however, it is not a matter of positing as a final goal the conversion of the church into a state, but rather the conversion of the state into a church. For it is the higher level that gives the previous stages their meaning and that sets their goal, not the other way around. A "state church" would be the absolute opposite of Leibniz's idea. He thus decisively rejects Hobbes's state absolutism,[14] and above all Hobbes's doctrine that the state should determine the religion of its citizens, for "Leibniz discerns in such a concept the concealed assertion that there is no such thing as a true religion, and that religion is a merely human invention."[15] The goal Leibniz has in mind is *not* the gradual absorption of the church into the state, but rather the gradual subordination of political and economic special interests to the ideals of the church, as a realization of the Augustinian *Civitas Dei*.

Christian Wolff (1679–1754) later developed *in practice* the doctrine and method propounded by Leibniz, and did so entirely in Leibniz's spirit. Wolff was "Leibniz's pupil, and although not a thinker of genius, was in his way also a master."[16] Wolff continued Leibniz's work not only by elaborating a system out of Leibniz's views on matters of principle

---

[14] "Auctoritas, non veritas facit legem" (*Leviathan*, chapter 20).

[15] *Geschichte der abendländischen Weltanschauung* [History of the worldview of western culture] (Würzburg, 1950), 4:196.

[16] Kuno Fischer, *Geschichte der neueren Philosophie* [History of modern philosophy] (Heidelberg, 1902), 3:620.

The "Grotians": Leibniz, Wolff, Vattel

(which had often been given in an almost aphoristic brevity) but also in the sense that he so extensively developed Leibniz's doctrine in accordance with the principle of *continuity*—in *one* of the two possible directions—that that system became "more" than Leibniz had achieved in the sense of "enlightened understanding" but "less" in the sense of its religious and mystical content. Wolff, that is, applied Leibniz's method of the gradual and continual transitions of concepts, ideas, and ideals (or to put it in Goethe's terms, their "metamorphoses") to Leibniz's own teaching. By emphasizing *one* aspect of these concepts, ideas, and ideals, while neglecting to afford their *other* aspect the same attention, he brought about a *transposition* of the whole of Leibniz's spiritual legacy from the "esoteric" to the "exoteric." Thus, for example, Leibniz understood purposiveness as the process of perfecting—i.e., of the self-unfolding—of substances or monads. In this sense, the *first cause* and the *final purpose* are one and the same. The blossoming and fruit-bearing plant is thus the final purpose of the process of the plant's growth, and also the first cause of the process of growth in the plant. In the kernel containing the seed, the blossoming and fruit-bearing plant is already prefigured, and its growth is thus "caused" by the germinating power of the seed, just as it is given its "purpose" by the state of blossoming and bearing fruit.

If the highest state of society, therefore, is the realization of the *pie vivere* ("to live in piety"), i.e., the state of being oriented towards God, it is not only a final purpose, but also the first cause, the *primus motor* of the whole development: everything *from* God and *towards* God. Or, put another way, all historical development leads from the primordial theocracy to the final theocracy. This is the content of the concept of purposiveness in Leibniz's sense. It is actually nothing other than a philosophical reshaping of the biblical formula, *I am the alpha and omega, the first and the last.*

Now, this concept of purposiveness was changed by Wolff into the concept of *utility*. But the truly purposive has its purpose *in itself*, whereas the useful serves an *alien* purpose. The former is a final purpose, the latter an intermediate purpose. Indeed, *inner* purposiveness was the principle of Leibniz's metaphysics in its authentic, esoteric sense—whereas *external* purposiveness, or *utility*, becomes the principle of Wolff's.[17] And this latter becomes the general point of view of the intellectual Enlightenment: "it considers, evaluates, and explains things according to their utility."[18]

> And thus there comes into being that metaphysics without living intuition, that empiricism without profundity, which give, together with philosophy, the appearance of a dry Scholastic wisdom, which was later greatly disparaged by thinkers of genius. In this way, Wolff founds the *intellectual Enlightenment*, in which he rounds off philosophy in encyclopaedic fashion, systematically subdivides philosophy, and subjects each of its parts to logical discipline. This intellectual Enlightenment is not the completion of Leibniz's philosophy, but a phase, indeed the first phase, of its development—the systematic expression of its exoteric spirit. . . . This intellect, which is incapable of grasping Leibniz's principle of identity, destroys the concept of the monad by seeing souls and bodies as different substances. As it divides souls from bodies, it is now compelled to divide clear from opaque knowledge, morality from nature,

---

[17] Ibid.
[18] Ibid., 3:633.

The "Grotians": Leibniz, Wolff, Vattel

and God from the universe. And so every spiritual bond that Leibniz held together in the concepts of the monad, and of the development of the order of all beings, is now dissolved . . . [things] are, to speak truly, not purposive. Rather, they *serve* a purpose, or are useful—for the intellectual Enlightenment.[19]

What is said here about the basic philosophical concepts also goes for their application to the field of law, in particular the field of natural law and international law. Of Wolff's sixty-seven works, some (in both German and Latin) are devoted to the problems of natural law and international law. Thus, among other works, he wrote *Rational Ideas on the Social Life of Human Beings* (1721); *Rational Ideas on Human Action and Omission. On the Promotion of Human Happiness* (1720); *Philosophia Practica Universalis* (1738–1739); *Jus Naturae* (8 vols, 1740–1748); *Jus Gentium and Philosophia Moralis* (4 vols, 1746–1753).

Wolff wrote his German works as a professor of philosophy in Halle and Marburg, but his Latin works were written as "teacher of the entire human race" (*praeceptor universi generis humani*).

A colossal body of material is thus before us, including material on the jurisprudence of international law. And yet, owing both to its sheer extent and its rigidly systematic construction, almost nothing can be done with it. The system is all there, and all its component parts have as their principle that clarity is the hallmark of truth. Yet none of these component parts is so conceived that it can be detached from the system as a whole and considered on its

---

[19] No reference is given for this quotation by Tomberg; presumably it too comes from Kuno Fischer's *Geschichte der neueren Philosophie*. ED

own. His work *Jus Naturae Methodo Scientifica Pertractatum* (8 vols, Frankfurt am Main, 1740–1748) is the result of what is universally agreed to be an excessive application of mathematical methods of exposition to the problems of natural law. This work foregrounds the Leibnizian principle that human beings should work together to the end of furthering the perfection of all. Accordingly, nations and states ought also to join together to achieve the goal specified by natural law. The principle underlying international law is thus not merely the keeping of the peace, and a protection against aggression (as well as the minimizing and humanizing of war), but also, beyond this, the international task of actively furthering universal progress—i.e., the enrichment and strengthening of the state of peace. For Wolff, as also for Leibniz, peace is not merely the absence of war, but is the activity of perfecting, i.e., of universal progress. From this universal progress, as a duty and task for the whole of civilized humanity, there also result the rights and duties of individual states. Each individual state, as a member of the *maxima civitas* of civilized humanity, has the right to maintain itself and to develop; but it is obliged to provide the same services to other states, which services it in turn receives from them—with the restriction, however, that it is only obliged to assist other states insofar as it does not harm itself in doing so. Duty to oneself takes priority over the group of duties towards other states. Consequently, each state has only an "imperfect right" to the assistance of other states—that is, the right to *seek* such assistance. But by means of concluding treaties, it can achieve a perfect right, that is, a right to *demand* assistance.

The "Grotians": Leibniz, Wolff, Vattel

If we wish to understand the detailed consequences of the principles of Leibniz and Wolff concerning natural law and international law, we must turn to the *Droit des Gens* [Law of nations] (1757) by Emer de Vattel (1714–1716). Where Leibniz only sows seeds, and where Wolff, by contrast, piles up a mountain of mathematical Latin paragraphs, Vattel, seeing what was missing, provided a systematic and complete exposition of his two teachers' theories of natural and international law—an exposition both adequately concise and written in a living language (French).[20] Leibniz provided a stimulus; Wolff elaborated this into a doctrinal edifice; but it was Vattel's contribution to expound this in a clear and accessible way. For this reason, the so-called "Leibniz-Wolff" doctrine—insofar as it made a contribution to the jurisprudence of international law—will be treated through Vattel, and the substantive distinctions and alterations of meaning that took place on the way from Leibniz through Wolff to Vattel will also be set out.

When Vattel says that he wishes to set out "to the leaders of the nations what natural law prescribes," he does not wish to offer a new solution to the question of the world legal order, but has in mind, rather, an exposition of the Wolffian system that will be intelligible to "the leaders of the nations." Since, however, this system rests on the concept of the monad—i.e., of the individual substance that, by developing itself, brings about a harmonious world

---

[20] Vattel began in 1741 by publishing a *Defence of Leibniz's System*. His final work in this field was *Questions de Droit Naturel ou Observations sur le Traité de la Nature par M. Wolff* [Questions of natural law, or observations on M. Wolff's treatise on nature], in 1762.

order—it is a *pluralistic* system, and Vattel therefore does not start with the question of the *unity* of the community of states, but with the question of the laws and obligations of individual states: "To establish on a solid foundation the obligations and rights of nations is the design of this work. *The law of nations is the science that teaches the rights subsisting between nations or states, and the obligations correspondent to those rights.*"[21]

What is the state for Vattel? "Nations or states are bodies politic, societies of men united together for the purpose of promoting their mutual safety and advantage by the joint efforts of their combined strength."[22] Each nation or state is thus a *legal* person that has come into existence as a result of the social contract, and that has the same rights and duties within the community of states as does the *natural* person within the civil community. "Its rights are naturally the same as those of any other state. Such are the moral persons who live together in a natural society, subject to the law of nations."[23] From the equality of persons, Vattel deduces the equality of states (I, §36). From the equality or equal rights of states follows their autonomy and their equal claim to self-rule. "Every nation that governs itself, under what form

---

[21] Emer de Vattel, *The Law of Nations*, trans. Thomas Nugent (Indianapolis, IN: Liberty Fund, 2008), 67.

[22] Ibid.

[23] The quotation as given by Tomberg reads: "Der Staat hat dieselben Rechte wie der Mensch" (I, §4). ["The state has the same rights as the human being."] The quotation as given in the text above is the sentence in the section specified that comes closest to the text of the quotation as given by Tomberg: Vattel, *Law of Nations*, 83. But cf. 75: "A nation then is mistress of her own actions so long as they do not affect the proper and perfect rights of any other nation . . . other nations are bound to acquiesce in her conduct, since they have no right to dictate to her." TR

soever, without dependence on any foreign power, is a *sovereign state*. [Foreign nations have no right to interfere in the governance of an independent state.]"²⁴ There are different forms of connections between states: unequal alliance (*alliance inégale*), a protectorate (*protectorat*) vassalage (*vassalité*), a league (*fédération*), etc., but none of these forms excludes sovereignty (self-rule), for "a nation is a being determined by its essential attributes, that has its own nature, and can act in conformity to it."²⁵

> A moral being is charged with obligations to himself, only with a view to his perfection and happiness: for to *preserve and to perfect his own nature* is the sum of all his duties to himself. . . . The *perfection* of a nation is found in what renders it capable of obtaining the end of civil society. . . . The *end* or *object* of civil society is to procure for the citizens whatever they stand in need of—the necessities, the conveniences of life, and, in general, whatever constitutes happiness. . . .²⁶

The duty of self-preservation, which becomes, in dealings with other states, a *right* to self-preservation, is the real basis for Vattel's system of international law. This right is expressed first of all in the form of the independence and sovereignty of states. The independence and self-rule of individual states is, according to Vattel, irreconcilable with a

---

²⁴ Vattel, *Law of Nations*, 83. The text enclosed in square brackets is translated directly from Tomberg's German, since it does not appear at this point either in the original French text of Vattel's treatise or in Nugent's English translation. *Le Droit des Gens, ou Principes de la Loi Naturelle* (London, 1758), 1:31. TR
²⁵ Ibid., 85.
²⁶ Ibid., 86.

civitas maxima in the sense of a universal legal order to whose laws the individual states must bow as before a person superordinate to them, as was held by Wolff—let alone with a supra-state jurisdiction of the emperor and the pope of the kind Leibniz had in mind. Furthermore, Vattel's conception of the self-rule of the state differs from that of Leibniz and Wolff. Vattel sees self-rule as a kind of highest value, as a basic right under international law and a basic duty in state law and in politics—a conception that has gradually achieved sole supremacy and has governed the world for almost two hundred years right up to the present day.

It must be noted here, however, that this conception results from a remarkable and conspicuous, yet hardly ever admitted, fallacy. For if the individual state was founded through the social contract to the end of guaranteeing to its citizens protection and security, as well as the enjoyment of all those things requisite to their needs, conveniences, pleasures of life (*agréments de la vie*), and above all to their happiness, then the will of the citizens who contract the agreement consists in the security of their own happiness rather than in the foundation of the *state for the state's sake*. Consequently, if a supra-state world-organization, or even a world-state in which individual states would be absorbed, is in a position to secure for *individual people* their life, their freedom, their property, and any progress better than an individual self-governing state surrounded by a plurality of self-governing states could do, then the original social contract (which is, of course, concluded for the *benefit* of individuals) will be better fulfilled by the world-organization or by the world-state—and the "duty and right to self-preservation" of the individual state will then not merely become superfluous but will instead count as one of those forces that breaks the contract and prevents the fulfillment of the contract. On this point, Leonard Nelson remarks in his critique of Jellinek's *General Theory of the State* that

> it is a quite baseless and demonstrably *false* assumption that, for its members, the survival of a state is a necessary condition for the satisfaction of those members' interests. For its members and for itself, the cessation of the independent existence of the state means nothing other than a change of governance. If, then, we set aside those who have an interest in the state's continuance because of their ruling position within the state, then it is *indeed possible, though not necessary*, that such a change of governance might damage the interests of individuals, or, indeed, be connected with their higher interests. May we at last cease to permit ourselves to be deceived by the short cuts and evasions that sully the name of the jurisprudence of international law with a euphemistic sophism that serves political self-interest![27]

The fallacy that underlies the doctrine of the unlimited sovereignty of the state consists in the confusion of means and end. The state is merely a means to the end of the happiness of its members; it loses its meaning when another means serves that same end better. This holds, however, only for those doctrines of international law and state law which recognize that a *social contract* is the basis of the state (irrespective of whether this is thought of as an historical event or as a mere construction). It is otherwise with views that see in states a kind of mystical, ideal, national, and biological essence. Here, however, we are discussing Vattel's doctrine, and Vattel was an explicit, and in many respects more consistent, supporter of the social contract theory. It

[27] Nelson, *Die Rechtswissenschaft ohne Recht*, 59.

was precisely the doctrine of unrestricted sovereignty, however, that conferred upon Vattel so much support and interest from the leading political circles of his time. His work was still much read and quoted in England and in America in the nineteenth century, perhaps because it seemed to support claims to unlimited sovereignty, which were on the rise.

Now, Vattel's doctrine of unlimited sovereignty not only puts him at odds with Leibniz and Wolff, but also creates contradictions within his own doctrinal edifice. For example, if one compares chapter twelve of the third book with chapter thirteen of the same book, one will see that the doctrine of unlimited sovereignty stands almost like a foreign body in relation to his other views, which accord with the great Western tradition, whereas in chapter twelve he speaks about the traditional Christian principles of the *just* war (as held, for example, by St Thomas and Vitoria). Moreover, in chapter eleven[28] he denies (in the interest of unlimited sovereignty) that the head of state has a right to judge the actions of another head of state, and leaves any decision on the question of whether a war is just to the conscience of the warring parties. There we find:

> He who is engaged in war derives all his right from the justice of his cause. The unjust adversary who attacks or threatens him (who withholds what belongs to him—in a word, who does him an *injury*) lays him under the necessity of defending himself, or of doing himself justice, by force of arms: he authorizes him in all the acts of hostility necessary for obtaining complete satisfaction. Whoever therefore takes up arms without a lawful cause can have absolutely no right whatever; every hostility that he com-

---

[28] Tomberg specifies chapter twelve, but the quotation given appears in Book III, chapter eleven. TR

mits is an act of injustice. He is chargeable with all the evils, all the horrors of the war. All the effusion of blood, the desolation of families, the rapine, the acts of violence, the ravages, the conflagrations, are *his* works and *his* crimes. He is guilty of a crime against the enemy, whom he attacks, oppresses, and massacres, without cause; he is guilty of a crime against his people, whom he forces into acts of injustice and exposes to danger without reason or necessity against those of his subjects who are ruined or distressed by the war—who lose their lives, their property, or their health, in consequences of it; finally, he is guilty of a crime against humankind in general, whose peace he disturbs, and to whom he sets a pernicious example. The one who causes the wrong is liable for reparations or for compensation, should the damage incurred be irreparable—indeed, he is himself liable to punishment, if punishment should prove to be necessary, either as an example to others, or to ensure the security of the victim of the wrong he has inflicted, or for the security of the human race.[29]

This, according to Vattel, is the position of a prince who is the author of an unjust war (bk III, chapter 11). In chapter twelve,[30] conversely, we find the following:

All the doctrines we have laid down in the preceding chapter are evidently deduced from sound principles—from the eternal rules of justice. They are so many separate articles of that sacred law which nature, or the divine author of nature, has prescribed to nations. He alone whom justice and necessity have armed has a right to make war; he alone is empowered to attack his enemy, to deprive him of life, and wrest from him his goods and possessions. Such is the decision of the necessary law of nations or of the law of

---

[29] Vattel, *Law of Nations*, 586.
[30] Tomberg mistakenly specifies chapter thirteen. TR

nature, which nations are strictly bound to observe—it is the inviolable rule that each ought conscientiously to follow. But in the contests of nations and sovereigns who live together in a state of nature, how can this rule be enforced? They acknowledge no superior. Who then shall be judge between them, to assign to each his rights and obligations—to say to the one, "You have a right to take up arms, to attack your enemy, and subdue him by force," and to the other, "Every act of hostility that you commit will be an act of injustice; your victories will be so many murders, your conquests rapine and robberies"? *Every free and sovereign state has a right to determine, according to the dictates of her own conscience, what her duties require of her, and what she can or cannot do with justice. If other nations take upon themselves to judge of her conduct, they invade her liberty, and infringe her most valuable rights.*[31] Moreover, each party asserting that they have justice on their own side will arrogate to themselves all the rights of war and maintain that their enemy has none, that his hostilities are so many acts of robbery, so many infractions of the law of nations, in the punishment of which all nations should unite. The decision of the controversy, and the justice of the cause, is so far from being forwarded by it, that the quarrel will become more bloody, more calamitous in its effects, and also more difficult to terminate. *Nor is this all: the neutral nations themselves will be drawn into the dispute, and involved in the quarrel....*[32] Let us then leave the strictness of the necessary law of nature to the conscience of sovereigns....[33]

In other words, Vattel announces in chapter eleven the principle of the "necessary and strict natural law" with

---

[31] Author's emphasis.
[32] Author's emphasis.
[33] Vattel, *Law of Nations*, 589–90.

The "Grotians": Leibniz, Wolff, Vattel

respect to the just war, yet in chapter twelve renounces this principle as an *objective norm of international law* because of the absence of any judge superordinate to the states, and because of the irreconcilability in principle of such a judge with the unlimited sovereignty of the states. And as a result, he relegates this principle to the realm of subjective matters of conscience for the heads of state.

Vattel's subjectivistic doctrine consequently prepared the way for the claims of heads of states, or of governments and electorates, to be their own sole judges in respect of their own affairs. It also prepared the way for the doctrine of "impartial neutrality" in the nineteenth century. Once the subjectivistic doctrine was accepted, the principle upheld by Grotius—that there can be "no neutrality in questions of justice"—was practically given up and the door opened wide to relativism. For if there is no objective, specifiable, and universally valid justice—that is, if it is a matter of the subjective *forum conscientiae* of the many heads of state—then justice becomes *relative*: there are two or more different, and even opposed, "justices" that can be considered trustworthy. The possibility, however, of several different simultaneous "persuasions of justice" in the domain of international dealings is in fact the basis of "impartial neutrality." A world of relativism stood behind Pilate's question, "What is truth?"—a world whose neutrality in questions of justice (there are no disputed cases where it is not a matter of justice) was expressed in the ritual of handwashing.

⊕

The relegation of the decision on the question of the justice of a war to the conscience of the heads of state concerned was, however, neither a new doctrine nor one that lacked a political foundation. In Vattel's time, it did not seem to be such a consequential risk to, or betrayal of, the matter of justice in the world as it may seem today. Grotius already "fell back on the lame conclusion that the only practical course was not to ask third states to judge of the lawfulness or otherwise of a war, but to leave that question to the conscience of the belligerents."[34] On the other hand, the general state of European humanity after the Reformation, and specifically after the Thirty Years' War, was such that the pope and the emperor, who had in the past exercised the office of arbitration or judging, and to whom this office fell as it were *ex officio*, could now themselves do nothing more than support one of the two parties into which "Christendom" had been split. The emperor, let alone the pope as head of the Church, could, as the head and defender of the Holy Roman Empire, only be Catholic. Protestants, however (and Vattel was the son of a Reformed church pastor from Couvet in the principality of Neufchâtel), could not acknowledge the authority of the pope as judge in international disputes, since they did not recognize his authority even in questions of religion or of conscience. The authority of the emperor, which as a consequence of the Thirty Years' War they had with great effort and at great cost brought to a minimum tolerable to themselves, could not henceforth be granted a judicial role over their states either. They therefore held to their states, in whose unlimited sovereignty they found protection for their freedom of faith and of conscience.

[34] J.L. Brierly, *The Law of Nations* (fourth edition, Oxford: Clarendon Press, 1949), 35.

The "Grotians": Leibniz, Wolff, Vattel

Finally, Vattel's subjectivistic doctrine, in his own time, by no means signified an abandonment of the principles of justice in the realm of international dealings. At that time, there was every reason to *trust* the heads of state. For the heads of state (who belonged to "Christian European humanity," even if it was split) were either faithful Christians or were enlightened humanists, or were both at once. They were also cultivated people who had been raised in the spirit of chivalry and the concept of honor. At that time, the monstrosities of the wolf of Berchtesgaden [Adolf Hitler], or of the clique in the Kremlin, could not even be dreamed of. If Vattel, therefore, leaves the decision to the conscience of heads of state, he knows, or thinks he knows, that this conscience really exists, and that its reality can be counted upon to act within set limits of honor, humaneness, and religion. A situation of the world in which there can be heads of state who are not only personally devoid of conscience (a monstrous phenomenon that was possible even in the eighteenth century) but who deny even the existence of conscience and of religion—in that they regard them as a merely "ideological" superstructure to the "realities" of economic class-interests or of race and biology—was still inconceivable in Vattel's time. This inconceivability excuses Vattel and many other authors of the past along with him from the reproach of having abandoned or even betrayed the matter of justice in dealings between states.

Beyond the trust in the humaneness and rationality of heads of state or of nations, Vattel's whole system of international-legal jurisprudence is underpinned by a faith in culture, i.e., in the progress of culture and its humanizing influence that serves the interests of justice. "Nations being obliged by nature reciprocally to cultivate human society are bound to observe towards each other all the duties that the safety and advantage of that society require," says Vattel.[35] By "human society" he does not mean a world-organization, but the cultivated community of civilized society as a whole. This cultivated community, and membership of it, bring with them a number of obligations to reciprocal assistance (*les offices de l'humanité*). This refers to the same mutual aid that human beings owe each other as human beings. For this reason, "the first general law that we discover in the very object of the society of nations is that each individual nation is bound to contribute everything in her power to the happiness and perfection of all the others."[36]

Cain's principle of "Am I my brother's keeper?" which attained sole supremacy in the nineteenth century not only in the practice of international law but also in its theory, is not admitted by Vattel, for each state is obliged to stand by another when the latter is threatened with oppression by a powerful enemy (II, §54). Each state is also bound to help another when the latter is afflicted by famine (II, §5). Even in the case of a civil war in another state, that party should be helped "which seems to have justice on its side," and "an unhappy nation ought to be protected against an unjust tyrant" (II, §56). Moreover, the states ought to facilitate and further mutual commerce among themselves. They ought to make their laws known to each other (II, §6). They ought not to monopolize trade (II, §35), but instead engage in mutual free trade (II, §21), which is to be furthered by means of the institution of the consulate (II, §34). The legal verdicts of courts should not discriminate against represen-

---

[35] Vattel, *Law of Nations*, 261.
[36] Ibid., 73.

tatives of other nations (II, §71). Each state is obliged to keep its borders open to foreigners under the sole condition that they obey the laws of the land (II, §101), and without refusing to allow them to leave the country, should they wish to do so (II, §108).

These are the most important duties of the state *as a member of human society*. However, the state *as a sovereign and free community* also has duties towards *itself*. These duties now appear as limitations of the international obligations given above; indeed, insofar as the principle of unlimited sovereignty is once again questioned, these limitations can go so far as to mean that they are freed from important international obligations—i.e., from obligations to render assistance (*offices de l'humanité*). The first limitation is that "in those particulars which a nation can itself perform, no succour is due to it from others." [262] A further limitation of the obligation to render international assistance is the condition that the state in need of help has to ask for it. "It belongs to each [nation] to consider whether her situation warrants her in asking or granting anything in this regard." [266] Assistance that is rendered without being asked for is impermissible, since it is the same as interfering in the affairs of a sovereign state. "It is strange to hear the learned and judicious Grotius assert that a sovereign may justly take up arms to chastise nations that are guilty of enormous transgressions of the law of nature, that treat their parents with inhumanity like the Sogdians. . . ." [265]

The most far-reaching limitation of international obligations to render assistance lies in the consequences of the principle that the right to self-preservation takes priority, in a doubtful case, over the duty to render assistance. This principle is inferred from the Leibnizian doctrine (which

Wolff, too, accepted) that the human being should shape his free deeds in harmony with the demands of nature, which drive all beings to self-preservation and self-development. Since an individual human being lacks the capacities needed to do this, he must unite his forces with those of others in order to contribute to the process of perfecting all. This is the basis of the duties of humankind. These duties are merely an extension and continuation of the natural duties of individuals—they are a means to an end. The human being ought, consequently, to concern himself with the process of making another human being perfect only when and to the extent that it does not harm his own becoming-perfect.

At this point, the paths taken by Leibniz, Wolff, and Vattel diverge. Leibniz saw the goal of self-development as lying in the attainment of the capacity for love, i.e., in "joy at the happiness of others," and thus saw the meaning of becoming perfect as lying in the gradual transformation of self-assertion into selflessness in accordance with the "rainbow" of the principle of continuity. Wolff and Vattel concluded, instead, that self-preservation took priority. Henceforth, within the spectrum of duties, duties towards oneself are now opposed to duties towards others. The duty to render assistance is valid only for so long as it is reconcilable with law and with the duty to self-preservation. The consequences for matters of juridical principle drawn from these philosophical doctrines—as Wolff and Vattel drew them—are as follows: there is a conflict between the law of self-preservation and the duty to render assistance; *self-preservation is the rule, and rendering assistance is the exception*; in a case of doubt, then, self-preservation takes priority over rendering assistance.

The "Grotians": Leibniz, Wolff, Vattel

What follows from this, however, is that in every case where the security of one state is placed at risk by rendering assistance to another, the state concerned is justified in refusing to another state the help that has been requested. Who is to decide, however, in a case of doubt, whether the assistance requested actually would endanger the security of the state? "These offices being due only in necessity, and by a nation that can comply with them without being wanting to itself; the nation that is applied to has, on the other hand, a right of judging whether the case really demands them, and whether circumstances will allow her to grant them consistently with that regard which she ought to pay to her own safety and interests...." [266]

International assistance is an *inner* commitment, since "it binds the conscience." At the same time, however, it is also an *outer* commitment, since it "is considered relatively to other men, and produces some right between them." [74] It is the source of an *imperfect* right (*droit imparfait*) since it confers only the right to seek assistance rather than a right to demand it. "The *perfect right* is that which is accompanied by the right of compelling those who refuse to fulfill the correspondent obligation; the *imperfect* right is unaccompanied by that right of compulsion. The *perfect obligation* is that which gives to the opposite party the right of compulsion; the *imperfect* gives him only a right to ask." [75]

How, though, can an imperfect right become a perfect right? That is, how can the mutual assistance of states be guaranteed? This can happen by means of the conclusion of a *treaty*. Every imperfect right can become a perfect one by means of a treaty. The state itself originated in a treaty—in the social contract. Through a treaty, too, the state guarantees the rights that are necessary to its self-preservation and further development. What, then, are the legal consequences of the treaty to which the state owes its origin—i.e., the social contract? What are, that is, the bases of the legal order of the state?

"The purpose of the state is the happiness of the people, not that of the prince." The state is therefore not a piece of property or an inheritance of the prince, or of the princely house. "A state *cannot* be a patrimony" [Tomberg's emphasis], says Vattel. [125] In this he differs from Grotius, who was careful to insist that sovereignty always and without exception belonged to the nation [*Volk*]. Vattel also, however, differs from Wolff, who, with Grotius and Leibniz,[37] recognized the existence of patriarchal kingdoms, which was henceforth denied by Vattel. "As it is absurd," he writes, "to suppose that a society of men can place themselves in subjection otherwise than with a view to their own safety and welfare, and still more that they can place their posterity on any other footing, it ultimately amounts to the same thing; and it must still be said that the succession is established by the express will or the tacit consent of the nation, for the welfare and safety of the state. . . ."[38] "The pretended proprietary right attributed to princes is a chimera produced by an abuse that its supporters would fain make of the laws respecting private inheritances. The state neither is nor can be a patrimony, since the object of patrimony is the advantage of the possessor, whereas the prince is established only for the advantage of the state." [114–15]

---

[37] Leibniz declared his support for hereditary monarchy.

[38] Vattel, *Law of Nations*, 114. [Page references for the numerous quotations from this text in the following section will be given in brackets at the end of the relevant quotation.]

The "Grotians": Leibniz, Wolff, Vattel

Vattel thus replaces the personhood and sovereignty of the prince with the personhood and sovereignty of the state, which has been given to it by the people by means of the social contract. The people, whose "sovereignty is unalienable" [123] (§69), is the master of the state's constitution; the people have the right to change that constitution, with the proviso that those who dissent from the change are free to emigrate (bk 1, chap. 3, §33). The citizen, the individual, is not the property of the state. He is free to leave his homeland and to seek another if his homeland has, for spiritual, political, or economic reasons, ceased to be "home" for him.[39] The right to migrate follows from the nature of the social contract, since the social contract does indeed contain obligations both of the individual towards the community and also of the community towards the individual. If, then, the community does not fulfill its obligations towards the individual, the individual is at liberty to abandon it. Indeed, this also goes for whole parts of the state—for provinces and cities. "This province or town, thus abandoned and dismembered from the state, is not obliged to receive the new master whom the state attempts to set over it. Being separated from the society of which it was a member, it resumes all its original rights; and if it be capable of defending its liberty against the prince who would subject it to his authority, it may lawfully resist him." [241]

---

[39] The Soviet Union and the so-called "people's democracies" today [1952] hold the opposite point of view, and consider all their citizens as belonging to them as the property of the state in accordance with the principle set out by Stalin: "human beings are the most valuable capital." That is, the citizen's power of labor creates all other values, and belongs to the state. Free migration would thus be an expense of capital without compensation, i.e., a waste of state property.

From International Law to World Peace

The cases in which a citizen is justified in leaving his country are as follows: (1) If he can find no way of making a living in his native land. (2) "If the body of the society, or he who represents it, absolutely fail to discharge their obligations towards a citizen, the latter may withdraw himself. For if one of the contracting parties does not observe his engagements, the other is no longer bound to fulfill his; for the contract is reciprocal between the society and its members." [223] (3) "If the major part of the nation, or the sovereign who represents it, attempt to enact laws relative to matters in which the social compact cannot oblige every citizen to submission, those who are averse to these laws have a right to quit the society, and go settle elsewhere."[223]

Membership of a state is to be understood in accordance with the concept of the social contract. In the view of feudal law, the land of one's birth determines one's membership of a state. However, it follows from the social contract, whose goal is the happiness of human beings, that "the natives, or natural-born citizens, are those born in the country of parents who are citizens . . . the country of the fathers is therefore that of the children; and these become true citizens merely by their tacit consent." [217–18] According to the feudal conception, membership of a state was permanent. Vattel, however, draws from the social contract a more liberal and more humane conclusion: "every man has a right to quit his country in order to settle in any other, when by that step he does not endanger the welfare of his country." [221]

Just as the individual has emergency law at his disposal in an emergency (a law that in case of a conflict between duties of the first rank and those of the second or third rank justifies neglecting the latter kind), so also the state is justified in cases of a conflict between the duties and rights that

The "Grotians": Leibniz, Wolff, Vattel

self-preservation brings with it and the duties and rights of the community of states, i.e., of the mutual dependence of states, in making use of a state of emergency.

A right of necessity (*droit de nécessité*) "we thus call the right that necessity alone gives to the performance of certain actions that are otherwise unlawful, when, without those actions, it is impossible to fulfill an indispensable obligation." [320] Under a right of necessity, the necessities of life can be obtained by force; foreign ships, vehicles, and horses, as well as the labor of foreign citizens, can be requisitioned (§§ 120, 121); the women of a foreign nation, indeed, can be abducted, following the example of the rape of the Sabines, even if "no nation was obliged to furnish the Amazons with males." [320] A right of necessity also justifies compelling a foreign territory to grant free passage (§123).

Apart from a right of necessity, every state also has a series of rights that follow from the construction of the original community (*communion primitive*). Among these rights are freedom of movement (i.e., the right to travel anywhere), freedom of commerce and freedom of trade insofar as no misuse is made of these rights, i.e., insofar as travel, commerce, and trade are conducted innocently (*d'une manière innocente*): "the refusal of an advantage that is manifestly innocent is an injury." [330]

An infringement of law or a legal claim that can in no other way be satisfied are unconditional prerequisites for a just war. The just war must meet two conditions: "first, some right which is to be asserted—that is to say, that we be authorized to demand something of another nation; second, that we be unable to obtain it otherwise than by force of arms." [488]

The presence of a legal claim does indeed justify a state in waging war against another; yet the war itself is not, in Vattel's view, a legal instrument, but merely an emergency measure that one has been forced to use in the absence of any legal means. For "it is an error, no less absurd than pernicious, to say that the purpose of war is to decide controversies between those who acknowledge no superior judge—as is the case with nations. Victory usually favors the cause of strength and prudence rather than that of right and justice." [489]

"Political" considerations, which bring with them a disturbance of the balance of power, yield no legal claim and are not a justification for war: "it is a sacred principle of the law of nations that an increase of power cannot, alone and of itself, give anyone a right to take up arms in order to oppose it." [492] The means available to the state concerned for the restoration of the balance of power is to contract alliances with other states (III, §49).

If a prince begins an unjust war, every other state is justified in rendering assistance to the victim of the attack.

The legal consequences of a state of war are as follows. All the citizens of the enemy state count as enemies (III, §70), irrespective of the place and the country in which these citizens might be located; this goes for women and children too (III, §72). However, women and children do not count as enemies who are offering resistance, and are therefore to be treated accordingly (III, §§140, 145).

The killing of prisoners of war is unconditionally prohibited. The same applies to the use of poisoned weapons (III, §156), in contrast to Wolff (*Jus Gentium*, §878). Buildings and objects of universal cultural value may not be plundered by troops (III, §168), while plunder must otherwise be tolerated as one of the victor's rights.

The "Grotians": Leibniz, Wolff, Vattel

The unjust war, as stated, justifies other states in rendering assistance to the unjustly attacked state. Here it is only a matter of a right to render an assistance that lies wholly in the free estimation of the state concerned, not of a duty. For this reason, any state may also decide upon *neutrality*. Vattel is the first to have used the word "neutrality" in a treatise on international law. Whereas Grotius speaks of "those who have taken up a middle position in a war" (*de his qui in bello medii sunt*), and Bynkershoek of "non-enemies" (*non-hostes*), Vattel speaks of "neutrals" (*neutres*) (III, §103) and gives this modern word its modern sense: "those who, in time of war, do not take any part in the contest, but remain common friends to both parties without favoring the arms of the one to the prejudice of the other." [523]

The idea of neutrality as a conscious setting aside of the justice or injustice of a matter for which one or other of the parties has gone to war, and the taking up of a stance towards *both* parties as if both were at the same time fighting for the just cause—i.e., a *friendly* stance towards both parties—is new, and is owed to Vattel's principle of the unlimited sovereignty of the state and the denial in principle of states' being subject to penal or other forms of legal verdict. *Grotius* sees neutrality as still containing a duty to refrain from all actions that might strengthen the party fighting for an unjust cause, or impede the party on whose side justice lies. *Bynkershoek*, conversely, held the view that the neutral state was justified in providing help to both parties at the same time. Vattel is the first to have put forward the principle that neutrality consisted not in rendering assistance in the same degree to both parties, but in refraining to the same extent from giving *any* help. The neutral state should not provide weapons to one party to the disadvantage of the other (III, §105), in contrast to Grotius's view, and ought, in contrast to Bynkershoek's view, to refrain from rendering equal assistance at the same time to both parties, since "it would be absurd that a state should at one and the same time assist two nations at war with each other." [524]

This principle of strict non-intervention is however qualified in two ways by Vattel: (1) "When a sovereign furnishes the moderate succor due in virtue of a former defensive alliance, he does not become an associate in the war." [524] (2) A grant of free passage for the armies of states waging war is not breach of neutrality (III, §123). If, however, the majority of unlimitedly sovereign states—of which each has to decide upon right and wrong, war and peace, and none is obliged to account for its decisions—constitutes, in Vattel's view, the basis of international law, then one cannot avoid bringing up the question of what sanctions are available to international law.

⊕

How are the norms of international law to be distinguished from ordinary well-meaning moral advice? Is there anything that makes these norms binding, not for the conscience, but for dealings among nations too? Wolff saw the basis for the sanctions of international law as lying in a universal community of nations. Vattel rejects this kind of sanction, saying in the foreword to his work that

> Monsieur Wolff deduces it ["the species of law of nations that we call *voluntary*"] from the idea of a great republic (*civitas maximae*) instituted by nature herself, and of which all the nations of the world are members. According to him, the *voluntary* law of nations is, as it were, the law of that great republic. This idea does not satisfy me; nor do

The "Grotians": Leibniz, Wolff, Vattel

I think the fiction of such a republic either admissible in itself, or capable of affording sufficiently solid grounds on which to build the rules of the universal law of nations that shall necessarily claim the obedient acquiescence of sovereign states. I acknowledge no other natural society between nations than that which nature has established between mankind in general. It is essential to every civil society that each member have resigned a part of his right to the body of the society, and that there exist in it an authority capable of commanding all the members, of giving them laws, and of compelling those who should refuse to obey. Nothing of this kind can be conceived or supposed to subsist between nations. Each sovereign state claims and actually possesses absolute independence on all the others. [14]

In denying that international law has any sanction at its disposal, Vattel believes that this does not signify any sort of difficulty, since the states are not governed by mere caprice in their actions.

States conduct themselves in a different manner from individuals. It is not usually the caprice or blind impetuosity of a single person that forms the resolutions and determines the measures of the public: they are carried on with more deliberation and circumspection: and, on difficult or important occasions, arrangements are made and regulations established by means of treaties. [15]

Vattel nevertheless admits that rationality and caution in the use of state power are not by themselves sufficient to maintain legal order in the world, in that he grants all nations the right to unite against nations that are guilty of a breach of international law and that are acting wickedly:

The laws of natural society are of such importance to the safety of all states, that, if the custom once prevailed of trampling them underfoot, no nation could flatter herself with the hope of preserving her national existence, and enjoying domestic tranquillity, however attentive to pursue every measure dictated by the most consummate prudence, justice, and moderation.... All nations have therefore a right to resort to forcible means for the purpose of repressing any one particular nation who openly violates the laws of the society that nature has established between them, or who directly attacks the welfare and safety of that society. [76–77]

If, then, there is anywhere a nation of a restless and mischievous disposition, ever ready to injure others, to traverse their designs, and to excite domestic disturbances in their dominions, it is not to be doubted that all others have a right to form a coalition in order to repress and chastise that nation, and to put it forever out of their power to injure them. [289]

Nations that are always ready to take up arms on any prospect of advantage, are lawless robbers: but those who seem to delight in the ravages of war, who spread it on all sides, without reasons or pretexts, and even without any other motive than their own ferocity, are monsters, unworthy of the name of men. They should be considered as enemies to the human race, in the same manner as, in civil society, professed assassins and incendiaries are guilty, not only towards the victims of their nefarious deeds, but also towards the state, which therefore proclaims them public enemies. All nations have a right to join in a confederacy for the purpose of punishing and even exterminating those savage nations. Such were several German tribes mentioned by Tacitus. [487]

What is the place, then, of the sanctions available to international law in Vattel's theory? States have the right—

The "Grotians": Leibniz, Wolff, Vattel

not the duty—to subdue criminals under international law and to chastise and (where necessary) to destroy them, if they find this right in order to defend their own and their common rights and to enforce the universal order (*les lois de la Société que la Nature a établie entr'elles*) ["the laws of society that nature has established among them"]. If, however, it is a matter, in such a case, of a single member of this "society that nature itself has founded" which has to defend its rights by armed force (when, for example, the other states have decided to remain neutral against an aggressor and criminal under international law), then this sort of sanction comes to the same thing as a *vendetta* between two states. If, however, it is a matter of a voluntary collective action of several states against a state that is trampling upon international law, or that is indulging in war for the most wicked reasons or without any reason, then this kind of sanction is equivalent to an international *lynching*. Just as, among the Corsican, Albanian, or Caucasian uplanders, vendettas in a case of conflict between two parties are settled by force of arms, so the essence of a sanction through an individual state towards another state consists in nothing other than the same sort of "settlement" as we have in the case of a "blood feud" or a vendetta. If, however, the behavior of a state disturbs the general peace and the universal legal order, then several or all states *can* ally together against the disturbers of the peace and law-breakers, not only after an impartial investigation and legal process has taken place, but whenever the parties themselves think it good to do so. *This, however, is nothing more than a lynch mob of international dimensions.* The lynch mob and the vendetta are thus the only forms of enforcement and protection for international law that, in Vattel's view, are compatible with the unlimited sovereignty of states. In other words, *the unlimited sovereignty of states, as long as it remains unlimited, demands a legal state of international dealings that is equivalent to that of the lynch mob and the carrying out of vendettas.*

The doctrine of the unlimited (and in principle unlimitable) sovereignty of the state and of a legal order that is only to be brought about by means of vendettas and lynch mobs became the dominant doctrine of the eighteenth, nineteenth, and the first quarter of the twentieth centuries. It is a cornerstone of so-called "modern international law" as it has come down to us, and today it stands at the center of the struggle for and against an enforceable legal order in the world.

⊕

Vattel's doctrine is also path-breaking for so-called "modern international law" in another very essential respect: in its distinction between natural law and international law; in its practical limitation of natural law to a merely consultative role *in foro conscientiae* ("in the forum of conscience"); and, finally, in the emphasis and stress laid upon the significance of *treaties* (i.e., of positive law at the expense of natural law) in the absence of any divine law (which no longer gets a mention). Vattel's system has two levels. In actuality, it consists of natural law and positive law, even if he divides these two levels into four subordinate levels, which he does as follows. First (1) natural law is the necessary or inner law, which is binding only upon conscience and consequently has only an ethical value (*Prélim.*, §7). Then come three kinds of positive international law: (2) law that depends upon the will, or voluntary law; (3) the law of treaties; and (4) the law of custom. All three of these latter kinds of law are grounded in the will of the states: voluntary law presupposes the agreement of the states; the law of treaties rests on their explicit agreement; and the law of custom on their silent agreement. This division, however, in no way alters the fact that we are dealing here with a system of law in which the level of divine law is missing, in which the level of natural law has been degraded so that it has only a subjective and advisory significance, and in which the level of positive law (now divided into three) is awarded the really essential role of binding international law.

Vattel himself characterizes his own system and its relationship to Wolff as follows:

> This glory [of distinguishing international from natural law] was reserved for the baron de Wolff. That great philosopher saw that the law of nature could not, with such modifications as the nature of the subjects required, and with sufficient precision, clearness, and solidity, be applied to incorporated nations or states without the assistance of those general principles and leading ideas by which the application is to be directed—that only by those principles are we are enabled evidently to demonstrate that the decisions of the law of nature respecting individuals must, pursuant to the intentions of that very law, be changed and modified in their application to states and political societies, thus to form a natural and necessary law of nations. From this he concluded that it was proper to form a distinct system of the law of nations, a task which he has happily executed. But it is just that we should hear what Wolff himself says in his Preface.
>
> "Nations," says he, "do not, in their mutual relations to each other, acknowledge any other law than that which nature herself has established. Perhaps, therefore, it may appear superfluous to give a treatise on the law of nations as distinct from the law of nature. But those who entertain this idea have not sufficiently studied the subject. Nations,

it is true, can only be considered as so many individual persons living together in the state of nature; and for that reason we must apply to them all the duties and rights that nature prescribes and attributes to men in general as being naturally born free and bound to each other by no ties but those of nature alone. The law that arises from this application, and the obligations resulting from it, proceed from that immutable law founded on the nature of man, and thus the law of nations certainly belongs to the law of nature. It is therefore, on account of its origin, called the *natural*, and, by reason of its obligatory force, the *necessary* law of nations. That law is common to all nations, and if any one of them does not respect it in her actions, she violates the common rights of all the others.

"But nations or sovereign states being moral persons (*personnes morales*) and the subjects of the obligations and rights resulting, in virtue of the law of nature, from the act of association that has formed the political body—the nature and essence of these moral persons necessarily differ in many respects from the nature and essence of the physical individuals, or men, of whom they are composed. When, therefore, we would apply to nations the duties that the law of nature prescribes to individual men, and the rights it confers on him in order to enable him to fulfill his duties—then, since those rights and those duties can be no other than what are consistent with the nature of their subjects, they must, in their application, necessarily undergo a change suitable to the new subjects to which they are applied. Why may it not therefore be separately treated of as a law peculiar to nations?" [...]

Both the necessary and the voluntary law of nations are therefore established by nature, but each in a different manner: the former, as a sacred law that nations and sovereigns are bound to respect and follow in all their actions; the latter, as a rule that safety and the general welfare oblige them to admit in their transactions with each other. The *necessary law* immediately proceeds from nature—which nature, as common mother of mankind, recommends the observance of the *voluntary law of nations* in consideration of the state in which nations stand with respect to each other, and for the advantage of their affairs. This double law, founded on certain and invariable principles, is susceptible of demonstration, and will constitute the principal subject of this work.

There is another kind of law of nations, which authors call *arbitrary* because it proceeds from the will or consent of nations. States, as well as individuals, may acquire rights and contract obligations by express engagements, by compacts and treaties: hence results a conventional law of nations, peculiar to the contracting powers. Nations may also bind themselves by their tacit consent: upon this ground rest all those regulations that custom has introduced between different states, and that constitute the *usage* of nations, or the law of nations founded on custom . . . it is a peculiar law, and limited in its operation, as the conventional law: both the one and the other derive all their obligatory force from that maxim of the natural law that makes it the duty of nations to fulfill their engagements, whether express or tacit. [10–12, 17]

A declaration by one side, by means of which the intention to give up an international custom is made known, suffices to free the state concerned from that custom's bindingness.[40] The usage of the *law of custom*, since it is a silent treaty, makes it possible for imperfect rights to be changed into perfect ones, just as a treaty does. Thus nations, for example, have the imperfect duty to receive the consuls of other nations, but the nations that receive them could

[40] "Preliminaries," *The Law of Nations*, §26.

always refuse them the necessary immunity: "Custom is to be the rule on these occasions." [280]

As far as its binding force is concerned, however, customary law stands far behind the *law arrived at by treaty*. For not only can it be invalidated by a declaration on the part of one party, but it is also invalid if it contradicts justice or contains something contrary to law; whereas a treaty, even if it is unjust or contrary to law, and thus invalid for *inner law* or "for the conscience," nevertheless retains its binding character as external (positive) law.[41] Now, just as the "inner law" or natural law gives way to a treaty (even one that contradicts natural law), and just as every court of arbitration has to give way in the face of the states' claim to unlimited sovereignty, so the law of custom must also give way to a treaty and to the explicit declaration of the states' will.

With Vattel, the doctrine of so-called "modern international law" is in all essential respects already with us—that is, the doctrine of the legal order of an *in principle* anarchic plurality of unlimitedly sovereign states, from which all the remnants of that principle that was crystallized in the Middle Ages as "emperor and pope" are henceforth excluded. Leibniz's ideas of a law with three levels were transformed by Wolff into a law with two levels in which the higher *natural law* had supremacy, and was then once more transformed by Vattel into a law with two levels in which *positive law* had supremacy. With this, there has already emerged in its essential features the doctrine of positive law that (once it had gotten rid of the "ethically and legally irrelevant"

[41] Ibid., §27.

The "Grotians": Leibniz, Wolff, Vattel

appendage of natural law) was to be the ruling doctrine at the time of the outbreak of war in 1914. This doctrine then underwent a further transformation in the same direction—from absolute principles to relative principles and from relative principles to the unprincipled *will to power* of the National Socialist and communist "theories of law."

In Vattel's work, the doctrine of modern international law is indeed already present in its fundamental outlines. The subsequent development consisted, on one hand, in the process of simply setting natural law aside, and on the other, in a struggle to retain it. This process can be described as the twilight of rationalistic natural law and the transition from a law with two levels to a "one-dimensional law."

PART VI

The Twilight of Rationalistic Natural Law and the Transition from a Law with Two Levels to a Law with One Level

1

The French Enlightenment's Ideas about International Law and the Revolutionary Politicizing of Law

n their commentary on the Austrian *Allgemeines bürgerliches Gesetzbuch* [Book of universal civil statutes], Pfaff and Hoffmann write: "The tamest and lamest theories, no less than the preaching of world reform from the guillotine and the French wars of conquest, were put forward in the name of the 'law of reason.' Natural law was a spiritual direction, not a regularly propounded doctrine." The "theocentric" approach to the field of jurisprudence, i.e., the approach that depended upon God, revelation, and divine law, had been given up (apart from the continuation of the tradition through Leibniz and the theologians). An "anthropocentric" standpoint had taken its place, an approach that looked for the norms of law in man and in his autonomous reason, ethical life, and will. The theologians' old opposition between realism and nominalism, as well as between the primacy of reason and the primacy of will (voluntarism), was taken over into the field of a henceforth secularized jurisprudence. Accordingly, two currents emerged. The first was that of the "believers in reason," who asserted the primacy of man's reason over his will and believed that all the norms of law could be axiomatically deduced from pure reason. The sec-

ond was that of the "law of will," that is, the current of the "believers in will," who asserted the primacy of man's will over his reason (Rousseau) and who thus believed that they could, as it were, "postulate" all the norms of law categorically out of "practical" reason.

Both currents alike are usually described as advocating the "law of reason," since both professed their membership of the "Enlightenment," both asserted the autonomy of humankind, and both made use of the language and arguments of emancipated reason, thereby emphasizing their opposition to the theologically oriented tradition. Yet the two currents are also very clearly distinct from each other. One need only compare Jean-Jacques Rousseau (1712–1778) and Christian Wolff (1679–1754) to put the distinction very clearly in view. For while Wolff, proceeding mathematically, saw in the statutes of law the statutes of reason itself, in Rousseau's case it was a matter of the will as the source of law; and indeed of the general will (*volonté générale*), which had emerged through the social contract that would determine the future. This general will is the will of the people, whose decisions

> always have the same rightness. You always will your own good, but you cannot always see it. The people is never corrupted, but it is often misled, and only then does it seem to will what is bad. There is often a great difference between the will of all and the general will: the latter takes account only of the common interest; the former takes account of private interest, and is only a sum of particular wills. But remove from these same wills the pluses and minuses that cancel each other out, and what is left as the sum of the differences is the general will. If, when a properly informed people deliberates, citizens held no commu-

nication with each other, the large number of small differences would always result in the general will, and the deliberation would always be good.¹

The general will is thus in principle infallible: "the general will is always rightful and always tends to public utility."² The state itself is the result of the general will, in that the creation of the state was the act of the general will, in the shape of the social contract. The social contract

> tacitly incorporates a commitment that alone can give force to the rest: namely, that whoever refuses to obey the general will shall be constrained to do so by the entire body. This means nothing other than that he shall be forced to be free. For such is the condition that, by giving each citizen to the Fatherland, guarantees him against all personal dependence: the condition that makes the artifice and play of the political machinery, and that alone gives legitimacy to civil engagements without which it would be absurd, tyrannical, and subject to the most enormous abuses.³

The question of how a man can be free if he has to fit in with what he is compelled to do by the will of the majority is answered by Rousseau as follows:

> The question is badly put. The citizen consents to all laws, even those passed in spite of him, and even those that punish him when he dares to violate one of them. The constant will of all members of the state is the general will; it is through this that they are citizens and free. When a law is

---

[1] Jean-Jacques Rousseau, *Of The Social Contract and Other Political Writings*, ed. Christopher Bertram, trans. Quintin Hoare (London: Penguin Books, 2012), 32.
[2] Ibid.
[3] Ibid., 23.

proposed in the people's assembly, what is asked of the members is not precisely whether they approve the proposal or reject it, but whether it is in conformity with the general will that is their own. In giving his suffrage, each expresses his opinion on this; and from the reckoning of the votes, the declaration of the general will is drawn. So, when the opposite opinion to mine prevails, that proves nothing other than that I was mistaken, and that what I considered to be the general will was not. If my particular opinion had prevailed, I should have done something other than what I had willed, and it is then that I should not have been free.[4]

Ernst von Hippel[5] says of Rousseau's doctrine of the general will, that if one tries

to disentangle what we have here from its lack of intellectual clarity and practical unreality (at least to understand it on its own terms), one will have to say something like the following. Rousseau's nominalistic approach has, as a necessary consequence, the loss of the *morally universal*—and thus, of world reason; and what Rousseau instead strives for (and thinks he has found as a kind of nominalistic universally-binding factor), is the will of the people, which thus takes the place of the divine will. So that this can appear to be grounded, however, the will of the individuals, if it is "purely" expressed (that is, for Rousseau, if it is not disturbed by influences lying outside it), must, as such, be directed towards the good.... Here Rousseau overlooks the fact that his own thinking is only a construction which, in the manner of a parallelogram made up of the forces of the individual wills (that in the end have in practice to be summarized), allows what is good in itself and thus bind-

---

[4] Ibid., 102–3.
[5] See Introduction to the present book.

ing in the universal will to be produced in the manner of a calculation. And if one sets aside what is unclear and unsupported in this merely artificial and emotional mysticism, all that remains that can be realized in practice is the principle of majority rule—which, as the tyranny of the merely quantitative, is almost deified by Rousseau.[6]

Rousseau's doctrine, as a scholarly achievement, would be completely irrelevant for the history of the jurisprudence of international law (since, quite apart from its deficiencies in form and content, it also makes no direct contribution to the problems of international law) had it not exerted a strong psychological influence upon views about the nature of the state as the subject of international law, as well as upon those about the nature of organized human community as such, and thus about the community of international law as well. His doctrine is also a telling symptom that is invaluable in helping us understand later tendencies in the field of international law—tendencies that see international law as having its source in precisely this "will of the state." Rousseau's passionate fanaticism had profound effects, and lived on in the men of the Terror of 1793. Indeed, his doctrine of the general will (*volonté générale*) was itself made part of the "Declaration of the Rights of Man and of the Citizen" of the National Assembly, which set out a new French constitution on August 4, 1789, a document unanimously approved by the National Convention on June 23, 1793. This "Declaration" was subsequently prefixed to every new French constitution as an introduction. Articles 3 and 4 run as follows.

[6] Ernst von Hippel, "Rousseaus Staatslehre als Mystik des Materialismus" [Rousseau's doctrine of the state as a mysticism of materialism], in *Neues Abendland* [New West] 6 (1951), 7.

From International Law to World Peace

ARTICLE 3
All men are equal, both by nature and before the law.

ARTICLE 4
Law is the free and solemn expression of the general will; before it, all are equal, whether the law protects or punishes; law can only prescribe what is right and useful to society; it can only forbid what is detrimental to it.

Rousseau's doctrine of the general will is here carved in granite. It has also, however, put down equally deep roots in modern theories of international law, specifically in the theory of the "will of the state." Thus, for example, Georg *Jellinek*, in his works *Die Lehre von den Staatenverbindungen* [Theory of the relations between states] (Vienna, 1882), and *Die allgemeine Staatslehre* [General theory of the state] (third edition, Berlin, 1914), provides a theory of the will of the state as the source of law as such, and of international law, which is really a continuation of Rousseau's theory. He says in *Die allgemeine Staatslehre* [hereafter AS, page(s)]: "either one tries to examine the nature of law as a power that is independent of human beings and is grounded upon the nature of what exists, or else one thinks of it as a subjective, i.e., always human, phenomenon." (AS 332) And he decides in favor of the idea of law as a phenomenon of subjective life: "Law exists in our heads, and the more detailed specification of law must explore which part of the content of our consciousness is to be described as law." (AS 332) This part, though, is the part that is at work in our actions, i.e., our will: "The necessary distinguishing feature of all law is its validity. A norm is valid if it has the capacity to supply a motive, if it determines the will. . . . This capacity arises from the conviction—a conviction that cannot be traced back any further—that we are obliged to obey it." (AS 333)

The validity of the legal norm "thus, in the first place, always rests on the conviction of its validity. On this purely subjective element, the whole legal order is built." (AS 333 ff) In order to distinguish a correct belief about law from an incorrect one, however, there is no other criterion available than the quantitative assessment of the "average" against the "minority." (AS 334) The "dominant belief about law" thus becomes "the criterion of law." (AS 481) The decision about what is legal and illegal is a problem to be assessed by "mass psychology" (AS 334), i.e., by determining the *average* will of the mass of the people, or, in Rousseau's terminology, the expression of the *general* will. This will determines the legal order, i.e., what is legal or illegal within a state; and it is also what is at work in relations between states as the "will of the state." Its independence is sovereignty.

In *Lehre von Staatenverbindungen* [hereafter LS, page(s)], Jellinek writes: "Sovereignty is that property of a state by virtue of which it can be legally bound only by its own will." (LS 34) And "sovereignty is the right to be bound and bindable by one's own will alone." (LS 55) Since the state is bound only by its own will, it is only bound by its own *declared* will for so long as this will continues. It is therefore, in truth, not bound in any way, and it has no duty to abide by treaties (LS 55),[7] since "in a struggle with the supreme interests of sovereign states, the duty of fidelity to treaties comes last" (AS 741), and since the state "stands higher than any individual legal statute." International law is there for the sake of the states; the states are not there for the sake of international law. (AS 337)

[7] Cf. Nelson, *Die Rechtswissenschaft ohne Recht*, chap. 2, 51 ff.

From International Law to World Peace

The conclusion one must inevitably draw from this doctrine is therefore that since states are bound only by their own wills, and since this binding is not binding at all (because the duty to observe a treaty lasts only for so long as it remains in the interest of the state that contracts the treaty), there is no such thing as international law, nor can there be such a thing—because what Jellinek calls "international law" is and can be in truth nothing other than an interaction among the political interests of unlimitedly sovereign states that are bound and guided by nothing but these interests.

Law is only law for so long as it has a meaning by means of which the intellect supplies norms to the will, which, that is, sets limits to it and gives it direction. If it is, instead, an expression of the will, even of the "general will" or the "average will" or even of a mass-psychological "conviction of law" (which all comes to the same thing), then it is no longer a matter of law, but of *politics*—i.e., of the struggle between, and balance among, aspirations to power. It is irrelevant in such a case whether it is a matter of Rousseau's "general will" or of Jellinek's "will of the state." Both authors make international law impossible, and thus deprive the jurisprudence of international law of any object. The dogma of the "will of the state" (etc.)—bound only by its own interests and owing no other obligation of any kind (i.e., the dogma of unlimited state sovereignty)—is, as Leonard Nelson has shown with a clarity that leaves nothing to be desired, completely incompatible with the existence of international law. On this question, Nelson says:

> This is admittedly a dogma shared by the ruling consensus among lawyers. But anyone who is able to free himself, if only for a moment, from blind faith in the supreme wis-

dom of the ruling consensus among lawyers, must upon even the slightest reflection come to the conclusion that there *cannot* be a right of sovereignty in the sense mentioned, since such a right would contradict the very concept of international law. It would be self-contradictory, since the sovereignty of one state immediately excludes that of the others. If one state *wishes* to abide by no limits with respect to the others (e.g., not to respect their independence), such a state can also have no sort of rights with respect to them, since these rights would *obligate* it to set limits to its own arbitrary will. Moreover, it would contradict the concept of international law. "The first principle of international law," says Jellinek (LS 21), "is the recognition of the equality of states, without respect to their size or political importance." It is obvious that this principle of international law, like all other such principles, is incompatible with the sovereignty of states. If there is a right of equality, or any other sort of right, among states, then this right is for that very reason removed from the arbitrary will of the states themselves; it therefore *limits* their sovereignty and thereby *removes* their sovereignty. Indeed, the fact that *a limitation of sovereignty is equivalent to its destruction* is also admitted by Jellinek. (AS 496) The possibility of international law thus completely contradicts the possibility of sovereignty.

Since Jellinek's doctrine of the sovereign wills of the states is only a consequence (within international law) of his and Rousseau's political and legal doctrines of the general will and the "ruling conviction of law," it can be concluded from this that the indirect influence of Rousseau was in principle hostile to international law. His influence was owed more to the pathos of his key teachings on "freedom" and "inalterable human rights," and had more of an effect on journalism and on political authors than on theorists of "natural and international law"; and rightly so, since his doctrine of the general will as the original source of law has precisely the significance of replacing law with politics, and positing that there is really no such thing as law at all—only politics.

⊕

The other current of the "rational law" of the "age of Enlightenment"—that is, the current of rationalistic natural law—also contributed, for its part, to the discrediting of natural law. In abandoning the trans-historical and universal principles of divine law and allowing emancipated reason alone to be considered the valid source of law, they fell victim to the relativism of subjective and historically-conditioned systems—which, however, all claimed to be "*the* system of natural law" or "*the* doctrine of reason concerning law." Thus, for example, from 1780 onwards, at every Leipzig book fair there were eight or more systems of "natural law," each claiming to be *the* system.

Compared with the deep intellectual and religious foundations of the doctrine of the *philosophia perennis* of the eternal three-note chord of law, the conceptions of law that deviate from it under the influence of the philosophy of the Enlightenment of the eighteenth century, and of the natural-scientific approach of the nineteenth, look as fleeting as mayflies. For if one sets aside the Scholastic doctrine of natural law, as well as the teachings of Hugo Grotius, Gottfried Wilhelm Leibniz, and even Christian Wolff, which still move in the same sphere of tradition, one leaves the domain of the great temple buildings and enters that of houses, huts, hovels, and, in the end, of barracks and dungeons.

If we contemplate, for example, the grandly comprehensive edifice built by Thomas Aquinas—in which *lex aeterna*

French Enlightenment's Revolutionary Politicizing of Law

(the divine *essence* of law in God) stands on high, and *lex divina* (positive divine law, the next level below *lex aeterna*) represents the *revelation* of eternal law to humankind, so that it may in turn arrive at the level of *lex naturalis* (the level of human *reason*) on the basis of which the decrees of *lex humana* (or positive law) are formulated by the legislator called to that vocation—then we have to admit that here *all* the levels of law are embraced in a single whole. Even as early as the work of Pufendorf (1632–1694), this building is no longer a temple, but a synagogue, a religious "school," since he does away with the highest level, the *lex aeterna*. But when we come to the French representatives of Enlightenment philosophy and to Friedrich Justus Thibaut (1772–1840), who can be seen as the leader of the natural law school in Germany, the edifice of law loses another storey: the revealed divine law, *lex divina*. All that remains is a purely human, two-storey habitation in which human reason hands down guidelines from the upper storey to the workshop of positive law found on the lower floor. But this third layer of legal consciousness, too, was brought to an end by modern *positivism*.

In sum, three of the levels of the earlier range of legal consciousness had by now been eliminated, and humanity was delivered up defenceless to the remaining area of "legislation" by the various tendencies of political power. For if *law* no longer traces its binding validity back to absolute divine law and to the dictates of universal human reason, then it can rest *only* on force. Thus the development of modern legal consciousness begins with the temple of Scholasticism (which was not even close to being finished, but to which much building work could and should have been added) and ends with dungeons and barracks (the *force majeure* of the interested parties)—that is, with unscrupulous positivism in its final and true shape.⁸

What is said here about jurisprudence also holds good for its corollary, the jurisprudence of international law.

> With all the defects and weaknesses of Enlightenment rational law, a historical retrospect must, admittedly, also acknowledge the great significance of that age of European legal history. The rational law of the eighteenth century provided for the first time a fully worked-out system of jurisprudence, which in principle wished to be without lacunae. It transformed the practice of punishment in a humane spirit, did away with torture, put an end to the scandal of witch-trials, and limited the caprice of judges in the presentation of evidence by means of the demand for legally appropriate means of knowledge and the imposition of the principle *nullum crimen sine lege* ["no crime without law"]. The lasting monument of these achievements are the law codes that emerged from the spirit of rational law in the eighteenth and early nineteenth centuries in Austria, Prussia, and Saxony, which provided individual citizens with a legal certainty that till then had been unknown on the European mainland. Finally, we must also make reference to the fact that the law of war in the eighteenth century showed unmistakable signs of progress towards a more humane approach under the influence of the Enlightenment.⁹

Despite the unmistakable progress towards a more humane approach, and the impulse towards the codification of law, the Enlightenment law of reason created a great deal of

---

[8] See author's *The Art of the Good...*, 28–29.

[9] Georg Stadtmüller, *Das Naturrecht im Lichte der geschichtlichen Erfahrung* [Natural law in the light of historical experience] (Recklinghausen, 1948), 23.

confusion in the field of jurisprudence precisely because of its proliferating productivity. Within this confusion, which affected almost all areas of the humanities, not least philosophy, there arose a man of twofold spirit. On the one hand, as a son of the Enlightenment within the Protestant tradition, this man was filled with a will to protect what was precious in "enlightenment" and the impulse towards individual freedom, and to rescue these from an inevitable future reaction. On the other, he took it upon himself to set limits to what had become the excessive claims of autonomous reason, to put an end to the free play of a subjectively influenced rational speculation, and to provide a new, solid, and once again universally valid foundation for reason's cognitive efforts—so that, freed from subjectivism, these efforts would once more be able to attain *objective* value and *objective* validity. The man who undertook to bring autonomous reason back within correct limits, and at the same time to provide it with a method and a certain and protected domain for its development, was the Königsberg philosopher, Immanuel Kant (1724–1804). His work and influence extend over almost all areas of human thought, including that of international law.

2

Kant and Kantianism

eary therefore of dogmatism, which teaches us nothing, and also of skepticism, which promises us absolutely nothing, not even the tranquillity of a permitted ignorance; summoned by the importance of the knowledge that we need, and made mistrustful, through long experience, with respect to any knowledge that we believe we possess or that offers itself to us under the title of pure reason, there remains for us but one critical question, the answer to which can regulate our future conduct: *Is metaphysics possible at all?*[1]

So asks Kant in his *Prolegomena to Any Future Metaphysics That Will Be Able to Come Forward as Science* (§ 4). He traces this question in turn back to the further question "how are synthetic *a priori* judgments possible?" (§ 5):

> Whether metaphysics is to stand or fall, and hence its existence, now depends entirely on the solving of this problem. Anyone may present his contentions on the matter with ever so great a likelihood, piling conclusion on conclusion to the point of suffocation; if he has not been able beforehand to answer this question satisfactorily, then I have the right to say: it is all empty, baseless philosophy and false wisdom. You speak through pure reason and pre-

---

[1] Immanuel Kant, *Prolegomena to Any Future Metaphysics*, trans. and ed. Gary Hatfield (Cambridge: Cambridge University Press, 1997), 25.

tend, as it were, to create *a priori* cognitions, not only by analyzing given concepts, but by alleging new connections that are not based on the principle of contradiction and that you nonetheless presume to understand completely independently of all experience; now how do you come to do this, and how will you justify such pretenses? You cannot be allowed to call on the concurrence of general common sense; for that is a witness whose standing is based solely on public rumor. . . . All metaphysicians are therefore solemnly and lawfully suspended from their occupations until such a time as they will have satisfactorily answered the question: "How are synthetic cognitions *a priori* possible?" For in this answer alone consists the credential that they must present if they have something to advance to us in the name of pure reason, in default of which, however, they can expect only that reasonable persons (who have been deceived so often already) will reject their offerings without any further investigation.[2]

Kant answers the question whether knowledge independent of sense perception and resting upon synthetic *a priori* judgments is possible (i.e., knowledge not resting on judgments of experience, which are "*ampliative* and augment the given cognition," in contrast to analytic judgments, which are "merely *explicative* and add nothing to the content of the cognition")[3] by saying that such knowledge of pure reason can by itself only know *forms*, but that the essence of the object, the "thing in itself"—as it is, and not merely as it *appears*[4] to a given kind of intuition—lies beyond the bor-

---

[2] Ibid., 28–30.

[3] Ibid., 16.

[4] "If our intuition had to be of the kind that represented things *as they are in themselves*, then absolutely no intuition *a priori* would take place, but it would always be empirical. For I can only know what may

ders of such knowledge. Such knowledge is thus merely a self-knowledge of the power of knowledge—of its categories, which are the *a priori* forms of intuition and thinking innate to it—and this, in reality, only as an ascertainment of the composition of these categories, not of why, whence, how, or for what purpose they are as they are. Thus, according to Kant, pure reason, i.e., the power of cognition that makes use of synthetic *a priori* judgments, can say nothing about the questions of God, freedom, or immortality. Since, however, on the other hand, scientific (i.e., necessary and universally valid) knowledge is only possible by means of the categories, it accordingly rests not on the truth-content of the *objects* of knowledge, but has its basis rather in the knowing subject's aptitude for the faculty of knowledge.

The essence of things thus cannot in principle be penetrated by knowledge directed towards the empirical realm. Kant unmistakably establishes the subjectivity of knowledge when he says that "we can cognize of things *a priori* only what we ourselves have put into them."[5] The knowledge of the world of appearances, which comes about by means of the categories of the human power of knowledge,

---

be contained in the object in itself if the object is present and given to me. Of course, even then it is incomprehensible how the intuition of a thing that is present should allow me to cognize it the way it is in itself, since its properties cannot migrate over into my power of representation; but even granting such a possibility, the intuition would still not take place *a priori*, i.e., before the object were presented to me, for without that, no basis for the relation of my representation to the object can be conceived; so it would have to be based on inspiration." Kant, *Prolegomena*, 34.

[5] Immanuel Kant, *Critique of Pure Reason*, trans. and ed. Paul Guyer and Allen W. Wood (Cambridge: Cambridge University Press, 1998), III.

may not be either a dream or a delusion, but it is in principle incomplete, and, indeed *qualitatively* incomplete. It is a process of approximation towards an object of knowledge as it is in itself, an object that is in principle infinite.

If, then, for knowledge, the *being* of things is simultaneously both made possible by and limited by the subjectivity of the knowing consciousness, the same is also true for the domain of the *ought*. Man is his own lawgiver. He is, morally speaking, completely autonomous, and Kant decisively rejects any heteronomy as conflicting with the dignity of a free being. "The moral law is given, as it were, as a fact of pure reason, of which we are *a priori* conscious and which is apodictically certain."[6] This moral law is revealed to practical reason as the categorical imperative: "act only in accordance with that maxim through which you can at the same time will that it become a universal law."[7]

Moral autonomy and the moral law thus yield, as it were, the axioms of the "moral logic" of practical reason, just as pure reason's forms of thought (categories) and of intuition yield axioms of "formal logic." These "axioms of moral logic" are the postulates of practical reason: "God, freedom, immortality." Indeed, moral striving for perfection would be meaningless if there were no goal and no ideal, i.e., no *God* of moral striving. Moral striving would not be moral if it were not *free*, and it would be unrealizable in practice if there were no *immortality*.

Thus the "ought-truths" of practical reason provide an answer to the essential questions of being human, questions

---

[6] Immanuel Kant, *Practical Philosophy*, trans. and ed. Mary J. Gregor (Cambridge: Cambridge University Press, 1996), 177.

[7] Ibid., 73.

From International Law to World Peace

to which pure reason was unable to provide any answer in the language of "being-truths." The formal knowledge of pure reason cannot tell us whether God *exists*, whereas practical reason's morally grounded capacity for conviction tells us that God *ought* to exist. Kant's real and great concern can be seen precisely in the fact that, to provide *certainty* about the important questions of life, he wished to open the door to a different human capacity than that of theoretical speculation—the capacity, that is, of practical reason's *moral logic*.

Just as Kant separated the sphere of pure knowledge from that of practical reason's moral "sphere of faith," so he also separated the latter from the sphere of *law*. For if the moral consists in the *inner* "ought" of the moral law, then the legal consists, according to Kant, in the *external* "must" of the law of the human social community. The distinction between morality and legality thus consists in the fact that legal obligations are enforceable, whereas moral duties belong to the realm of individual freedom. The highest maxim of law is thus the formula "Act *externally* in such a way that the free use of your will is consistent with the freedom of everyone under a universal law."

Now, the distinction between moral life and law, when conceived in such a way that it refers to the whole human being and his inner attitude—and that this then refers to an external order—is an ancient tradition, as was shown above. The new element that was introduced by Thomasius, and that Kant perfected, is the *separation* between morality and law. Thomasius assigned to morality the goal of the inner peace of the soul of the individual, while he saw the purpose of law as the external peace of society. Kant replaced inner peace with autonomous freedom: "a person is subject to no other laws than those he gives to himself (either alone or at least along with others)."[8] Morality is the domain of inner freedom. It is distinguished from legality, not by means of the difference of duties, but rather by means of the difference of law-giving. The moral law is given by man to himself; here the free human being is at once law-giver and the law's addressee in one person. The legal statute, however, has separate people as legislators and addressees. The purpose of legislation is the maintenance of external freedom, i.e., the freedom to do anything that does not harm the freedom of other members of the community. The maintenance of external freedom necessarily demands binding laws, so as to protect the freedom of the individual. Thus, an inner legislation (i.e., moral legislation) can, according to Kant, never be external, and no external (i.e., legal) legislation can ever be inner legislation, i.e., it can never have a moral significance. The whole of natural law thus contracts, in Kant's work, into the concept of *formal external freedom*. Here Heinrich Rommen comments as follows:

> Freedom, as the starting point and basic principle of natural law, in its purely formal character, makes a substantive natural law impossible. . . . Kant's formalism, the theory of the mere conditions of the possibility of knowledge and of moral autonomous freedom, is the basis for this characteristic (moral rationalism) of Kantian ethics. It does not permit Kant to arrive at substantive values, but only at the theory of the conditions under which such values could be given. The principle of freedom is too formal and thus too unproductive to allow any substantive *ordo*, either of *ought* or of *essential being*, to be arrived at, whether in the domain

[8] Ibid., 378.

of knowledge or in that of the will. . . . Consequently, that external way of acting (in which the freedom of the wills of our fellow legal subjects is not contracted) must appear to be legal. That is, the reciprocal agreement and consent of our fellow legal subjects must be able positively to make any possible action a legal one, quite apart from its substantive moral quality (here the famously strong influence of Rousseau on Kant shows through). Thus it would be possible, on condition of the formal freedom of others, for actions, in themselves immoral, to be legal ones (e.g., usury, suicide, adultery)—as, indeed, Ockham also accepted where *lex naturalis* was concerned, since Ockham taught the same dualism of theoretical and practical reason.[9]

It is nevertheless possible for usury, suicide, adultery, and still other immoral actions to become legal actions, on the condition that the formal freedom of others is maintained. This is a possibility, however, that did not occur to Kant himself. So innocent and pure was his imagination that, in regard to the principle of *the protection of external freedom* as a purpose of the legal order, he was unable to arrive at such possibilities of misuse. His whole being was still too much rooted in the Christian tradition to arrive at the consequence that a law which was in *theory* freed from moral life could also be freed from moral life in *practice*—i.e., that immoral actions might not only be legally tolerated, but would even be legally prescribed. Kant was instead of the conviction (self-evident to a decent person) that even if law is separated from ethics, it will nevertheless be applied in an ethical manner. Indeed, in Kant's time and for more than a century thereafter each Prussian official (that model of

[9] *Die ewige Wiederkehr des Naturrechts*, 118.

dutiful and incorruptible conduct to the officialdom of the European continent) *did* apply it.

For this reason, in his theory of law, Kant himself drew such practical consequences from the formal principle of freedom as are to be found in, for example, his text devoted to the basic problem of international law, *Perpetual Peace* (1795). In this text, occasioned by the Peace of Basel with the French Republic, Kant draws the consequences of his general theory of law for the domain of international law.

The first problem of international law, namely the nature of the legal community of states, or the international legal community, is answered by Kant as follows:

> Peoples who have grouped themselves into nation-states may be judged in the same way as individual men living in a state of nature, independent of external laws; for they are a standing offence to one another by the fact that they are neighbors. Each nation, for the sake of its own security, can and ought to demand of the others that they should enter along with it into a constitution, similar to the civil one, within which the rights of each could be secured. This would mean establishing a *federation of peoples*. But a federation of this sort would not be the same thing as an international state. For the idea of an international state is contradictory, since every state involves a relationship between a superior (the legislator) and an inferior (the people obeying the laws), whereas a number of nations forming one state would constitute a single nation. And this contradicts our initial assumption, as we are here considering the right of nations in relation to one another insofar as they are a group of separate states that are not to be welded together as a unit.
>
> We look with profound contempt upon the way in which savages cling to their lawless freedom. They would

rather engage in incessant strife than submit to a legal constraint that they might impose upon themselves, for they prefer the freedom of folly to the freedom of reason.... We might thus expect that civilized peoples, each united within itself as a state, would hasten to abandon so degrading a condition as soon as possible. But instead of doing so, each *state* sees its own majesty (for it would be absurd to speak of the majesty of a *people*) precisely in not having to submit to any external legal constraint.... And the main difference between the savage nations of Europe and those of America is that while some American tribes have been entirely eaten up by their enemies, the Europeans know how to make better use of those they have defeated than merely making a meal of them. They would rather use them to increase the number of their own subjects, thereby augmenting their stock of instruments for conducting even more extensive wars.

Although it is largely concealed by governmental constraints in law-governed civil society, the depravity of human nature is displayed without disguise in the unrestricted relations that obtain between the various nations. It is therefore to be wondered at that the word *right* has not been completely banished from military politics as superfluous pedantry, and that no state has been bold enough to declare itself publicly in favor of doing so. For Hugo Grotius, Pufendorf, Vattel, and the rest (sorry comforters as they are) are still dutifully quoted in *justification* of military aggression, although their philosophically or diplomatically formulated codes do not and cannot have the slightest *legal* force, since states as such are not subject to a common external constraint. Yet there is no instance of a state ever having been moved to desist from its purpose by arguments supported by the testimonies of such notable men. This homage that every state pays (in words at least) to the concept of right proves that man possesses a greater moral capacity, still dormant at present,[10] to overcome eventually the evil principle within him (for he cannot deny that it exists), and to hope that others will do likewise. Otherwise the word *right* would never be used by states that intend to make war on one another, unless in a derisory sense, as when a certain Gallic prince declared: "Nature has given to the strong the prerogative of making the weak obey them." The way in which states seek their rights can only be by war, since there is no external tribunal to put their claims to trial. But rights cannot be decided by military victory, and a *peace treaty* may put an end to the current war, but not to that general warlike condition within which pretexts can always be found for a new war. And indeed, such a state of affairs cannot be pronounced completely unjust, since it allows each party to act as judge in its own cause.

Yet, while natural right allows us to say of men living in a lawless condition that they ought to abandon it, the right of nations does not allow us to say the same of states. For as states, they already have a lawless internal constitution, and have outgrown the coercive right of others to subject them to a wider legal constitution in accordance with their conception of right. On the other hand, reason, as the highest legislative moral power, absolutely condemns war as a test of rights, and it sets up peace as an immediate duty. But peace can neither be inaugurated nor secured

---

[10] Even if the word law had "never passed the states' lips," and even if there were no sort of moral aptitude among human beings (even an aptitude "temporarily slumbering"), law and ethics are, as Kant unequivocally asserts here, connected with each other in the closest possible manner. Here Kant is speaking about the ethical meaning of law, since, with due deference to the "Gallic prince," it can be the case that the weaker party is in the right against the stronger, which demonstrates the primacy of the ethical order over any merely physical order.

From International Law to World Peace

without a general agreement between the nations; thus a particular kind of league, which we might call a *pacific federation* (*foedus pacificum*), is required. It would differ from a *peace treaty* (*pactum pacis*) in that the latter terminates *one* war, whereas the former would seek to end *all* wars for good. This federation does not aim to acquire any power like that of a state, but merely to preserve and secure the *freedom* of each state in itself,[11] along with that of the other confederated states—although this does not mean that they need to submit to public laws and to a coercive power that enforces them, as do men in a state of nature.

---

[11] That is, even a freedom without any substantive content would still be a matter of a federation of tyrannically-ruled states, of slave-holding states, of states seeking to conquer the world by means of subversion (if it were a question *only* of war, this would indeed be permitted), of states conquering the world by means of choking other states economically, of states governed by authoritarian regimes, of democratic states, and so on. If the freedom that was to be protected or secured by these peace federations also had the meaning of the unimpeded suppression or extirpation of religious, racial, national, and class minorities, then the curse of countless victims of this "freedom" would lie upon it and upon the peace bought at such a price. Now, Kant well understood that it would not do to create a worldwide (federalistic) peace federation, without its members having something in common in their internal constitutions. For this reason, he preceded the chapter "International Law Ought to Rest on a Federalism of Free States" with a chapter bearing the title "The Civil Constitution in Every State Ought to be Republican." By a "republican constitution," Kant understands a representative form of government in which the legislature is separated from the executive, according to Montesquieu's principle of the separation of powers. "Republicanism is the state principle of the separation of the executive power (the government) from the legislative power." ("Perpetual Peace," first article) The peace federation states suggested by Kant ought as a matter of principle to consist of "republics, i.e., of states with representative constitutions and separated powers."

It can be shown that this idea of *federalism*, extending gradually to encompass all states and thus leading to perpetual peace, is practicable and has objective reality. For if by good fortune one powerful and enlightened nation can form a republic (which is, by its nature, inclined to seek perpetual peace),[12] this will provide a focal point for federal association among other states. These will join up with the first one, thus securing the freedom of each state in accordance with the idea of international right, and the whole will gradually spread further and further by a series of alliances of this kind.

It would be understandable for a people to say: "There shall be no war among us; for we will form ourselves into a state, appointing for ourselves a supreme legislative, executive, and judicial power to resolve our conflicts by peaceful means." But if this state says: "There shall be no war between myself and other states, although I do not recognize any supreme legislative power that could secure my rights and whose rights I should in turn secure," it is impossible to understand what justification I can have for placing any confidence in my rights, unless I can rely on some substitute for the union of civil society, i.e., on a free federation. Indeed, if the concept of international right is to retain any meaning at all, *reason* must necessarily couple it with a federation of this kind.

The concept of international right becomes meaningless if interpreted as a right to go to war. For this would make it a right to determine what is lawful, not by means of universally valid external laws, but by means of one-sided

---

[12] "If (as cannot be otherwise in this constitution) the consent of the citizens is required in order to decide whether there ought to be war or not, nothing is more natural than that—since they must take upon themselves all the hardships of war—they will reflect seriously before beginning such a bad business." ("Perpetual Peace," first article)

maxims backed up by physical force. It could be taken to mean that it is perfectly just for men who adopt this attitude to destroy one another, and thus to find perpetual peace in the vast grave where all the horrors of violence and those responsible for them would be buried. There is only one rational way in which states coexisting with other states can emerge from the lawless condition of pure warfare. Just like individual men, they must renounce their savage and lawless freedom, adapt themselves to public coercive laws, and thus form an *international state* (*civitas gentium*), which would necessarily continue to grow until it embraced all the peoples of the earth. But since this is not the will of the nations according to their present conception of international right (so that they reject *in hypothesi* what is true *in thesi*), the positive idea of a *world republic* cannot be realized. If all is not to be lost, this can at best find a negative substitute in the shape of an enduring and gradually expanding *federation* likely to prevent war. The latter may check the current of man's inclination to defy the law and antagonize his fellows, although there will always be a risk of it bursting forth anew.[13]

Seeing no other way to replace the order of force with an order of law in dealings between states, Kant thus suggests the same path that individual people either explicitly or tacitly follow when they found a state or enter into a state, and provide this state with enforceable laws. Yet at the same time, he sees in the "concept of international law" (i.e., in the kind of international law that the states *wish* to have and the ideas of such a law that had been disseminated by

---

[13] Immanuel Kant, "Perpetual Peace: A Philosophical Sketch," in *Political Writings*, trans. H.B. Nisbet (second edition, Cambridge: Cambridge University Press, 1991), 93–130, 102–5. [Hereafter, frequent citations from this same text will be indicated by page numbers in brackets.]

means of Vattel's doctrine) a temporarily insuperable obstacle. He therefore suggests a *reasonable* compromise to the states that are insisting on their unlimited sovereignty (in Kant's sense of "freedom of folly, instead of the freedom of reason"). Instead of the actually effective solution of a world republic, which, because of the claim to unlimited sovereignty, has proved to be unfeasible, he suggests a *peace federation*, which rests on the basis of a treaty, and which would thus, in preserving the sovereignty of the states, serve the merely *negative* purpose of preventing war.

A peace federation or league of nations of this kind means, however, a lessening and restriction of a sovereignty that is supposedly unlimited and illimitable under "international law," since, by virtue of renouncing war as a means of settling disputes, each state entering into this league would either have to renounce any attempt to settle international conflicts, or would have to abide by the judgment of a court of arbitration or of some other international court. That is, they would have to acknowledge a judge standing *above* them, and thus would also have to drop the claim to be themselves their own sole judges. This, however, would be equivalent to renouncing unlimited sovereignty, since the latter stands and falls on the claim to have no judge over oneself.

Kant creates a hope that states could decide to renounce sovereignty in this way as a result of the *republican* constitution of the states that would be founding this "league of peace." Kant sees in the republican constitution the first step in the direction of "perpetual peace"—i.e., to a world legal order: "A state of peace among men living together is not the same as the state of nature [*status naturalis*], which is rather a state of war. For even if it does not involve active hostilities, it involves a constant threat of their breaking out. Thus the state of peace must be *formally instituted*...."[98] The first step on the way to instituting peace among nations would consist in realizing the demand that "the civil constitution in every state ought to be republican." Now, what Kant means by a republican constitution is not the usual opposition between a "republic" and a "monarchy," but a representative form of state in which the legislative, executive, and judicial powers are separated:

> A *republican constitution* is founded upon three principles: firstly, the principle of *freedom* for all members of a society (as men); secondly, the principle of the *dependence* of everyone upon a single common legislation (as subjects); and thirdly, the principle of legal *equality* for everyone (as citizens). It is the only constitution that can be derived from the idea of an original contract, upon which all rightful legislation of a people must be founded. Thus, as far as right is concerned, republicanism is itself the original basis of every kind of civil constitution, and it only remains to ask whether it is the only constitution that can lead to a perpetual peace. [99–100]

Kant answers this question in the affirmative, for the republican constitution "is not only pure in its origin (since it springs from the pure concept of right)," [99–100] but has the further advantage that it is the least favorable to war, and the most favorable to peace. For in such a constitution, the citizens themselves decide if they wish for war, with its burdens, or not, since they themselves are the ones "doing the fighting ... supplying the costs of the war from their own resources, painfully making good the ensuing devastation," and will therefore "have great hesitation in embarking on so dangerous an enterprise.... But under a constitution where the subject is *not* a citizen, and which is therefore *not* republican, it is the simplest thing in the world to go to war. For the head of state is not a fellow citizen, but the owner of the state, and a war will not force him to make the slightest sacrifice so far as his banquets, hunts, pleasure palaces, and court festivals are concerned."[100]

> The following remarks are necessary to prevent the republican constitution from being confused with the democratic one, as commonly happens. The various forms of state (*civitas*) may be classified either according to the different persons who exercise supreme authority, or according to the way in which the nation is governed by its ruler, whoever he may be. The first classification goes by the form of sovereignty (*forma imperii*), and only three such forms are possible, depending on whether the ruling power is in the hands of an *individual*, of *several persons* in association, or of *all* those who together constitute civil society (i.e., *autocracy, aristocracy*, and *democracy*: the power of a prince, the power of a nobility, and the power of the people).
>
> The second classification depends on the form of government (*forma regiminis*), and relates to the way in which the state, setting out from its constitution (i.e., an act of the general will whereby the mass becomes a people), makes use of its plenary power. The form of government, in this case, will be either *republican* or *despotic*. *Republicanism* is that political principle whereby the executive power (the government) is separated from the legislative power. *Despotism* prevails in a state if the laws are made and arbitrarily executed by one and the same power, and it reflects the will of the people only insofar as the ruler treats the will of the people as his own private will. Of the three forms of sovereignty, *democracy*, in the truest sense of the word, is necessarily a *despotism*, because it establishes an executive power through which all the citizens may make decisions about (and indeed against) the single individual without his con-

sent, so that decisions are made by all the people and yet *not* by all the people; and this means that the general will is in contradiction with itself, and thus also with freedom. [...]

We can therefore say that the smaller the number of ruling persons in a state and the greater their powers of representation, the more the constitution will approximate to its republican potentiality, which it may hope to realize eventually by gradual reforms. For this reason, it is more difficult in an aristocracy than in a monarchy to reach this one-and-only perfectly lawful kind of constitution, while it is possible in a democracy only by means of violent revolution. [100–1]

Republicanism is the only perfectly lawful constitution because it guarantees *freedom* and *equality*, "these innate and inalienable rights, the necessary property of mankind." [99, note] External (legal) *freedom* is "a warrant to obey no external laws except those to which I have been able to give my own consent." [100, note] External (legal) *equality* in a state is "that relationship among the citizens whereby no one can put anyone else under a legal obligation without submitting simultaneously to a law which requires that he can be put under the same kind of obligation by the other person." [100, note] This is precisely the nature of the republican constitution. The republican constitution is not only, as it were, "the original basis of every kind of civil constitution" (since any constitution conforms with law only insofar as, and only because, it approximates to the republican constitution and carries that constitution's elements within itself); not only is it the goal of the legal order that includes all of humanity (the "positive idea of a world republic," which alone can really support perpetual peace), but it can also be thought of as the "constitution of the world"—i.e., as a constitution that embraces heaven and earth, earthly and purely spiritual beings. Just as Leibniz thought of the whole world as a "republic of free spirits" ("monads"), a *hierarchically gradated* world monarchy with God as its monarch, so Kant thinks of the world order as a republic of free spirits who are, however not only *free* but also—with the *sole* exception of God—in principle, all *equal*.[14]

> The validity of these necessary and inalienable rights, the necessary property of mankind, is confirmed and enhanced by the principle that man may have lawful relations even with higher beings (if he believes in the latter).[15] For he may consider himself as a citizen of a transcendental world, to which the same principles apply. And as regards my freedom, I am not under obligation even to divine laws (which I can recognize by reason alone) except insofar as I have been able to give my own consent to them; for I can form a conception of the divine will only in terms of the law of freedom of my own reason. As

---

[14] Here we see the essential difference between Kant's *Protestant* approach and Leibniz's traditional Christian (i.e., *Catholic*) approach. For the *hierarchical* principle, the principle of gradation and rank ordering, is essentially Catholic, while Protestantism does not in principle recognize the mediating significance of the saints and the hierarchies of angels between God and man. For Protestantism, the connection between the human I and God is immediate. All beings, with the exception of God, are thus *equal*, i.e., not composed in the same or a similar fashion, but *equally justified* before God.

[15] The qualification "if he believes in the latter" contains the following "logical" propositions: (1) Anyone who has accepted the supreme being, God, as a postulate of practical reason, can also conceive of *other* beings who are higher than humans, but they need not do so (Protestantism); (2) these beings can only be *conceived of*; that is, since all experience is only of a sensory kind, only in thought can a relation to supersensible beings be fashioned.

for the principle of equality[16] in relation to the most exalted being I can conceive of, apart from God (e.g., a power such as an Aeon), there is no reason—if I and this higher being are both doing our own duty in our own stations—why it should be my duty to obey while he should enjoy the right to command.[17] But the reason why this principle of equality (unlike that of freedom) does not apply to a relationship towards God, is that God is the

---

[16] *Gleichheit* ("equality") means also "analogousness, likeness, similarity"—an important point to bear in mind especially in the present context of hierarchy or rank-ordering (or the *analogia entis*). ED

[17] Here there is a mischaracterization of the first of the three ancient Christian vows and virtues: *obedience*, chastity, and poverty. For obedience, as a free vow (i.e., as an act of individual freedom), is only intelligible if one acknowledges that there is a hierarchical gradation of beings and values, and is thus able to acknowledge that there are higher (as it were, more "existent" beings) and higher values in comparison to one's own being and one's own value. If we were to see matters from the viewpoint argued for here by Kant, then Abraham's obedience, for example, would not be a virtue at all, but a surrender of the use of his own reason—i.e., voluntary madness. Leibniz's principle of continuity, by contrast, makes it possible to understand obedience and fittingly honor it. For if the free human I is connected to God by the path of gradual, graduated approximation (the ranked levels of the hierarchies, and of the levels of consciousness), then his freedom goes beyond the boundaries of his self, and can even transplant the center and the starting-point of his actions into another being that seems to him (rightly or wrongly) to stand closer to the primordial source of wisdom and goodness than does he himself at the stage of consciousness at which he stands at any given time. Human consciousness does not need to be condemned to the lifelong prison of its own freedom. It can leave that prison. This abandonment of the restricted space of one's personal freedom in the service of a higher stage of freedom than that which has been experienced up to that point, is *obedience* in the true sense. True obedience can only be fully understood from the perspective of the *moral value of love*, never from

only being for whom the concept of duty ceases to be valid. [99, note]

Once Kant has suggested that the "republican constitution" is both the constitution of the state essential for peace and the legal order necessary for the whole of humankind to be able to arrive at world peace (and is thus envisaged as the final goal), and once he has also given it, as it were, a *metaphysical* superstructure (by suggesting that the world of supersensible beings should be thought of as consisting of "citizens" of a cosmic republic), he then turns to the *physical*—i.e., the natural side of the problem of perpetual peace, with a supplement [108] under the title: "On the Guarantee of a Perpetual Peace," where we read:

> Perpetual peace is *guaranteed* by no less an authority than the great artist *Nature* herself (*natura daedala rerum*). The mechanical process of nature visibly exhibits the purposive plan of producing concord among men, even against their will, and indeed *by means of* their very discord. This design, if we regard it as a compelling cause whose laws of operation are unknown to us, is called *fate*. But if we consider its purposive function within the world's development, whereby it appears as the underlying wisdom of a higher cause, showing the way towards the objective goal of the human race and predetermining the world's evolution, we call it *providence* . . . we can and must *supply it mentally* in order to conceive of its possibility by analogy with human artifices. [108–9]

that of the *concept of duty* alone. Only for love can another being seem to a person more essential or existent than he himself is, or a value appear more valuable than his own freedom. For Abraham, the God who had appeared to him was more *full-of-being* (i.e., more existent and more living) than himself and everything that belonged to him.

From International Law to World Peace

Nature, who "has taken care that human beings are able to live in all the areas where they are settled," and this even "by means of *war*, so that they inhabit even the most inhospitable regions," [109–10] takes care that this same war also works towards perpetual peace. This, however, does not happen in such a way that she imposes a duty on human beings, but rather "she does it herself, whether we are willing or not: *fata volentem ducunt, nolentem trahunt.*"[18] [112] In this sense, war is to be thanked for the fact that in the foundation of the state, the first significant step in the direction of universal peace was taken, or, rather, came into being. For "if people were not compelled by internal dissent to submit to the coercion of public laws, war would produce the same effect from outside. . . . Each people would find itself confronted by another neighboring people pressing in upon it, thus forcing it to form itself internally into a *state* in order to encounter the other as an armed *power.*" [112] The next step accomplished by nature in the direction of perpetual peace is the balance of power between the states:

> The idea of international right[19] presupposes the separate existence of many independent adjoining states. And such a situation is essentially a state of war, unless there is a federal union to prevent hostilities breaking out. But in the light of the idea of reason, this state is still to be preferred to an amalgamation of the separate nations under a single power that has overruled all the rest and created a universal monarchy. For the laws progressively lose their impact as the government increases its range, and a soulless despo-

---

[18] Literally, "fate leads the willing, drags the unwilling." ED

[19] That is, the doctrine that prevailed in Kant's time of the plurality of unlimitedly sovereign states as the only prerequisite for international law.

tism, after crushing the germs of goodness, will finally lapse into anarchy. It is nonetheless the desire of every state (or its ruler) to achieve lasting peace by thus dominating the whole world, if at all possible. But *nature* wills it otherwise, and uses two means to separate the nations and prevent them from intermingling: *linguistic* and *religious* differences. These may certainly occasion mutual hatred and provide pretexts for wars, but as culture grows and men gradually move towards greater agreement over their principles, they lead to mutual understanding and peace. And unlike that universal despotism which saps all man's energies and ends in the graveyard of freedom, this peace is created and guaranteed by an equilibrium of forces and the most vigorous rivalry. [113–14]

The third measure nature takes to compel humanity to join together is the peaceful effect of "mutual self-interest." "The *spirit of commerce* sooner or later takes hold of every people, and it cannot exist side-by-side with war.... In this way, nature guarantees perpetual peace by the actual mechanism of human inclinations. And while the likelihood of its being attained is not sufficient to enable us to *prophesy* the future theoretically, it is enough for practical purposes. It makes it our duty to work our way towards this goal, which is more than an empty chimera." Among other things, this work towards perpetual peace means a struggle against a politics freed from morality. Kant here *expressly* understands morality as identical with law!

> It is also necessary that we should know what the condition is under which its maxims [the maxims of "morality (in the sense of a theory of right)"] will agree with international right.... The condition that must be fulfilled before any kind of international right is possible is that a *lawful state* must already be in existence. For without this,

there can be no public right, and any right that can be conceived outside of it, i.e., in a state of nature, will be merely a private right. Now, we have already seen above that a federative association of states whose sole intention is to eliminate war is the only *lawful* arrangement that can be reconciled with their *freedom*. Thus, politics and morality can only be in agreement within a federal union, which is therefore necessary and given *a priori* through the principles of right. And the rightful basis of all political prudence is the founding of such a union in the most comprehensive form possible; for without this aim, all its reasonings are unwisdom and veiled injustice. This kind of politics has its own *casuistry*. . . .

But *both* aspects, philanthropy and respect for the *rights* of man, are obligatory. And while the former is only a *conditional* duty, the latter is an *unconditional* and absolutely imperative one; anyone must first be sure that he has not infringed it if he wants to enjoy the sweet sense of having acted justly. Politics can easily be reconciled with morality in the former sense (i.e., as ethics), for both demand that men should give up their rights to their rulers. But when it comes to morality in its second sense (i.e., as the theory of right), which requires that politics should actively defer to it, politics finds it advisable not to enter into any contract at all, preferring to deny that the theory of right has any reality and to reduce all duties to mere acts of goodwill. This subterfuge of a secretive system of politics could, however, easily be defeated if philosophy were to make its maxims public, would it but dare to allow the philosopher to publicize his own maxims.

With this in mind, I now put forward another transcendental and affirmative principle of public right. It might be formulated as follows: "All maxims that *require* publicity if they are not to fail in their purpose can be reconciled both with right and with politics." [129–30]

Kant and Kantianism

This much, then, on Immanuel Kant's immediate contribution to the main problem of the jurisprudence of international law. It is now time to turn away from this clear, transparent, and luminous jewel drawn from the spiritual treasury of the human race, and turn back to the further course of the history of the problems and methods of the jurisprudence of international law.

The separation between law and moral life that was completed by Kant, as well as the primacy of the *formal* over the *substantive* that he presented as a necessary condition of scientific method, are still alive today, and are the common basis for the three schools of legal philosophy now prevailing, schools that all undertook to continue Kant's work: the *neo-Kantian* school, the *logical* school, and the school of pure *phenomenology*.

The *neo-Kantian* tendency found its main proponent in the so-called Marburg School of philosophy (founded by Hermann Cohen in the 1860s), whose most important representative in the realm of law, Rudolf Stammler, put forward a formal yardstick whose application to historically existing law was to provide a *direction* [*Richtung*] so that "correct [*richtiges*] law" could result: "The law now reveals itself in the domain of social willing. For this concept is meant to regulate cooperation. It takes the form of a willing that is oriented towards the pursuit of common purposes by the people who are brought together by it."[20]

By contrast, the *logical school*, also known as the Vienna School (founded by Hans Kelsen), frees law from all its

---

[20] No reference given. ED

connections with metaphysics, ethics, psychology, sociology, or politics, and leaves the concept of law subsisting only as a formal category within a "*pure* theory of law." The "pure theory of law" is thus a formal *instrument* of a specific mode of juridical thinking, and a theory of the law "that is in force," without concerning itself with the content, value, or making of law. Law can thus have any content whatsoever here, and can have come into being in any way whatsoever. As long as it is *in force*, it falls within the scope of the method of the "pure theory of law."

The *phenomenological school* (following Edmund Husserl, who founded a *pure* phenomenology and phenomenological philosophy as an *a priori* science in contrast to empirical psychology), seeks to establish the *a priori* propositions of law that can be grasped through introspection or "through reason" [*einsichtig*] and are valid without exception, like the axioms of mathematics and logic (Reinach, Felix Kaufmann).

The influence of Kantianism, i.e., of the critical and transcendental method, on the jurisprudence of international law in particular, consisted and consists in subjecting to examination, analysis, and reformulation all those concepts that belonged to the theory and practice of international law, and to which Vattel, for example, simply helps himself—concepts such as that of "international law" itself, of "the state as the subject of international law," of "the subject of international law," of "state sovereignty," of "a state of war or peace," and so on. The pre-Kantian period of proliferating productivity at the level of the creation of systems (particularly systems of natural law), was then followed by a period of critical examination and of an uncreative "detail work" of the clarification of all the concepts—as well as a detection of the remnants of "dogmatic" and "natural-law" (understood here in its dogmatic sense) elements in them. This period itself gave way to an almost incalculable overproduction of *critical* works in the face of which it was impossible any longer to be certain where one stood. Thus, for example, the concept of "war," whose meaning had been clear to everyone for centuries, was lately subjected to a thoroughgoing re-examination. Fritz Grob listed *seventy* definitions of the legal concept "war" that had been formulated by jurisprudentialists of international law in the period between 1900 and 1940, and investigated their respective validity. In his study *The Relativity of War and Peace: A Study in Law, History, and Politics*,[21] Grob came to the conclusion that there simply does not yet exist any single clear and valid *legal* concept of "war," or of "a state of war," that satisfies all the requirements. From this conclusion, however, it follows that if there is no concept of war, there can also be no concept of peace. But if there is no concept of peace, there cannot be any concept of "peaceful dealings" of states with each other either—and so on, until it becomes clear that the whole of international law is a pointless word-game and is incapable of pointing to a single valid concept.

Fritz Grob, however, is no Kantian, and belongs, according to his own account, to the tendency of legal positivism. But the very extensive and thoroughgoing work he has done on the critical examination of the single concept of "war," and the result of this work, are very indicative of the now barely stoppable avalanche of criticism, which was initially stimulated by justified and moderate doubt about the

---

[21] New Haven, CT: Yale University Press, 1949.

pretensions of Enlightenment rationalism, but now threatens to tear everything up and bury it.

That the critical approach by itself does not suffice, and that the creative principle has primacy over the critical one, was the conviction that underpinned the work of the Traditional School; and this was also understood in the first half of the nineteenth century by those "free" spirits who had left the ground of tradition. Johann Gottlob Fichte (1762–1814), for example, gave up the idea of the "thing in itself" as the hidden true essence behind appearances, which latter were inevitably reshaped by subjectivity, and instead proposed the rational *I*, no longer hidden but revealing itself as the *subjective-objective* both on the scene of consciousness and on that of external events. The I as the "absolute subjectivity-objectivity" also posits itself as the "not-I." The I, insofar as it is determined by the not-I, is the intuiting I, and as such is the object of a "*theoretical* doctrine of science" or "epistemology." By contrast, the I that determines the not-I, and acts, is the topic of the "*practical* doctrine of science."

Freedom and absolute independence of action for its own sake are no longer, as in Kant's work, the condition of and prerequisite for moral life; instead, they are its *content* and highest task. Accordingly, *law*, for Fichte, following Kant, is freedom as an innate and original (i.e., natural-legal) *given*—a given that underpins all legal life. Just as the will of the I creates the laws of ethics, so it is the *consciousness* of the I that sets out the progressive and forward-looking rational movement between thesis, antithesis, and synthesis. The knowledge of *being* as an object of philosophical cognition is given up, together with Kant's "thing in itself." Instead, philosophical cognition is now directed exclusively towards *becoming*. With this turn away from *being*, and towards *becoming*, Fichte took an important and consequential step towards emancipation from the scruples of Kantian criticism—scruples that, as mentioned above, proved so disabling to creative metaphysical cognition.

The completion of this emancipation from Kant's "cognitive timidity," and the drawing out of the final consequences of the thesis that the "subjective" and "objective" are identical (as well as the final consequences of the *replacement* of being by becoming as the topic of philosophical cognition), was reserved to Georg Wilhelm Friedrich *Hegel* (1770–1831)— along with all the consequences this completion entailed for the treatment and solution of the problems of international law.

3

Hegel and the Theory of the Sovereignty of the State

egel's philosophy appeared against a background in which criticism's "timidity of cognition" was growing—and in this connection, tending to content itself with the "detail work" of specialists as a strong reaction to cognitive ambition and to the striving for an all-embracing and organically ordered knowledge. Hegel's philosophy did away with paralyzing scruples about the problem of knowledge, of how our concepts and thought processes relate to the things and processes outside it, by means of his "Eureka" moment: the identity of the process of thought, of logic, with what takes place, in world history—the identity of the concept with being. This became one of the most influential and strongest demonstrations of trust in thinking and cognition to have appeared in world history. It rests on Kant's criticism, followed through to its ultimate consequences, and on the choice of one of the two consequences that follow from Kant's work. If, on the one hand, it is the case that all experience is incapable of leading to necessary and universal cognition as well as that an inductive metaphysics grounded on experience is impossible, and on the other, it

is the case that a necessary and universal cognition can only be acquired through the categories of the capacity for knowledge, through thinking itself—then this "categorial" cognition is either in principle all-encompassing and absolute (i.e., extends to everything now conceivable and to everything that will or can become conceivable tomorrow and in the centuries to come) or else it is an illusion, as there is simply no such thing as necessary and universal cognition. If one decides that there *is* cognition without sense experience, then one neither can nor need be content with acquiring this or that degree of cognition and stopping at some limit or other (such as, for example, the "thing in itself"); rather, the greatest possible *use* both can and should be made of such knowledge. In this latter case, any limits of cognition will be displayed *after* it has been used, not in advance (i.e., as crippling and restricting obstacles that consciousness has put in its own way). What is productive and favorable to cognition is not a lack of faith in thinking, but a trusting use of thinking. If, then, the categories of the capacity for thinking themselves carry within them the properties of necessity and universality, then one should regard the forms of the capacity for thinking themselves as universal and necessary. This, however, means recognizing that they [the forms of the capacity for thinking] are identical with the lawlike nature of world history—in which case logic and metaphysics are one and the same—and that the dialectical movement of positing, negating, and assimilating that negation in turn to a higher state is the essence both of thinking and of world history. "The *element* of the *universal spirit's* existence [*Dasein*] is: intuition and image in art, feeling and representational thought in religion, and pure and free thought in philosophy. In *world history*, it is spiritual actuality in its entire range of inwardness and externality."[1]

Even the opposition between reason and will, between rationalism and voluntarism, comes to an end in Hegel's philosophy—or in his logic. Thinking and willing are identical. *Spirit* is first of all *intelligence*, and it goes through those states that, "from *feeling* to *representational thinking* [*vorstellen*] to *thought* are the way by which it produces itself as *will*—which, as practical spirit in general, is the proximate truth of intelligence." [47, §4] So that "those who regard thinking as a particular and distinct *faculty*, divorced from the will as an equally distinct *faculty*, and who in addition even consider that thinking is prejudicial to the will—especially the good will—show from the very outset that they are totally ignorant of the nature of the will. . . ." [37–38, §4] Even the opposition between "right" or law [*Recht*] and morality [*Sittlichkeit*] is overcome (one ought to say "overcome *once more*"), like the oppositions of the subjective and the objective, and of thought and will. For law and morality are expressions of the abstract concept of the idea of the will that is nothing other than "in general, *the free will that wills the free will.*" [57, §27]

> Right is something *utterly sacred*, for the simple reason that it is the existence [*Dasein*] of the absolute concept, of self-conscious freedom. But the *formalism* of right—and also of duty—arises out of the different stages in the development of the concept of freedom. In opposition to the more formal (i.e., *more abstract* and hence more limited) kind of

[1] G.W.F. Hegel, *Elements of the Philosophy of Right*, trans. H.B. Nisbet (Cambridge: Cambridge University Press, 1991), 372 (§341). In the following section, citations from this work will be limited to bracketed page numbers following the cited text.

Hegel and the Theory of the Sovereignty of the State

right, a higher right is possessed by that sphere and stage of the spirit in which the spirit has determined and actualized within itself the further moments contained in its Idea—for it is the *more concrete* sphere, richer within itself and more truly universal. Each stage in the development of the Idea of freedom has its distinctive right, because it is the existence of freedom in one of its own determinations. When we speak of the opposition between morality or ethics and *right*, the right in question is merely the initial and formal right of abstract personality. Morality, ethics, and the interest of the state: each of these is a distinct variety of right, because each of them gives determinate shape and existence to freedom. [59, §30]

Accordingly, freedom (or law), whose bearer and subject is the "world-spirit" ("only the right of the world-spirit is absolute in an unlimited sense [59, §30])" stands at the top; immediately below it, one level down, is the law (or freedom) of states or "national spirits" (which "have their truth and their destiny in the concrete Idea as *absolute universality*, i.e., in the world-spirit, around whose throne they stand as the agents of its actualization and as witnesses and ornaments of its splendor [376, §352]"). Last comes the stage of the freedom (or law) of the "abstract individual": "as the *particular* individual, as the will of the single person in his distinctive arbitrariness [58, §29]." A more precise gradation of the "idea of the will that is free in and for itself" (i.e., of law) in the opposite direction, that is, from bottom to top, is as follows:

> the sphere of *abstract* or *formal* law, where the *individual* faces an "immediately external thing";
>
> the sphere of *morality*, where the will "as a subjective unity" faces the *universal* ("partly as something inward, the good, partly as something external, a world that is present");

the sphere of *morality*, as the "*unity* and *truth*," i.e., the synthesis of the two moments of individuality and universality ("so that freedom, as the *substance*, exists no less as *actuality* and *necessity* than as *subjective* will." [62, §33]).

Moral substance, however, first appears as a "natural spirit" in the *family*, then "in its *division* and *appearance*" in *civil society*, so as, at last, to be revealed in the *state*—and, indeed, in the state "as freedom, which is equally universal and objective in the free self-sufficiency of the particular will. This actual and organic spirit (a) of a people (b) actualizes and reveals itself through the relationship between the particular national spirits (c) and in world history as the universal world-spirit whose *right* is *supreme* [62–63, §33]."

Since, then, *individuality* has only a derivative right (an "abstract" right, in Hegel's terminology), while it is the state that as "the actual and organic spirit of a people" ascends to a true, non-derivative right (a "concrete" right, in Hegel's usage) by means of its relation to other national spirits, and, through the course of world history, to the universal world-spirit, it is thus the *state* that is the true subject of law—not the individual. The individual is a subject of law only in the sphere of "abstract or formal law," which, as it were, is limited to the triangle of one person's relation to another person and of both persons to the "external matter [*Sache*]." The command of abstract law is thus "*be a person and respect others as persons.*"

The *state*, conversely, "is the actuality of the moral Idea —the moral spirit as substantial will, *manifest* and clear to itself, that thinks and knows itself and implements what it knows insofar as it thinks it." [275, §257] "The state is . . . the *rational* in and for itself. [It is] an absolute and unmoved end in itself; and in it, freedom enters into its

Hegel and the Theory of the Sovereignty of the State

highest right, just as this ultimate end possesses the highest right in relation to individuals, whose *highest duty* is to be members of the state." [275, §258]

The author asks the reader to pause a moment here, so as to become aware of the grave consequences (grave, too, for the problems of international law) of the actual content that is being expressed in these propositions, along with its inevitable limitations of verbal symbolization. The reader is asked to become a little more aware of all this than is usual when familiarizing oneself with "views expressed in the historical past." In order to offer one or two helpful pointers to the reader in doing so, the author permits himself to pose an apparently far-fetched question: How would Hegel have expressed these ideas about law as freedom, about the levels of law as formal law, morality, and ethical life, and about the primacy of the universal, of the all-embracing community, over the particular individual, if, instead of being a professor of philosophy in the capital city of Prussia in the nineteenth century, he had been a bishop of the Catholic church at the beginning of the fifth century? In the latter case, might he not perhaps have said that the Logos alone suffices—the God-become-flesh who reveals himself in world history by becoming immanent to humanity ("I am with you until the end of the world!") and henceforth walks step by step with humankind, "until the end of the world"—so that in the end, through the whole of humankind as its organ, world history comes—*in* Him and *from* Him and *through* Him— to the full awareness of itself at the Last Judgment? Would he not then, instead of speaking of the "world-spirit," have spoken of *Christ*? And instead of speaking of the stages of the world-spirit's being-in-itself, being-outside-itself, and returning-to-itself, would he not have spoken instead of the Logos "in God and with God," of His incarnation in world-history, and, beyond that, of His resurrection and ascension? Would he not then have spoken of the "mystical body of Christ"—the community embracing all of humankind—inspired by the "revealed, self-transparent, substantial will, that thinks and knows itself and that brings to pass what it knows, and does so insofar as it knows it"? Would he not have set in opposition to the secular state, the *civitas terrena* (as it appears as an accidental historical phenomenon with its aspirations to power and its dirty political machinations), a community that necessarily follows from freedom itself—a community that is essentially identical with freedom as a *civitas Dei*, a "city of God"?

For Hegel, "God's presence on earth" would certainly not have been the Caesar-state, but the *church*, because as the "mystical body of Christ," the church is indeed by very definition "God's presence on earth." Indeed, if one defines a community as "an unmoved end in itself, in which freedom comes to its highest right," so that—"as this ultimate end possesses the highest right in relation to individuals, whose *highest duty* is to be members of the state"—one is in very truth giving a definition of what is meant by the *church*. And if one starts out, not from accidental historical facts that happen to be in front of one, let alone from denominational, national, or personal sympathies and antipathies, but rather from *logic* as metaphysics (which is where Hegel wanted to start out from)—that is, if one holds to *ideas* and *concepts* alone, free from any experience—then Hegel's definitions just quoted in fact *mean* the church; indeed, they mean the church alone and nothing but the church.

Hegel and the Theory of the Sovereignty of the State

That Hegel *in fact* projected the idea of the church onto the state changes nothing about the matter. Hegel, as a professor of philosophy in Prussia in the nineteenth century, projected the idea of the church onto the state that happened, historically, to be in front of him; he did so, not out of the inner necessity of the Idea, but as a result of a contingent external influence—even if this was the influence of his own, extra-logical human nature. But this (to speak in purely Hegelian terms and in complete accord with Hegel's own spirit, i.e., with what he really wanted to offer to the world as a method and as a result) changes nothing about the matter, because in *truth*, and in the realm of *substantive, concrete truth*, Hegel was speaking of the church—which, for whatever reason, he had merely happened to lose sight of in the realm of empirical experience, or of which he happened to have an image that did not correspond to its reality (whether by his own fault, or not, we can set to one side). For this reason (or for any other reasons you like), he thought he found it in the state, which he put forward as a sort of "church-state" or "state-church" (i.e., a state with churchly qualities)—as a unity of, or as an identity of, the church and state, which had historically come to appear as opposites of each other. But here, it was the state to which he ascribed total significance, while he granted the church only that of being an aspect of the state, which appeared as a unity. For him, the church represented subjective conviction, whereas the state was "the agent of knowing [*der Wissende*]." (§270)

Now let us imagine, on the other hand, that St Augustine had emerged as a Protestant-educated professor of philosophy in Berlin in the first half of the nineteenth century. What would he have taught, had he wanted to express the essential elements of Augustinian thought in the intellectual language of that time and its environs? Would he not have spoken of the spirit immanent to world-history, which gathers together in its being a humanity falling prey to schism and leads it to ever higher stages of ethical life and of reason until, in the end, it becomes one with humankind ("Not I, but Christ in me")? Would he not also have taught that this process of gathering humankind, in and through the being of moral life and reason, was at the same time a process of growth and ascent on the part of a community that, in principle, embraced all of humankind—a community related to the particular existing communities (such as for example states) as a whole to its parts, or as an organism to its individual organs (when these organs serve the organism), or as health to sickness (when the organs resist the organism)? And would he not have insisted on the independence, or even upon the absolute significance, of this world-community whenever any of the individual states made a claim to be, itself, this all-embracing whole? Would he not then have said, with Hegel, that "only the right of the world-spirit is unlimited in an absolute sense," and that the right of the state (irrespective of whether these are many or one) is subordinate to the right of the world-spirit, because they "have their truth and their destiny in the concrete Idea as *absolute universality*—i.e., in the world-spirit, around whose throne they stand as the agents of its actualization and as witnesses and ornaments of its splendor"?

Then, with the inner fire of a St Augustine, he would have postulated the absolute necessity of this "absolute universality" as goal and as ideal: a universality that, precisely because of its universal character, must stand far above all national, racial, class, or other forces that divide and fragment humanity. It ought not, however, to be universal merely according to its *nature*, but ought also to strive for the realization of this universality in time and space. Since it is now, as it were, the "body of the world-spirit," it can only be *one*, and *holy*; since it is essentially universal, it is *catholic*; and since this universality is realized by means of growth and dissemination in time and space, it is *apostolic*. This doctrine of the presence of the world-spirit in world-history, a doctrine that is contained in the very ideas of the moral and of the rational, and that is developed out of those ideas, could thus be summarized in the following sentence from the Christian profession of faith: *I believe in one holy catholic and apostolic church*.

Now, as an individual citizen working in the kingdom of Prussia in the first half of the eighteenth century, Hegel was unable or unwilling to utter this sentence from the Creed. Instead, he uttered roughly the following sentence, replacing "church" with "state": "It is an absolute necessity that for each person there is only one state, which is, to him, holy, universal, and endowed with a claim to absoluteness." From this sentence, however, there follows a doctrine of the state that in all its particulars is constructed as a "religion of the state," in which, since the state is "the *self-knowing* actuality of spirit, its form must become distinct from that of authority and faith" [§270], which it managed to achieve thanks to its separation from the church, since "only then [when it stands] above the *particular* churches can the state attain *universality* of thought as its formal principle and bring it into existence [*Existenz*].... Consequently, far from it being, or ever having been, a misfortune for the state if the church is divided, it is *through this division alone* that the state has been able to fulfill its destiny as self-conscious rationality and moral life." [301–2, §270] This "religion of the state" also puts an end to the ancient oppositions and quarrels between the kings and the prophets of the Old Testament, between the Caesars and early Christianity, and between emperor and pope in the Middle Ages. The medieval doctrine of the "two swords, the secular and the spiritual" (cf. the *Saxon Mirror*) now acquires the significance that it is the *state* to which *both* swords belong. In other words, the state alone *knows* what it does; and thus, as a knowing agent, what it alone is justified in doing. The sphere of existence left to the church is no sort of "sword" at all; that is, it is not an *objective* function that is promulgated by and promotes *truth* and *moral life*, but is merely the *subjective* realm of "faith and feeling." For "when the church proceeds to put forward *doctrines* (although there are and have been churches that confine themselves to doctrine, and others in which worship is the principal concern, and doctrine and a more educated consciousness are merely secondary), and its doctrines relate to *objective principles*, to moral and rational thoughts, its expression of these doctrines immediately brings it into the province of the state." [299, §270]

Since, then, the state is the *reality* of the world-spirit, it is above not only the church, but also the *individual*. It owes neither its origin nor its survival to the individual, and cannot, therefore, depend on any sort of "social contract." "If the state is confused with civil society, and its purpose is equated with the security and protection of property and personal freedom, *the interest of individuals as such* becomes the ultimate end for which they are united, from which it also follows that membership of the state is an optional matter. But the relationship of the state to the individual is of quite a different kind. Since the state is *objective* spirit, it is *only* through being a member of the state that the individual himself has objectivity, truth, and ethical life." [276, §258] Here the state once again comes forward as *church*, since man only has "objectivity, truth, and moral life" as a member of the state. That is, *extra ecclesia non est salus* becomes here the proposition *extra statu non est salus*.[2] Hence, like the church, the state cannot be "grounded" on a contractual basis through the agreement of individuals; rather, whatever empirical and historical forms may have *accompanied* its coming-into-being, it can only ground itself in its own nature.

> The philosophical approach deals only with the internal aspect of all this (i.e., apart from the *historical* circumstances of the origin of each particular state—*Author*), with the *concept as thought*. As far as the search for this concept is concerned, it was the achievement of *Rousseau* to put forward the will as the principle of the state, a principle that has *thought* not only as its form (as with the social instinct, for example, or divine authority) but also as its content—and that is, in fact, *thinking* itself. But Rousseau considered the will only in the determinate form of the *individual* will (as Fichte subsequently did also), and regarded the universal will not as the will's rationality in and for itself, but only as the *communal element* arising out of this individual will *as a conscious will*. In this way, the union of individuals within the state becomes a *contract*, based accordingly on their arbitrary will and opinions, and on their express consent given at their own discretion— and the further trivially rational consequences following

---

[2] That is, "there is no salvation outside the church," and "there is no salvation outside the state." ED

from this—which destroy the divine element that has being in and for itself, and its absolute authority and majesty. [276–77, §258]

However, the church (which Hegel replaces with the concept "state") cannot have "arbitrary will and opinions" as its basis, since the "trivially rational consequences" following therefrom would be of the kind that could only have destroyed "the divine element that has being in and for itself, and its absolute authority and majesty." The church is in any case, by virtue of its concept, its idea, and its ideal, no work of human hands, nor an association founded by human beings. For this reason, not even Hegel, who was inwardly wholly under the spell of the greatness and magnificence of the idea of the church, could see the state (in which he believed he had found the realization of the idea of the church) as an association grounded on a merely contractual basis. This is why, although he acknowledges Rousseau's "general will," he also criticizes Rousseau's view of the way this general will comes into being as a result of the expression of particular individual wills. Rousseau's doctrine is "Protestant" in relation to the state as a church, while Hegel himself propounds the purely "Catholic" doctrine that the church ("state") is *ex Deo, per Deum, ad Deum* ("from God, for God, to God").

Since the state has "absolute authority and majesty," it also self-evidently has absolute sovereignty. For just as, for example, the Lutheran church, the Eastern Orthodox church, and the Roman Catholic church could not relate to each other in any other way than by asserting their own unlimited sovereignty in matters of doctrine, liturgy, church law, and church organization (for if they had not asserted this sovereignty they would have ceased to be particular church communities), so the individual states (which are like "individual churches") can only be unlimitedly sovereign. There can, therefore, be no supra-state international law that is binding for individual states. Only the *world-spirit* stands above the states, and the only court that judges the states, as well as the only sanctioning power of this court, is world-history. All law is thus *state law*, and, indeed, *internal state law*, insofar as it is a matter of the individual state "as a self-related organism." When it is a case of a relationship of one state to other states, law is *external state law*; and then also, beyond this—as "the universal Idea (i.e., as *genus* and absolute power in relation to individual states)—it is the spirit that gives itself its actuality in the process of *world history*." [281, §259] Internal law is the state's relationship to itself. "As present-spirit *unfolding* as the actual shape and organization of a *world*, the state *is* the divine will. Those who refuse to go beyond the form of religion when confronted by the state behave like those who, in the cognitive realm, claim to be right even if they invariably stop at the *essence* instead of proceeding beyond this abstraction to *existence*, or like those who . . . will only the *abstract good* and leave it to the arbitrary will to determine *what* is good." [366, §330] It is internal state law, rather than the arbitrary will that determines what is good. *External state law*, which takes the place of international law, "applies to the *relations* between independent states. What it contains *in and for itself*, therefore, assumes the form of an *obligation*, because its actuality depends upon *distinct* and *sovereign wills*."[3]

---

[3] Ibid., 366 (§330).

From International Law to World Peace

"The nation-state or 'folk as state' [*das Volk als Staat*] is the spirit in its substantial rationality and immediate actuality, and is therefore the absolute power on *earth*; each state is consequently a sovereign and independent entity in relation to others." [366, §331] Its "primary and absolute entitlement" is to be recognized as such by other states. "But this recognition requires a guarantee that the state will likewise recognize those states that are supposed to recognize it, i.e., that it will respect their independence. Accordingly, these other states cannot be indifferent to its internal affairs." [367, §331]

> The principle of *international law*, as that *universal* right which ought to have international validity in and for itself (as distinct from the particular content of positive treaties), is that *treaties*, on which the mutual obligations of states depend, *should be observed*. But since the sovereignty of states is the principle governing their mutual relations, they exist to that extent in a state of nature in relation to one another, and their rights are *actualized*, not in a universal will with constitutional powers over them, but in their own particular wills. Consequently, the universal determination of international law remains only an *obligation*, and the [normal] condition will be for relations governed by treaties to alternate with the suspension of such relations. There is no praetor to adjudicate between states, but at most arbitrators and mediators; and even the presence of these will be contingent, i.e., determined by particular wills. Kant's idea of a *perpetual peace* guaranteed by a federation of states that would settle all disputes and that, as a power recognized by each individual state, would resolve all disagreements so as to make it impossible for these to be settled by war, presupposes an *agreement* between states. But this agreement, whether based on moral, religious, or other grounds and considerations,

400

would always be dependent on particular sovereign wills, and would therefore continue to be tainted with contingency. [368, §333]

Consequently, if no agreement can be reached between particular wills, conflicts between states can be settled only by *war*. Since the sphere of the state is extensive and its relations through its citizens are extremely varied, it may easily suffer injuries on many occasions. But, which of these injuries should be regarded as a specific breach of treaties or as an injury to the recognition and honor of the state remains "in itself" indeterminable; for a state may associate its limitlessness and honor with any one of its individual interests, and it will be all the more inclined to take offence if it possesses a strong individuality which, as a result of a long period of internal peace, is encouraged to seek and create an occasion for action abroad. [369, §334]

Decisions about peace and war, reasons for war, and so on, thus belong to the domain of an estimate freely made by the state, *every* state; and there are in principle no such things as "just or unjust" wars, because "a state may associate its limitlessness and honor with any one of its individual interests," and because even the efforts of "a strong individuality" to find "an occasion for action abroad" is enough to produce reasons for war—within the sphere of reasons for war that are "in themselves indeterminable."

Moreover, the relationship between states may not be measured and judged against criteria drawn from private law or morality, since

> states are not private persons but completely independent totalities in themselves, so that the relations between them are not the same as purely moral relations or relations of private right. Attempts have often been made to apply private right and morality to states, but the position of pri-

vate persons is that they are subject to the authority of a court that implements what is right in itself. Now, a relationship between states ought also to be inherently governed by right, but in worldly affairs, that which has being in itself ought also to possess power. But since no power is present to decide what is right in itself in relation to the state and to actualize such decisions, this relation must always remain one of *obligation.* The relationship between states is a relationship of independent units that make mutual stipulations, but at the same time stand above these stipulations. [366, addition to §333]

War is therefore not merely something that belongs to law, i.e., to the freedom of states, but is also a necessity that is occasioned by the nature of the state and that belongs to the state as an ethical substance.

> It is a grave miscalculation if the state, when it requires this sacrifice [of property and life—*Author*], is simply equated with civil society, and if its ultimate end is seen merely as the *security of the life and property* of individuals. For this security cannot be achieved by the sacrifice of what is supposed to be *secured.* On the contrary, the *ethical moment of war* is implicit in what was stated above. For war should not be regarded as an absolute evil and as a purely external contingency whose cause is therefore itself contingent, whether this cause lies in the passions of rulers or nations [*Völker*: "folk" or "peoples"], in injustices, etc., or in anything else that is not as it should be.
>
> Whatever is by nature contingent is subject to contingencies, and this fate is therefore itself a necessity—just as, in all such cases, philosophy and the concept overcome the point of view of mere contingency and recognize it as a *semblance* whose essence is necessity. It is *necessary* that the finite—such as property and life—should be *posited* as contingent, because contingency is the concept of the finite.

Hegel and the Theory of the Sovereignty of the State

On the one hand, this necessity assumes the shape of a natural power, and everything finite is mortal and transient. But in the moral essence (i.e., the state), nature is deprived of this power, and necessity is elevated to a work of freedom, to something moral in character. The transience of the finite now becomes a *willed* evanescence, and the negativity that underlies it becomes the substantial individuality proper to the moral essence.

War is that condition in which the vanity of temporal things and temporal goods (which tends at other times to be merely a pious phrase) takes on a serious significance; and it is accordingly the moment in which the *ideality* of the *particular* attains its right and becomes *actuality*. The higher significance of war is that, through its agency (as I have put it on another occasion), "the moral health of nations is preserved in their indifference towards the permanence of finite determinacies, just as the movement of the winds prevents the sea from the stagnation that a lasting calm would produce—a stagnation that a lasting, not to say perpetual, peace would also produce among nations." [no citation]

Since "a lasting, not to say, perpetual peace" threatens a state with stagnation, Hegel's view of any world-organization whose purpose is to secure peace (i.e., his view of Kant's views and suggestions in his work on *Perpetual Peace*) also follows from this. On that topic, Hegel says the following:

In peace, the bounds of civil life are extended. All its spheres become firmly established—and, in the long run, people become stuck in their ways. Their particular characteristics become increasingly rigid and ossified. But the unity of the body is essential to its health, and if its parts grow internally hard, the result is death. Perpetual peace is often demanded as an ideal to which mankind should approximate. Thus, Kant proposed a league of sovereigns to settle disputes between states, and the Holy Alliance was meant to be an institution more or less of this kind. But the state is an individual, and negation is an essential component of individuality. Thus, even if a number of states join together as a family, this league, in its individuality, must generate opposition and create an enemy. Not only do peoples emerge from war with added strength, but nations troubled by civil dissension gain internal peace as a result of wars with their external enemies. Admittedly, war makes property insecure, but this *real* insecurity is no more than a necessary movement. [362, addition to §324]

Accordingly, it is not the peaceability of states and their citizens that matters, but their *valor*. "Valor is in itself a *formal* virtue, because it is the highest abstraction of freedom from all particular ends, possessions, pleasure, and life. . . . [364, §327] The significance of valor as a disposition lies in the true, absolute, and ultimate end: the *sovereignty* of the state." [Ibid., §328]

The state, like the church, thus also stands in need of confessors and martyrs, for otherwise it will "go to ruin," i.e., it will decline to a "merely bourgeois society" that exists only for the protection of property and of the lives of its members. In any case, what would a church or a religious community be worth if it was concerned only with the temporal and transient, and if it cared only for the property and the lives of its members in this world? And would not the state of the spiritual life of humanity be absolutely lamentable if all religious communities (Christianity, Judaism, Islam, Buddhism, Brahmanism, and others) had completely, and as a matter of principle, given up their claim to *truth*, and their *opposition* to other confessions, and had concluded a "perpetual peace"—a peace in which fatalism would live "peacefully" side-by-side with freedom of the will, belief in the eternity of the world alongside belief in its temporality and transience, belief in redemption through one's own efforts alongside belief in redemption through grace, etc., without making any claim to truth, and without any mutual opposition? Would such a "tolerance" not be just the same as perfect *indifference*, in which each would say of his brother, "Am I my brother's keeper?" And might one not justly compare this state of general indifference to stagnant marsh-water, and, along with Hegel, bid welcome to "the movement of the winds that prevents the sea from stagnating"?

All the details of Hegel's doctrine of the state and of international law demonstrate the fact that he was seized by the *idea of the church*, which he projected onto the state. Therefore *war* means, for him, exactly the same thing as a *schism*, and true citizens amount to *confessors* and *martyrs*. For him, too, all wars are thus *wars of religion*, all military campaigns are *crusades*, and all wars of conquest are *apostolic*.

PART VII

International Law With One Level: Pure Positivism and Its Problems

ince states function as *particular* entities in their mutual relations, the broadest view of those relations will encompass the ceaseless turmoil, not just of *outer* contingency, but also of of passions, interests, ends, talents and virtues, violence, wrongdoing, and vices in their *inner* particularity. In this turmoil, the ethical whole itself—the independence of the state—is exposed to contingency. The principles of the *spirits of nations* are in general of a limited nature, and this because of that particularity in which they have their objective actuality and self-consciousness as *existent* individuals. Moreover, in their mutual relations, their deeds and their destinies are the manifest dialectic of the finitude of these spirits. It is through this dialectic that the *universal* spirit, the *spirit of the world*, produces itself in the "freedom from all limits," and it is this spirit that exercises its right—which is the highest right of all—over finite spirits in *world history* as the *world's court of judgment*.[1]

This doctrine of Hegel essentially expresses the idea that

---

[1] Hegel, *Philosophy of Right*, 371 (§340).

One-Level International Law: Positivism and Its Problems

world-history, as a totality of both external and internal events, proceeds as if on three levels. First, there is the level of the immediate facts of events, deeds, passions, interests, purposes, and so on. *Behind* this, as if above the heads of individual people, lies the level of the effects and development of the "national spirits"; and behind this, in turn, lies the level of the world-spirit. These three levels correspond to the three levels of law: abstract or formal law; law as morality; and law as ethical life. From this, however, it follows that all law is in the process of *coming to be*, and that the legal unities that are in principle absolute—the states—are in fact *not* absolute as historical facts. Furthermore, they never *can* be absolute, since there are *several* of them but only *one* "spirit of the world," which is absolute. Thus emerges the thesis that all law is relative insofar as it *appears*, but that at the same time it represents a level and an aspect of the absolute law that is revealed only in the *totality* of world-history.

The relativity of everything that comes to be, but that nonetheless points towards the absolute, was precisely the founding intuition and decisive impetus of the so-called Historical School founded by Friedrich Karl von Savigny (1779–1861). This school, which was dominant in Germany for two generations, put forward the view that law has its origin neither in arbitrary human will nor in the conscious thinking of individual human beings, but that it gradually rises from the unconscious depths of nations and slowly ascends in the course of history to the surface, as it were, of the broad daylight of consciousness. Conscious unification and legislation are not the origins of law; they are, rather, sympto-matic appearances of it, *promulgations* of the unconscious common will of the nation. Law is the creation of the "folk or national spirit."[2]

"The colorful world of the forms of law, like language, or art, or customs, does not develop by virtue of a willed natural observation or by rational considerations of utility; instead, it springs from the common conviction of the people, from the same feeling of inner necessity, which excludes all ideas of contingent or arbitrary origin," says Savigny.[3] Just as the languages of the nations differ, therefore, so also do the laws of the nations vary. Roman law was the law of the Romans, German law is the law of the Germans, Anglo-Saxon law is the law of the Anglo-Saxons. The stages by which law comes into existence (which are at the same time "the sources of law") are as follows. First we have the *law of custom*. With the progress of the state and of the consciousness of the state's mission, the law of custom is supplemented by means of *legislation*. Then, as the third stage, we have jurisprudence, which *collects* the law of *custom*, *interprets* the law of *statute*, and *brings* the two spheres *into concord* with each other. *Scholarship* makes explicit those legal statutes that are contained as basic elements in the law of custom and in the positive law of the state.

As practice, statute, and contract, law is present as a fact. The task of scholarship does not consist in testing and judging, let alone in improving these facts. Its task, instead, is merely that of getting to know the facts and penetrating analytically to their basic components. This, precisely, is *positivism* as a *method* of jurisprudence. When, however, this method depends on the standpoint that sheer knowl-

---

[2] *Volksgeistes*.
[3] Quoted from Rommen, *Die ewige Wiederkehr des Naturrrechts*, 128.

One-Level International Law: Positivism and Its Problems

edge of, and analysis of, the legal material before one is not merely necessary, but is *the only thing* needed, so that no efforts are *permissible* beyond these (since they would be "unscientific"), then this becomes *positivism as a school.*

The Historical School, which replaced the rational law of the Enlightenment (or rationalistic "natural law") with the subconscious depths of the law-creating folk or national spirit, and saw the law of custom as the first and original source of law, was, when compared with Hegel's system of law, a step in the direction of banalization. This is analogous to Vattel's doctrine when compared with that of Leibniz, or to the rational law of the early Enlightenment (e.g., that of Pufendorf) in relation to St Thomas Aquinas's three levels of law. For if the Historical School has to do with positive law (the law of statute and of contract) on the one hand, as well as, on the other, with the law of custom as the immediate promulgation of the folk or national spirits, it *follows* Hegel's teaching to the extent that Hegel did indeed see the origin of the law in force as residing in the folk or national spirits, thus putting the law currently in force in an historical perspective. And yet, it is *distinct* from Hegel's doctrine at the same time, in that Hegel, like Aquinas, taught that there were *three* levels of law, whereas the Historical School let the highest level of absolute law, the level of ethical or moral life—or the law of the world-spirit (whose rank corresponds to that of the "divine law" in St Thomas)—fall away, as it were, leaving in place only two of the levels of Hegel's system of law: the level of "formal law" and that of the law of the folk or national spirits. Thereby, however, the whole domain of the life of law moves into the sphere of relativity, both of time ("historicism") and of space ("national individualism").

From International Law to World Peace

For jurisprudence (and thus, for the jurisprudence of international law too) nothing then remains but to "get to know" the law and the international law in force at any given time as actual phenomena, and to investigate their basic elements. So as to have anything at all to hold on to, and not drown in the ocean of relativism, the very relativism that necessarily results from the mere "historicism" and "national individualism" of the Historical School harbors within it the irrefutable demand to stick to the facts of the law in force. This firm ground may not be abandoned, for everything else is unreliable and subjective (even if "nationally" subjective); that is, it is not really a matter for jurisprudence, but instead for *psychology* (even for "national psychology"). This is roughly the line of thought that takes the Historical School towards pure positivism, i.e., along the path from the three levels of law in Hegel, through the two levels of law in Savigny's Historical School, to, finally, law with a single level alone in positivism.

Positivism also came to dominate in practice soon after Savigny's death in 1861 and then dominated roughly three-quarters of the field of the jurisprudence of international law until the end of the First World War. Since that time, it has had to yield one part of the territory it ruled to a revived current of thought oriented towards natural law. Thus, at the time of the outbreak of the Second World War, positivism and a natural-law approach more or less balanced each other. After that war, more progress on the part of natural-law thinking can be detected within the free world. In the part of the world ruled by communism, on the other hand, natural law was extirpated root and branch, both in theory and in practice.

One-Level International Law: Positivism and Its Problems

⊕

With positivism and the current state of the problem of international law, the *historical* part of this study, whose subject is the history of the jurisprudence of international law, comes to an end. For the second half of the nineteenth century and the first half of the twentieth century are, so far as the *problems* of international law are concerned, part of the *present day*. From a journalistic standpoint, recent decades may appear to belong to the "historical past," but, seen from a scholarly standpoint, this period resounds as "the present" (in the sense of the current set of problems) in relation to which the *distance* necessary for the formulation of the history of the problem is not yet at hand.

In the sense of the history of the problem and the history of the method of the jurisprudence of international law, pure positivism signifies an endpoint—not only in time, but also in terms of content. For what peculiarly characterizes positivism is that it neither has, nor wishes to have, anything to do with *problems*; Instead, it limits itself to the practical *task* of investigating and getting to know the international law currently in force in such a way that the individual points of the objective domain of international law can be brought together in a manageable system of international law. It is a task in which the individual legal statutes that make up this system are to be obtained from the realm of the international law that lies in front of us by means of observation, analysis, and abstraction—for "law is whatever is in force." To establish a *certain* answer to the following questions is thus the task, the method, and the content of positivism:

(1) States as *legal subjects*: their legal capacity to act (cases and conditions, their mitigation and aggravation), the realm

From International Law to World Peace

of the state (its vocation, gain and loss), the people of the state, the law of aliens (expulsion, naturalization), means of dealings between states (envoys and consuls), international administrative bodies, legal relationships between states (treaties, crimes under international law).

(2) Regulation of the interests of the *community of states*: commerce and business (freedom of the seas, sea voyages, air traffic, railway traffic, etc.; trade, trading institutions, weights and measures), administration of justice (international private law, protection of intellectual and commercial property, mutual assistance in law enforcement, extradition), social and ideal interests (protection of health and life, safety at work, slave trading, the white slave trade, trade of smoking materials).

(3) Disputes *among states*: prevention of war, disarmament, courts of arbitration, international courts, self-defence, war (land war, naval war, air war, neutrality, ending wars).

Almost every textbook of international law that has been published in the last fifty years, whether in German, English, French, or other languages, is concerned with this "series of topics" or "questionnaire," and it is outside the scope of this work to provide yet another introductory exposition of modern international law as currently in force. What *should* be noted with respect to positivism, however (not as a method, but as a school), is the fact that very different uses are made of it. For as a school that is in principle "free from ideology," positivism serves such ideologies as an instrument precisely *because* of this supposed freedom from ideology—since a system of law without law is essentially in accord with, and works to the advantage of, these ideologies. Thus, the Positivist School finds in the

One-Level International Law: Positivism and Its Problems

champions of totalitarian theories of the state some of its most eager defenders, since it is the only school that puts no sort of obstacles in the way of states that claim their power, not only on the basis of absolute self-rule, but also on the basis that they alone have any value; and it is thus well suited to serve them as an instrument. By becoming a tool at the service of such claims to power, however, positivism loses its last connection with jurisprudence as a *science* and with the legal consciousness as such, a connection that it inherited from Europe's past. It is, as it were, swallowed alive by politics. Then begins the twilight of the last and third stage of the former consciousness of law, a consciousness with three levels—*then law is no longer present at all.*

PART VIII

The Dawn of One-Dimensional Law: Positivism as International Law

he entire area of dealings between states, as a whole and in detail, always faces a dilemma. Is it to be *law* or *politics*? Every state, and every group of states, is daily and continuously faced with the choice of whether to decide upon the deeds and omissions of states according to *principles* of law, or instead by following the *interests* of power. In the practice of states' dealings with each other, the feeble attempt to delimit law and politics from each other as two different spheres has only led to a situation wherein those states to which a legal solution of a contested case was inconvenient tend to declare that such cases were ones of politics; whereas other cases that were just as much or just as little to be described as purely political (but where the state in question lacked the power needed to enforce a solution favorable to it) were declared to be *legal* cases. Both outcomes are nonetheless always possible, because—as regards dealings between states—there is not actually anything that could not just as well be described as a "political" matter as it could be described as a "legal"

matter. The *actual* problem thus consists, not in how one can separate out one part of dealings between states as belonging to "the sphere of politics" (i.e., as lying outside law and law-breaking) and another as belonging to the "sphere of law," but in *whether the whole field of dealings between states is to take place in accordance with principles of law or in accordance with the interests of power and advantage*—whether, in other words, politics is to give way to law and disappear into law, or whether law is to give way to politics and to disappear into politics.

The latter standpoint is precisely that of the proponents of totalitarian theories of the state, both of the Fascist and Nazi sort, and of the Marxist and communist variety. From the point of view of the totalitarian national state, everything that works to the advantage of the state is legal, and everything that harms it is illegal. According this theory, in the field of dealings between states, the interests of the state are identical with law itself. Georg Jellinek's doctrine that "wherever it conflicts with the existence of the state to observe international law, the rule of law withdraws,"[1] and, further, that "when the highest law of the state, its self-preservation, imperatively demands it, then the lower duty of keeping to a treaty must give way,"[2] was modified by the proponents of national totalitarianism insofar as they took it to its logical conclusion. Where the observation of international law comes into conflict with the *interests* of the state, the rule of law withdraws, because it is only there to serve the interests of the state. And when the highest duty

---

[1] *Allgemeine Staatslehre*, 377.
[2] *Lehre von den Staatsverbindungen*, 53.

of the state, its self-preservation, expansion, and ruling position imperatively demands as much, the lower duty of keeping to a treaty must give way. This is how Georg Jellinek's propositions would read if they had been uttered by a proponent of the national totalitarian theory of the state. The meaning of these propositions, however, is none other than that there is no international law, because there is no binding law that stands above the interests of the state, and because treaties are valid only for so long as it is *advantageous* for them to be valid.

The same goes for the Marxist and communist theory. Thus, Andrei J. Vyshinsky writes:

> In his survey of Hegel's *Science of Logic*, Lenin wrote, on the subject of the relationship between form and substance, that "form is substantial. Substance is formed in one way or another, depending on the substance."[3] This is the basic thesis of Marxist-Leninist philosophy on the unity of form and content, of form and substance, on their mutual interpenetration, of the transition from one into the other. When applied to law, this means that the form of law depends on its substance. A foundational alteration of the substance of law inevitably brings with it an alteration of its form.

And further on:

> Although the economic foundation of socialism was built upon further [during the first fifteen years of the communist regime—*Author*], law was already socialist. This does not contradict the theses of Marxism, according to which,

---

[3] Lenin, *Philosophische Schriften* [Philosophical writings] (1947), 119; Lenin, *Aus dem philosophischen Nachlass* [From the philosophical legacy] (Berlin, 1949), 61.

One-Dimensional Law: Positivism as International Law

in the last instance, law is conditioned by and determined by the economic basis of society—or by the further Marxist thesis that not only does economics have an effect on politics (and consequently on law), but, conversely, the political and legal superstructure also affects the economic base. Socialist law has not only consolidated what has already been achieved, but has also influenced the direction the economy of its socialist state had to take.[4]

In other words: the dictatorship of the working class over the two or three other classes, and of the communist party over the working class, and of the party leadership over the communist party—this three-level dictatorship is precisely the *essence* of Soviet law; and the sum-total of the measures taken to maintain and promote them is the *form* of that law, for

> socialist Soviet law is the totality of the rules of conduct established by the state within a socialist society. Its norms are an expression of the will of the working class, and of the representatives and allies of all workers—i.e., of the will of the overwhelming majority of the people. And since the last class of exploiters remaining in the USSR, the kulaks, have been got rid of, these norms are an expression of the will of the entire Soviet people. [...] Soviet law, however, not only wishes to compel, but also to educate the mass of the population in the spirit of socialist discipline. (Vyshinsky)

But this "will of the working class," which represents the "will of all workers" and thus also the "will of the over-

---

[4] A. J. Vyshinsky, "Socialist Soviet Law," article in the *Enzyklopädie der Union der Sozialistischen Sowjet Republiken* [Encyclopedia of the USSR], (Berlin, 1950), 2:156.

whelming majority of the people," is itself represented by the "will of the communist party," whose "will" is in turn expressed in the shape of its leading group. The "will of the whole Soviet people" thus comes about in *two* ways: on the one hand, by establishing the "will of the proletariat *in itself*," as is done by Marx, Engels, Lenin, and Stalin with the help of the dialectical method "appropriated" from Hegel, and as it is converted into a program that is correctly interpreted by the leading group of the communist party and is transplanted into praxis, i.e., becomes the "will of the communist party." When the expression of the will of the party leadership becomes the "will of the party," however, it also becomes the "will of the working class," for the party is supposed to be nothing but the "organized will of the working class." Thus it becomes, at the same time, the "will of all workers," since the working class is "the representative and ally of all workers"—i.e., it becomes the "will of the overwhelming majority of the people." Indeed, it also becomes so in principle, even in a case when the people (by means of a free vote), by a *statistical* majority, might itself (by an "overwhelming majority") have spoken against it—as happened in Russia itself in the vote for the constitutional assembly in 1917. For in such a case, the people is not aware of what its own will really is.

On the other hand, so as not to obtain only an "overwhelming majority," but the "whole people" *statistically* as a unity of will, a second method was adopted: that is, actually to *create* first a "majority," and then "unity," by making those who are *in principle* in the "minority" disappear by "educating" or "eliminating" (i.e., destroying) them. Thus, for example, the unity of the "intelligentsia" with the "working class" is brought about by annihilating the intelli-

One-Dimensional Law: Positivism as International Law

gentsia or sending them into exile, and by re-educating their children. The "unity" of the peasantry with the "working class" is brought about by "eliminating the kulaks," that is, the peasants who through industry and persistence had attained a certain prosperity, modest indeed by Western standards, and who therefore did not want to be robbed of the fruits of their efforts and labor. The "unity" of the "will of the party," however, was managed by "purging" (*chistka*) the party of the "bourgeois-fascist" elements of the Right Opposition, and of the—also—"bourgeois-fascist" elements of the Left Opposition, the Trotskyists.

The "unity" of the nations living in the USSR was also achieved by making certain nations disappear from the population map of the USSR—for example, the Crimean Tartars in Crimea, the Chechens and Ingush in the Caucasus, and the Volga Germans in the Volga region. In all these cases, unity of the will was accomplished by the "elimination" of those elements that spoiled it, irrespective of whether they were minorities or majorities (which, from a "merely statistical" point of view, was irrelevant, since *in principle* whatever resists the dictatorship of the proletariat is *always* a "minority"). And this "unity of the will" is precisely the *essence*, the substance, of "Soviet law," while its form consists of the laws, provisions, and—externally—the treaties that are to preserve this "unified will," to further it, and to help it come to rule by conquest of the whole world. Following Lenin's doctrine, the form and substance of this "law"—of *Soviet* law—are, however, one and the same. And they are also one and the same in *politics*—in the politics of attaining in one country the three-stage dictatorship detailed above, as well as of extending this dictatorship across the whole world.

From International Law to World Peace

For this reason, Soviet authors of the twenties[5] denied even the possibility of the existence of a universal international law. Instead, they spoke of an "international law of the transitional period," a law that consisted, and *rightly* consisted, in particular treaties between individual states. (This was in contrast to the general or universal treaties for the transitional period that would be brought to an end once the Soviet regime had spread across the whole world.) Then this "international law" too would disappear and be replaced by the relationship between the local and national sections of the communist party, and perhaps also by trade union federations. Measures of global scope serving the preservation and furthering of the world-dictatorship of the communist party and its leading groups would then take the place of the former "international law." A "science of the goals and methods of the world-dictatorship of the communist party" would replace the former "jurisprudence of international law."

When Gumplovicz, one of the proponents of dialectical materialism's "theory of law," conceives of law as "the limits that the social groups competing for power and influence in

---

[5] Cf. Korowin, *Die Völkerrecht der Übergangszeit* [International law in the transitional period], 7, 24, et al. The later, as it were "official," alteration of this standpoint, which is connected to the Soviet Union's joining the League of Nations, was only a political chess move. The treaty relationship with the League of Nations was also regarded as a "particular treaty" of the transitional period, which, like the relationship to the United Nations today [1952], was also a "transitional measure." One may, as Lenin taught, take *two* steps back, so long as one will thus be in a position to take *three* forward. On the later "alteration" of the Soviet relationship to international law, see Mannzen, *Sowjetunion und Völkerrecht* [The Soviet Union and international law] (1932).

One-Dimensional Law: Positivism as International Law

the state set to their rule and their influence at any given time," i.e., when he conceives of law merely as a *clock hand* pointing to power relationships of an economic and political kind, then it is the goal of a "dialectical materialism," of communism, carried out in the most consistent way, to bring this clock hand to an eternal standstill, so as to be able to announce—together with Mephistopheles—the great hour of world history:

> (*Faust sinks back, the spirits of the dead take him and lay him on the ground.*)
>
> MEPHISTOPHELES:
> No bliss satisfied him, no enjoyment,
> And so he tried to catch at shifting forms:
> The last, the worst, the emptiest of moments,
> He wished to hold at last in his arms.
> Though against me he tried to stand,
> Time is master: age lies on the sand.
> The clock stands still—
>
> CHORUS:
> Stands still! As midnight: silent.
> The hand moves.
>
> MEPHISTOPHELES:
> It falls, and all is spent
>
> CHORUS:
> It is over[6]

Such an hour of "perpetual peace" would be the perfect, unlimited triumph of one power; thus the end of all struggle, of all opposition between power and power: one power, all else sand.

---

[6] *Faust*, Part II, Scene VI.

PART IX

The Present Movement Towards the Rebirth of International Law Through a Return to Natural Law and Divine Law

oday [1952], the choice "politics or law" faces both the theorist and the practitioner with such decided clarity that it is no longer possible to avoid it. Those politicians endowed with a sense of responsibility have thus in recent times taken measures which, if they have any meaning at all, signify the relinquishment of the principle of the unlimited sovereignty of the state in favor of the supra-state authority of the federation of states in the United Nations, which was set up with the purpose of preventing war. This, however, faces positivism (which is oriented towards the law in force, and limits itself to that law) with a new fact—namely, the presence of positive legal obligations that limit the sovereignty of the state insofar as the individual state is henceforth no longer its own sole judge in questions of war and peace.

The Soviet Union's participation in the UN organization does indeed have the purpose of transforming it from an instrument of world-law into an instrument and arena for world-politics, with the aim of suppressing and casting doubt upon law, and replacing the unpleasant situation of an opposition between law and politics with a situation in which there is a purely political opposition. But this could not, and cannot, change anything about the fact that the part of humanity that still makes its decisions freely has decided to bring an end to the state of international relations that is brought about by the theory and practice of the unlimited sovereignty of the state. For an understanding has spread across the remaining free world that it can simply no longer go on with the absolute sovereignty of the state, and that it is henceforth high time to put an end to the anarchic state of international world-law that is owed to that absolute sovereignty (i.e., to the primacy of politics) and to replace it with an international *legal* order.

This understanding has now found expression in the fact of the United Nations and its statutes. With this, all those doctrines of legal positivism that rest on the *fact* of unlimited (or even unlimitable) sovereignty, collapse. For example, we witness the collapse of Jellinek's doctrine that "the community of states ... is of a purely anarchic nature—and that international law, because it originates in an authority that is not organized and that does not possess any ruling power, can justifiably be described as an anarchic law...."[1] And Lasson's dictum also collapses: "The state can ... never be subjected to a legal order or to any will outside itself. Thus, the situation that prevails among states is a completely lawless one."[2]

---

[1] *Allgemeine Staatslehre*, 378.

[2] *Prinzip und Zukunft des Völkerrechts* [The principle and the future of international law] (Berlin, 1871), 22.

From International Law to World Peace

Today, upholding the claim to unlimited self-rule is in every way a lost cause. For not only do religion, morals, and reason—not to speak of the bitter experience of centuries of world history, and the fact of the dangers that threaten humankind today—demand the limitation of state sovereignty in favor of a world legal order, but the side that, for political reasons, supports unlimited state sovereignty (the states of the Soviet bloc) is really in theory and practice working towards its *end*, in favor of *the unlimited sovereignty of an internationally organized political party*. Which of the so-called "satellite states" of the Soviet Union has retained an unlimited state sovereignty? Does not the essence of the "betrayal" of the Yugoslavian "traitor" Tito consist precisely in the fact that he claimed a greater degree of state sovereignty for Yugoslavia with respect to Moscow than had been provided by Moscow to the satellite states?

Thus, in the final analysis, every state—and every person—faces a decision whether to *renounce* unlimited state sovereignty, or to *lose* it. The conscious and free renunciation of unlimited state sovereignty in favor of a worldwide legal order is one path that can be taken; and the forcible loss of state sovereignty in favor of a worldwide order of power, which has been undergone by nine European states in the last decade, is the other. All attempts to find a "third way"—that is, to remain at the standpoint of the eighteenth and nineteenth centuries—are at best a politics of thrusting one's head in the sand. Who can doubt what would happen to Sweden or to Switzerland, for example, if their neighboring states had lost their independence? Or do the politicians leading these states calculate that the neighboring states, which have entered into an alliance, will protect *them* too, and that it is more advantageous to hide behind others—so that in this way the sacrifices necessary to the common cause can be spared them?

Do the politicians who are leading India *really* believe, for example, that the current holders of power in China will show them more sympathy, peaceability, and humaneness than they are willing to afford their own compatriots and co-citizens, whose rights have found a refuge on the island of Taiwan? Or do they think they still have time quietly to make all the necessary preparations for fleeing to the island of Ceylon, so as there, under the protection of the American and perhaps also the English fleet, to await the "hour of liberation" of their "beloved fatherland"? If not, why have they not been willing to do anything more or anything better for Korea than to send an ambulance? Can they *really* not see that what happened to Korea the day before yesterday, or to Tibet yesterday, can happen to Burma today and to India tomorrow? Or are they really not thinking anything definite at all, and instead hoping in a general way that they will be lucky, in the sense of the philosophy of "perhaps it will turn out all right"?

The author and the reader will never get a clear answer to these simple questions, but will receive instead a torrent of words of "political wisdom," or pithy and empty dicta such as that one "should have good neighborly relations with all neighbors" and the like. The reason why the above questions will remain unanswered lies in the fact that they *cannot* be answered—precisely because there is no answer to them, since an answer is only attainable as the result of a process of reflection resulting in clarity, whereas the choice of the "third way" or of "holding the balance" rests precisely on the fact that no such process of reflection has taken place.[3]

Nevertheless, it is not here a question of a "political" impossibility, since in politics *everything* is possible, but rather of the *inconceivability* of a solution without the renunciation of the unlimited sovereignty of the state in favor of a world legal order. Even pure legal positivism (if it holds to the *facts* of the law in force) must today give up the unlimited sovereignty of states as the sole basis of international law and acknowledge either the authority of a supra-state organization of states that aims at a world legal order, or that of a supra-state party organization that aims at a world-order of power. Both the pure legal positivist and the jurist following the traditional Western school of justice can agree on *one* point, if only on this: that the doctrine of unlimited state sovereignty has in the end shown itself to be a grave error (for the proponents of the legal tradition), and that the existence of several states with unlimited sovereignty is henceforth both politically and legally an impossibility (for the pure positivists).

If the principle of unlimited state sovereignty is relinquished, however, one has taken a step leading of necessity to further steps, even if this initial step consists at first of "shifting" unlimited sovereignty to the supreme instrument of a league of states. The first step that necessarily results is the recognition of a *field of basic norms* that is superordinate to all positive law and that takes precedence over such law—i.e., basic norms that are not enforceable and on which the whole edifice of enforceable norms rests. One may call this

---

[3] The author would be happy if he could be convinced that he is in error, and would be obliged to any who might be able to teach him better.

"field of basic norms" whatever one would like; we see, however, no reason why it should not be described using the traditional expression "natural law," since this expression describes quite precisely the law that precedes positive law and that is superordinate to it.

In this sense, it can be said that once the principle (i.e., the principle of *power*) of the unlimited sovereignty of the state is relinquished, the way is cleared to acknowledge the authority of natural law—the principle of *law in itself.* Thus, one of the greatest, one of the most celebrated, and also one of the most attacked legal scholars of the present day, *Hans Kelsen*, has worked out a "pure theory of law" in the sense of the "juridical logic" that underlies all legal systems currently in force. He has done this both by means of a comparative study of the various positive systems of law, as well as by using Kant's transcendental method (that is, by starting out from the question, "how is jurisprudence possible?"). The "pure theory of law" is a universal theory of positive law—a structural analysis of positive law—rather than a psychological or economic explanation of its conditions, or a moral or political critique of the value of its goals. It *limits* itself to the knowledge of positive law; it does not discuss how law is made.[4]

Kelsen's concern is to completely separate the purely legal element from all the fields neighboring it—morality, metaphysics, psychology, social and economic life—and to treat it *purely on its own account.* Kant's transcendental method is at the basis of this work, but *not* Kant's theory of law, since Kelsen, together with the Marburg School of neo-

---

[4] Hans Kelsen, *General Theory of Law and State* (Cambridge, MA: Harvard University Press, 1945).

Kantianism, is of the view that in his theory of law Kant was unfaithful to his own transcendental method and was influenced by metaphysics. In Kelsen's "pure theory of law" we find once again the concept of the "ought" (as it has been separated from ethics in Windelband's sense) in that of Husserl's logicism (in opposition to psychologism) and in the sense of Cohen's epistemological dictum that the *direction* of knowledge determines the *object* of knowledge.

Law itself is a *system of norms*, and jurisprudence is an "ought-science"[5] in the sense that norms are connected—i.e., one "ought" follows necessarily from another "ought." For this reason, jurisprudence treats the domain of (legal) norms separately from any *content* those norms might have, just as logic does not teach particular opinions, but instead the technique of correct thinking.

There is no objection to such a study in itself, and one can only be grateful that it has been done—so long as it is conceived of as it is essentially intended: the field of purely-legal laws observed and discussed *for its own sake*. If, however, the "pure theory of law" is seen not only as a valuable contribution to the necessary education and training for advocates, civil servants, judges, civil lawyers, journalists, and jurisprudentialists, but also as a requirement to restrict oneself to that theory if one wants to be "scientific"—if, that is, the view is put forward that one is only a "true jurist" if one's thinking and judgments are limited to a purely formal approach, and if one pays no heed to any moral, religious, philosophical, philological, natural-scientific, psychological, political, social, or economic factors when think-

---

[5] *Soll-Wissenschaft*.

ing and judging—then the results are catastrophic. For the demarcation of a special field is only meaningful if, when analysis is complete, it can then be reintegrated into that whole from which it was separated *for the purpose of clarification*. A judge who pays no attention to morality, psychology, or society, is of no use as a judge; an international lawyer who does not trouble himself about the affairs of humankind—history, politics, culture—will not be in any position to understand what international law is about, either as a whole or in detail.

Now, it is of the greatest interest to establish that Kelsen's "pure theory of law" also hangs by a thread, and that this thread (the "basic norms," as Kelsen calls them) itself derives from *natural law*! The basic norms imply a minimum (or "smallest degree") of natural law, as Kelsen himself admitted.[6]

The necessity of these basic norms and their essential nature result in the following way. Law is a system of norms. Each norm is posited; that is, among other things, it is enforceable or has sanctions supporting it. This series of sanctions, however, cannot be infinite, and must come to an end somewhere—i.e., must lead to an *unsanctioned* norm. This unsanctioned norm is, precisely, the "basic norm" that, since it is not enforceable, is not a posited but a presupposed norm, and so is not a "legal norm." It is thus a *moral* norm. The part of morality, however, that determines the norms of law, and upon which legal norms are dependent, is precisely what is meant by "natural law." As

---

[6] As L.L. Fuller of the Harvard Law School notes: cf. his *The Law in Quest of Itself* (1940), 35, 85.

an example of unsanctioned legal authority, we can think of the Supreme Court of many countries, since the Supreme Court has no court above it and itself decides definitively on the interpretation and application of the law—and even, as in the USA, on the constitutionality or unconstitutionality of these laws. The same goes as well for the International Court of Justice.

Thus, the "pure theory of law" (also called the Austrian School) that is so influential today, even if it wishes *only* to be an instrument or method of positive law, is compelled, precisely because of its *purity*, to testify in favor of natural law. Truly, Balaam blessed the people of Israel, even though he had set out to curse them!

The "pure theory of law" dominates the jurisprudence of international law in South America, and also exercises a strong influence in North America, where Kelsen himself found a new home. Among the American proponents of the "pure theory of law," the study by Josef L. Kunz is of value as a symptom of the further development of the doctrine. Kunz fully acknowledges the value of the "pure doctrine of law . . . in its *limited* sense" as a "special, concrete science of positive international law" and as a "universal, abstract jurisprudence, which, on the basis of a comparative analysis of the various positive legal orders, examines the formal structure of the legal norm of the legal order and its construction, and provides fundamental concepts with which the *jurist* can describe a concrete positive legal order."[7] But as a "scholar of legal policy," he goes beyond the task of "describ-

---

[7] J.L. Kunz, "Was ist die Reine Rechtslehre?" [What is the pure theory of law?] *Österreichische Zeitschrift für öffentliches Recht* [Austrian periodical for public law], Vienna (1.3, new series).

ing concrete, positive legal orders" and argues, in contrast to Kelsen, for scholarly discussion of "the *dynamic* problems of international law" too. He regards Kelsen's treatment of this problem as defective. That treatment is consistent with Kelsen's "pure theory of law," "but here, where he [Kelsen] departs from his formal limitation, and discusses problems of the *politics* of law [which are, however, legal problems, not purely political ones—*Author*], the problem of justice cannot be excluded; nor can the solution of international problems of 'peaceful change,' which are by their nature problems of international *legislation*, be entrusted to an international court of justice that is bound to the *positive* law from which the conflict itself has resulted."[8] In other words, Kunz cannot be content with the idea that the jurisprudence of international law, or jurisprudence *tout court*, may not go beyond the description of the *positive* existing law in "fundamental basic concepts" of the "pure theory of law." Instead, he sees the task of jurisprudence, beyond description, as also participating in the *making* of law, which he calls "legal policy"—i.e., in the solution of the *dynamic* problems of international law. This task, however, also includes the "problem of *justice*," which "*cannot* be excluded."

Thus, the task of "two generations" of the development of the "pure theory of law" is as follows. Kelsen's "pure theory of law" wishes only to be a scientific instrument of *positive* law, but also arrives at a necessary acknowledgement of a supra-positive legal norm—the basic norm as the "smallest degree of natural law." The "pure theory of law" in its

---

[8] Ibid.

further development, as instanced at a high level by the work of J.L. Kunz, transcends its limitation to positive law alone (and thus its static quality), and the concepts acquired by that theory are transposed into the field of the *making of law*—a field that is indissolubly bound up with justice. We therefore see here a progression from the "smallest degree of natural law," the *basic norm*, to the full extent of natural law, *justice*. For the objection that justice is not "natural law," but morality, cannot hold good, since the moral element that determines, or helps to determine, the making of law and the validity of law is, precisely, natural law. The recognition of natural law, however—that is, the recognition of reason, justice, and humaneness as factors that determine law—brings along with it everything else necessary for the development of the jurisprudence of international law. The jurisprudence of international law is thus saved from death and will continue to *live*. Balaam *had* to bless the people of Israel; now his blessing shows itself to be efficacious, and new life unfolds where it was not to be looked for.

⊕

If, among the scholars whose work derives from Kelsen's, Kunz does indeed take a step beyond the purely formal nature of the "pure theory" towards the substantive element of the dynamic problems of jurisprudence connected with justice, and yet still depreciates the "introduction of natural law into the juridical treatment of positive law," another world-renowned English scholar of international law whose work is also influenced by Kelsen's, Hersch Lauterpracht, goes further in this direction. In the introduction to his book *An International Bill of the Rights of Man* (New York, 1945), Lauterpracht explained that a return to natural law was necessary. The return to natural law means, however, among other things, giving up the principle of the unlimited sovereignty of the state in favor of a world legal order, and the shaping of this world legal order for the purposes of justice. In other words, it means the primacy of *law* over *politics*.

Alongside the current turn towards natural law (a current in the jurisprudence of international law that goes back ultimately to Kant), a revival is also simultaneously taking place, in theory and in practice, of the surviving traditional natural law, or natural law perspectives in the field of the problems of international law—a tradition that was never completely eliminated. Maine, Pollock, and Lauterpracht have repeatedly shown that it is a commonplace of jurisprudence that the historical task of natural law always consisted in supplementing and correcting the law in force. One of the simplest formulations of the role that traditional natural law plays in international law is contained, for example, in the note of the United States to Mexico about the question of expropriation on August 22, 1938: "There is indeed no mystery about international law: it is nothing more than the recognition between nations of the rules of right and fair dealing such as ordinarily obtain between individuals and that are essential for friendly intercourse."

If the current that comes from Kant leads to a return to postulating natural law, and if Hegel proclaims the unity of law, morality, and ethical life, then, in the present day—as in all centuries of the history of the problem of international law—it is the Catholic School[9] that is cultivating,

---

[9] By "Catholic" is meant here not the denomination to which the legal scholar in question belongs, but his positive attitudes towards the

developing, handing down, and proclaiming the doctrine of the *complete* law—that is, the doctrine of a three-part law in contrast to the two-level law of the rational Enlightenment, to the one-dimensional law of legal positivism, and to the lawless law (the degree zero of law) of political totalitarianism.

Alfred Verdross-Drossberg (Vienna) gives such a striking account of the basic views of this school that it should be quoted in full.

> The multiplicity of the theories of natural law only shows us that there are different conceptions of natural law, but not that the *object* to which all these conceptions refer does not exist.[10] From this it results that most theories of natural law are in principle in accord in their *foundations*. They all recognize that man is *by his nature a rational and social being*, since he can only develop his strengths within the human community. Since, however, every community requires an ordering, a second proposition results from this first one with compelling necessity: that man, by virtue of his social nature, is obliged to obey the order of the community. If, further, one holds that the social order is anchored in the nature of the *human being*, then there follows the conclusion that the order of the community possesses an existence that is not separate from human beings and independent of them, but that it may only be put to the purpose of serving the physical, spiritual, and moral development of human beings. This three-part structure of

---

traditional Catholic doctrine of a law with three levels: positive law, natural law, and divine law. In this sense, *Leibniz*, for example, belonged to the Catholic School, even though he was well known to be a Protestant.

[10] Just as, for example, it may not be concluded from the fact of the existence of multiple worldviews that there is no such thing as the world.—*Author*

Return to Natural Law and Divine Law

norms forms the common basis of all theories of natural law from *Aristotle* up to the present day.[11]

Only in their further *conclusions* do theories of natural law partly differ from each other. These differences, in some measure, result from the fact that the highest propositions are applied to different social states of affairs, and must therefore necessarily lead to different results. This also explains the conservative or progressive tendencies of the different theories of natural law. Those scholars who anchor existing norms in natural law appear to be conservative, whereas those who posit *new* norms on the basis of natural law are taken to be revolutionary. Apart from this, however, any system of natural law that goes beyond the exposition of general principles is more or less subjective, since its application to particular relations is not an exact science, but passes through the scholar's value-judgments. We must therefore strictly distinguish between *primary* natural law (together with its immediate conclusions) and the further consequences that are drawn from it.

A *universal* codex of natural law is also impossible because social relationships are continually in flux, so that conclusions adequate to one situation are seen to be inappropriate to another. Thus, for example, the rule of the eight-hour day, which is normally appropriate in the modern industrial state, may be irrational and thus contrary to natural law when other relationships pertain, for instance, in a closed domestic economy or in times of emergency. The Historical School of law and the legal positivism

---

[11] Cf. A. Verdross-Drossberg, *Grundlinien der antiken Rechts- und Staatsphilosophie* [Basic features of the ancient philosophy of law and of the state] (1946; second edn., 1948), 139 ff.

derived from it are thus to be agreed with *in toto*—to the extent that they merely question the universal validity of the system of natural law.

The *original* jurisprudence of international law, however, already avoided this error, since it did not occur to it to set up such systems. Instead, it limited itself to the application of primary natural law to relations between states. Its line of thought is the following. Just as human beings are prompted by their rational and social nature to enter into connection with each other, so states, which are nothing other than human associations, are obliged by their social nature to acknowledge each other as members of the universal human community, and to live according to the order of this community. This consequential conclusion was first come to by the Spanish School of international law. Grotius took up this idea and saved it from the division over faith. In complete agreement with this, Christian Wolff speaks of the *civitas maxima*, and Vattel of the *Société des Nations*. This idea of natural law forms the normative basis for the community of states, without which that community would fall apart into different and mutually competing power complexes. Nietzsche actually comes to this same conclusion, since he denies universal morality and the universal legal order connected to it.[12]

This shows us, however, that without this foundation in natural law, positive international law also would dissolve into an infinite multiplicity of diplomatic emissaries, state treaties, and arbitrations. One has the separate parts in one's hand, but the spiritual bond connecting them is unfortunately missing. This insight, however, also underpins the

[12] Nietzsche, *On the Genealogy of Morals*, §11.

modern theory of international law, which, in contrast to the old legal positivism, attempts to found international law in a supra-positive *basic norm*. Anzilotti considers the proposition *pacta sunt servanda* ("agreements must be kept") to be such a basic norm. Against this, Kelsen objects that this norm already presupposes the law of custom, for which reason the basic norm must read that the states ought to behave according to previous practice:

> These and like formulas all presuppose the existence of states and their connection to a community. Without them, there can neither be any state treaty nor the practice of international law. Hence, if their sociological and natural-legal background is left out of account, these formulas are completely empty of content. If the latter are instead taken into consideration, it is shown that we must proceed to specify the content of the basic norm of international law from the *legal principles* that are acknowledged by all civilized nations,[13] since the norms of the law of custom were first formed on the basis of the *consensual legal consciousness of the states*. The law of treaties is also rooted in such a *legal principle*, namely in the principle of *bona fides*, not in that practice which often contradicts this principle. Hence, the basic norm of international law requires that the subjects of international law ought to follow the legal principles under discussion, as well as the more precise form those principles take in treaties and in their reception.

This is one of the best concise expositions of how international law is founded on natural law. Nevertheless, it is not, in my opinion, complete. For if Verdross refers to the *original* theory of international law and the Spanish School, and

---

[13] Article 38 of the statutes of the International Court of Justice.

praises both its prudent restraint and its staunchness, this School owes both of these qualities not least to the fact that it acknowledged, over and above the positive law, a natural law that was founded on the nature of man itself: as reason, justice, and humaneness. But this natural law was *also* founded on *divine* law. For the original theory of international law, grounded and worked out by theologians, was always aware of the fact that there is indeed a natural law grounded in human nature, but that as a consequence of the Fall, this human nature cannot be *absolutely* dependable. The proposition *natura vulnerata, non deleta* ("nature is wounded, but not destroyed"), which underpins the views of the Spanish theory of international law, brings two conclusions along with it. First, that there is a "law written in the hearts of men" (natural law); second, however, that this law, when handled by human beings, itself stands in need of correction, supplementation, and guidance from a *still higher, purer,* and *absolute* source. This source is, precisely, "God as lawgiver," or the source of *divine* law. If positive law acknowledges the human authority of the lawgiver, and if natural law recognizes the authority of human reason and of the conscience, divine law signifies the source of the very existence of human reason and conscience, which is superordinate to them—a source that human beings look up to as a final test of what reason and conscience have made of that source. For although this reason and conscience are a mirror of truth and justice, they are also, because of the Fall, not so faithful a mirror that they never distort anything.

So much is either clearly known by most people, or is felt with varying degrees of clarity. This knowing and this feeling protest against the assertion that natural law is the *highest* authority, just as they protest against the many systems of natural law stemming from the rationalist Enlightenment, each claiming for itself universal validity. Reason, justice, and humaneness as sources and as definitive guiding principles for the making of positive law, for its judgments, and for the filling-out of its lacunae, are acknowledged by every person of sound mind—i.e., every person who has retained a sense of objective responsibility for what happens in the world (irrespective of national, class, and other passions). And yet, the recognition of the primacy of natural law over positive law leaves one remaining, nagging doubt: whether everything that *appears* to be reason, justice, and humaneness, *really is* reason, justice, and humaneness.

Injustice, and inhumanity too (for example, the laws National Socialism passed against the Jews, or the laws communism passed against the nobility, the bourgeoisie, and the peasantry), appealed (and still appeal in the case of communism) to "reason," indeed even to "*true* justice and *true* humaneness." For if one starts out from the *presupposition* that the principle Darwinism set up for the *animal* kingdom (the struggle for existence and the survival of the fittest) applies to the *human* kingdom as well, and that, accordingly, race is set against race and class against class in a struggle for existence—then any conclusion that sets out from this presupposition (and thus favors the victorious survival of a race, a people, or a class) can *appear* to be "rational, just, and humane."

From this standpoint, would it not then be rational, in view of the naturally-occurring process of the demise of innumerable less-valuable individuals (i.e., those deemed unworthy to live, and whom wear and tear, degeneration, sickness, and decrepitude ceaselessly destroy so many), to take this *process* into one's own hands and properly undertake to *do* what, in nature, just "happens"? And why should the destruction of a race, a nation, or a class be unjust if that race, class, or nation is in any case destined *by their very nature* to disappear? Viewed thus, should not whatever avails those who are capable of life and are worthy of having a future be considered just? Nor would such a destruction be inhumane, since *humane* conduct is precisely what serves humankind—and what greater service could one show to humankind than to free it from the elements of backwardness, sickness, and decadence clinging to it?

In practice, all these inferences signify *legislation*. Indeed, such inferences were all actually drawn, and "systems of positive law" corresponding to them were actually brought into force. What, however, does it mean that *reason* could have arrived at such inferences and at such legal norms corresponding to them? It means that "reason as such" cannot be taken for the ultimate criterion and the sole source of law, but only "true reason," that is, reason of a *particular kind*, and *only* that one kind of reason—as also one kind of justice and humaneness. Now, what kind of reason, justice, and humaneness is it that can count as the ultimate criterion and true source of law in the world?

The inferences of the "reason" that led to the permissibility, indeed to the wish for and the necessity of, the annihilation of particular national groups and social strata, are indeed "correct," are "in accordance with reason," *if the presupposition lying behind them is true*—that the principle of the struggle for survival which holds true in the animal kingdom is valid for the human kingdom also. It is the *presuppositions*—not the *inferences*—that determine the nature of true reason, justice, and humaneness as the ultimate criterion and source of law. *There must and ought to be presuppositions that are absolute and that neither can nor may be shaken.* They must and ought also to be *absolute* presuppositions in the sense that they are themselves not inferences, but presuppositions of *all* possible inferences, and thus so fashioned that *any* train of ideas can be tested by its according with or contradiction of them. Such absolute presuppositions, which also bind reason in its activity, just as reason binds the activity of the making of positive law, represent precisely the *divine law* that was taught by Thomas Aquinas, acknowledged by the Spanish School of international law, and explicitly acknowledged or silently included in the views put forward by the current school that is still at work in the present day, which we have called the Catholic School. Divine law sets out the absolute *presuppositions* for reason, justice, and humaneness as sources and criteria of valid law.

Since divine law ought only to have the character of something presupposed—and so, not of something derived or inferred—its content is *revelation*. That is to say, it derives neither from experience together with inferences drawn from experience, nor from the analysis of concepts or from a deduction from the universal to the particular. Rather, divine law stands before the knowing, ethical, and legal consciousness as a primordial phenomenon and primordial norm: there it stands, as it were, as the final and absolute criterion for that consciousness. It is "discernment of spirits" that makes possible accord with, or contradiction of, divine law—that is, whether what comes forward as natural law, (as reason, justice, and humaneness) is *true* natural law (*true* reason, *true* justice, and *real* humaneness).

Thus, for example, because the *brotherliness* or *sisterliness* of the whole human race is an absolute norm of divine law, it is *impossible* ever to arrive at conclusions that declare any part of the human race to be in principle of less value on the basis of a reason oriented towards divine law that knows itself to be honestly bound by divine law—regardless of whatever experience might teach, and whatever a reason "emancipated" from divine law might have to say.

The whole edifice of law can only be built and maintained on the firm ground, the "rock," of divine law. Positive law cannot stand on its own, for it falls victim to *politics* and becomes a mere tool of power. Natural law as autonomous human reason and knowing can always fall victim to *erroneous presuppositions*. Only an accord with the absolute presuppositions of divine law gives certainty to natural law, as well as true validity (i.e., a validity resting not merely on power, but on *right*) to positive law.

Positive law can only escape the *swamp* of politics if it is founded on natural law. Natural law can only be protected from the dangers of the *sand* of subjectivism if it is itself supported by the *rock* of divine law. The doctrine of a law with three levels contains not only the *substantive* guarantee that the consciousness of law will not be submerged in the swamp, nor wobble and collapse amid shifting sands, but has also as a matter of fact resisted such swampings and collapses of history up to the present day: the much older doctrine was formulated by Thomas Aquinas in the thirteenth century, and these present lines were written in the year 1952.

Return to Natural Law and Divine Law

⊕

Law bears within itself the demand, made by its very nature, for stability, for *legal certainty*. It does so, not in the sense that there are sanctions behind it, that it can be enforced, but, in the first place (since we are talking about free and rational beings, about *human* beings), in the sense that its *content* is certain. Such certainty about law's content cannot be achieved in any other way than by legal scholars and scholars of international law, of jurisprudence, and of the jurisprudence of international law, bearing witness once more to God in all seriousness of maturity and consciousness of responsibility—and granting Him that place which He deserves.

Will this mean losing the "scientific character" of jurisprudence? Will those legal scholars who in the course of the centuries have learned to bow before the authorities of reason, of the facts, of the state, of precedent, and so on, thereby become less able to work creatively and critically in their field—less able to establish facts and offer interpretations—if, above the multiplicity of mutable and temporary authorities, they acknowledge an authority that can be touched by no *temporal* passions, and that provides an unshakable and immutable foundation for law, reason, justice, and humaneness? Well, if no one, for example, accuses the *natural scientist* of being unscientific when he considers the indisputable *fact* of experience as the final criterion for his views and is always ready to alter his views in accordance with its requirements, why should the pro-ponent of a humanistic *spiritual science*,[14] whose branch is that of jurisprudence, have objections made to him if he, too, obeys an

---

[14] *Geisteswissenschaft*.

absolute *ought*—just as the natural scientist obeys a fact, i.e., obeys *being*?

All science, whether natural science or a humanistic-spiritual science, must rest on something that lies outside the domain of human arbitrariness. For natural science, this something is the pure fact of extrahuman being; for jurisprudence, it is the pure commandment of the extrahuman ought. The "extra-human ought," which is just as withdrawn from human arbitrariness and subjectivity as are the pure facts of experience, is precisely divine law—as the final criterion of all contents of jurisprudential consciousness.

Quis custodiat custodes?—Deus.
"Who will guard the guardians?—God."

APPENDICES

Appendix A: Francisco de Vitoria[1]

And as St. Augustine shows, the reason for this lies in John the Baptist's words to the warrior (Luke 3), when he says "Do violence to no man, neither accuse any falsely." Augustine says, though, that if Christian teaching were to condemn war as such, then those in the gospel who asked for advice about salvation would have been given the answer that they should throw away their weapons and give up being warriors altogether; instead of that, however, what is said is "do violence to no man . . . and be content with your wages."

In the *second place*, there is also a reason that follows from the meaning of the object (St. Thomas, II–II, qu. 40, art. 1). It is permitted, that is, to draw one's sword and to use weapons against internal evildoers and rebels, in accordance with chapter 13 of the letter to the Romans: "he beareth not the sword in vain: for he is the minister of God, a revenger to execute wrath upon him that doeth evil." Thus it is also permitted to use the sword and weapons against external enemies. . . .

In the *third place*, this was also allowed by natural law, as can be seen from the example of Abraham, who fought against the four kings (Genesis 14), as well as from the written law that follows from the examples of David and

---

[1] See page 108, fn 6 for the original location of this lengthy quotation. Cf. Vitoria, *Political Writings*, ed. Pagden and Lawrance, 297–324. The Latin quotation is from Horace, *Epistles*, i.2, line 14. TR (see 108, fn 11)

the Maccabees. The law of the gospel, however, prohibits nothing that is permitted by natural law, as Thomas so well demonstrated (I–II, qu. 107), and this is precisely why it is called the law of freedom (James, chapters 1 and 2). What is permitted according to natural law is therefore no less permitted by the law of the gospel.

In the *fourth place*, it cannot be doubted that in the case of a war of self-defence, force can be made use of in order to fend off force (*Digests* 1.1.3). This is also the case in relation to a war of attack, i.e., a war in which we are not only defending ourselves or attempting to get back what we own, but in which we are also attempting to right a wrong that has been done. This, I say, is supported by the authority of St Augustine (*Liber 83 Quaestionum*) in a passage also to be found in the canon *Dominus Deus noster* (*Decretum*, chap. 23, 2.2): "Those wars will be called just that revenge injustices, if a state or a city is to be punished that has either neglected to punish a wrong carried out by its citizens or has unjustly neglected to give back something it has taken away."

In the *fifth place*, it can be said in justification of an offensive war that even a defensive war cannot be waged satisfactorily if the enemy who has done a wrong or attempted to do a wrong is not first chastised—for if one did not first deter them by means of fear of retribution, one would merely encourage the enemy to attack again.

It can be adduced as a *sixth reason* that, as Augustine says (*De Verbo Domini*, and in the letter to Boniface), the purpose and the goal of war is the peace and the security of the state. But there can be no security for the state if enemies are not stopped from doing wrong by the fear of war, since the situation would obviously be unpropitious for war if the state that was unjustly attacked were not permit-

Appendix A: Francisco de Vitoria

ted to do anything more than merely to defend against attack, without being able to take further steps.

A seventh reason follows from the purpose, goal, and welfare of the whole world. No happiness would be possible in the world, and, indeed, the situation of the world would be one of the greatest wretchedness, if oppressors, robbers, and plunderers could act according to their nature with impunity and oppress the decent and innocent, while the latter for their part were not permitted to punish the evildoers.

My *eighth and last ground* is one that has the greatest weight—that is, the authority and example of good and holy people. Such people have not only defended their country and their possessions in wars of self-defence, but have also striven to extract satisfaction for the wrongs done them or attempted upon them by their enemies. . . .

SECOND QUESTION: Who is empowered to declare war and to wage war?

My *first position* on this question is as follows: everyone, even a private person, can undertake and wage a war of self-defence. This results from the fact that force may be warded off by force (*Digests*, as above). This kind of war can consequently be waged without being empowered to this end by anyone, for the defence not only of one's person, but also of one's possessions and one's goods.

A doubt arises in relation to this position, however; that is, whether someone who is attacked by a robber or by an enemy may strike the attacker back when it is possible instead of escaping by fleeing. . . . Bartolus . . . in his commentaries on the *Digests* (*Dig.* 48.19 and 48.8.9) teaches that self-defence is justified without qualification, and that there is no obligation to flee, since being occasioned to flee is itself a wrong (*Dig.* 47.10.13). . . . Accordingly, even if the natural law does not permit killing in order to defend possessions, it is permitted under the civil law, and to the extent that it prompts no resistance is not only allowed for lay people, but also for spirituals and those in holy orders.

Second position: Every state is empowered to declare and to wage war. . . . [In] my opinion . . . everyone who is attacked in a way that injures his honor can immediately strike back, even in the case where the attacker has no intention of undertaking a further attack, since everyone who is, for example, struck in the face, may immediately, in order avert shame and dishonor, lay hand on his "sword"—and this not in order to revenge himself, but, as I have said, to avoid shame and dishonor. A state, conversely, is not merely justified in protecting itself, but also in avenging itself and its subjects, and in compelling the making-good of the wrong done. . . . The state is not in a position to protect the common weal and itself effectively if it does not revenge a wrong, or if it may not take any measures against its enemies, since evildoers would be all the more ready to do evil, and all the more audacious if they were able to do wrong with impunity. It is therefore necessary for order in human affairs that states should have the authority to do this.

THIRD QUESTION: What may be a valid reason and cause for a just war?

My *first position* here would be this: difference of religion (*diversitatis religionis*) is no cause of a just war. This was thoroughly demonstrated in the previous *relectio* ["De Indis," the fifth *relectio—Author's note*], where we explained that the fourth supposed legal reason for the subjection of the Indians—that is, their refusal to adopt Christianity—was invalid. It is also the opinion of St Thomas (II–II 94.66, art. 8) and the common conviction of the Doctors—in fact I know none among them who is of the opposite view.

Appendix A: Francisco de Vitoria

Second position: Extension of one's own territory (*amplificatio imperii*) is not a just reason for war. . . .

Third position: Neither the personal fame of the prince. nor any other advantage to him is a just reason for war. . . .

Fourth position: There is only a single just reason for beginning a war, that is, a wrong that has been suffered (*unica est sola causa justa inferendi bellum, injuria accepta*) . . . which is the conclusion at which St Thomas arrived (II–II, qu. 40), and is also the opinion of all the Doctors.

Fifth position: Not every kind or every degree of wrong suffered (*injuria quaelibet et quantavis*) suffices for beginning a war. . . . It is not permitted to wage a war on account of a small wrong done by him who is guilty of it, since the degree of punishment must correspond with the degree of misconduct (Deuteronomy 25).

The FOURTH QUESTION concerns the law of warfare, that is, what kind and what degree of force is permissible in a just war?

First position: My first position here is as follows: In war everything is permitted that the defense of the common good demands (*licet omnia facere quae necessaria sunt ad defensionem boni publicii*). . . .

Second position: It is permitted to wrest control of everything that one has previously lost, and also of all its component parts. . . .

Third position: It is justified to recompense the expenses of war (*impensatum belli*) from the property of the enemy, as also all damage caused illegally by the enemy (*omnia damna ab hostibus injuste illata*). . . . Thus, even an authorized judge, if there were such a person set above the two warring parties, would have to sentence the illegal aggressor and author of the injustice not only to restore what was taken, but also to pay the costs of the other side, as well as those of any damages inflicted. . . .

From International Law to World Peace

Fourth position: Not only is the prince waging a just war justified in doing all the things named above, but he may also, in the case of a just war, go further himself, and take such measures as are necessary to protect peace and security from his enemies. He may, for example, destroy a stronghold of the enemy, or even erect such a stronghold on enemy territory, if this should be necessary in order to avert a dangerous attack by the enemy. Such conduct is justified by the fact that, as said above, the purpose and the goal of war is peace and security. . . . It follows from this that even after victory has been won and the wrong suffered has been made good, the enemy can, further, be compelled to give up hostages, ships, weapons, and other things, if this is actually necessary to keep the enemy to the fulfillment of his obligation and to prevent his once more becoming a danger.

Fifth position: Not only is all this permitted, but also— even when victory has been won, reparations have been made, and peace and security have been guaranteed—it is, beyond this, justified to retaliate for the wrong suffered at the hands of enemies (*vindicare injuriam ab hostibus acceptam*) and to take measures against them so as to punish them for the wrong inflicted (*et animadvertere in hostes, et punisre illos pro injuriis illatis*). . . . Everything necessary for directing and preserving society is justified in natural law, and in no other way can it be shown that the state is authorized by natural law to threaten or to execute punishments of its citizens, if the latter should place these things under threat. If, however, the state may do this to its own citizens, it may certainly do the same to the larger community as such of all wicked and dangerous people, which it can only do through princes, as its instrument. . . .

FIRST DOUBT: A first doubt arises, however, in relation to the justice of a war, whether it suffices for a war to be held

Appendix A: Francisco de Vitoria

to be just that the prince himself believes that he has a just reason for it.

First position: On this point, my first position is as follows: This belief does not always suffice. . . . "Princes" almost always believe that their cause is just. All those waging war would accordingly be innocent (*innocentes*), and it would consequently not be permitted to kill them. Also, if belief were enough, then even Turks and Saracens would be able to wage war against Christians, because they believe that they are serving God by so doing.

Second position: It is an essential precondition of a just war that an extremely careful examination of the justification for and the reasons for the war has been undertaken in advance, and that the reasons of those who oppose the war on grounds of fairness are heard. . . .

SECOND DOUBT: Whether subjects are obliged to examine the reasons for war, or if they may provide military service without undertaking such a careful investigation, just as the lictors used to enforce the provisions of the praetors, without examining those provisions.

First position: In relation to this doubt, my first position is as follows: If a subject is convinced of the injustice of a war, he is not obliged to perform military service—not even on the order of the prince. This is obvious, because no one can be empowered to kill an innocent person. . . . Even soldiers are not excused if they fight in bad faith. . . . The consequence results that subjects whose consciences deny the justice of a war may not take part in such a war, whether they are right or wrong about its justice. This is clear, because "whatsoever is not of faith is sin." (Romans 14)

Second position: Senators, dependent princes, and, in general, everyone who belongs to the state council or to the prince's council, ought to and must seek for reasons that make a war unjust.... Nor is the king in a position to examine the reasons for a war (to examine its justice) on his own, since the possibility of a mistake on his part is not improbable—which mistake, however, would mean great evil and ruin for great numbers of people. Thus, the war ought not to be begun upon the judgment of a few people, but only on the basis of the judgment of many people, and those wise and honorable.

Third position: Other, lesser, people, who have no seat in nor access to the prince's council or the council of state, are not obliged to examine the reasons for war, and may perform service in it, trusting to the judgment of their betters....

Fourth position: It can, nevertheless, come about that proofs and indications of the injustice of a war are so formed that ignorance can no longer count as an excuse, even for subjects of this kind, for participating in a war. This is very clearly the case, since such ignorance can be intentional, and can be accepted out of an evil motivation towards the enemy....

THIRD DOUBT: How should one proceed in a case where the justice of a war is dubious, i.e., where there are actual and possible arguments on both sides?

First position: As far as princes themselves are concerned, they ought ... not to make any use of armed force while the doubt remains.... The reason for this can be seen in the fact that in a case of doubt, the party that is in possession is in a more favorable position. For this reason it is not legal to take an owner's possessions away from him for a dubious legal reason (*causa*).... Moreover, war would otherwise be just on both sides, and could never be arbitrated.

Second position: If one party wishes to end the dispute by means of arbitration, and has suggested a division or a

Appendix A: Francisco de Vitoria

compromise in respect of part of a claim, the other party is obliged to accept the suggestion, even if this other party is stronger and might be in a position to seize control of the whole by force of arms; then they would still have grounds for a just war. . . .

Third position: Anyone who is in doubt about his own legal title is obliged, even if he is in actual possession, demanding peace, to undertake a careful examination of this title, and to give a calm hearing to the reasons of the other side, if only to achieve certainty in his own favor or in favor of the other party. . . .

Fourth position: It is beyond doubt that in a war of self-defense the subjects—even in a case where there is doubt about the justice of the war—may follow their prince into war, and indeed, are obliged to do so, even in an offensive war. In a case of doubt, the safer direction should be taken. If the subjects did not follow their prince into war in a case of doubt, then they would create a danger of the state's being betrayed to the enemy, which would be much more serious than fighting against the enemy despite the presence of a doubt. . . .

FOURTH DOUBT: The fourth doubt is: Whether a war can be just on both sides. My answer is as follows:

First position: Apart from the case of ignorance, this cannot happen, since if there were certain right and justice on both sides, it would not be permitted to fight against them, either offensively or defensively.

Second position: Granted that there be a perceptible uncertainty either in relation to the facts of the case or in relation to the legal situation, it can happen that, on the side that is justified, the war is just in itself, whereas on the other side, the war is just in the sense that it can be cleared of sin on the grounds of good faith (*bona fides*), since an invincible ignorance offers complete exculpation. This can even, at least on the side of subjects, happen frequently. . . .

FIFTH DOUBT: From this there arises a fifth doubt: Is someone who has engaged in an unjust war out of ignorance, and who is later convinced of its injustice, obliged to make amends? The question applies to princes as well as to their subjects.

First position: If the proof of the injustice of the war was within the realm of attainability for him, he is obliged, once he has recognized the injustice of the war, to reimburse what he has appropriated and has not yet used—i.e., to the extent that he has enriched himself. He is, however, not obliged to do so in relation to what he has already used, since it is a principle of law, that no one who is not in the wrong should be incriminated.

Second position: My second position would accordingly be as follows: Our man is as little obliged to restore what he as used as the other side is, because, as has been said, his fight was just and in good faith. . . .

Now, much heed must also be given to the acknowledged fact that a war can indeed be just in itself, and yet can be impermissible because of certain additional circumstances. For it is recognized that one can be in possession of a justified claim to a city or to a province, and that making good this claim by means of force can nevertheless be completely impermissible—for example, because of the offensive character of such an attempt. For since (as explained above) wars ought only to be waged for the common good, but a city cannot be reconquered without a greater evil, such as, for example, the destruction of several cities, a large-scale bloodbath, provocations towards other princes, occasions for further wars that lead to the destruction of the Church (where, for example, an opportunity is given to the heathen to intrude into Christian countries and to seize control of them), it is beyond doubt that the prince is obliged to renounce his rights and to refrain from war. . . .

Appendix A: Francisco de Vitoria

In respect to another question, that is, the extent to which far-reaching measures are permissible in the context of a just war, there are also several doubts.

FIRST DOUBT: The first doubt is whether it is permitted to kill the innocent (*innocentes*) in war. . . . In respect of this doubt, my first position is as follows: it is never permitted to kill the innocent knowingly. . . . It follows from this that even in a war against the Turks it is impermissible to kill children. This is obvious, since children are innocent. The same, however, goes for the wives of infidels—which is reasonable, since (insofar as it is a question of war) it is to be presumed that they are innocent. This does not hold, however, in the individual case of a woman whose guilt is certain. Moreover, the same judgment is valid, among Christians, for harmless peasants; it is no less valid for the whole remaining peaceful population, since all these are covered by a presumption of innocence, as long as the opposite has not been established. From this principle it also follows that it is against the law to kill foreigners or guests who are staying with the enemy, for the presumption of innocence holds for them too—they too are indeed, in reality, not enemies. The same principle holds for clergy and for members of religious orders, since they are presumed to be innocent in war, unless the opposite has been demonstrated—for example by their participation in actual combat.

Second position: sometimes one is justified, because of certain additional circumstances, in killing innocent parties, even knowingly—if, for example, a stronghold or a city is stormed in a just war, even though it is known that it harbors a number of innocent parties, and that guns and other engines of war cannot be used, nor buildings set on fire, without afflicting innocent parties as well as the guilty. . . . Great heed must, however, be paid to the point that was already emphasized above, namely, the duty to take care that there does not arise out of the war an evil greater than the one the war is undertaken to avert. And thus, whenever only a small influence on the final outcome of the war is to be expected from the storming of a stronghold or of a fortified city in which many innocent people are located, it would be against the law, in order to attack a few guilty people, to kill many innocents—by means of fire or war-engines or other means so fashioned as to destroy the innocent and the guilty alike, without distinction. The final result is thus that it is never permitted to kill innocent people, even as an indirect and unforeseen consequence, except in a case where there is no other means or way to continue a just war—in accordance with the passage from Matthew 13: "Nay [do not gather the tares], lest while ye gather up the tares, ye root up also the wheat with them."

SECOND DOUBT: The second point concerning which there is doubt is the question whether it is permitted, in a just war, to rob innocent subjects of the enemy of their goods and belongings.

First position: it is doubtless permitted to take such things from innocent parties as the enemy might use against us, such as, for example, weapons, ships, and engines of war.... Indeed, it is even permitted to take money from innocent parties, to destroy their grain and to kill their horses, if this should be seen to be necessary in order to undermine the enemy's strength....

All this can be summarized in a few canons or rules for waging war.

First rule: assuming that a prince is empowered to declare and wage war, he ought not in the first place to seek opportunities and reasons for war, but should strive as far as possible to live in peace with all people, as St Paul bids us (Romans 12). He ought, moreover, to consider that

Appendix A: Francisco de Vitoria

other people are his neighbors, whom we are to love as ourselves, and that we all have in common one Lord over us, to whose court we must give an account of ourselves. For it is the utmost savagery to seek and to delight in finding reasons to kill and to destroy people whom God has made, and for whom Christ died. Only under compulsion and with reluctance should a prince arrive at a recognition of the necessity of war.

Second rule: when war has broken out for a just cause, then it may not be waged in such a way that the demise of the opponent's people is striven for, but only so as to enforce the validity of one's own right, so as to defend one's own country, and thus, in time, to come out of this war with peace and security.

Third rule: after victory has been achieved, and the war is ended, the victory should be made use of with moderation and Christian humility. The victor ought to occupy the judgment seat between the two states—the one that has suffered the injustice and the one that carried out this injustice—so that he has to pronounce, as a judge rather than as a prosecutor, the judgment by which reparation is awarded to the state that has suffered the injustice, and this ought as far as possible to happen in such a way that it ought to bring with it the smallest degree of calamity and misery to the guilty state, by limiting the chastisement to the guilty persons, within the bounds of the law. There is a particular reason for this, namely that among Christians responsibility is to be unconditionally ascribed to princes, since subjects as a rule act in good faith when they fight for their princes, and it is completely unjust to act according to the poet's words: *quidquid delirant reges, plectuntur Achivi* ("for any madness of their kings, it is the Greeks who take the beating").

From International Law to World Peace

As far as concerns the chastisement of "guilty persons," as is the right and the duty of the victor after he has secured victory over the guilty state in the case of a just war, in accordance with his office as judge, Vitoria puts forward the principle that "the punishment should not exceed the degree and the nature of the misdemeanor. Indeed, punishments should be determined restrictively, and rewards extensively.[2] This is not merely a principle of human (positive) law, but of natural law and of divine law."

---

[2] That is, punishments should be restricted to the minimum possible consistent with the law, and, in a case of doubt, the lighter punishment should be decided upon, while in cases of reward the opposite holds: the highest possible reward consistent with the law is to be striven for, and in a case of doubt, the higher amount is to be preferred.

Appendix B: Francisco Suárez[1]

Just as it is necessary that there be a legal force within a state in order to punish crime and to preserve internal peace, so, in order for the different states to live in concord, there must in the world as a whole be a power to punish any law-breaking committed by one state towards the another. Since this power cannot be found in any superordinate court (for we assume that the states in question have no universally recognized superordinate power standing over them), this power must rest with the sovereign prince of the state that has been wronged. The prince of the state that has committed the wrong is now subordinated to the prince of the state that has been wronged, precisely because of the wrong done. *Thus, war of this kind is a court that replaces the missing criminal court.*

Against this, the objection is made that, in consequence, the same party comes forward both as accuser and as judge, which contradicts natural law. This objection is also confirmed by the fact that the right to self-defense is not available to private persons, and this for the reason that it would go beyond the limits of justice. The same

---

[1] See page 173, fn 7. This lengthy quotation from Suárez is not specifically referenced. Since it picks up and further develops the theme of the views of Suárez on the right to declare war cited just a few pages earlier (169–170), the source of the citation is almost certainly the same: Suárez's text *De triplici virtute theolgica: fide, spe, charitate* (1621), "Disputatio XIII, De Bello," section II. ED

danger, however, also exists in the case of a prince who resorts to self-defense. Furthermore, the same objection is strengthened even more by the fact that (if princes were able to come forward both as accusers and as judges in their own causes) then any private person who is for any reason unable to obtain punishment of the guilty party by judicial means could take the enforcement of the law into his own hands, since this prerogative belongs to princes only in a case where they cannot achieve a legal punitive settlement in any other way. We answer to this, that it cannot be denied that in this case the same person comes forward at once as accuser and as judge. . . . Nevertheless the justifying grounds for this lie simply in the fact that such an act of punitive justice is indispensable to humanity, and that no more appropriate means for the execution of this act could be found within the natural order and using human powers alone. This holds all the more strongly, because we must presume that before the beginning of the war a refusal to make reparations had taken place on the part of the party who had broken the law. If the latter then finds himself a subject of the injured party, he has only himself to thank for his misfortune.

The case is also different in its nature from that of a private person.[2] For a private person acts according to his own personal judgment, and will therefore readily go beyond the limits of law-enforcement, while the public power behaves according to the public counsel tasked with overseeing it, and it is therefore in a better position to avoid the disadvantages of personal inclinations. Furthermore, the power of enforcing punishment is a purpose

---

[2] The text actually reads, "The case is the same in its essential nature as that of a private person." Given that the paragraph goes on to explain the differences between the two kinds of case, it seems likely that there is a textual error here.—TR

Appendix B: Francisco Suárez

belonging not to a private, but to the public, good; for this reason, it is not entrusted to a private person, but to the public corporation.

Further (third), I assert that everyone who begins a war without just cause offends not only against love but also against justice, and that he is consequently obligated to pay compensation for any damage arising therefrom.

The only question that arises in connection with this point is whether there can be grounds for war that are free from the guilt of injustice, but not free from the guilt of sinning against love. The answer is that such a situation comes about only seldom, but that it is by no means inconceivable. For just as in dealings between private persons it happens that one demands from another what is due him, a deed that does not conflict with justice, but sometimes does conflict with love (especially in a case where the debtor suffers great harm as a result, while the matter is of no great significance to the creditor), a similar situation can come about in dealings between princes and states. Nevertheless, in this connection it must be considered that in the case of a war of this kind, *three states of affairs* can be considered: first, harm to the state against which the war is waged; second, harm to the state that is waging war; and, third, the possible harm to the whole Church.

As far the *third* possibility is concerned, it is easy for us to find confirmation of our position here. Even if a Christian king has particular just grounds for war, he can nevertheless sin against the love he owes to the Church by insisting on his rights. He can foresee that as a result of a gain in power for the enemies of religion, etc., it would be a sin to start a war; and yet no obligation to pay compensation for damages would arise to him, since the particular just grounds he has for war would erase any such obligation.

In relation to the *second* possibility, the following is to be said. If a prince were to begin a war against another prince, even upon just grounds, and were thereby to expose his own kingdom to disproportionate damage and danger, then he would have violated not only love, but also the justice he owes to his own state. Consequently, a prince is obliged by justice to take more care of the common welfare of his state than he does of his own welfare. For if he behaves otherwise, he becomes a tyrant. Thus, for example, a judge who condemns a criminal to be hanged—a criminal who indeed deserves the punishment, but of whom the state has great need—is acting against the duty of his office and consequently also against justice. In the same way, a doctor would violate the justice of his profession if he prescribed a medicine that did indeed cure the present ailment, but would at the same time cause another, and significantly worse, ailment.

Furthermore [as regards the *first* possibility], we should take into account the conclusion Cajetan (II–II, qu. 96, art. 4) draws from these considerations of matters of principle, namely that the prince who is to wage a just war must possess a degree of power such that he is morally certain of victory. The first reason for this conclusion is that the prince would otherwise run the risk of harming the state more than he benefits it. Similarly, Cajetan says, a judge would be wrong to try to arrest a criminal without being certain that the force assigned for this purpose was strong enough not to be overpowered. Second, the principle holds that the party who begins a war thereby takes an active role upon itself; the active side must always be the stronger side, if it is to defeat the passive side. Nevertheless, the condition that one must be certain of victory does not seem to me to be requisite without qualification. First, because it is hardly humanly achievable; second, because it is often in the interest of the state not to wait for such a

Appendix B: Francisco Suárez

degree of certainty, but instead to test its power to defeat the enemy, even if this capacity is still doubtful; third, because, if the conclusion is correct, a weaker prince would never be in a position to declare war on a more powerful prince, since he would never be able to be certain that he would win, which Cajetan holds to be requisite. The following rules should therefore be observed:

A prince who intends to declare war is indeed obliged to achieve as much certainty as is possible about the prospects of victory. He ought also to weigh up the prospect of victory and the risk of defeat, so that, after careful consideration of all the circumstances, he can determine whether the prospect of victory is greater. If such a degree of certainty is impossible to achieve, he ought at least either to have a more probable prospect of victory, or an equally probable prospect of victory and defeat, in relation to what is necessary for the state and for the general good. If, however, the prospect of victory is smaller than the prospect of defeat, and if the war is a war of aggression in its nature, then war must in almost all cases be refrained from. If, however, it is a matter of a war of self-defense, then it should be risked, since in this case war is a necessity, whereas the war of aggression depends a voluntary decision. These conclusions are all sufficiently solid, and are grounded in the principles of conscience and justice.

Appendix C:
Thomas Hobbes[1]

In chapter thirteen, "Of the Naturall Condition of Mankind, of his major work *Leviathan: or the Matter, Forme, and Power of a Commonwealth Ecclesiastical and Civil* (1651),[2] Thomas Hobbes provides the reasons for the natural equality of human beings, and develops a concept of equality that is derived from the capacity for evil.

> Nature hath made men so equall, in the faculties of body, and mind; as that though there bee found one man sometimes manifestly stronger in body, or quicker of mind then another; yet when all is reckoned together, the difference between man, and man, is not so considerable, as that one man can thereupon claim to himselfe any benefit, to which another may not pretend, as well as he. For as to the strength of body, the weakest has strength enough to kill the strongest, either by secret [69] machination, or by con-

---

[1] See page 221.

[2] Thomas Hobbes, *Leviathan*, ed. Richard E. Flatman and David Johnston (New York and London: W.W. Norton, 1997), 68–74; 79; 95; 9. As the page numbers given will make clear, this long quotation from Hobbes's *Leviathan* is constructed by Tomberg out of passages in some cases widely separated, and from a number of different chapters of the book, so that ellipses within it indicate gaps in some cases of a few words or lines, but in others of many pages. Nor do these passages follow sequentially, as their position in the text might imply. For example, the final passage is taken from the very beginning of the book. Page numbers in brackets have been inserted for the convenience of the reader, indicating that text subsequent to each such number begins on that page.—TR

Appendix C: Thomas Hobbes

federacy with others, that are in the same danger with himselfe.

And as to the faculties of mind, (setting aside the arts grounded upon words, and especially that skill of proceeding upon generall, and infallible rules, called Science; which very few have, and but in few things; as being not a native faculty, born with us; nor attained, (as Prudence,) while we look after somewhat else,) I find yet a greater equality amongst men, than that of strength. For Prudence, is but Experience; which equall time, equally bestowes on all men, in those things they equally apply themselves unto. . . .

From this equality of ability, ariseth equality of hope in the attaining of our Ends. And therefore if any two men desire the same thing, which neverthelesse they cannot both enjoy, they become enemies. . . .

And from this diffidence of one another, there is no way for any man to secure himselfe, so reasonable, as Anticipation; that is, by force, or wiles, to master the persons of all men he can, so long, till he see no other power great enough to endanger him: And this is no more than his own conservation requireth, and is generally allowed. . . .

Againe, men have no pleasure, (but on the contrary a great deale of griefe) in keeping company, where there is no power able to over-awe [70] them all. For every man looketh that his companion should value him, at the same rate he sets upon himselfe: And upon all signes of contempt, or undervaluing, naturally endeavours, as far as he dares . . . to extort a greater value from his contemners, by dommage [damage]; and from others, by the example.

So that in the nature of man, we find three principall causes of quarrell. First, Competition; Secondly, Diffidence; Thirdly, Glory.

The first, maketh men invade for Gain; the second, for Safety; and the third, for Reputation. . . .

From International Law to World Peace

Hereby it is manifest, that during the time men live without a common power to keep them all in awe, they are in that condition which is called Warre; and such a Warre, as is of every man, against every man. For WARRE, consisteth not in Battell onely, or the act of fighting, but in a tract of time, wherein the Will to contend by Battell is sufficiently known: and therefore the notion of *Time*, is to be considered in the nature of Warre; as it is in the nature of Weather. For as the nature of Foule weather, lyeth not in a showre or two of rain; but in an inclination thereto of many dayes together: So the nature of Warre, consisteth not in actuall fighting; but in the known disposition therein, during all the time there is no assurance to the contrary. All other time is PEACE. . . . [71]

To this Warre of every man against every man, this is also consequent; that nothing can be Unjust. The notions of Right and Wrong, Justice and Injustice have there no place. Where there is no common Power, there is no Law: where no Law, no Injustice. Force, and Fraud, are in Warre the two Cardinall vertues. Justice and Injustice are none of the Faculties neither of the Body, nor Mind. If they were, they might be in a man that were alone in the world, as well as his Senses, and Passions. They are Qualities, that relate to men in Society, not in Solitude. . . .

The Passions that encline men to Peace, are Feare of Death; Desire of such things as are necessary to commodious living; and a Hope by [72] their Industry to obtain them. And Reason suggesteth convenient Articles of Peace, upon which men may be drawn to agreement. These Articles, are they, which otherwise are called the Lawes of Nature. . . .

THE RIGHT OF NATURE, which Writers commonly call *Jus Naturale*, is the Liberty each man hath, to use his own power, as he will himselfe, for the preservation of his own Nature; that is to say, of his own Life. . . .

Appendix C: Thomas Hobbes

By Liberty, is understood, according to the proper signification of the word, the absence of externall Impediments. . . .

A Law Of Nature (*Lex Naturalis,*) is a Precept, or generall Rule, found out by Reason, by which a man is forbidden to do, that, which is destructive of his life, or taketh away the means of preserving the same; and to omit, that, by which he thinketh it may be best preserved. For though they that speak of this subject, use to confound *Jus,* and *Lex, Right* and *Law;* yet they ought to be distinguished; because Right consisteth in Liberty to do, or to forbeare; Whereas Law, determineth, and bindeth to one of them: so that Law, and Right, differ as much, as Obligation, and Liberty. . . .

And because the condition of Man . . . is a condition of Warre of every one against every one; in which case every one is governed by his own Reason; and there is nothing he can make use of, that may not be a help unto him, in preserving his life against his enemyes; It followeth, that in such a condition, every man has a Right to every thing; even to one another's body. And therefore, as long as this naturall Right of every man to every thing endureth, there can be no security to any man, (how strong or wise soever he be) of living out the time, which Nature ordinarily alloweth men to live. And consequently it is a precept, or generall rule of Reason, *That every man, ought to endeavour Peace, as farre as he has hope of obtaining it; and when he cannot obtain it, that he may seek, and use, all helps, and advantages of Warre.* The first branch of which Rule, containeth the first, and Fundamentall Law of Nature; which is, *to seek Peace, and follow it.* The Second, the summe of the Right of Nature, which is, *By all means we can, to defend our selves.*

From this Fundamentall Law of Nature, by which men are commanded to endeavour Peace, is derived this second Law; *That a man be willing, when others are so too, as farre-*

forth, as for Peace, and defence [73] *of himselfe he shall think it necessary, to lay down the right to all things; and be contented with so much liberty against other men, as he would allow other men against himselfe.* . . .

To *lay downe* a mans *Right* to any thing, is to *devest* himselfe of the *Liberty*, of hindring another of the benefit of his own Right to the same. . . .

Right is layd aside, either by simply Renouncing it; or by Transferring it to another. . . . And when a man hath in either manner abandoned, or granted away his Right; then is he said to be OBLIGED, or BOUND, not to hinder those, to whom such Right is granted, or abandoned, from the benefit of it. . . .

Whensoever a man Transferreth his Right, or Renounceth it; it is [74] either in consideration of some Right reciprocally transferred to himselfe; or for some other good he hopeth for thereby. For it is a voluntary act; and of the voluntary acts of every man, the object is some *Good to himselfe*. . . .

The mutuall transferring of Right, is that which men call CONTRACT. . . . [79]

[The] definition of INJUSTICE, is no other than *the not Performance of Covenant*. And whatsoever is not Unjust, is *Just*. . . . [95]

The agreement of these ["irrationall"] creatures is Naturall; that of men, is by Covenant only, which is Artificiall: and therefore it is no wonder if there be somwhat else required (besides Covenant) to make their Agreement constant and lasting; which is a Common Power, to keep them in awe, and to direct their actions to the Common Benefit.

The only way to erect such a Common Power . . . is, to conferre all their power and strength upon one Man, or upon one Assembly of men, that may reduce all their Wills, by plurality of voices, unto one Will: which is as much as to say, to appoint one Man, or Assembly of men, to beare

Appendix C: Thomas Hobbes

their Person; and every one to owne, and acknowledge himselfe to be the Author of whatsoever he that so beareth their Person, shall Act, or cause to be Acted, in those things which concerne the Common Peace and Safetie; and therein to submit their Wills, every one to his Will, and their Judgments, to his Judgment. This is more than Consent, or Concord; it is a reall Unitie of them all, in one and the same Person, made by Covenant of every man with every man, as if every man should say to every man, *I Authorise and give up my Right of Governing my selfe, to this Man, or to this Assembly of men, on this condition, that thou give up thy Right to him, and Authorise all his Actions in like manner.* This done, the Multitude so united in one Person, is called a COMMON-WEALTH, in latine CIVITAS. This is the Generation of that great LEVIATHAN, or rather (to speake more reverently) of that *Mortall God,* to which wee owe under the *Immortal God,* our peace and defence. . . .

[9] For seeing life is but a motion of Limbs, the beginning whereof is in some principall part within; why may we not say, that all *Automata* (Engines that move themselves by springs and wheels as doth a watch) have an artificiall life? For what is the *Heart,* but a *Spring;* and the *Nerves,* but so many *Strings;* and the *Joynts,* but so many *Wheeles,* giving motion to the whole Body, such as was intended by the Artificer? *Art* goes yet further, imitating that Rationall and most excellent worke of Nature, *Man.* For by Art is created that great LEVIATHAN called a COMMON-WEALTH, or STATE, (in latine CIVITAS), which is but an Artificiall Man; though of greater stature and strength than the Naturall, for whose protection and defence it was intended; and in which, the *Soveraignty* is an Artificiall *Soul,* as giving life and motion to the whole body.

If, then, the state is the "great Artificiall Man" whose cells and organs are individual people and groups of individual people, how do matters stand, according to Hobbes, with spiritual life, with the individual's freedom of conscience, and with religion?

In the twenty-ninth chapter of *Leviathan*, where Hobbes discusses things *"that Weaken, or tend to the Dissolution"* of the state, the above questions are answered with a clarity that leaves nothing to be desired:

> I observe the *Diseases* of a Common-wealth, that proceed from the poyson of seditious doctrines; whereof one is, *That every private man is Judge of Good and Evill actions.* This is true in the condition of meer Nature, where there are no Civill Lawes; and also under Civill Government, in such cases as are not determined by the Law. But otherwise, it is manifest, that the measure of Good and Evil actions, is the Civill Law; and the Judge the Legislator, who is always Representative of the Common-wealth. From this false doctrine, men are disposed to debate with themselves, and dispute the commands of the Common-wealth; and afterwards to obey, or disobey them, as in their private judgements they shall think fit.[3]
>
> It hath been also commonly taught, *That Faith and Sanctity, are not to be attained by Study and Reason, but by supernaturall Inspiration, or Infusion,* which granted, I see not why any man should render a reason of his Faith; or why every Christian should not be also a Prophet; or why any man should take the Law of his Country, rather than his own Inspiration, for the rule of his action. And thus wee fall again into the fault of taking upon us to Judge of Good and Evill. . . .[4]

---

[3] Hobbes, *Leviathan*, 163.
[4] Ibid., 164.

Appendix D:
John Locke[1]

§4. To understand political power right, and derive it from its original, we must consider what state all men are naturally in, and that is, a state of perfect freedom to order their actions and dispose of their possessions and persons, as they think fit, within the bounds of the law of nature; without asking leave, or depending on the will of any other man. A state also of equality, wherein all the power and jurisdiction is reciprocal, no one having more than another [...]

§5. This equality of men by nature the judicious Hooker looks upon as so evident in itself, and beyond all question, that he makes it the foundation [102] of that obligation to mutual love amongst men, on which he builds the duties we owe one another, and from whence he derives the great maxims of justice and charity. . . .

§6. But though this be a state of liberty, yet it is not a state of licence: though man in that state have an uncontrollable

---

[1] John Locke, "The Second Treatise: An Essay Concerning the True Original, Extent, and End of Civil Government," in Locke, *Two Treatises of Civil Government and A Letter Concerning Toleration*, ed. Ian Shapiro (New Haven, CT: Yale University Press, 2003), 100–209, 101–82. As will be evident, this long quotation from Locke is woven together by Tomberg from passages appearing at widely separated parts of Locke's book. Tomberg does not always mark elisions, which are all, however, indicated here, together with parenthetical page references to the edition cited. TR (See page 233 of present text.)

liberty to dispose of his person or possessions, yet he has not liberty to destroy himself, or so much as any creature in his possession, but where some nobler use than its bare preservation calls for it. The state of nature has a law to govern it, which obliges every one: and reason, which is that law, teaches all mankind, who will but consult it, that being all equal and independent, no one ought to harm another in his life, health, liberty or possessions. . . .

§7. And that all men may be restricted from invading others' rights, and [103] from doing hurt to one another, and the law of nature be observed, which willeth the peace and preservation of all mankind, the execution of the law of nature is, in that state, put into every man's hands, whereby every one has a right to punish the transgressors of that law to such a degree as may hinder its violation: for the law of nature, would, as all other laws that concern men in this world, be in vain, if there were nobody that in the state of nature had a power to execute that law, and thereby preserve the innocent, and restrain offenders. And if any one in the state of nature may punish another for any evil he has done, every one may do so: for in that state of perfect equality, where naturally there is no superiority or jurisdiction of one over another, what any may do in prosecution of that law every one must needs have a right to do.

§8. And thus, in the state of nature, "one man comes by a power over another". . . .

§95. [141] Men being, as has been said, by nature all free, equal, and independent, no one can be put out of this estate, and subjected to the political power of another, without his own consent. The only way whereby any one [142] divests himself of his natural liberty, and puts on the bonds of civil society, is by agreeing with other men to join and unite into a community, for their comfortable, safe,

Appendix D: John Locke

and peaceable living one amongst another, in a secure enjoyment of all their properties, and a greater security against any that are not of it. This any number of men may do, because it injures not the freedom of the rest; they are left as they were in the liberty of the state of nature. When any number of men have so consented to make one community or government, they are thereby presently incorporated, and make one body politic, wherein the majority have a right to act and conclude the rest.

§96. For when any number of men have, by the consent of every individual, made a community, they have thereby made that community one body, with a power to act as one body, which is only by the will and determination of the majority; for that which acts any community being only the consent of the individuals of it, and it being necessary to that which is one body to move one way; it is necessary the body should move that way whither the greater force carries it, which is the consent of the majority: or else it is impossible it should act or continue one body, one community, which the consent of every individual that united into it agreed that it should; and so every one is bound by that consent to be concluded by the majority. . . .

§97. And thus every man, by consenting with others to make one body politic under one government, puts himself under an obligation to every one of that society to submit to the determination of the majority, and to be concluded by it; or else this original compact, whereby he with others incorporate into one society, would signify nothing, and be no compact, if he be left free, and under no other ties than he was before in the state of nature. . . .

§99. [143] Whosoever therefore out of a state of nature unite into a community, must be understood to give up all the power necessary to the ends for which they unite in society, to the majority of the community, unless they expressly agreed in any number greater than the majority. And this is done by barely agreeing to unite into one political society, which is all the compact that is, or needs be, between the individuals that enter into, or make up a commonwealth. And thus that which begins and actually constitutes any political society, is nothing but the consent of any number of freemen capable of a majority, to unite and incorporate into such a society. And this is that, and that only, which did or could give beginning to any lawful government in the world. . . .

§ 111. [149] But though the golden age (before vain ambition, and *amor sceleratus habendi*, evil concupiscence, had corrupted men's minds into a mistake of true power and honour) had more virtue, and consequently better governors, as well as less vicious subjects; and there was then no stretching prerogative on the one side, to oppress the people; nor consequently on the other, any dispute about privilege, to lessen or restrain the power of the magistrate; and so no contest betwixt rulers and people about governors or government; yet, when ambition and luxury in future ages would retain and increase the power, without doing the business for which it was given; and, aided by flattery, taught princes to have distinct and separate interests from their people; men found it necessary to examine more carefully the original and rights of government, and to find out ways to restrain the exorbitancies, and prevent the abuses of that power, which they having intrusted in another's hands only for their own good, they found was made use of to hurt them. . . .

§ 128. [155] For in the state of nature, to omit the liberty he has of innocent delights, a man has two powers. The first is to do whatever he thinks fit for the preservation of himself [156] and others within the permission of the law of

Appendix D: John Locke

nature: by which law, common to them all, he and all the rest of mankind are one community, make up one society, distinct from all other creatures. And, were it not for the corruption and viciousness of degenerate men, there would be no need of any other; no necessity that men should separate from this great and natural community, and by positive agreements combine into smaller and divided associations. The other power a man has in the state of nature, is the power to punish the crimes committed against that law. Both these he gives up when he joins in a private, if I may so call it, or particular politic society, and incorporates into any commonwealth, separate from the rest of mankind. . . .

§131. But though men, when they enter into a society, give up the equality, liberty, and executive power they had in the state of nature, into the hands of the society, to be so far disposed of by the legislative as the good of the society shall require; yet it being only with an intention in every one the better to preserve himself, his liberty and property (for no rational creature can be supposed to change his condition with an intention to be worse); the power of the society, or legislature constituted by them, can never be supposed to extend farther than the common good. . . . And so whoever has the legislative or supreme power of any commonwealth, is bound to govern by established standing laws, promulgated and known to the people, and not by extemporary decrees; by indifferent and upright judges, who are to decide controversies by these laws; and to employ the [157] force of the community at home, only in the execution of such laws; or abroad to prevent or redress foreign injuries, and secure the community from inroads and invasion. And all this to be directed to no other end but the peace, safety, and public good of the people.

From International Law to World Peace

§175. [178] Though governments can originally have no other rise than that before mentioned, nor politics be founded on any thing but the consent of the people; yet such have been the disorders ambition has filled the world with, that in the noise of war, which makes so great a part of the history of mankind, this consent is little taken notice of: and therefore many have mistaken the force of arms for the consent of the people, and reckon conquest as one of the originals of government. But conquest is as far from setting up any government, as demolishing a house is from building a new one in the place. . . .

§ 176. That the aggressor, who puts himself into the state of war with another, and unjustly invades another man's right, can, by such an unjust war, never come to have a right over the conquered, will be easily agreed by all men, who will not think that robbers and pirates have a right of empire [179] over whomsoever they have force enough to master, or that men are bound by promises which unlawful force extorts from them. Should a robber break into my house, and with a dagger at my throat make me seal deeds to convey my estate to him, would this give him any title? Just such a title, by his sword, has an unjust conqueror, who forces me into submission. The injury and the crime are equal, whether committed by the wearer of the crown or some petty villain. . . . From whence it is plain, that he that conquers in an unjust war, can thereby have no title to the subjection and obedience of the conquered.

§177. But supposing victory favours the right side, let us consider a conqueror in a lawful war, and see what power he gets, and over whom. . . .

§178. [180] Let us see next what power a lawful conqueror has over the subdued: and that I say is purely despotical. He has an absolute power over the lives of those who by an unjust war have forfeited them: but not over the lives or

Appendix D: John Locke

fortunes of those who engaged not over the war, nor over the possessions even of those who were actually engaged in it.

§179. Secondly, I say then the conqueror gets not power but only over those who have actually assisted, concurred, or assented to that unjust force that is used against him: for the people having given to their governor no power to do an unjust thing, such as to make an unjust war (for they never had such a power in themselves) they ought not to be charged as guilty of the violence or oppression their governors should use upon the people themselves, or any part of their fellow-subjects, they having empowered them no more to the one than to the other. . . .

§180. [181] Thirdly, the power a conqueror gets over those he overcomes in a just war, is perfectly despotical: he has an absolute power over the lives of those who, by putting themselves in a state of war, have forfeited them; but he has not thereby a right and title to their possessions. This I doubt not but at first sight will seem a strange doctrine, it being so quite contrary to the practice of the world; there being nothing more familiar in speaking of the dominion of countries, than to say such a one conquered it; as if conquest, without any more ado, conveyed a right of possession. . . .

§181. [S]upposing we are in such a state that we have no common judge on earth whom I may appeal to, and to whom we are both obliged to submit; for of such I am now speaking. It is the unjust use of force then, that puts a man into the state of war with another: for quitting reason, which is the rule between man and man, and using force, the way of beasts, he becomes liable to be destroyed by him he uses force against, as any savage ravenous beast, that is dangerous to his being.

§182. But because the miscarriages of the father are no faults of the children, and they may be found rational and peaceable, notwithstanding the brutishness and injustice of the father; the father, by his miscarriages and violence, can forfeit but his own life, but involved not his children in his guilt or destruction. His goods, which nature, that willeth the preservation of all mankind as much as is possible, hath made to belong to the children to keep them from perishing, do still continue to belong to his children. . . . [182] So that he that by conquest has a right over a man's person to destroy him if he pleases, has not thereby a right over his estate to possess and enjoy it [...] it is damage sustained that alone gives him title to another man's goods: for though I may kill a thief that sets on me in the highway, yet I may not (which seems less) take away his money and let him go: this would be robbery on my side. His force, and the state of war he put himself in, made him forfeit his life, but gave me no title to his goods. The right then of conquest extends only to the lives of those who joined in the war, not to their estates, but only in order to make reparation for the damages received, and the charges of the war; and that too with reservation of the right of the innocent wife and children.